Intel® Integrated Performance Primitives

How to Optimize Software Applications Using Intel® IPP

Stewart Taylor

ISBN 0-9717861-3-5

This book is printed on acid-free paper. ♾

Publisher: Richard Bowles
Editor: David Clark
Managing Editor: David B. Spencer
Content Manager: Stuart Goldstein
Text Design & Composition: Wasser Studios
Graphic Art: Wasser Studios (illustrations), Ted Cyrek (cover)

Library of Congress Cataloging in Publication Data:

Printed in the United States of America

10 9 8 7 6 5 4 3 2 1

First printing, February 2004

Contents

Acknowledgements

A book of such broad subject material relies very heavily on domain experts for accuracy. This book depended more than most on the aid of such experts. For their careful reviews and constructive comments, I would like to thank Alexey Fadeev, Asia Nezhdanova, Iliya Slavutin, Sergey Komolov, Alexey Bulanov, Boris Sabanin, Igor Astakhov, Nikolay Degtarenko, Vladimir Dudnik, Gary Bradski, Mark Buxton, James Abel, Will Damon, Guru Nagendra, Nathaniel Chichioco, Amanda Sharp, Tim Trumbull, Todd Rosenquist, Ying Song, Bruce Rady, Bryan Cook, Christopher Lund, Dan Staheli, Judi Goldstein, Shobhan Jha, Mike Schauf, and Suneel Bhagat.

For their contributions to this book and to Intel IPP, I'd particularly like to thank Shinn Lee, Davis Frank, Ken Dellinger, Vladimir Tatarinov, and Boris Sabanin.

Chapter 1

Introduction

The effort to create the Intel libraries grew out of our group's recognition of three facts about software development:

- We could identify a set of common computationally-intensive functions that developers needed on Intel processors.
- Developers would have to optimize these functions carefully to get adequate performance.
- This optimization process was complicated and time-consuming.

With each successive generation of processors, the number of developers who wanted to program in assembly has diminished. Further, every generation has required a new round of assemblers and compilers and a new set of developer expertise. Recognizing a need to provide developers with software tools to support every processor release, Intel began to develop a storehouse of optimized code for developers.

At first, Intel built special-purpose libraries for each technology domain. The Performance Libraries consisted of the Intel Image Processing, Signal Processing, Recognition Primitives, and JPEG Libraries. In addition, Intel has been responsible for the Open Source Computer Vision Library and other limited-release arithmetic and media codec libraries. Most of this functionality grew out of earlier research and product work.

The Intel® Integrated Performance Primitives (Intel® IPP) is the second generation of Intel libraries. It started as an effort to provide a lower-level API to the Image Processing Library, but it quickly became clear that a single, unified low-level library offered great benefits. As a result,

Intel IPP grew to encompass the broad range of functionality covered by all the earlier libraries.

This chapter explains the general features of Intel IPP and then describes what you can expect from the remainder of this book.

What Are the Intel® Integrated Performance Primitives?

This question has several reasonable answers. One way to break down the interesting features of the library is to explain the motivation of the name "Integrated Performance Primitives." The following sections present the ideas behind those terms one by one.

A Broad Multimedia and Computational Library ("Integrated")

Intel IPP is a single umbrella with a unified set of conventions. It covers a range of functionality that includes functions for a broad class of computational tasks and almost every media type. Almost any time-consuming function, particularly those that operate on arrays of data at a time, is a reasonable candidate for Intel IPP.

One obvious advantage to integrating all this functionality in one library is an increase in programming efficiency. Moving from domain to domain within this one library requires less development time than adopting the new set of conventions that separate libraries would require.

The API covers the following functional areas:

- *Arithmetic and Logical*: From simple vector addition to complex transcendental functions with fixed accuracies
- *Signal Processing and Audio*: Includes core DSP functions, audio and speech coding functions and examples, speech recognition primitives
- *Image Processing and Video and Image Coding*: Includes two-dimensional signal processing, image manipulation, computer vision, and JPEG, MPEG, DV, and H.26x coding
- *Matrix Arithmetic and Linear Algebra*: Emphasis on small matrices for graphics and physics
- *Strings:* A small library of functions for manipulating strings
- *Cryptography:* Implementations of several cryptographic algorithms and support functions

A Software Optimization Layer ("Performance")

The key to low-level optimization is processor-specific code.. With each successive generation, Intel processors have added new technologies and capabilities. Many of the new capabilities can't be accessed easily or uniformly from high-level languages. Most prominent among these features are single-instruction multiple-data (SIMD) instruction set enhancements like MMX™ technology, SSE, SSE-2, SSE-3, and Intel® Wireless MMX™ technology. Higher-level languages don't usually have standard constructs for fine-grained parallelism; they require use of specialized tools or programming in assembly language.

However, some computational routines have multiple applications and recur in innumerable programs. These routines are good candidates for inclusion in a library, so that they can be optimized in assembly language once per processor type and that optimized code reused many times. That's what Intel IPP is, the product of careful processor-specific optimization. Intel IPP raises the processor capabilities up to the level of C and C++ for the array of technologies listed in the previous section.

Applications targeted at PCs have remained largely processor-neutral. Most applications are compiled into a single version for all Intel architecture processors. Intel IPP is intended to allow such code to take advantage of processor-specific features. Code using Intel IPP can continue to be processor-agnostic while still getting performance benefits of using processor-specific code. The use is hidden in Intel IPP.

The dispatching mechanism is the key to maintaining ease of use while providing multiple versions of the code. Intel IPP supplies multiple implementations of each function. The dispatching methodology determines the processor type at startup and, using a jump table or processor-specific dynamic library, ensures that the most appropriate version of each function is executed. Figure 1.1 illustrates CPU-based dispatching.

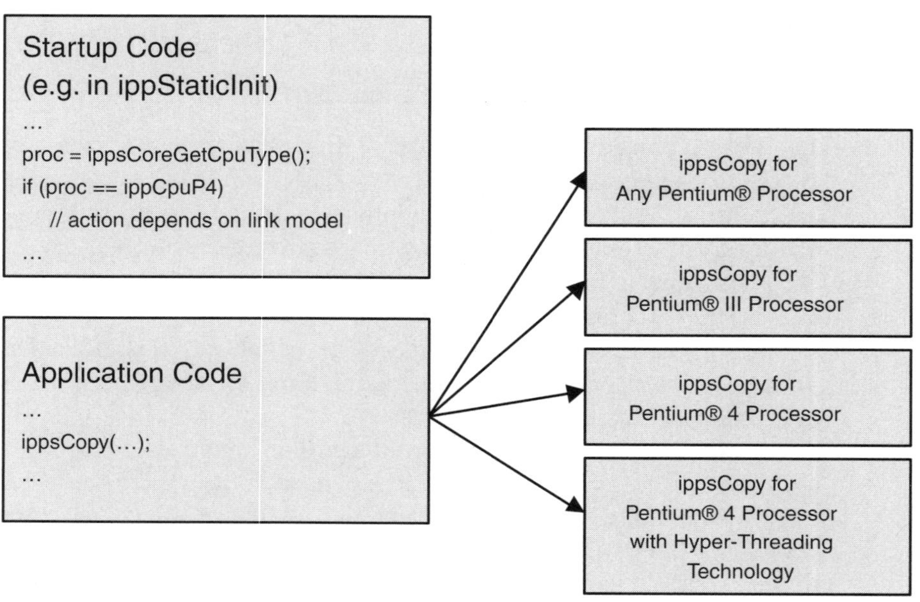

Figure 1.1 CPU Detection and Dispatching (32-bit processors)

An Extensive Set of Low-Level Operations ("Primitives")

Although they had the same goal of multimedia optimization, earlier Intel libraries contained higher-level constructs and functionality. These constructs often occluded the real benefits of the libraries: performance and generality. The Intel IPP emphasis is on primitives. The functions in Intel IPP were designed to be short, low-level, low-overhead functions.

One advantage of this approach is that each function contains fewer branches. The small functions in Intel IPP tend to support one data type and one flavor of the function. As a result, they incur no overhead in switching to branches supporting different data types.

Another advantage is that smaller functions have a smaller memory and disk footprint. Usually, an application will need only one or two versions of a function, and the fine-grained approach allows that application to link in exactly the needed functions.

A disadvantage of a low-level API is that it may not be as powerful or full-featured as a high-level API. In particular, some common components such as video compression are difficult to implement even if multiple kernels are already written. For this reason, Intel provides about two dozen coding samples for Intel IPP 4.0, most of which are for image, video, audio, and speech compression and decompression. These samples are provided in source code, allowing you to enhance and expand them. While not part of the Intel IPP API, they do make extensive use of the primitives as their optimization layer. Figure 1.2 illustrates the relationship between these samples and Intel IPP.

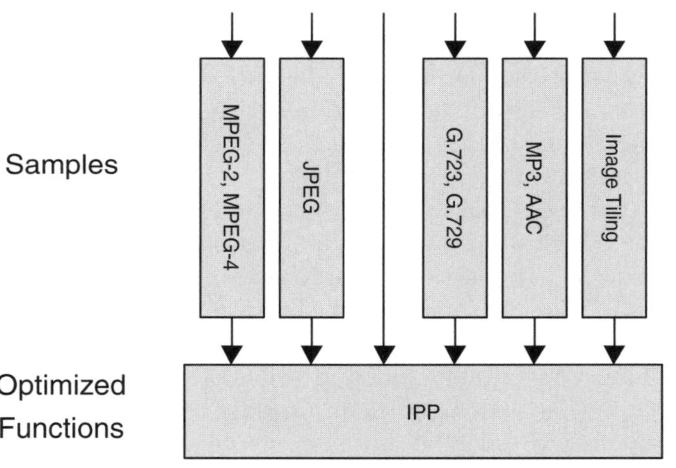

Figure 1.2 Primitives and Samples

A Cross-Platform API

Intel IPP is also a cross-platform compatibility layer, with an API similar between some platforms and identical between others. The API supported for Intel architecture processors and the Itanium® family of processors is identical, and is the same on both Windows† and Linux† operating systems. The handheld version, for Intel Personal Internet Client Architecture (Intel PCA), is a scaled-down version of that API, restricted to integer and fixed-point operations and lacking a few of the domains. It is also identical across Windows and Linux.

The level of difference between the Intel architecture version and the Intel PCA version is comparable to that of the operating system services and APIs. Regardless of the total coverage, Intel IPP use makes cross-platform development easier than it would be without Intel IPP.

Why This Book?

The documentation for the Intel® Integrated Performance Primitives is extensive–perhaps too extensive for the reader new to Intel IPP. For Intel IPP version 4.0, the four-volume manual set tops 3,000 pages. That should give some idea of the extent of the API. But it also means that the manual is more useful for reference than for reading sequentially. If you know what you are looking for, you should be able to find it. But while the manual describes every function of the entire API, it includes few examples or detailed explanations of usage. For the most part it provides little context for the uninitiated.

This book takes a teach-by-example approach. It addresses every area of the API, but it by no means covers every function, much less every flavor of every function. Chapters and sections include background and context for a functional area and examples of Intel IPP use in that area. These examples show the use of many of the important functions in the area, walking you through function selection and argument preparation. Most examples also attempt to demonstrate a useful algorithm or technique. In some cases you will be able to apply these implementations directly.

Who's the Reader?

Many of the application topics in this book, such as signal and image processing, are advanced and somewhat specialized domains of expertise. I attempt to make them accessible with the introductory sections of each topic. In most cases, I believe that the sections will be comprehensible with little or no background in the topics. If you already feel comfortable with, say, digital signal processing or JPEG, you may find yourself skimming over or skipping those sections to get to the Intel IPP-specific explanations and code examples.

Readers are expected to be comfortable with C and C++ but need not be experts. Some examples use Win32†, MFC†, or OpenGL†, but no experience with these interfaces is expected.

What are the Contents?

This book contains four parts. Chapters 1 through 4 introduce Intel IPP architecture and use, and explain a few functions. Chapters 5 through 7 deal with signal processing and audio. Chapters 8 through 10 contain information on image processing and video. Finally, Chapters 11 and 12 handle other topics, including graphics, strings, and cryptography. Each is described in more detail below.

- Chapter 1: Introduction gives you the background for the library itself and for this book about it.
- Chapter 2: Using Intel IPP shows you four approaches to building an application with Intel IPP.
- Chapter 3: Architecture and Interface provides a detailed explanation of Intel IPP data types, structures, and naming conventions.
- Chapter 4: Basic Tricks contains usage examples from "Hello World" to advanced performance tricks.
- Chapter 5: Digital Signal Processing explains the fundamentals of filtering, windowing, and transforming data with Intel IPP.
- Chapter 6: Audio Processing focuses on application of Intel IPP functions to audio signals.
- Chapter 7: Audio Coding explains MP3 and AAC standards, Intel IPP support, and samples of each.
- Chapter 8: Image Processing introduces the Intel IPP imaging conventions and functions.
- Chapter 9: Image Filtering and Manipulation shows you how to use Intel IPP image filters and geometric functions in C++ programs.
- Chapter 10: JPEG and MPEG explains JPEG and MPEG-2 standards, Intel IPP support, and samples of each.
- Chapter 11: Graphics and Physics covers implementations of graphics algorithms using Intel IPP.
- Chapter 12: Special-Purpose Domains is a quick introduction to strings, cryptography, and computer vision in Intel IPP.

CD-ROM

The included CD-ROM contains all of the examples from this book and the trial version of Intel IPP 4.0. The file `index.htm` on the root of the CD explains how to install Intel IPP and the code examples.

All the examples include workspaces and project files with the correct settings to build these examples using Microsoft† Visual C/C++ 6.0. Each workspace has the examples for one chapter. Generally, each project file in that workspace corresponds to one section, class, or example. The project files assume that Intel IPP is in its default Windows† location:

`c:\program files\intel\ipp40.`

In some cases, a single example is broken into two projects, one containing a class or functions built as a library and the other a short executable that tests that library. For example, the project defined in the project file `imaging\filter\filter.dsp` builds the `Filter` class into a library file, and the class `imaging\filtertest\filtertest.dsp` builds a short test that demonstrates a sample image filter.

Note Most core sample code will work on Linux†, but in general the interface will not. For example, the interface for the graphics examples in Chapter 11 is built using MFC† and is specific to Windows, but the model manipulation code is OS-independent and the model viewer uses OpenGL†.

Chapter 2

Using Intel® Integrated Performance Primitives (Intel® IPP)

To support a broad range of application use, the Intel® Integrated Performance Primitives supports several different linkage models for Pentium® and Itanium® architectures. None of them is difficult to use, but choosing the correct one is important and can be tricky. This chapter explains four models for linking Intel IPP into an application, including step-by-step instructions on using each. The last section contains a comparison of the options to help you choose the one that best suits a particular development environment and deployment constraints.

Linkage Options Overview

You have three ways to choose among processor-specific code versions: automatic dispatching using the provided *dispatcher dynamic libraries*, automatic dispatching using the dispatchers in the dynamic link library (DLL)-finding static library, or skipping dispatching by statically linking to a particular version.

All of the linkage options are divided into four parts: *dynamic linkage*, *static linkage with dispatching*, *custom dynamic linkage*, and *static linkage without dispatching*. They differ among themselves in size, distribution, and processor coverage. Dynamic linkage is separated from custom dynamic linkage by the size of the DLLs, and from static linkage by the distribution method and processor coverage.

Note The below descriptions generally refer to the dynamic linkage in Windows†. The same concepts are present in Linux†, as shared objects instead of DLLs.

The four options are as follows:

- Dynamic Linkage

  In the dynamic linkage model, the application links to stub libraries that are provided with the Intel IPP distribution. At run time, the startup code in the dispatcher DLLs automatically loads the best processor-specific DLLs. Any calls to Intel IPP functions go to the version of the function in that processor-specific DLL. The package distributed with the application includes all dispatcher and processor-specific DLLs.

Note All examples in this book except those in this chapter use dynamic linkage.

- Static Linkage with Dispatching

  With this model, you use provided dispatching wrappers for each function and statically link them into your application. The linker creates a self-contained application of approximately the same size as all the custom DLLs with automatic dispatching for multiple processor types. This model is most appropriate for distribution of a single Intel IPP-based application where code sharing enabled by DLLs provides no benefit.

- Custom Dynamic Linkage

  In the custom dynamic linkage model, you build your own stubs, dispatcher DLLs, and processor-specific DLLs. These DLLs use the same dispatching mechanism but are much smaller, since they only contain the functions used by the application. The custom DLLs must be shipped with the application.

- Static Linkage Without Dispatching

  This model is the simplest but least flexible. The application links to one or more processor-specific static libraries. Instead of calling and linking to a stub, the code calls the processor-specific function directly, using a modified name. The code is optimized only for one target processor type and usable only on processors that have those features. It is most appropriate for kernel-mode or driver use. All functions can link into a single executable for distribution.

  Using this method, it is also possible to create a custom dispatching solution or use the functions from different processors for different functions.

As with Intel IPP 4.0, the version for the Itanium® processor family supports only dynamic linkage and static linkage without dispatching, since there is currently only one processor-specific code version.

The basic steps to build an application or DLL with Intel IPP are:

1. Determine which headers are necessary. This information is listed in the manual entry for every function.
2. Include either `ipp.h` or all necessary headers.
3. Add the appropriate static libraries, either stubs or full implementations, to the application or DLL link step. The libraries containing the implementation for the functions declared in each header are listed in Table 2.1.

Other steps may be necessary, depending on the linkage model. The remainder of the chapter provides more detail for each model, including a detailed explanation of the mechanism, usage, and distribution for each, followed by a comparison of the four models.

Table 2.1 Libraries Linked for Each Linkage Model in Intel IPP 4.0

Header File	Dynamic Linkage[1]	Static Linkage with Dispatching or Custom Dynamic Linkage[2]	Static Linkage without Dispatching[2]
ippac.h	ippac20.lib	ippacemerged.lib ippacmerged.lib	ippacmerged.lib
ippch.h	ippch20.lib	ippchemerged.lib ippchmerged.lib	ippchmerged.lib
ippcore.h	ippcore.lib[3]		ippcorel.lib[3]
ippcp.h	ippcp20.lib	ippcpemerged.lib ippcpmerged.lib	ippcpmerged.lib
ippcv.h	ippcv20.lib	ippcvemerged.lib ippcvmerged.lib	ippcvmerged.lib
ippi.h	ippi20.lib	ippiemerged.lib ippimerged.lib	ippimerged.lib
ippj.h	ippj20.lib	ippjemerged.lib ippjmerged.lib	ippjmerged.lib
ippm.h	ippm20.lib	ippmemerged.lib ippmmerged.lib	ippmmerged.lib
ipps.h	ipps20.lib	ippsemerged.lib ippsmerged.lib	ippsmerged.lib
ippsc.h	ippsc20.lib	ippscemerged.lib ippscmerged.lib	ippscmerged.lib
ippsr.h	ippsr20.lib	ippsremerged.lib ippsrmerged.lib	ippsrmerged.lib
ippvc.h	ippvc20.lib	ippvcemerged.lib ippvcmerged.lib	ippvcmerged.lib
ippvm.h	ippvm20.lib	ippvmemerged.lib ippvmmerged.lib	ippvmmerged.lib

Custom dynamic linkage requires the listed files to create the custom DLL and stub library. The application links to that created stub library.

Versions of Intel IPP before 4.0 did not support all of these domains. Files in `stublib` for the Itanium processor family have `64` added to the name before `20`. Files in lib have `i7l` instead of `emerged` or `merged`. The Linux versions of these files start with `lib` and have the suffix `.a` instead of `.lib`.

[1] Located in the `stublib` directory

[2] Located in the `lib` directory

[3] Core libraries have no processor-specific code, so only one 32-bit and one 64-bit version are supplied.

Dynamic Linkage

The simplest and probably the most commonly used linkage model is the dynamic linkage model. This method takes full advantage of the dynamic dispatching mechanism in Windows† dynamic link libraries (DLLs) or Linux† shared objects (SOs). It has the benefits of run-time code sharing among multiple Intel IPP-based applications, automatic dispatching of processor-specific optimizations, and the ability to provide updated processor-specific optimizations without relinking or redistribution.

The dynamic linkage model works by detecting the CPU type during the initialization of the DLL or SO using `ippCoreGetCpu`. The library that dispatches the calls, `ipp??20.dll` or `ipp??.so` then loads the most appropriate processor-specific library available using a waterfall procedure. All calls to Intel IPP functions go to that processor-specific DLL or SO. This means that the optimizations of `ippsCopy_8u` for Pentium® 4 processors will be used on Pentium 4 processor-based systems, and the optimizations for Pentium® III will be used on Pentium III processor-based systems. This mechanism is illustrated in Figure 2.1.

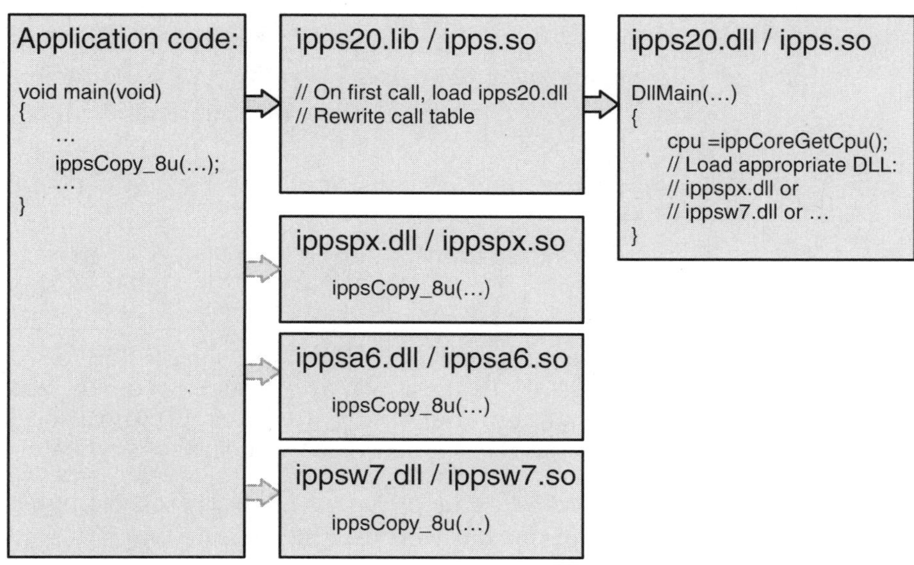

Figure 2.1 Graph of Dynamic Linkage

Each processor-specific DLL or SO is associated with a processor identifier. This two-letter code is used as a suffix for the processor-specific files containing functions optimized for that processor. For example, the processor-specific functions for signal processing on the Pentium® 4 chip are located in `ippsw7.dll` and `ippsw7.so`. The identifiers are listed in Table 2.2.

Table 2.2 Identification Codes Associated with Processor-Specific Libraries and Functions

ID Code	Processor(s)
`px`	Any Pentium® processor
`m6`	Pentium II processors (only in Intel IPP versions previous to 4.0)
`a6`	Pentium III processors
`w7`	Pentium 4 and Xeon™ processors, and processors based on Intel Centrino™ mobile technology
`t7`	Pentium 4 processor with Hyper-Threading Technology
`i7`	Itanium® and Itanium 2 processors

Most applications are good candidates for using this linkage model, which is the recommended linkage model for Intel IPP.

Usage

Link Intel IPP dynamically into an application by following these steps:

1. Include `ipp.h` or corresponding domain include files in your code.
2. Use the normal Intel IPP function names when calling Intel IPP functions.
3. Link corresponding domain import libraries, as listed in Table 2.1. For example, if you use the `ippsCopy_8u` function, link against `ipps20.lib` or `ipps.so`.
4. The run-time libraries, for example `ipps20.dll` or `ipps.so`, must be available to the application, such as on the executable search path, at run time. Using the Intel IPP Run-Time Installer, found in `ipp\tools\runtime`, is the simplest way to ensure this.

Figure 2.2 shows code that uses dynamic linking. All examples in this book, except those in this chapter, use this method and will appear similar to this code sequence.

```
#include "ipp.h"

void main(int argc, char* argv[])
{
    const int SIZE = 256;
    Ipp8u pSrc[SIZE], pDst[SIZE];

    int i;
    for (i=0; i<SIZE; i++)
        pSrc[i] = (Ipp8u)i;

    ippsCopy_8u(pSrc, pDst, SIZE);

    printf("pDst[%d] = %d\n", SIZE-1, pDst[SIZE-1]);
}
```

Figure 2.2 Code for Dynamic Linking

Distribution

The distribution of applications based on this linkage model is simplified by the presence of pre-packaged Intel IPP run-time libraries, which may be redistributed with Intel IPP-based applications. The Run-Time Installer or RTI package automatically installs a full set of Intel IPP run-time libraries in the system or specified directory.

Static Linkage with Dispatching

There is an easy way to reduce the size of the installation package without sacrificing performance. Reduction is accomplished by linking the application statically with the Intel IPP DLL-finding static libraries and the merged static libraries. The former provide statically linked stubs for the processor-specific functions in the latter. The distribution of applications based on this linkage model is quite simple since the application is self-contained.

Figure 2.3 illustrates the relationships between the static libraries used with the static dispatching model.

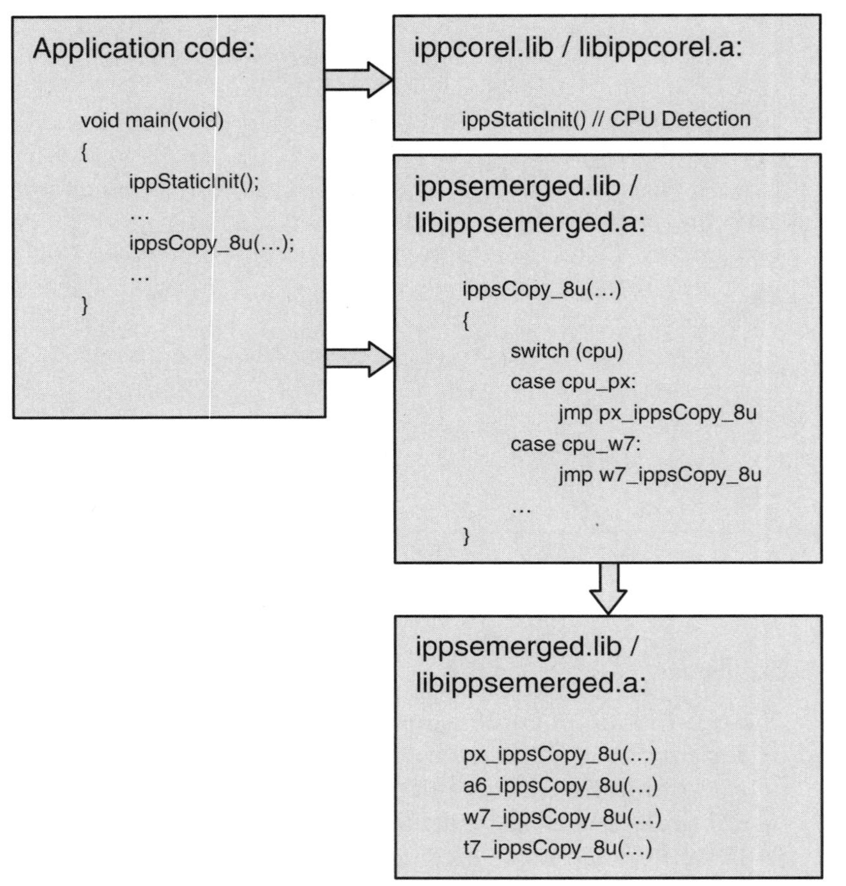

Figure 2.3 Graph of Static Linkage with Dispatching

The core static library `ippcorel.lib` or `ippcorel.a` contains the runtime processor detection functions for initializing the dispatch mechanism.

The dispatching static libraries, such as `ippsemerged.lib` or `libippsemerged.a`, provide an entry point for every Intel IPP function. The application calls via this entry point. These libraries contain no implementation code, only the dispatcher.

The dispatcher chooses among the available processor-specific implementations, checking for any available newer DLL on the system, and then passes the call on to that implementation. Since these checks are done once at startup, there is actually very little overhead in this dispatching process; only a single jump instruction is added relative to undispatched code.

The merged libraries, such as `ippsmerged.lib` or `libippsmerged.a`, contain one version of each Intel IPP function for each supported processor. To prevent symbols from conflicting and to identify each function, each target processor is assigned a two-letter code. These processor identifiers are used as prefixes for processor-specific function names. Table 2.2 lists the codes associated with each processor.

For example, `ippsmerged.lib` and `libippsmerged.a` contain several flavors of `ippsCopy_8u`. In Intel IPP 4.0, those flavors are `px_ippsCopy_8u`, `a6_ippsCopy_8u`, `t7_ippsCopy_8u`, and `w7_ippsCopy_8u`.

The dispatching static libraries require initialization before any non-decorated function names can be called. The best function is `ippStaticInit()`, which initializes the library to use the best optimization available. This function uses the same waterfall procedure as in the dynamic linkage model. It is also possible to substitute the function `ippStaticInitBest`, which does not look for new processor models, or `ippStaticInitCpu`, which designates one specific CPU type. The latter is particularly good for debugging, since it can force any processor type.

Because of the combined benefits of size, convenience, performance, and capability, this model is appropriate in most cases. The model is particularly useful when distributing a single Intel IPP-based application, in which case the code sharing made possible by dynamic linkage provides no benefit.

Usage

Follow these steps to use static linkage with dispatching:

1. Include `ipp.h` or corresponding domain include files.
2. Before calling any Intel IPP functions, initialize the static dispatcher by calling `ippStaticInit()`, which will perform the complete dispatching process. This function will call `ippStaticInitBest()` if no better code is available. These functions are declared in `ippcore.h`.
3. Use the normal Intel IPP function names, such as `ippsCopy_8u`, to call Intel IPP functions.

4. Link the application with corresponding dispatching static libraries, merged libraries, and the core library. For example, if ippsCopy_8u is used, link to the libraries ippsemerged.lib, ippsmerged.lib, and ippcorel.lib, in that order, to build under Windows. For Linux, link to the libraries libippsemerged.a, libippsmerged.a, and libippscorel.a, in that order.

Figure 2.4 shows a short example of code using static linkage in this way.

```
#include "ipp.h"

void main(int argc, char* argv[])
{
    ippStaticInit();

    const int SIZE = 256;
    Ipp8u pSrc[SIZE], pDst[SIZE];

    int i;
    for (i=0; i<SIZE; i++)
        pSrc[i] = (Ipp8u)i;

    ippsCopy_8u(pSrc, pDst, SIZE);

    printf("pDst[%d] = %d\n", SIZE-1, pDst[SIZE-1]);
}
```

Figure 2.4 Code for Static Linkage with Dispatching

In some cases, you might want to use ippStaticInitCpu instead of ippStaticInit. This will force the use of the code for a specified processor, so it may be useful in debugging results on a particular processor. This function can also be helpful in doing performance comparisons on a single platform. It should be used with caution, since using code for the wrong processor can cause the execution of illegal instructions.

Distribution

In this case, application distribution requires no additional files, since the result of the build is a compact, self-contained application with automatic dispatching for multiple processor types.

Custom Dynamic Linkage

It is also possible to use a dynamic linkage model and still get high-performance code with a small footprint. By creating a custom DLL, you can retain the benefits of full processor coverage and code sharing, but a custom DLL contains only the functions needed. This model is often used in application designs where multiple applications or products within a single company utilize a subset of Intel IPP.

This model is similar to the static linkage with dispatching, except that you link the Intel IPP functions into a separate DLL instead of the application proper. The DLL uses the same Intel IPP dispatching static, merged, and core libraries.

Figure 2.5 shows how this model works.

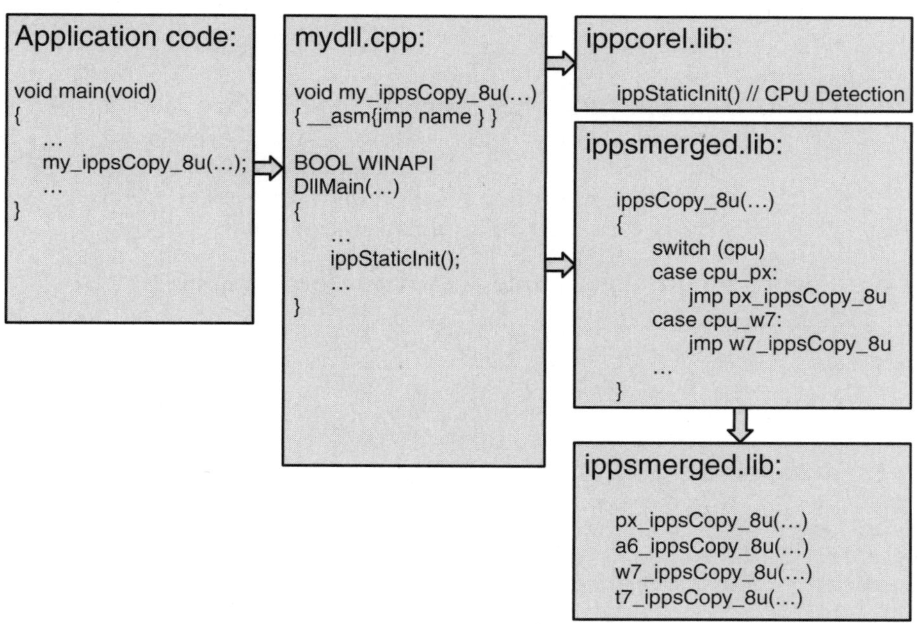

Figure 2.5 Graph of Custom Dynamic Linkage

Usage

To create a custom DLL, you need to create a separate build step or project that generates the DLL and stubs. To do so, perform these steps:

1. Copy the function prototypes of all Intel IPP functions used from the Intel IPP include files into a header file. This example uses the filename `mydll.h`.
2. Write a DLL initialization function called `DllMain`. Call the function `ippStaticInit` from the function to initialize the dispatching mechanism. This example uses the filename `mydll.cpp`.
3. In the same file (`mydll.cpp`), write a wrapper function for each Intel IPP function prototyped in `mydll.h`. The wrapper function serves as a direct jump to the correct processor-specific optimized version of the Intel IPP function. These wrapper functions can be automatically generated by redefining the macro IPPAPI before including `mydll.h`:

   ```
   #define IPPAPI(type,name,args) \
   __declspec(naked dllexport) \
   void __STDCALL my_##name args \
   { __asm {jmp name } }
   ```

4. Compile the file containing `DllMain` as a DLL link in `ippcorel.lib` and both the `ippXXmerged.lib` and `ippXXemerged.lib` files containing every Intel IPP function used. The compiler should generate both the DLL and an import library to which an application can link.

Figure 2.6 lists an example of the code for a custom DLL.

```
========= mydll.h ==========
#ifndef __MYDLL_H__
#define __MYDLL_H__

#ifndef IPPAPI
#define IPPAPI(type,name,args)
#include "ipps.h"
#undef  IPPAPI
#define IPPAPI(type,name,args) extern type __STDCALL my_##name
args;
#endif
```

```
#ifdef __cplusplus
extern "C" {
#endif

/* List Function Prototypes Here */
IPPAPI(IppStatus, ippsCopy_8u,( const Ipp8u* pSrc, Ipp8u* pDst,
int len ))
IPPAPI(IppStatus, ippsCopy_16s,( const Ipp16s* pSrc, Ipp16s*
pDst, int len ))

#ifdef __cplusplus
}
#endif
#endif // __MYDLL_H__

//======== mydll.cpp =========

#define WIN32_LEAN_AND_MEAN
#include <windows.h>
#include <ipp.h>

#undef  IPPAPI
#define IPPAPI(type,name,args) \
    __declspec(naked dllexport) \
    void __STDCALL my_##name args { __asm {jmp name } }
#include "mydll.h"

BOOL WINAPI DllMain(HINSTANCE hinstDLL,
DWORD fdwReason, LPVOID lpvReserved)
{
    switch( fdwReason )
    {
    case DLL_PROCESS_ATTACH:
         ippStaticInit
    default:
         hinstDLL;
         lpvReserved;
         break;
    }
    return TRUE;
}
```

```
//======== customdynamictest.cpp =========
void main(int argc, char* argv[])
{
    const int SIZE = 256;
    Ipp8u pSrc[SIZE], pDst[SIZE];

    int i;
    for (i=0; i<SIZE; i++)
        pSrc[i] = (Ipp8u)i;

    my_ippsCopy_8u(pSrc, pDst, SIZE);

    printf("pDst[%d] = %d\n", SIZE-1, pDst[SIZE-1]);
}
```

Figure 2.6 Code for Custom Dynamic Linkage

More advanced techniques are also possible. For example, other shared code may be merged into this DLL to reduce the total number of files in the application. It is also possible to write function wrappers that link only a subset of the processor-specific optimizations; the next section contains information on how to do so.

For debugging, you can replace the call to the `ippStaticInit` function with a call to the `ippStaticInitCpu` function that loads the code for a particular processor.

Distribution

The output of the custom DLL process is a single DLL that contains versions of all functions needed for each processor. This DLL needs to be available to the application on the target machine.

Such DLLs are considerably smaller than the entire Intel IPP DLL set.

Static Linkage Without Dispatching

The absolute smallest memory and disk footprint is obtained by linking directly with the merged static libraries. These merged libraries, such as `ippsmerged.lib` or `libippsmerged.a`, contain one version of each Intel IPP function for each supported processor. Each function name is prefixed with a processor identification string as outlined in the custom dynamic linkage section above. When the application links statically to this library, only one of these processor-specific versions is included for each function. Macros in the code can specify which processor-specific version of the code the linker should use, eliminating the need for the initialization and dispatching code contained in `ippcorel.lib` or `libippcorel.a` and the dispatching static libraries.

> **Note** The code optimized for Itanium processors is in a separate library due to the different 64-bit format.

This method does not dispatch and as a result may produce code that attempts to execute illegal instructions on some processors. Therefore, developers need to be mindful of the target processor capabilities to confirm correct installation of processor-specific code. In addition, this method produces less-than-optimal code if the code is chosen to support the least-common denominator processor. For these reasons, its use should be restricted to cases in which it is necessary, such as processor-specific applications and embedded or kernel mode code.

Figure 2.7 illustrates static linkage. Only the processor-specific function referenced in the application code is linked into the application executable from the merged static library.

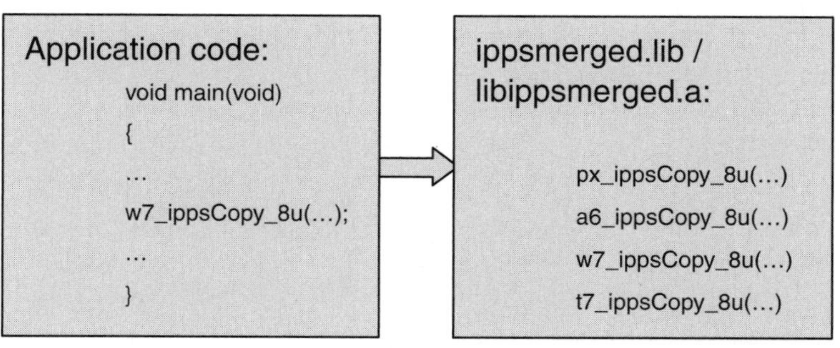

Figure 2.7 Graph of Static Linkage Without Dispatching

Usage

To link with Intel IPP static libraries without dispatching, follow these steps:

1. Prior to including `ipp.h`, define the following preprocessor macros:

   ```
   #define IPPAPI(type,name,arg) \
   extern type __STDCALL w7_##name arg;
   #define IPPCALL(name) w7_##name
   ...
   #include "ipp.h"
   ```

   The first macro adds the processor code, in this case `w7`, to the function names in Intel IPP header files. All declarations of functions in Intel IPP header files will be changed by this macro. The second defines a macro through which Intel IPP functions can be called without adding the processor code to each call explicitly. Include `ipp.h` after this statement.

2. Wrap each Intel IPP function call in your application with an `IPPCALL` macro. For example, a call to `ippsCopy_8u` would be expressed as:

   ```
   IPPCALL(ippsCopy_8u)(…)
   ```

3. Link against the appropriate merged static library or libraries, such as `ippsmerged.lib` or `libippsmerged.a`.

Figure 2.8 shows a short example of code using static linkage in this way.

```
#define IPPAPI(type,name,arg) \
extern type __STDCALL px_##name arg;
#define IPPCALL(name) px_##name

#include "ipp.h"

void main(int argc, char* argv[])
{
    const int SIZE = 256;
    Ipp8u pSrc[SIZE], pDst[SIZE];

    int i;
    for (i=0; i<SIZE; i++)
        pSrc[i] = (Ipp8u)i;

    IPPCALL(ippsCopy_8u)(pSrc, pDst, SIZE);

    printf("pDst[%d] = %d\n", SIZE-1, pDst[SIZE-1]);
}
```

Figure 2.8 Code for Static Linkage Without Dispatching

There are alternatives to this procedure. For one, the Intel IPP package includes header files, such as `ipp_w7.h`, in `ipp\tools\staticlib` that define macros individually for every Intel IPP function. If used, these header files replace the `IPPCALL` macro.

Alternatively, it is possible to use the modified name in each call. The disadvantage of this approach is that every function call must be changed individually to change the target processor. However, this approach does allow the usage of different processor versions for each function call.

For the Itanium family of processors, Intel IPP 4.0 has only one code version and therefore does not require the prefix when using static linkage. The files linked, such as `ippsi71.lib`, contain only the `i7` version of the code with unmodified names. However, it is reasonable to assume that this will change in future versions of the library, and it is safest to use the `IPPCALL` macro as a placeholder:

```
#define IPPCALL(name) name
```

Finally, it is possible to mix this version with the merged static library with dispatching, particularly as a workaround or for debugging purposes. Mixing can force the use of a particular processor-specific version of a particular Intel IPP function while still using dispatching for others. To do this, combine the instructions above and those in the previous section. When listing functions, follow the above instructions for the non-dispatched functions and the previous section's instructions for the dispatched functions. To use dispatching, call the function using the normal name, but to avoid dispatching call it by the prefixed name.

If attempting this mixed-model approach, do not use the automatic header files such as `ipp_w7.h`.

Distribution

The distribution in this case contains the same files as it would without Intel IPP. Because this model includes only one processor version, the size can be the smallest of all the models. However, if you currently create one executable per processor type, the total incremental size will be comparable to that in the static linkage with dispatching model.

Linkage Model Comparison

The basic trade-off among the linkage models is complexity versus performance size. Dynamic linkage is the simplest model and ensures the highest performance overall. Static linkage is the smallest model but is not full-featured; custom dynamic linkage and static linkage with dispatching are about the same size. Only static linkage is appropriate to kernel mode code.

The following are the main questions to consider when choosing a linkage model:

- Are there limitations on how large the application executable can be? Are there limitations on how large the application installation package can be?
- When installing the application, are there restrictions on placing files in system folders?
- How many Intel IPP-based executables are in the application? Are there other Intel IPP-based applications that often co-exist on the users' systems?
- Is the Intel IPP-based application a device driver or similar "ring 0" software that executes in kernel mode at least some of the time?
- Is the application supported on a range of processor types, or is the application explicitly only supported on a single type of processor? For example, is the application part of an embedded or custom hardware/software system for which only one type of processor is used?
- How important is ease-of-use?
- How often will the application be updated? Will application components be distributed independently or always packaged together?

The answers to these questions should determine which linkage model is best for a given application. The features of each are listed in Table 2.3 and summarized in more detail in the next section.

Table 2.3 Linkage Models Quick Comparison

Feature	Dynamic Linkage	Static Linkage with Dispatching	Custom Dynamic Linkage	Static Linkage Without Dispatching
Processor updates	automatic	automatic	recompile and redistribute	release new processor-specific application
Optimizations	all processors	all processors	all processors	one processor
Build	link to stub static libraries	link to static libraries and stubs	build separate DLL	link to processor-specific libraries
Calling	regular names	regular names	modified names	processor-specific names
Distribution	provided run-time installer	no extra distribution	distribute custom DLLs	no extra distribution
Total Binary Size	large	small	small	smallest
Executable Size	smallest	small	smallest	small
Kernel Mode	no	no	no	yes
Multi-Threading Support	yes	no	yes	no

Linkage Features Summary

This last section summarizes the key comparison points of the four linkage models, and expands on the notes in Table 2.3.

Dynamic Linkage

Dynamic linkage enables updates with new processor optimizations without recompiling or relinking.

This type of linkage is easy to use for several reasons. Usage is facilitated because it allows the use of unmodified function names. Building is facilitated because dynamic linkage does not require an additional build step and adds only one static library per Intel IPP header file. The distribution is facilitated by the prepackaged run-time installer package that installs the DLLs or SOs.

Only the dynamic libraries get additional performance from multi-threaded implementations.

If it is not already installed, the complete Intel IPP installation requires about 50 megabytes of additional disk space. If it was previously installed, it requires no additional disk space. This requirement is constant regardless of the number of executables using Intel IPP.

If not already loaded, the process of loading the DLLs or SOs into memory at startup takes a certain amount of time and memory.

Dynamic linkage is not appropriate for code with restricted OS access, such as drivers, or for applications or components that require a very small download, such as applets or plug-ins.

Static Linkage with Dispatching

Static linkage with dispatching enables updates with new processor optimizations without recompiling or relinking.

The installation footprint is smaller the full DLL or SO installation.

Using static linkage with dispatching is almost as easy as dynamic linkage. It allows the use of unmodified function names, though it does require a call to `ippStaticInit`. Building with this model adds two static libraries per Intel IPP header file but does not require an additional build step. Because it produces a self-contained application executable, installation and packaging are no more difficult.

This model might be slightly larger or less efficient than the DLL models because code will be duplicated for multiple Intel IPP-based applications.

Static linkage with dispatching is not appropriate for code with restricted OS access, such as drivers.

Custom Dynamic Linkage

The installation footprint is smaller than the full DLL or SO installation. Further, this method produces the smallest installation package when multiple applications use some of the same Intel IPP functions

The custom DLLs or SOs require an additional build step and must be rebuilt to integrate new processor-specific optimizations.

The custom DLLs contain modified Intel IPP function names, which must be used throughout your code.

Custom dynamic linkage is not appropriate for code with restricted OS access, such as drivers.

Static Linkage Without Dispatching

Static linkage results in the smallest, but least flexible, executable. Each function call supports only one processor type, so supporting multiple processors requires multiple executables. Updates to a new library with new processor optimizations require the creation of a new executable.

Using static linkage without dispatching is a little more complicated than with dispatching because it requires the use of processor-specific names. Other than that, usage and building are the same but with only one static library per header file.

This model is suitable for kernel-mode/device-driver use.

Chapter 3

Architecture and Interface

This chapter introduces readers to the interface and architecture of the Intel® Integrated Performance Primitives (Intel® IPP). The Intel IPP is a large API containing thousands of functions. To make these thousands of functions intelligible to the developer, Intel IPP follows naming and interface conventions. The goal is to make Intel IPP behavior predictable by making it uniform and consistent across all functions in the API. The experienced Intel IPP user should be able to determine the name and arguments of a complicated Intel IPP function without relying excessively on the manual.

The goal of this chapter is to lay groundwork that is needed for all subsequent chapters, with a particular focus on understanding the scope of the functions. Within each function group, the data types, data layouts, structures, and protocols are described. Additional emphasis is placed on the function naming and calling conventions.

The Three Input Types

Intel IPP operations can be divided into three large groups, each of which has a corresponding function prefix and a volume in the Intel IPP manual. The fundamental distinction among the groups is the type of input array on which each operates. The three types for these groups are:

- Signals and Arrays

  This category includes most functions operating on one-dimensional arrays of data. Functions in this group have the prefix `ipps`, because in many cases the one-dimensional array is a signal and many of the operations are signal-processing operations.

  Examples of array operations include:

  - Vectorized scalar arithmetic operations, such as adding two arrays element-wise into a third array
  - Vectorized math.h-type functions, such as taking the sine of each number in an array
  - Digital signal processing (DSP) operations
  - Audio processing and encoding
  - Speech recognition primitives
  - Cryptographic operations
  - String operations

- Images

  An image is a two-dimensional array of pixels. Images are distinguished from general two-dimensional arrays in two main ways. First, they usually have multiple channels; these channels represent separate color planes. Second, many functions that operate on images, such as filters and geometric operations, expect pixels adjacent in space to be related.

  Image functions in Intel IPP have the prefix `ippi`. The following are some examples of imaging functions:

  - Arithmetic, logical, and statistical functions for images
  - Image filtering and manipulation functions
  - Two-dimensional signal processing functions, such as might support radar imagery or medical imagery
  - Computer vision functions
  - Video coding primitives
  - Raster-based graphics functions, such as drawing primitives

- Vectors and Matrices

  Vectors and matrices are one- and two-dimensional arrays that are treated as linear equations or data vectors and subjected to linear algebra operations. In Intel IPP, these functions have the prefix `ippm`. Some examples of matrix and vector operations are:

  - Multiplication and addition of vectors and matrices
  - Dot product, cross-product, and inversion
  - Equation solvers

A few administrative functions in Intel IPP do not operate on one of these three data types. These functions have `ipp` as a prefix. They are described in more detail below under "Core Functions".

Functions are primarily grouped according to the data array arguments they take, but in some cases functions don't take data arrays. In those cases, the functions are usually grouped with the related functions. For example, the function `ippsUnpackSideInfo_MP3` takes a bit stream as input rather than a signal. This function is grouped with the signal functions because it is part of a group of audio coding functions for MP3 that do operate upon signals.

Fundamental Data Types

C, C++, and most other languages emphasize architecture independence for fundamental types at the expense of some specificity. For example, at the language level, the `int` type has always been described in general terms as the core type of the executing architecture. Even though the `int` type now almost universally indicates a 32-bit integer even on 64-bit architectures, the long-term future of such types is hard to predict. For example, at the inception of Intel IPP, the future size of the type `long` on 64-bit architectures was uncertain.

Because Intel IPP functions rely so heavily on vector operations, the exact size of data elements in bits is a key characteristic of input and output data. For this reason, the types of arrays in Intel IPP are specified to be of a certain bit length. Support for complex numbers, which are not fundamental types in C or C++, is an added advantage of these definitions.

Fundamental types are of the form:

```
IppNN<u|s|f>[c]
```

The code `NN` represents the number of bits in the type, such as 8 or 32. The characters `u` and `s` indicate signed and unsigned integers, respectively, `f` indicates a floating-point number, and `c` indicates that the number is interleaved complex.

Table 3.1 is a complete list of types defined in Intel IPP. The "code" column in the table below indicates the characters found in the function name for functions that take arrays of that type. Multiple versions of the same function that take different data types are distinguished in this way.

Table 3.1 Fundamental Types in Intel® Integrated Performance Primitives (Intel® IPP)

Code	Intel IPP Type	Usual C Definition
8u	Ipp8u	unsigned char
8s	Ipp8s	char
16u	Ipp16u	unsigned short
16s	Ipp16s	short
32u	Ipp32u	unsigned int
32s	Ipp32s	int
32f	Ipp32f	float
64f	Ipp64f	double
1u	Ipp8u	unsigned char* bitstream, int offset
16sc	Ipp16sc	struct { Ipp16s re; Ipp16s im; } Ipp16sc;
32sc	Ipp32sc	struct { Ipp32s re; Ipp32s im; } Ipp32sc;
32fc	Ipp32fc	struct { Ipp32f re; Ipp32f im; } Ipp32fc;
64fc	Ipp64fc	struct { Ipp64f re; Ipp64f im; } Ipp64fc;

Signals and Arrays

While functions supporting each of the three data types share common elements, such as argument order, each of the three also has characteristics particular to the conventions of its data type. These are particularly visible in the function name.

To provide a very efficient and flat function hierarchy, almost every flavor of every function has its own entry point. The function name is required to differentiate all of these flavors. The convention used in Intel IPP is to compose the name from series of largely orthogonal components. The behavior of each function in Intel IPP can be understood by breaking the name down into these components. This section and the two following explain the syntax of Intel IPP function names, so that even a complicated operation can be easily understood if read and found if sought.

For one-dimensional signals and arrays, the name is constructed as follows:

```
ippsBasename[_modifiers]_types[_descriptors]
```

The `Basename` component is one or more words, acronyms, and abbreviations that identify the algorithm/operation.

The `Modifiers` are abbreviations that choose among flavors of the base name that recur across more than one entry point. Modifiers are function-specific, and new modifiers can be created to make function groups. Modifiers are often used to indicate when a function is specific to a particular algorithm, or to differentiate similar operations on different algorithms or data layouts.

The `Types` are shorthand codes for the input and output data types. These are listed in the first column of Table 3.1. If the input and output types are different, both are listed with the input first.

The `Descriptors` are individual characters that indicate particulars of the operation. Table 3.2 lists the descriptor codes used for functions with prefix `ipps`. If more than one descriptor is used, they are listed in alphabetical order. Many functions have no descriptors, and rely entirely on the default behavior.

Some examples of functions on one-dimensional arrays with an `ipps` prefix are:

- `ippsAdd_32f` (prefix, base name, and type)
- `ippsConvert_16s32f_Sfs` (prefix, base name, input and output types, and a descriptor)
- `ippsFIROne_Direct_32f_ISfs`(prefix, base name, modifier, type, and two descriptors)

Table 3.2 Descriptor Codes for ipps Functions

Code	Description	Example
Axx	For advanced arithmetic operations, specifies the bits of **accuracy** of the result.	ippsSqrt_32f_A11 and ippsSqrt_32f_A24 ippsCos_64f_A50 and ippsCos_64f_A53
I	The operation is **in-place**. The result of the operation is written back into the source, and one argument is both a source and a destination.	ippsFlip_16u takes three arguments, src, dst, and len. ippsFlip_16u_I takes two arguments, srcdst and len.
Sfs	The function **scales** the result of the operation, shifting it right by the scaleFactor argument. This generally takes place at a higher bit resolution to preserve precision.	ippsAddC_16s_Sfs(src, val, dst, len, scaleFactor) adds val to each element of src, divides by scaleFactor, and puts the result in dst.

Images

The names of functions that operate on images are constructed from the same elements as the signal functions. The form is the following:

```
ippiBasename[_modifiers]_types[_descriptors]
```

The biggest difference lies in the decoding of descriptors. The descriptors for imaging functions are more extensive. Table 3.3 lists the descriptor codes used for functions with prefix ippi in the order in which they occur in the function name.

Gray images generally have a single channel of data, the intensity of the image. Color images generally have three channels of data; the most common image is the three-channel red-green-blue (RGB) image. The next section illustrates the layouts of these and other multichannel images in more detail.

Unlike the other descriptors, every function that operates on image data will have a channel count descriptor, since no default channel count is defined. Every image is either interleaved and is described as Cn or is planar and is described as Pn.

Table 3.3 Descriptor Codes for `ippi` functions

Code	Description	Example
`AC4`	The images have 4 channels, the fourth of which is the alpha channel. When identified in this way, the alpha channel will be excluded from the operation.	`ippiAddC_8u_AC4R`, `ippiMean_8u_AC4R`
`C1, C3, C4`	The images have 1, 3 or 4 channels of data interleaved in memory. C1, indicating one channel, can also be used for multiplane images in most cases.	`ippiDCT8x8Fwd_16s_C1I`, `ippiRGBToYUV_8u_C3R`
`C2`	The images have *interleaved channels* in memory. This is a special case, in which frequently the second "channel" is itself two interleaved, subsampled channels. The sizes and other arguments, though, are based on a 2-channel image.	`ippiYCbCr422ToRGB_8u_C2C3R`, `ippiJoin422_8u_P3C2R`
`I`	The operation is performed *in place*. The result of the operation is written back into the source, and one argument is both a source and a destination.	`ippiDCT8x8Fwd_16s_C1` takes three images as arguments, `src1`, `src2`, and `dst`. `ippiDCT8x8Fwd_16s_C1I` takes two images as arguments, `src` and `srcdst`.
`M`	The operation uses a *mask* to determine which pixels on which to operate.	`ippiSet_8u_C1MR(val, dst, dstStep, size, mask, maskStep)`
`P3, P4`	The images have 3 or 4 channels of data arranged in separate planes; the operation takes an array of pointers to image planes.	`ippiRGBToYCbCr420_8u_C3P3R` takes interleaved RGB input and writes the result into three separate output arrays.
`R`	The function operates on a defined *Rectangle of Interest* (ROI) for each of the input images. Most image-processing functions have this descriptor and use ROI.	
`Sfs`	The function scales the result of the operation, shifting it right by the `scaleFactor` argument. This shift generally takes place at a higher bit resolution to preserve precision.	`ippiAddC_8u_AC4Sfs(src, values, dst, size, scalefactor)` adds `values` to each element of `src`, divides by `scaleFactor`, and puts the result in `dst`.

When input and output channel layouts don't agree, both source and destination are listed, in that order. For example, the function `ippiCopy_8u_C3P3R` copies the three channels of an interleaved image into three separate one-channel planes.

Channel-order Images

Images of type `C3` or `C4` are interpreted as having three or four interleaved channels. Images of type `AC4` are also interpreted as having four interleaved channels, but the fourth channel is not read or written.

Table 3.4 shows the data layouts for the possible channel-order images. Each number represents a different data channel, such as "red" or "green".

Table 3.4 Data Layouts for Channel-Order Images

Descriptor	Index 0	1	2	3	4	5	6	7	8
C1	1	1	1	1	1	1	1	1	1
C3	1	2	3	1	2	3	1	2	3
C4	1	2	3	4	1	2	3	4	1
AC4	1	2	3	A	1	2	3	A	1
C2	1	2	1	2*	1	2	1	2*	1

* Depending on data type, this entry may be a subsampled channel different from the other "2".

Planar Images

The planar image format has separate arrays for each channel. Planar images are passed to Intel IPP functions as an array of pointers and, when the `R` specifier is also used, an array of step parameters.

These functions take interleaved RGB input and write the result into three separate output arrays:

```
ippiRGBToYUV422_8u_C3P3(const Ipp8u* pSrc, Ipp8u*
    pDst[3], IppiSize imgSize)
ippiRGBToYCbCr420_8u_C3P3R(const Ipp8u* pSrc,
    int srcStep, Ipp8u* pDst[3], int dstStep[3],
    IppiSize roiSize)
```

Most functions don't require a separate function to handle planar images. An image with multiple channels arrayed in separate planes can generally be treated as multiple images with a single channel, and handled by multiple calls to the `C1` version of the function. Color conversions and other cross-channel operations are the obvious exception to this rule, so such functions generally have `P3` versions.

Rectangle of Interest (ROI)

Most operations expect that the size of the operation is not exactly the size of the images. These operations have the `R` descriptor. In these operations, every image pointer is followed by a `step` parameter. This parameter identifies the width in bytes of the lines of the image.

Chapter 8 explains the memory layout of images and the interpretation of image parameters in more detail.

Mask ROI

Some Intel IPP functions support bit masks. The mask for an image is another image of the same dimensions, though the memory stride can be different and the data type is always `Ipp8u`. Figure 3.1 illustrates the behavior of one operation that takes a mask, `ippiSet_8u_C1MR`.

1	**1**	**1**	0	0	0
1	**1**	0	0	0	0
1	**1**	0	0	0	0
1	0	0	0	0	0
1	0	0	0	0	0

Mask

1	2	3	4	5	6
1	2	3	4	5	6
1	2	3	4	5	6
1	2	3	4	5	6
1	2	3	4	5	6

Source Image

99	**99**	**99**	4	5	6
99	**99**	3	4	5	6
99	**99**	3	4	5	6
99	2	3	4	5	6
99	2	3	4	5	6

Destination Image

Figure 3.1 Operation of `ippiSet_8u_C1MR` with a `value` Argument of 99

Matrices

Understanding the function name for matrix and array functions, those with the prefix `ippm`, requires a little more information than is in the previous two sections. Fortunately, functions in this group support operations, data types, object types, and memory layouts in the most orthogonal way; that is, for any given operation, Intel IPP is very likely to have a function supporting a needed layout, object type, and data type. The result is that there are a large number of functions, but it should be easy to determine any one that is needed by constructing its name.

The name of functions with an `ippm` prefix takes the following form:

```
ippmBasename_objects_type[_objectsize][_descriptors]
```

Some examples are `ippmAdd_vv_32f`, `ippmMul_mva_32f_3x3`, and `ippmLUDecomp_ma_32f_6x6_LS2`.

Because of the nature of linear algebra and vector and matrix operations, there are few operations in this group. The entire list is: `Copy`, `Extract`, `LoadIdentity`, `Saxpy`, `Add`, `Sub`, `Mul`, `CrossProduct`, `DotProduct`, `L2Norm`, `LComb`, `Transpose`, `Invert`, `FrobNorm`, `Det`, `Trace`, `Gaxpy`, `LUDecomp`, `LUBackSubst`, `QRDecomp`, and `QRBackSubst`.

The `ippm` functions support only floating point inputs. Almost all functions support `Ipp32f` and `Ipp64f` equally.

Objects

There are two new fields in this function name. The first is the objects field. This field indicates the basic layouts or object types of the sources. It takes the form

```
<srccode1>[srccode2]
```

If an operation has two sources, both sources are indicated even if they are the same. The destination object types are not specified because they are uniquely determined by the input object types.

There are three basic types: constants, vectors, and matrices, indicated by `c`, `v`, and `m`. For example, `ippmMul_mv_32f` multiplies a matrix by a vector and puts the result in a vector of the same size.

If a matrix should be transposed on input, that transposition is specified by an additional `T` in the object code. For example, `ippmMul_vmT_32f` multiplies a vector by a transposed matrix and puts the result in a vector of the same size.

Arrays of vectors and matrices can be passed in to `ippm` operations. The operation on an array of vectors or matrices proceeds exactly as would multiple calls of the same operation on the individual vectors and matrices. For example, ippmMul_mva_32f multiplies a matrix against each vector in an array and puts the result in an array of vectors of the same size.

Table 3.5 lists all the object codes and their meanings.

Table 3.5 Object Codes for ippm Functions

Code	Meaning	Description
c	Constant	Single value / scalar
V	Vector	One-dimensional array of values
M	Matrix	Two-dimensional array of values
mT	Transposed Matrix	Matrix to be treated as if flipped over the diagonal
Va	Array of Vectors	Array, list, or sequence[1] of vectors
Ma	Array of Matrices	Array, list, or sequence of matrices
maT	Array of Transposed Matrices	Array, list, or sequence of transposed matrices

Sizes

Many matrix and vector functions are written to take only a specific size of matrix or vector. The objectsize field indicates the size of the matrix, if there is a matrix involved, or the size of the vector if not. Objects of differing sizes are frequently involved in the operation, but these sizes are uniquely determined by the size of the matrix and the operation type. For example, ippmMul_vc_32f_3x1 multiplies a 3-by-1 vector by a constant, and ippmMul_mv_32f_3x3 multiplies a 3-by-3 matrix by a 3-by-1 vector.

If no size is specified, the size is taken as an argument. If specified, the options for vector size are 3x1, 4x1, 5x1, and 6x1, and the options for matrix size are 3x3, 4x4, 5x5, and 6x6.

Descriptors

The functions with prefix ippm have just three descriptors: L, P, and S2. The first two indicate layouts that are alternatives to the default. The last allows an additional stride as a parameter to the function. This descriptor is independent of the layout, so a total of five descriptor combinations other than the default are used: L, P, S2, LS2, and PS2.

[1] The exact layout of an "array-of" object depends on the descriptors. See Figure 3.2 for more details.

Table 3.6 Descriptor Codes for `ippm` Functions

Code	Description	Example
None	Each input is a pointer to the first in an array of objects.	`ippmMul_mam_32f_3x3 ( const Ipp32f* pSrc1, Ipp32s src1Stride0, Ipp32s src1Stride1, const Ipp32f* pSrc2, Ipp32s src2Stride1, Ipp32f* pDst, Ipp32s dstStride0, Ipp32s dstStride1, Ipp32u count);`
`L`	Each input is an array of pointers to objects.	`ippmMul_mam_32f_3x3_L(` **`const Ipp32f** pSrc1,`** `Ipp32s src1ROIShift, Ipp32s src1Stride1,` **`const Ipp32f* pSrc2,`** `Ipp32s src2Stride1,` **`Ipp32f** pDst,`** `Ipp32s dstROIShift, Ipp32s dstStride1, Ipp32u count);`
`P`	Each input is an array of pointers to elements, each pointing to that element in the first object.	`ippmMul_mam_32f_3x3_P(` **`const Ipp32f** pSrc1,`** `Ipp32s src1ROIShift,` **`const Ipp32f** pSrc2,`** `Ipp32s src2ROIShift,` **`Ipp32f** pDst,`** `Ipp32s dstROIShift, Ipp32u count);`
`S2`	An extra stride exists between each element of an array or matrix.	`ippmMul_mam_32f_3x3_S2( const Ipp32f* pSrc1, Ipp32s src1Stride0, Ipp32s src1Stride1,` **`Ipp32s src1Stride2,`** `const Ipp32f* pSrc2, Ipp32s src2Stride1,` **`Ipp32s src2Stride2,`** `Ipp32f* pDst, Ipp32s dstStride0, Ipp32s dstStride1,` **`Ipp32s dstStride2,`** `Ipp32u count);`

Bold lines are the arguments that are distinct for each descriptor code

The function `ippmCopy` is a special case. Since differing source and destination layouts are supported, the source code is listed first, then the destination. In this case, if the source or destination is the default layout, that fact is represented with the code `S`.

Table 3.6 lists the descriptors and gives an example of each.

Figure 3.2 shows the default, L, and P layouts graphically.

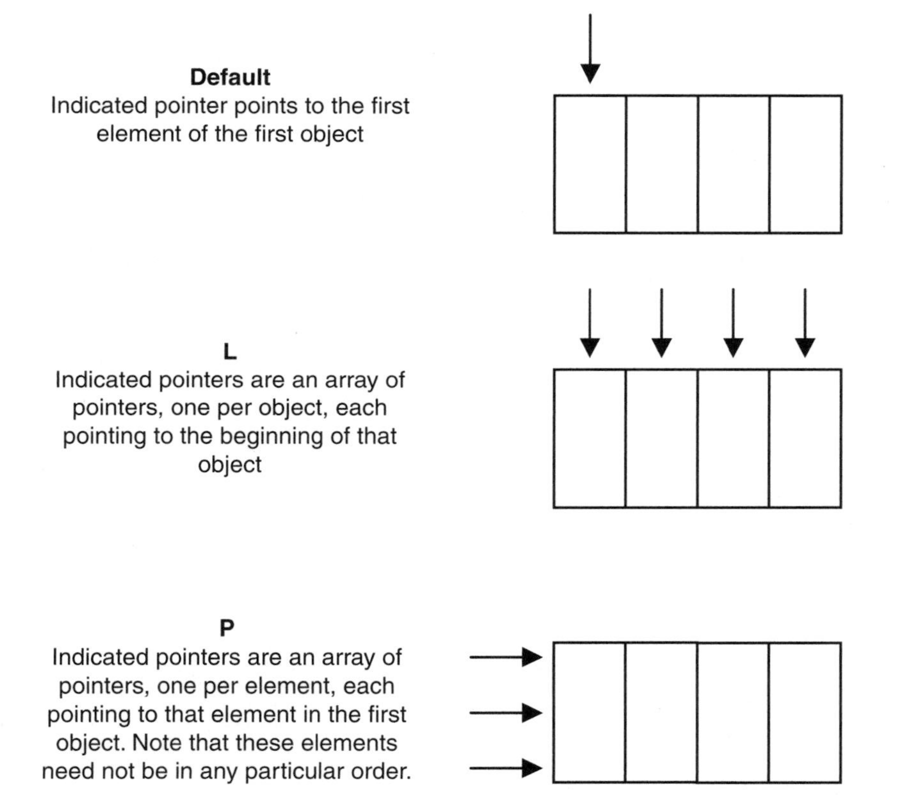

Default
Indicated pointer points to the first element of the first object
L
Indicated pointers are an array of pointers, one per object, each pointing to the beginning of that object
P
Indicated pointers are an array of pointers, one per element, each pointing to that element in the first object. Note that these elements need not be in any particular order.

Figure 3.2 `ippm` Data Layouts in Graphical Form

See the Intel IPP manual for further details on these data layouts and strides, and Chapter 11 for usage examples for many matrix and vector functions.

Core Functions

The library contains a few type-neutral operations for detecting and setting system and Intel IPP configuration. These functions are generally prefixed with `ippCore`. Some examples are:

- `ippCoreGetCpuType` gets the CPU type
- `ippGetLibVersion` returns the library version
- `ippCoreGetCpuClocks` reads the processor clock

Domains

For organizational purposes, the Intel IPP is internally divided into subdivisions of related functions. Each subdivision is called a *domain*, and generally has its own header file, static libraries, DLLs, and tests. The Intel IPP manual indicates in which header file each function can be found, but doesn't explain the individual domains. Table 3.7 lists each domain's code, header and library names, and functional area.

Table 3.7 Domains in Intel IPP 4.0

Code	Header	Libraries	Description
ippAC	ippac.h	ippac*.lib	Audio Coding
ippCP	ippcp.h	ippcp*.lib	Cryptography
ippCV	ippcv.h	ippcv*.lib	Computer Vision
ippIP	ippi.h	ippi*.lib	Image Processing
ippJP	ippj.h	ippj*.lib	JPEG
ippMX	ippm.h	ippm*.lib	Small Matrix Operations
ippSP	ipps.h	ipps*.lib	Signal Processing
ippSC	ippsc.h	ippsc*.lib	Speech Coding
ippSR	ippsr.h	ippsr*.lib	Speech Recognition
ippVC	ippvc.h	ippvc*.lib	Video Coding
ippVM	ippvm.h	ippvm*.lib	Vector Math

Library names refer to the version for Windows†. The wildcard (*) refers to one of the following: `i7l, emerged, merged, 20, 6420.`

These domains frequently map easily to the three data types and the prefixes `ipps`, `ippi` and `ippm`, but the match is not perfect. For example, while the functions in `ippSP.h`, `ippSC.h`, and `ippSR.h` all operate on signal data, and `ippCV.h` is almost exclusively imaging functions, `ippMP.h` is divided between signal and image functions.

Multi-step Operations

As a library of primitives, Intel IPP functions are stateless; that is, they don't "remember" data about previous data arrays, other arguments, or operations. Functions do not maintain static variables, and structures external to the functions contain many tables and the state necessary to execute complex functions efficiently. This is important for predictability, as well as to enforce thread safety and reentrancy.

Many functions can be divided into an initialization phase that needs to be performed only once per set of parameters and an execution phase that is performed on every block of data. For efficiency, it is desirable to separate these operations into two functions so that one may be called once and the other called once per loop.

To maintain the results of the initialization, and sometimes to maintain the state that evolves between function calls, these operations have associated structures, maintained by the user but not defined publicly, that either contain a static state or dynamic state. The static structures are called "Spec" or specification structures, and the dynamic state structures are called "State" structures.

When such a multi-step operation is called for, it follows one of two formats, and may also have a related "direct" function version. Both formats have a function that initializes the State or Spec structure and a function that performs the operation; they differ in how the memory for the structures is allocated. The three possible calling sequences to call such Intel IPP functions are:

- The sequence that optimizes for multiple loops and is the easiest to use is the `InitAlloc` sequence. This sequence allocates the memory for the specification or state structure and initializes any tables or state needed to execute the function. This sequence has three steps:

  1. Allocate memory and initialize state: `ippFooInitAlloc`
  2. Execute operation: `ippFoo`
  3. Free the memory for the state structure: `ippFooFree`

- The sequence that allows for multiple steps and gives control over memory is the `Init` sequence. This sequence provides a function to indicate how much memory is necessary for the specification or state structure and a separate function to initialize whatever tables or state are needed to execute the function. There are also three steps for this sequence, excluding the user-controlled memory allocation:
  1. Get the amount of memory needed: `ippFooGetSpecSize`
  2. Initialize the memory allocated by the user: `ippFooInit`
  3. Execute operation: `ippFoo`
- Many operations that have multi-step versions as described above also support a single-step version. In that case, the modifier direct indicates the single-step version. Such functions require only one step: Initialize tables if necessary then execute: `ippFoo_Direct`.

Examples of the `Init` and `InitAlloc` sequences are described below.

The State and Spec structure's content is not meant to be accessible directly by the user of the library. In many cases, the fields are machine dependent. For this reason, the structures should not be dereferenced, nor can they be; the field definitions are only contained in internal header files, while in the public header the structures are declared as merely `struct IppsXXXSpec`.

`Init` Sequence

At least three functions are defined for an `Init` sequence. The first gets the size of the structure and possibly an additional memory buffer. This function takes enough arguments to describe the operation sufficiently to calculate the memory needed to create its tables. In some cases more than one function is provided to get the sizes of multiple buffers.

The second function initializes the structure to a usable state. The parameters of this function include all the arguments describing the operation that are necessary to initialize the tables and, if initializing a State structure, the initial state.

The third function performs the operation. This function takes arguments just as any other operation would, except that many of the inputs are replaced by the single Spec or State structure. That is, arguments used to build the structure are not provided a second time to the operation.

The `Init` version of the filter function FIR requires the following three functions:

```
ippsFIRGetStateSize_32f(int tapsLen, int* stateSize);

ippsFIRInit_32f (IppsFIRState_32f* pState, const Ipp32f*
   pTaps, int tapsLen, const Ipp32f* pDlyLine);

ippsFIROne_32f (Ipp32f src, Ipp32f* pDstVal,
   IppsFIRState_32f* pState);
```

The code sequence in Figure 3.3 executes FIR using user-controlled memory.

```
IppsFIRState_32f* pState;
int size;

ippsFIRGetStateSize_32f(tapsLen, &size);
pState = (IppsFIRState_32f*) ippsMalloc_8u(size);
ippsFIRInit_32f(pState, pTaps, tapsLen, pDlyLine);

for (i=0; i<tapsLen; i++)
      ippsFIROne_32f(pSrc[i], &pDst[i], pState);

ippsFree(pState);
```

Figure 3.3 FIR Executed with `ippsFIRInit`

`InitAlloc` Sequence

Three functions are generally defined for an `InitAlloc` sequence. The first allocates and initializes the State or Spec structure, the second performs the operation, and the third frees the memory assigned to State or Spec structure. If a function sequence has both an `InitAlloc` and an `Init` version, the function actually performing the operation is almost always the same for both.

For example, the filter function FIR provides the following three related functions, the second of which is identical to that used above:

```
ippsFIRInitAlloc_32f (IppsFIRState_32f** pState, const
   Ipp32f* pTaps, int tapsLen, const Ipp32f* pDlyLine)

ippsFIROne_32f (Ipp32f src, Ipp32f* pDstVal,
   IppsFIRState_32f* pState)

ippsFIRFree_32f(IppsFIRState_32f* pState)
```

The code sequence in Figure 3.4 uses these functions to execute a filter without having to explicitly allocate memory.

```
IppsFIRState_32f* pState;
ippsFIRInitAlloc_32f(&pState, pTaps, tapsLen, pDlyLine);

for (i=0; i<tapsLen; i++)
      ippsFIROne_32f(pSrc[i], &pDst[i], pState);

ippsFIRFree_32f(pState);
```

Figure 3.4 FIR Executed with `ippsFIRInitAlloc`

Return Values

All Intel IPP functions return an `IppStatus` code. Each code is assigned a name prefixed with `ippSts` and fixed number. These codes are enumerated in `ippdefs.h`. Figure 3.5 lists a few of these codes.

By convention, positive status codes are warnings. Warnings indicate that the operation was able to complete, but some abnormality occurred, such as an overflow or division by zero. Negative status codes represent errors. Errors indicate that the operation was interrupted before completion. A status code of zero, defined as `ippStsNoErr` or `ippStsOK`, indicates that the operation completed successfully and without incident.

The function `ippCoreGetStatusString` provides an explanatory text string associated with an error code.

```
ippStsStepErr                = -14,
ippStsScaleRangeErr          = -13,
ippStsDataTypeErr            = -12,
ippStsOutOfRangeErr          = -11,
ippStsDivByZeroErr           = -10,
ippStsMemAllocErr            = -9,
ippStsNullPtrErr             = -8,
ippStsRangeErr               = -7,
ippStsSizeErr                = -6,
ippStsBadArgErr              = -5,
ippStsNoMemErr               = -4,
ippStsSAReservedErr3         = -3,
ippStsErr                    = -2,
ippStsSAReservedErr1         = -1,

 /* no errors */
ippStsNoErr              =   0,

 /* warnings */
ippStsNoOperation        =   1,
ippStsMisalignedBuf      =   2,
ippStsSqrtNegArg         =   3,
ippStsInvZero            =   4,
ippStsEvenMedianMaskSize=   5,
ippStsDivByZero          =   6,
ippStsLnZeroArg          =   7,
ippStsLnNegArg           =   8,
ippStsNanArg             =   9,
```

Figure 3.5 Sample Intel® Integrated Performance Primitives (Intel® IPP) Error Codes

Arguments

The order of arguments passed to Intel IPP functions is consistent throughout the API. Knowing the rules and guidelines for the order of these arguments makes calling Intel IPP functions much quicker. The graph in Figure 3.6 breaks down the argument hierarchy.

First Argument	....	Last Argument		
Data			Operation-Specific Arguments	General Arguments
Source Data	Source / Dest. Data	Destination Data		

For each data element:

Array, Image, or Matrix				
Pointer to data array	Index for `Ipp1u` data	Stride(s) or step(s)	Size information	Other information about the data

Figure 3.6 Argument Hierarchy in Intel IPP

The data arrays are the arrays, matrices, and images that are the fundamental type for the operation. Constants for arithmetic operations such as `AddC` are also considered source data, and scalar outputs are considered destination data.

The size and other data characteristics such as memory stride are placed after the last array to which that size applies. For example, the function `ippsAddC_16s_Sfs(src, value, dst, len, scaleFactor)` has the constant value next to the other source, and has the length argument after both the source and destination pointers.

Operation-specific arguments are used by only one group or a small subset of functions. These include filter taps, FFT scale values, operation-specific flags, and State and Spec structures.

General arguments are common across any function. Examples include the scale factor and memory buffers. They are passed last.

Structures

Use of structures is limited in the Intel IPP API. Almost all structures fall into one of the following categories:

- Fundamental types unsupported by the compiler, implemented as structures
- Basic structures
- State and Spec structures for multi-step operations
- Structures for codec-specific, "vertical" functions

Fundamental Type Structures

Intel IPP expands the number of fundamental types to include interleaved complex numbers by defining structures that give a type to arrays of these numbers. The following are a few of the complex numbers used in Intel IPP:

```
typedef struct { Ipp8u  re; Ipp8u  im; } Ipp8uc;
typedef struct { Ipp16s  re; Ipp16s  im; } Ipp16sc;
typedef struct { Ipp32f  re; Ipp32f  im; } Ipp32fc;
```

These types are treated the same as the other fundamental types; that is, they are passed by value if a scalar or as a pointer if in an array. For example, the `Set` function has the following prototype:

```
ippsSet_16sc(Ipp16sc val, Ipp16sc* pDst, int len);
```

Basic Structures

The basic structures in Intel IPP are `IppiPoint`, `IppiSize`, and `IppiRect`. They are defined as follows:

```
typedef struct { int x; int y; } IppiPoint;
typedef struct { int width; int height; } IppiSize;
typedef struct { int x; int y;
int width; int height; } IppiRect;
```

These structures are also passed into Intel IPP functions by value, such as in the `Resize` function:

```
ippiResize_8u_C1R (const Ipp8u* pSrc, IppiSize srcSize,
      int srcStep, IppiRect srcROI,
      Ipp8u* pDst, int dstStep, IppiSize dstRoiSize,
      double xFactor, double yFactor, int interpolation)
```

Multi-step Operation Structures

As noted above, the public definition of these Spec and State structures does not expose any of the fields in the `struct`. This is to maintain cross-platform and cross-processor compatibility without sacrificing performance. Within the structure, the table alignment, layouts, and other characteristics are each specific to the microarchitecture.

These structures are publicly declared as `structs` with no definition. As a result, they can be handled only as pointers to the structures. Figure 3.7 shows an example.

```
// Public header file declaration
struct FFTSpec_C_16sc;
typedef struct FFTSpec_C_16sc IppsFFTSpec_C_16sc;

// Internal header file (platform-specific):
typedef struct FFTSpec_C_16sc {
int order;
int bufSize;
#if defined(MMX_SUPPORTED)
...
```

Figure 3.7 Multi-step Operation Structures Example

Chapter 4

Basic Techniques

This chapter provides basic and general examples that are intended to increase your comfort level with Intel® Integrated Performance Primitives (Intel® IPP) while introducing generally useful functions in various domains. Many of these examples demonstrate techniques that might not be obvious even to experienced users.

Many of the Intel IPP functions perform basic operations, basic enough to be written in one to four lines of C++. Some of them even duplicate or extend functionality available in the standard libraries, such as `sin` and `memcpy`. The main distinction is that the vectorized versions in Intel IPP operate much more quickly than they would if written in a higher-level language. However, it can be tricky to adapt code from the standard scalar version of such functions to the Intel IPP vector version.

Other Intel IPP functions perform complex arithmetic functions. In many cases, these arithmetic functions are aimed at a particular domain but have more than one application.

This chapter shows how to write code that uses these functions, and some clever ways to apply these functions. The breadth of applicability of these functions may not be immediately obvious, so many of the examples below show very useful alternate applications for these basic functions.

Measuring Performance with `CoreGetCpuClocks`

Processors use electronic clocks to organize their operations. Each time the processor clock changes state, the processor performs some calculation. In almost all cases, the clock oscillates at a fixed rate, so counting ticks of this clock is an excellent way to measure time. To allow the use of this clock for performance measurement, the core of many Intel processors includes a register that counts the ticks of this clock.

The Intel IPP function `CoreGetCpuClocks` polls this 64-bit register. Subtracting two successive polling results gives a very accurate measurement of elapsed time. This result is the most fine-grained measurement of elapsed processor time, although, depending on the application, it may not be the most accurate measure of algorithm performance.

Figure 4.1 lists a short example using this function to make two measurements.

```
#include "ipp.h"
int main(int argc, char* argv[])
{
    Ipp64u start, end;

    start = ippCoreGetCpuClocks();
    end = ippCoreGetCpuClocks();

    printf("Clocks to do nothing: %d\n",
     (Ipp32s)(end - start));

    start = ippCoreGetCpuClocks();
    printf("Hello World\n");
    end = ippCoreGetCpuClocks();

    printf("Clocks to print 'hello world': %d\n",
     (Ipp32s)(end - start));

    return 0;
}

Results:

Clocks to do nothing: 99
Hello World
Clocks to print 'hello world': 26750
```

Figure 4.1 Simple Code and Results for Performance Measurement

Notice that the time "to do nothing", measured in this example by two adjacent `ippCoreGetCpuClocks` calls, is still around a hundred cycles. One refinement on this method, useful when measuring short code sequences, is to subtract the overhead to get the CPU clock from the time measured. The overhead limits the precision of the measurement, and subtracting it out allows you to capture code segments that take as little as 10 cycles to execute. This code performs this calculation:

```
start = ippCoreGetCpuClocks();

start = ippCoreGetCpuClocks() * 2 - start;

// Code to be measured goes here

end = ippCoreGetCpuClocks();
```

This method almost always gives more accurate results, but can occasionally produce anomalous results, including, rarely, negative cycle counts. These anomalous results occur because `CoreGetCpuClocks` returns a count of *processor* ticks and not *process* ticks. The operating system always has multiple processes that are competing to use the processor, so there is no assurance that the entire time between the two calls to `CoreGetCpuClocks` is spent executing that code. If the operating system switches to another thread or process done during a performance test, the resulting clock count includes any other operation that occurs between the two CPU clock checks.

The time slices used by non-real-time operating systems, including Microsoft Windows†, are large enough that a single performance measurement is accurate most of the time. But no matter how short, every operation is interrupted some of the time. For this reason, it may be preferable to perform the operation multiple times then take the average of the executions. This method has the added advantage that it warms the cache, but it can take considerably longer and is only suitable for performance tests, not production code. This method is used for most performance measurements in this chapter.

For more accurate readings, a further improvement is to perform the operation multiple times and record the cycle count of each, as above, then use the median of the result. This approach almost completely removes the effect of truly anomalous readings.

The performance comparisons done in this chapter are relative to other code. For these comparisons, clock ticks are a good unit. When an absolute time measurement is needed, divide the number of clock ticks by the processor frequency to get the time. For example, the clock of a processor at 2 gigahertz counts $2*10^9$ ticks per second. On that processor, a clock measurement of 200,000 cycles would correspond to $2*10^5$ cycles/($2*10^9$ cycles / second) = 10^{-4} seconds = 0.1 milliseconds.

This calculation is best performed using `float` or `double` rather than `Ipp64s`.

The function `ippsGetCpuFreqMhz` estimates the CPU frequency through empirical measurement.

Note

To get consistent and fair performance measurements, the data should be always in cache (warm) or always out of cache (cool). Clock counts throughout this chapter and elsewhere in the book have been taken using a warm cache that has already loaded the data of interest. In most cases, either pre-performing the operation or performing the operation multiple times warms the cache.

It's preferable to choose a warm cache because:

- A test program can reliably warm a cache but it is harder to reliably cool it. Therefore, always using a warm cache produces more consistent results.
- Intel IPP optimizations are focused more on processor performance than on main memory performance. This is another reason that the measurements can be more consistent when the data is in cache.
- The best possible performance is only achievable by using good memory management techniques and keeping data in cache. Therefore, this method provides a good performance target for carefully programmed code.

Because a warm cache is used, the performance results are accurately reflective of some situations, particularly if memory is managed carefully, but results may vary if memory is not managed carefully.

Copying Data

The `ippsCopy` function is useful any time you need to copy medium to large chunks of data, whether the data is an array, string, or structure. This function is a very high-performance memory copy, but the call and other function overhead are justified only for copies over a certain size. To base the decision to use `ippsCopy` on actual performance data, compare three methods of copying `short` data. The first is written in C:

```
for (i=0; i<len; i++) pDst[i] = pSrc[i];
```

The second is this C standard library call:

```
memcpy(pDst, pSrc, len*2);
```

The third is this Intel IPP call:

```
ippsCopy_16s(pSrc, pDst, len);
```

The results are graphed in Figure 4.2. The array size necessary to justify the library function call is surprisingly small. Based on this data, a crossover point at length 16 is reasonable for this function on this system. For smaller arrays, writing inline code is preferable; for larger arrays, calling Intel IPP functions is better. These results are specific to a particular configuration, but this derived crossover point is unlikely to vary widely much from system to system.

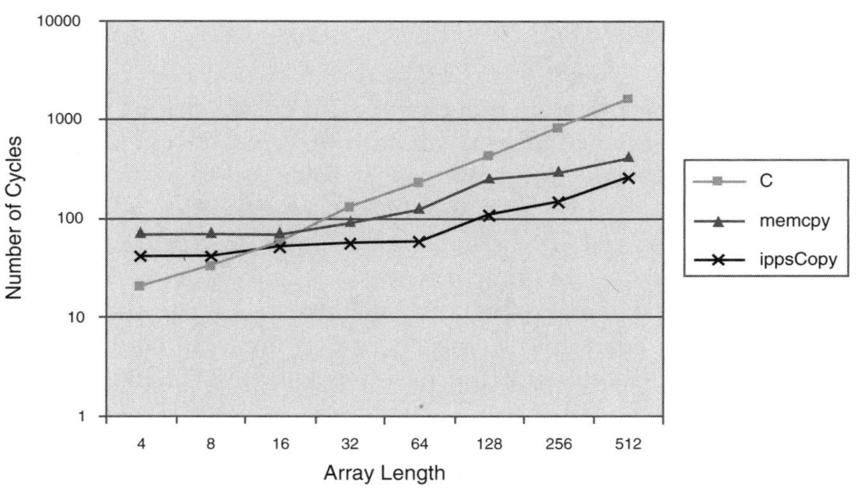

Figure 4.2 Performance Crossover Point Illustrated for Copy Using C++, `memcpy`, and `ippsCopy`

Converting Types and Layouts

One of the areas covered the most strongly by Intel IPP is conversions. As a practical matter, a library such as Intel IPP cannot support every data type and every data layout for every function. Therefore, some data layouts and a few data types are supported only through conversions. Obviously, conversion can't degrade application performance with too much overhead, so particular emphasis is placed on the performance of these conversions.

This section will look at two types of conversions:

- Converting data from one fundamental data type to another
- Rearranging data layouts, including converting from one structure to another

Converting Data Types with Convert

C and C++ implicitly convert between two integer types or between an integer and a floating-point type. The downsides of this conversion are slow performance and an uncontrolled loss of precision. Explicitly converting data with Intel IPP can be faster and give more control, but as with `copy`, call overhead should be considered.

The conversion functions of the form `ippsConvert_<Type1><Type2>` copy data out of an array of type `Type1` into an array of type `Type2`. If the destination type has greater or equal dynamic range and precision, the data is merely copied into a larger space as the new type, perhaps with sign extension. However, if the new type has less precision or less dynamic range than the old type, the conversion usually includes a scale factor or a rounding mode.

The following is a simple example. This line performs an explicit `short`-to-`float` conversion using a C-style cast:

```
for (i=0; i<len; i++) pDst[i] = (float)pSrc[i];
```

This call performs the same short-to-float conversion in a batch:

```
ippsConvert_16s32f(pSrc, pDst, len);
```

The graph in Figure 4.3 shows the performance of the two methods of conversion. Based on this data, even an array length of eight justifies the overhead of a call to Intel IPP. These numbers are system and compiler dependent, but do illustrate how inefficient the built-in numeric conversions can be.

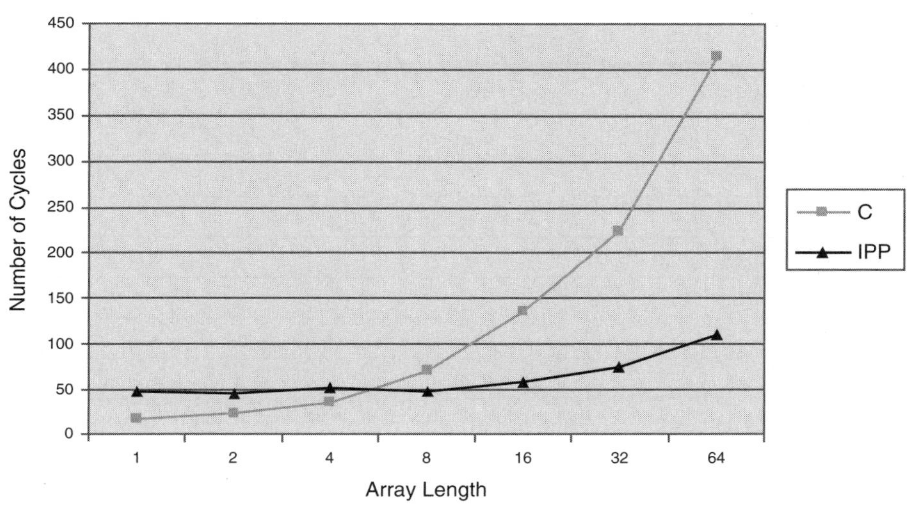

Figure 4.3 Comparison of Time to Execute Conversions Using C and Intel IPP

In copying data from type `short` to type `float` there is no potential loss of precision, so both operations just copy each short value into the float format. If the conversion were from `float` to `short`, there could be a precision issue and a dynamic range issue. The C automatic conversion between the types would clamp the result, forcing it into the dynamic range of the destination type, but the Intel IPP version takes additional parameters to control the operation. The `scaleFactor` parameter sets the number of bits by which to shift the result right. The `rndMode` parameter specifies the rounding mode, either **round-to-zero** or **round-to-nearest**. Most rounding in Intel IPP is round-to-nearest, which rounds floating point results to the nearest integer, except for numbers ending in .5 which are rounded to the nearest even integer.

The result of an Intel IPP conversion from `float` to `short` can be written as

```
Min(32767, Max(-32768, Round (src >> scaleFactor)))
```

For reference, Table 4.1 lists all of the available conversions. Note that the "signal" and "image" conversions in this table are neither perfectly overlapping nor completely disjoint. The focus in these two areas is on conversions to and from the core types for that area, which are `Ipp16s` and `Ipp32f` for signals and `Ipp8u` for images.

Table 4.1 Conversion Functions in Intel IPP 4.0

	To						
From	**8u**	**8s**	**16u**	**16s**	**32s**	**32f**	**64f**
8u	-		i	i	i	s,i	
8s		-		s	i	s,i	
16u	i		-			s,i	
16s	i	s		-	s	s,i	
32s	i	i		s	-	s	s
32f	s,i	s,i	s,i	s,i	s	-	s
64f					s	s	-

Note: "i" indicates that the function exists as a version of `ippiConvert`. "s" indicates that it exists as a version of `ippsConvert`. "-" indicates that the types are the same.

Rearranging Data with `Real`, `Imag`, `RealToCplx` and `CplxToReal`

Intel IPP supports, to a greater or lesser extent, three formats for real and complex data:

- Real or imaginary data in a single array (RRR…)
- Complex data, interleaved (RIRIRI…)
- Complex data, separated (RRR… III…)

Most data arrays are real arrays of the first category, and all but a few Intel IPP functions support this type of data. The second format is represented by the types ending in "c" such as `Ipp16sc` and `Ipp32fc`. The third is automatically supported by any function that supports the first category that is closed to the real and imaginary domains; that is, for which real or imaginary inputs produce real or imaginary outputs, respectively. Real filters, for example, can be applied to real and imaginary components in separate calls. For other functions, this type is supported only through the conversions in Table 4.2. The functions `Real`, `Imag`, and `CplxToReal` separate interleaved channels. The function `RealToCplx` inverts this operation, reassembling an interleaved signal from separated data.

Table 4.2 Some Interleaving Functions in Intel® Integrated Performance Primitives (Intel® IPP)

Function name	Description
`ippsReal`	Extract even-numbered channels into a separate array
`ippsImag`	Extract odd-numbered channels into a separate array
`ippsRealToCplx`	Interleave two arrays into a single array
`ippsCplxToReal`	De-interleave an array

These conversion functions are ostensibly intended for converting between real and complex domains, but the operations they perform are fundamental and have broader applications. They have many applications to real signals, including stereo audio. In this case, instead of real-imaginary-real-imaginary data, the input or output might be right-left-right-left channel data.

Take, for example, the function `ippsRealToCplx`, which interleaves two arrays of "real" numbers into a single array of "complex" numbers. The complex type `Ipp32fc` is defined in C as follows:

```
typedef struct {
    Ipp32f  re;
    Ipp32f  im;
} Ipp32fc;
```

Passing `ippsRealToCplx` a right-channel array as the real-array parameter and a left-channel array as the imaginary-channel parameter efficiently interleaves two stereo channels. This transfer is likely to require that the type be cast from `Ipp32f*` array to `Ipp32fc*`.

Interleaving two signals or channels may be done in C with the code:

```
for (i=0; i<len; i++) {
      pDstStereo[i*2] = pSrcR[i];
      pDstStereo[i*2+1] = pSrcL[i];
}
```

Both source and destination are of type `Ipp32f`. The same operation is performed by this call to `RealToCplx`:

```
ippsRealToCplx_32f(pSrcR, pSrcL, (Ipp32fc*)pDstStereo,
   len);
```

The performance of these two code snippets is summarized in Figure 4.4.

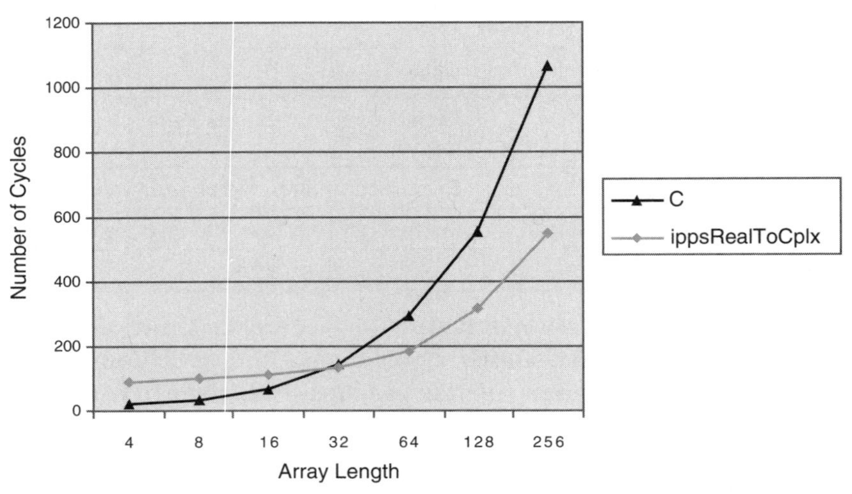

Figure 4.4 Comparison of Time to Interleave Data Using C and Intel® Integrated Performance Primitives (Intel® IPP)

Initializing Arrays

Often it's necessary to fill an array `pDst` with a sequence of results of function such that pDst[x] = f(x). Many functions can be calculated most efficiently by performing the operation on several inputs in a single function call. When you have a way of executing f() in a vectorized fashion and a potential performance advantage to doing so, a good method for calculating the elements of `pDst` is to fill an array with a sequence of numbers from 0 to `len and` then pass this array of values into `f()`. Essentially, instead of calling f(x) many times in a loop using many values for `x`, call `f(x)` once on an array of inputs for x, and structure `f()` accordingly.

For efficiency, this input array can be filled by vector code. Several Intel IPP functions can be adapted for this purpose. This section implements and compares the efficiency of possible methods of generating input arrays for functions.

Initializing One-Dimensional Arrays with `ippsVectorRamp`

Intel IPP has functions that are capable of generating data that could be adapted to this purpose. These functions are listed in Table 4.3. Of these, the desired functionality is clearly implemented in `ippsVectorRamp`, but that is not necessarily the highest performing method.

Table 4.3 Data Sequence Generation Functions in Intel® Integrated Performance Primitives (Intel® IPP)

Function name	Description
`ippsTriangle_Direct`	Generate a triangle wave
`ippsVectorRamp`	Generate a sequence of linearly increasing or decreasing values
`ippsAddC`	Add a constant to each value of an array

The simplest C code that fills a vector with increasing values is

```
for (i=0; i<len; i++) pIndex[i] = i;
```

The function `ippsTriangle` generates a triangle wave with controllable period, symmetry, magnitude, phase, and offset. This function can be made to generate a rising sequence of values by generating only a quarter of a single wave, the portion of the wave that rises from 0 to the magnitude. The "triangle wave" that emulates this code above has amplitude `len` and offset 0.0:

```
ippsTriangle_Direct_16s(pIndex, len, len,
   0.25/(double)len, 0.0, &phase);
```

The function `VectorRamp` is intended only to create a single ramp, not multiple periods of rise-and-fall, so it *should* be faster. It takes only a starting offset (0.0) and a slope (1.0):

```
ippsVectorRamp_16s(pIndex, len, 0.0, 1.0);
```

The results of this comparison are in Figure 4.5.

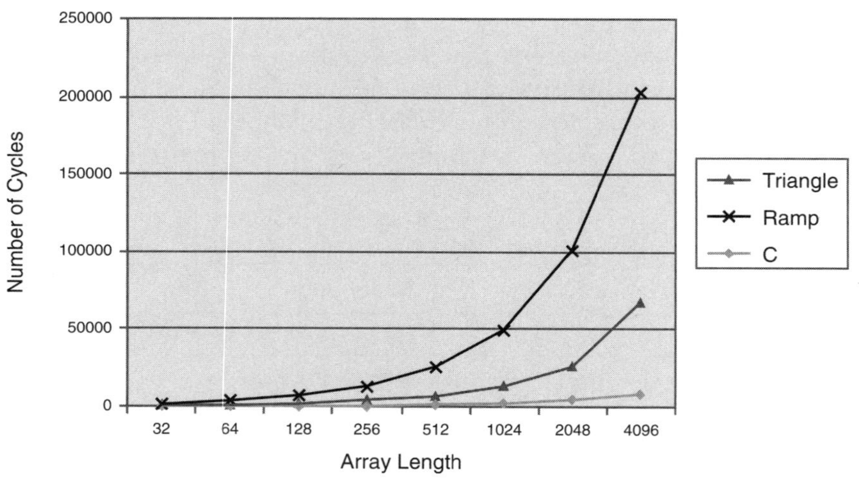

Figure 4.5 Comparison of Time to Create a Ramp Signal

These results indicate that even `VectorRamp` is not a good substitute for simple C/C++ code, perhaps because it is too general, perhaps because it uses floating point for internal calculation. That being the case, an integer function probably better suits this need.

Since there is no purely integral version of `ippsRamp`, the function `AddC` can be used to create one. Starting with a ramp created in C, `AddC` can be used to create a new range of a ramp of the same slope. For example, a ramp from 0…255, plus 256, creates a ramp from 256…511.

The process starts with a ramp, created with C/C++, in the first block of an array. Each successive loop uses `AddC` to fill another block as the sum of the previous block's elements and a constant. The following code does this for cases in which `len` is an integer multiple of `buflen`:

```
for (i=0; i<buflen; i++) pIndex[i] = i;
for (i=buflen; i<len; i+=buflen)
   ippsAddC_16s_Sfs(pIndex+i-buflen, buflen, pIndex+i,
      buflen,0);
```

Note that the source block runs from `pIndex[i-buflen]` to `pIndex[i-1]` and the destination block runs from `pIndex[i]` to `pIndex[i+buflen-1]`. Each loop adds the constant `buflen` to the source block and stores it in the destination.

The performance of this code is significantly better than all previous versions, as shown in Figure 4.6.

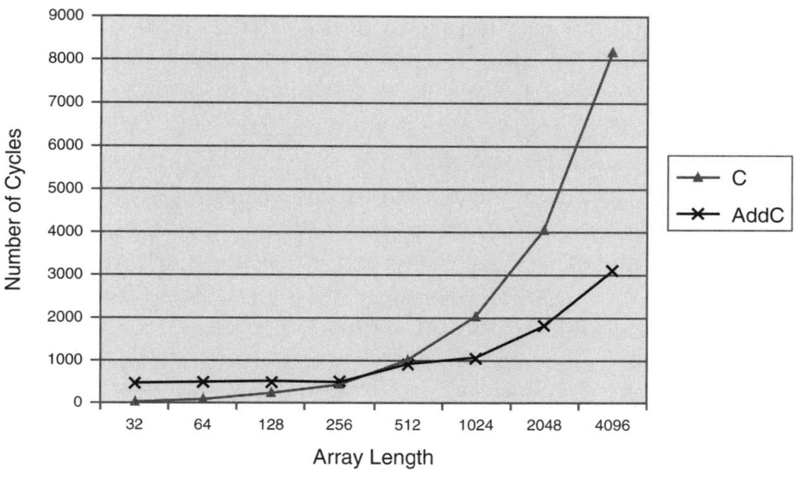

Figure 4.6 Comparison of Time to Create a Ramp Signal Using `IppsAddC`

At least in Intel IPP 4.0, use of the `VectorRamp` functions should be restricted to cases for which a non-integral slope is needed. In other cases, it is preferable to create a simple ramp as described. Creating ramps of other integral slopes, including decreasing slopes, should require only minor modifications.

Initializing Two-dimensional Arrays with `ippiImageRamp`

The two-dimensional analog to this problem, in which the function `image[y][x] = f(x,y)` is needed, can be handled in a similar manner. Instead of a single index array, the two-dimensional version uses an "x-map" and a "y-map". Every entry in the x-map is equal to the column or x-value of the image. Every entry in y-map is equal to the row or y-value of the image. The function `ippiImageRamp` fits this need, or the above process can also be used.

Removing Loops and Branches

Traditional conditional execution, in particular the branch, is not possible on vector operations. Every operation must perform the same instruction on each of the data elements. This is true for both fine-grained data in *single-instruction multiple-data* (SIMD) parallelism and vector operations in Intel IPP. However, when converting code to use Intel IPP, it is possible to remove some inner-loop conditionals with a little extra computation. In many cases there is a performance advantage even though extra calculations are necessary.

The basic method, which may well be familiar to programmers used to SIMD assembly or Matlab,[†] is to execute both sides of a conditional operation then somehow overlay the results. Usually the two results are combined using one or more comparison operators. In Intel IPP, the useful functions are `Compare`, which generates a separate mask for the data, and `Threshold`, which modifies the source data directly.

This technique should be used with some caution, since it is appropriate only when the benefit from the parallelism outweighs the approximately doubled number of operations. The SIMD registers and operations in MMX™ instructions, SSE, and SSE-2 are up to 16 elements wide, meaning that between two and 16 operations happen each opcode. Since Intel IPP relies heavily on these operations, an optimal simple function performs between 2 and 16 times as fast. As a result, it is often possible to perform both branches of a conditional, roughly double the number of operations, in the same or less time as the equivalent scalar operation with a conditional branch.

Removing Branches with `Threshold`

To demonstrate loop removal, this section compares implementations of "square root of real numbers with complex result," a function not contained in Intel IPP.[1] This function takes the square root of real numbers, including negative numbers that will produce an imaginary result, and stores the result in an interleaved-complex array.

The prototype for this function, using roughly the same naming conventions as Intel IPP, is:

```
mySqrt_32f32fc(Ipp32f* pSrc, Ipp32fc* pDst, int len);
```

[1] Intel IPP doesn't have a real-to-complex square root, but does have a complex-to-complex square root. This sequence, the performance of which is still better than the C reference code, uses the complex-to-complex root on real data:

```
ippsZero_32f(pTmp, len);
ippsRealToCplx_32f(pSrc, pTmp, pDst, len);
ippsSqrt_32fc_I(pDst, len);
```

The most straightforward way to implement this uses the standard library square root function. This code uses only C++ and the standard library call `sqrt()` to perform the calculation:

```
for (i = 0; i < len; i++)
    if (pSrc[i]<0.0f)
    {
        pDst[i].re = 0.0f;
        pDst[i].im = sqrt(-pSrc[i]);
    }
    else
    {
        pDst[i].re = sqrt(pSrc[i]);
        pDst[i].im = 0.0f;
    }
```

Most of the Intel IPP functions for calculating square root are considerably faster than the square root from the standard library for even very short arrays of inputs. Replacing the standard library call with the Intel IPP call is simple, but the "`if…then`" branch makes calling it on an array of inputs not so easy. The result must be conditionally placed in the real field if the input is positive or the imaginary field if the input is negative.

As noted earlier, removing branches doesn't always improve the performance of a sequence of code. It is worth trying to replace just the `sqrt` call first. There are two Intel IPP square root functions that are most applicable to the situation. The first such function is `ippsSqrt_32fc`, which calculates the square root of a complex array. This function has the right output type, but the input is also expected to be complex. The function `ippsRealToCplx` performs this conversion efficiently. The code sequence looks like this:

```
ippsRealToCplx_32f(pSrc, 0, pDst, len);
ippsSqrt_32fc(pDst, pDst, len);
```

Passing zero as the imaginary array argument tells the real-to-complex conversion to fill the imaginary portion of the output array with zeros. The result, placed in the array `pDst`, is the real data expanded into a complex array. The square root calculation is then performed in-place.

The other option is to replace each call to the function sqrt with a call to the function ippsSqrt_32f. It is possible to do this directly, as in this code:

```
for (i = 0; i < len; i++)
    if (pSrc[i]<0.0f)
    {
        pDst[i].re = 0.0f;
        pSrc[i] = -pSrc[i];
        ippsSqrt_32f_A11(&pSrc[i], &pDst[i].im, 1);
        pSrc[i] = -pSrc[i];
    }
    else
    {
        ippsSqrt_32f_A11(&pSrc[i], &pDst[i].re, 1);
        pDst[i].im = 0.0f;
    }
```

This requires some unpleasant modification of the source array and unnecessary pointer math by the compiler. For efficiency, the results are best placed in a temporary array, with a single call to the Intel IPP square root function. This code precomputes the roots of the absolute value of the input with an Intel IPP call and performs the branch as before:

```
ippsAbs_32f(pSrc, pTmp, len);
ippsSqrt_32f_A11(pTmp, pTmp, len);
ippsZero_32fc(pDst, len);
for (i =0; i<len; i++)
if (pSrc[i]<0.0f)
        pDst[i].im = pTmp[i];
else
        pDst[i].re = pTmp[i];
```

This code takes around half the computation time of the standard library version and about 25 percent less time than the version using ippsSqrt_32fc. A close look at the performance of this implementation shows that only 25 percent of the time is spent in the Sqrt and Abs calls. The remaining 75 percent of the time, 20 cycles per element or so, is spent in the rather plain overhead code that performs the conditional copy. Given that unbalance, there is a good chance that this C code can be profitably replaced with Intel IPP calls.

The general idea of the threshold technique for loop removal is to take the code

```
if (x > val) y = fp(x);
else y = fn(x);
```

and replace it with

```
if (x < val) xn = x; else xn = 0;
if (x > val) xp = x; else xp = 0;
y = fp(xp) + fn(xn);
```

The functions `fp` and `fn` can be any functions for which a zero input results in a zero output. Square root is one such function.

The second version still appears to have a conditional statement. However, this conditional statement is now in a standard form implemented by the functions `ippsThreshold_LTVal` and `ippsThreshold_GTVal`. If `val` is zero, the functions `ippsThreshold_LT` and `ippsThreshold_GT` can be used instead.

The square-root example is of a form similar but not identical to the above:

```
if (x > 0) y.re = f(x);
else y.im = f(-x);
```

This code is equivalent to:

```
if (x > 0) xp = x; else xp = 0; // Threshold_LT
y.re = f(xp);                   // Sqrt
if (x < 0) xn = x; else xn = 0; // Threshold_LT
x = -x;                     // MulC
y.im = f(xn);                   // Sqrt
```

Each line of code above maps to the single Intel IPP call in the comment. Since the output of the square root function is a real or imaginary array, final call to `ippsRealToCplx` is necessary to interleave the real and imaginary results. The precise code is in Figure 4.7.

```
ippsMulC_32f_I(-1.0f, pTmp, len);
ippsSqrt_32f_A11(pTmp, pTmp, len);
ippsRealToCplx_32f(pRe, pTmp, pDst, len);

// if (pSrc[i] < 0) pTmp[i] = 0.0; else pTmp = Src[i];
ippsThreshold_LT_32f(pSrc, pTmp, len, 0.0f);

// pRe[i] = sqrt(pTmp[i]);
ippsSqrt_32f_A11(pTmp, pRe, len);

// if (pSrc[i] > 0) pTmp[i]=0.0; else pTmp[i]=pSrc[i];
ippsThreshold_GT_32f(pSrc, pTmp, len, 0.0f);

// pSrc[i] = -pSrc[i];
ippsMulC_32f_I(-1.0f, pTmp, len);

// pTmp[i] = sqrt(pTmp[i]);
ippsSqrt_32f_A11(pTmp, pTmp, len);

// pDst[i].re = pRe; pDst[i].im = pTmp;
ippsRealToCplx_32f(pRe, pTmp, pDst, len);
```

Figure 4.7 Final Code for `mySqrt_32f32fc()`

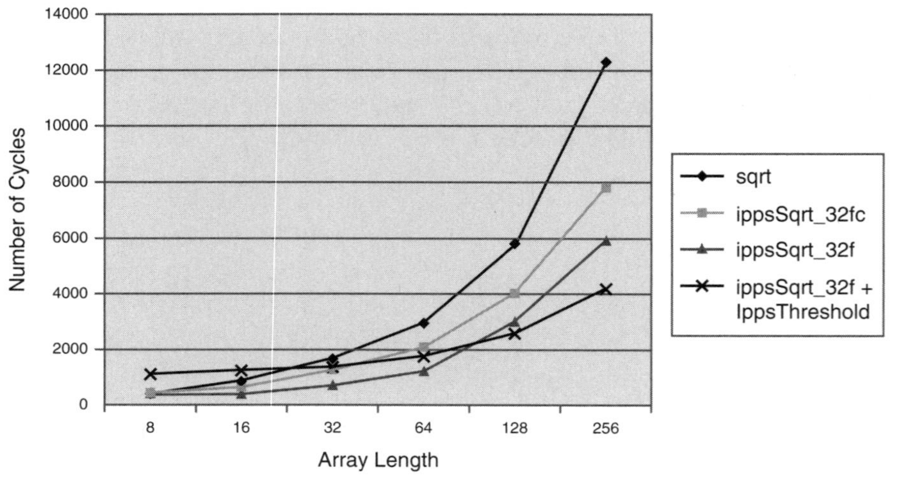

Figure 4.8 Relative Performance of Methods for `mySqrt_32f32fc()`

The performance of all of the described implementations is shown in Figure 4.8. Beyond an array size of 64, the version that replaces the branch with calls to `Threshold` is significantly faster than the other versions. At 64 and below, the version that keeps the branch but performs the square root in a single Intel IPP call is the fastest.

Removing Loops with Compare and Logical Operations

The `threshold` function is useful only when the source data is being compared to a constant value and the conditional branch or loop is based on that comparison. That is, the condition for the branch can only be a direct comparison against the source data. When it is necessary to remove a branch or loop based on any other type of condition, the threshold method doesn't apply. In those cases, there is a more general method that uses the `Compare` function and logical functions `And`, `Not`, and `Or`.

This method is useful where there is a construction such as the following:

```
if (condition) y = ftrue(x) else y=ffalse(x)
```

This construction can be broken into two steps by using a mask to store the results of the conditional. The two steps are mask creation and mask usage:

```
// Create the mask
if (condition) mask = 0xff else mask=0

// Use the mask
y = (mask & ftrue(x)) | (~mask & ffalse(x))
```

This code is illustrated in Figure 4.9.

The first step can be performed on a vector of inputs by the function `ippiCompare`. There are many variants of compare that are capable of producing a mask based on a greater-than, greater-or-equal, less-than, less-or-equal, or equal-to condition. The second step can be performed either by logical operations or by one of the functions that support masks explicitly.

Since the imaging compare function creates an 8-bit mask, this technique is supported well for 8-bit data, such as most pixels. For this reason, creating a new function `Abs_8s8u_C1R` is a good demonstration of this loop removal technique. The function will take the absolute value of elements of an array of 8-bit signed values and puts them in an array of 8-bit unsigned values. The function does not exist in the Intel IPP API, though other absolute value functions do.

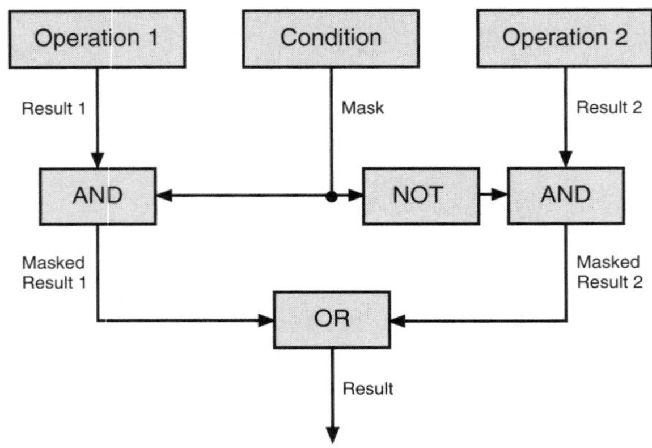

Figure 4.9 Illustration of Branch Removal Using Logical Operations

The absolute value operation on a single input is:

```
if (x > 0) y = x; else y = -x;
```

Breaking this operation into two steps, as above, results in the following code:

```
if (x > 0) mask = 0xff; else mask = 0;
y = (x & mask) | (-x & ~mask);
```

Implementing the first line for an array of inputs is easy. A single `ippiCompare` call performs exactly that operation. Implementing the second line is more involved, as every operator must become its own function call, as in the following:

```
Or ( And (x, mask) , And ( Mul (x, -1), Not (mask) ) )
```

A further complication is that the Intel IPP API has few functions that operate on `Ipp8s` data. This is not a problem as long as only logical functions are used, such as `And`, `Or`, and `Not`; for these logical functions, the 8-bit unsigned versions of functions can be used. However, multiplication and arithmetic negation behave differently on signed and unsigned data, and neither function is supported by Intel IPP for 8-bit signed values. Fortunately, arithmetic negation can be done using only logical functions for two's complement. For numbers represented in two's complement format, `-x = ~x + 1`.

Figure 4.10 and Figure 4.11, respectively, show the code before and after loop removal. The code in Figure 4.10 uses the built-in compiler translation to perform the signed-to-unsigned conversion.

```
Ipp8s *pSrc, *pTmpS;
Ipp8u *pDst, *pTmpD;
...
{
  pTmpS = pSrc + i*srcStride;
  pTmpD = pDst + i*dstStride;
  for (j=0; j<w; j++)
  {
      if (*pTmpS < 0) *pTmpD++ = -*pTmpS++;
      else *pTmpD++ = *pTmpS++;
  }
}
```

Figure 4.10 C/C++ Code for Absolute Value

The code in Figure 4.11 starts by determining whether the `Ipp8s` data is negative by casting, but not converting, the data to `Ipp8u` then comparing it to `(Ipp8u)127`. If it is greater than 127, the number is negative. The result of this comparison is a mask that has `0xff` for every positive entry and `0` for every negative entry. An `And` operation between this mask and the source data effectively copies the positive entries into the destination unmodified and inserts zero instead of the negative entries.

Next, the source is negated into a temporary buffer using `Not` and `Add`, and the mask is logically inverted in place. Repeating the mask operation zeros the positive numbers and negates the negative numbers. This is then inserted into the destination with a call to the `Or` function, completing the absolute value operation.

The performance results of these routines, as well as the routine in the next section, are shown in Figure 4.13.

```
// Calculate mask
// mask = (((Ipp8u)src <= 127) ? 0xff : 0)
ippiCompareC_8u_C1R((Ipp8u*)pSrc, srcStride, 127,
    pMask, maskStride, size, ippCmpLessEq);

// Copy only positive numbers to destination
// dst = mask & src
ippiAnd_8u_C1R((Ipp8u*)pSrc, srcStride, pMask,
    maskStride, pDst, dstStride, size);

// Invert mask to pass only negative numbers
// mask = ~mask
ippiNot_8u_C1IR(pMask, maskStride, size);

// Negate source
// tmp = -src
ippiNot_8u_C1R((Ipp8u*)pSrc, srcStride, pTmp,
    tmpStride, size);
ippiAddC_8u_C1IRSfs(1, pTmp, tmpStride, size, 0);

// Zero out numbers that were positive, now negative
// tmp = tmp & mask
ippiAnd_8u_C1IR(pMask, maskStride, pTmp, tmpStride,
    size);

// Overlay negated negative numbers on destination
// dst = dst | tmp
ippiOr_8u_C1IR(pTmp, tmpStride, pDst, dstStride, size);
```

Figure 4.11 C++ Code for Absolute Value Using Intel® Integrated Performance Primitives (Intel® IPP)

Note The function `ippsCompareC` is considerably faster using the flag `ippsCmpLessEq` than using `ippsCmpLess`. Using the latter it is almost impossible to beat the C/C++ code.

Removing Loops with Compare and Copy with Mask

Some Intel IPP imaging functions support masks. When a mask is taken as an argument, the operation is performed only on those pixels for which the corresponding "pixel" in the mask is nonzero. Copy is one such function; the masked version either copies a pixel or leaves the destination unmodified. In the example above, this function would take the place of most of the logical function calls. Figure 4.12 shows the code after this substitution. The performance results in Figure 4.13 indicate that this code, in addition to being somewhat simpler and not requiring temporary storage, is also slightly faster than the previous version.

```
// Generate mask
ippiCompareC_8u_C1R((Ipp8u*)pSrc, srcStride, 127,
    pMask, maskStride, size, ippCmpLessEq);

// pDst = -pSrc
ippiNot_8u_C1R((Ipp8u*)pSrc, srcStride, pDst,
    dstStride, size);
ippiAddC_8u_C1IRSfs(1, pDst, dstStride, size,0);

// if (mask) pDst = pSrc
ippiCopy_8u_C1MR((Ipp8u*)pSrc, srcStride, pDst,
    dstStride, size, pMask, maskStride);
```

Figure 4.12 Alternate Code for Absolute Value Using Copy with Mask

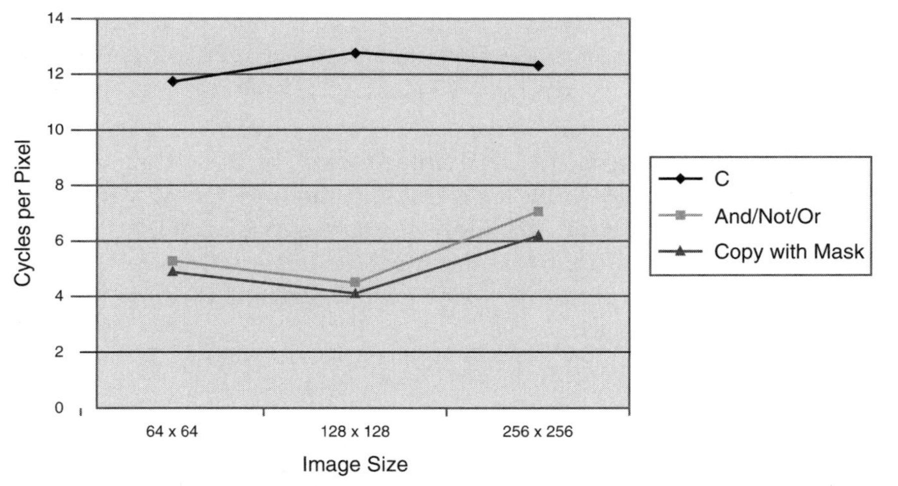

Figure 4.13 Relative Performance of Methods for `myAbs_8s8u()`

Performing Arithmetic Efficiently

Intel IPP contains quite a few functions that are designed as special-purpose imaging or video functions but that implement general mathematical formulae. These functions generally combine multiple arithmetic operations into a single compound operation tailored to a particular domain. The operations they implement are, in many cases, generally useful even outside that domain, if the appropriate function can be found.

This section describes several functions of this type. The functions are highlighted here because it is not always obvious that these functions have general applications.

Performing Arithmetic Between Integers and Floating Point Values with `AddWeighted` and `AddProduct`

There are two functions that operate on arrays of 8-bit integers but store results in 32-bit floating-point array. The `AddWeighted` function is designed to take running averages of a sequence of images. The target medium is a video stream; the function is capable of averaging pixels across multiple frames of video. It averages two images using the formula:

```
Dst = a * Src1 + (1-a) * Src2
```

The constant `a` is the weighting factor. In the original application, the running average would be `Src2` and the new image would be `Src1`. The larger the constant, the more the average is weighted toward the most recent image and the less the previous images are weighted.

The `AddProduct` function accumulates the products of two images into a third image:

```
Dst += Src1 * Src2
```

Both of these functions implicitly convert the `Ipp8u` source data to `Ipp32f` on the fly, performing the operation in the floating-point domain for better precision and dynamic range. Converting the data in this way saves temporary buffer space, and therefore cache space, as compared to a block-by-block or image-by-image conversion.

Table 4.4 lists these two functions and their formulae.

Table 4.4 Functions for Integer/Floating-Point Arithmetic

Function name	Function	Notes
`ippiAddWeighted`	`dst = a*src1 + (1-a) * src2`	`a` and `dst` are `32f`
`ippiAddProduct`	`dst += src1 * src2`	`dst` is `32f`

Performing Linear Combinations of Two Sources with Alpha Composition

Alpha composition functions are intended to simulate transparency in overlaid images. Each pixel is assigned an alpha value, or opacity, between zero and one. The functions that composite based on these alpha values calculate the intensity for each pixel when transparency is considered; generally, this is done by multiplying each pixel by one or more alpha values. There are several flavors, such as *over*, *atop*, and *plus*, each operating on an implicit model of the interaction between the images. Atop, for example, assumes that the first image is placed on top of the second, and calculates the intensity of combined image at each pixel accordingly.

The imaging interpretations of alpha composition functions aside, the mathematical formulae are also of general interest. These functions can be adopted for other purposes. All of the flavors of compositing functions are linear combinations of one or two images and one or two channels of alpha values.

The Intel IPP function that performs alpha composition is `ippiAlphaComp`. It supports six models for image-image interaction. The most general form, and thus perhaps the most broadly useful, is *plus*. Plus combines the two images and the two alpha channels as follows:

```
Dst = a * Src1 + b * Src2
```

The alpha values `a` and `b` can be constants or they can be arrays. In the Intel IPP integer implementations, these constants are normalized by the operation. That is, the entire dynamic range of the input type maps linearly to the range 0.0 – 1.0. For example, when using `Ipp8u` an input value of 0 is interpreted as 0.0 and a value of 255 is interpreted as 1.0.

In addition to plus, there are five other versions of alpha composition that implement different equations. All six are listed in Table 4.5.

Table 4.5 Types of Image Compositing Operations

Function	Intel IPP Enum Code	Formula	Alpha Formula
Over	`ippAlphaOver`	a *A+(1-a)* b *B	a +(1-a)*b
In	`ippAlphaIn`	a *A * b	a * b
Out	`ippAlphaOut`	a *A* (1-b)	a *(1-b)
Atop	`ippAlphaAtop`	a *A*b +(1-a)*b *B	a * b +(1-a)*b
Xor	`ippAlphaXor`	a *A*(1-b)+(1-a)*b *B	a *(1-a)+(1-a)*b
Plus	`ippAlphaPlus`	a *A + b *B	a + b

a and b are alpha channels, and may be constants or arrays. A and B are the corresponding data arrays or images.

This is an implementation of `ippiAlphaComp` for the plus type in C/C++:

```
for (i =0; i<h; i++)
{
    pTmpS1 = pSrc1 + i*src1Stride;
    pTmpS2 = pSrc2 + i*src2Stride;
    pTmpD = pDst + i*dstStride;
    for (j=0; j<w; j++)
    {
        *pTmpD++ =
            a * *pTmpS1++ / 256 + b * *pTmpS2++ / 256;
    }
}
```

Unfortunately, the actual precision used by the compiler-generated code is not clear from the above, and the performance of this simple code is rather poor.

A second way to perform this operation is by using two calls to `MulC` to pre-multiply each array by the constant and one to `Add` to sum the results. The code below does this using the destination array `pDst` to hold one multiplication result and a temporary array to hold the other:

```
ippiMulC_8u_C1RSfs(pSrc1, src1Stride, a, pDst, dstStride, size,8);
ippiMulC_8u_C1RSfs(pSrc2, src2Stride, b, pTmp, tmpStride, size,8);
ippiAdd_8u_C1IRSfs(pTmp, tmpStride, pDst, dstStride, size,0);
```

Note the `scaleFactor` argument is set to 8 for the multiply operations. A scale factor of 8 is equivalent to dividing the result by 256, but this division is done carefully to save precision without unnecessarily sacrificing performance.

This same operation can be performed in a single call to `AlphaCompC`. To perform this operation, use `ippAlphaPlus` as the type argument, and other parameters as follows:

```
  ippiAlphaCompC_8u_C1R(pSrc1, src1Stride, a, pSrc2,
src2Stride, b, pDst, dstStride, size, ippAlphaPlus);
```

Figure 4.14 shows the relative performance of these three methods. Assuming this is the exact construction needed, the alpha composite function is the fastest.

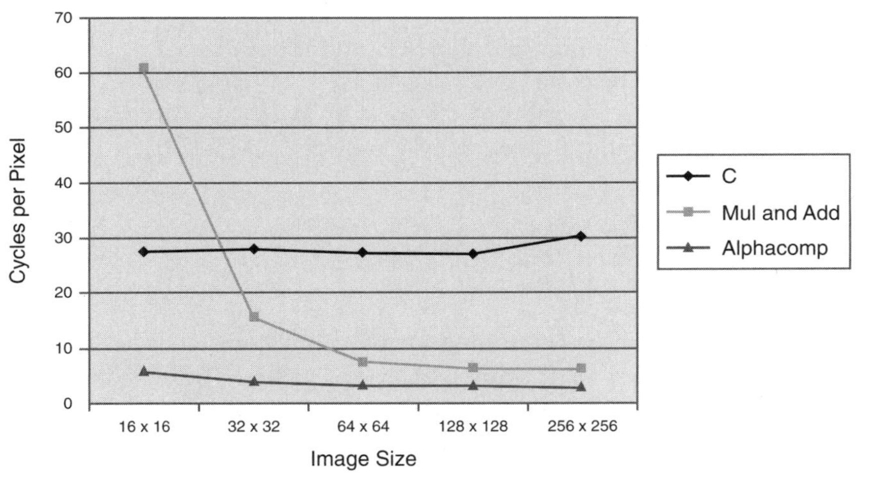

Figure 4.14 Relative Performance of Implementations for `Dst = a * Src1 + b * Src2`

Performing Linear Combinations of Three Sources with `ColorToGray` and `ColorTwist`

Certain functions are intended to convert between color spaces that are also useful as general arithmetic functions. These functions supplement the alpha composition functions because they perform linear combinations of three arrays of data instead of two.

The function ColorToGray is intended to linearly weight each channel of a three-channel image, then sum the results. Often, the channels are the RGB components red, green, and blue. Mathematically, the operation is the following:

```
Y = aR + bG + cB
```

The variables R, G, and B are arrays; a, b, and c are constants. This function is mathematically equivalent to the matrix operation ippmDotProduct_vav, which takes the dot product of a vector and each of an array of vectors. However, ippmDotProduct supports only floating point types for the data arrays, while ippiColorToGray supports integral input types Ipp8u, Ipp16u, and Ipp16s.

The function ColorTwist is intended to perform a complete color conversion from one color space to another. Three weighted sums are taken to calculate three new channels, as if ColorToGray were called three times:

$$R_{new} = a_1R_{old} + b_1G_{old} + c_1B_{old} + d_1$$
$$G_{new} = a_2R_{old} + b_2G_{old} + c_2B_{old} + d_2$$
$$B_{new} = a_3R_{old} + b_3G_{old} + c_3B_{old} + d_3$$

This function is mathematically equivalent to the matrix operation ippmMultiply_vav, but like ColorToGray, the ColorTwist function supports the integral input data types Ipp8u, Ipp16u, and Ipp16s.

In both ColorToGray and ColorTwist, the constant inputs are expressed as floating point values even if the input arrays are integral.

In the "C3" versions, these are uninterrupted interleaved data arrays (RGBRGBRGB). In the "AC4" versions, these are padded with an unused alpha channel (RGBARGBARGBA). The most useful of the versions of this function may be the three-plane "P3" version, supported by ColorTwist only. The three-plane version takes an element-wise linear combination of three separate arrays.

Optimizing Table-Based Functions Using a Look-Up Table

The look-up table function LUT transforms ranges of source pixels into the corresponding destination ranges. The function takes two arrays, Values and Levels. Values are the source ranges; Levels are in the destination ranges. Every pixel that meets (Values[n] <= pixel < Values[n+1]) maps to Levels[n]; that is, where a pixel in that Value range exists in the source, the destination will be set to the appropriate Level.

Table 4.6 shows part of a sample set of input tables.

Table 4.6 `ippiLUT` Tables Example

Index	Values	Levels
0	0	0
1	4	16
2	8	64
3	16	256
...		

In this example, an input from 0 to 3 will be mapped to 0, an input from 4 to 7 will map to 16, and so on.

Two other versions of the function are `LUT_Linear` and `LUT_Cubic`. These versions don't map the source to an exact level if the source isn't exactly equal to a value in the list. Instead, they interpolate between two levels to find a best-fit result. For a sparse `Levels` table, `LUT_Linear` produces a much more reasonable result than the nearest-fit `LUT`. See Table 4.7 for a comparison of results using inputs from Table 4.6.

In some cases, the additional curve fitting of `LUT_Cubic` might produce a more accurate result.

Table 4.7 LUT Results

Input	`LUT` Result	`LUT_Linear` Result
0	0	0
2	0	8
4	16	16
6	16	40
10	64	112
12	64	160

The function is intended to perform color histogram operations such as white-balancing or gamma correction. The reason this function is of general interest is that it can be used to execute any kind of table-based function efficiently.

When the inputs are `Ipp8u` it's easy to create a complete table, one for which every source input has a corresponding value. If the tables are complete, then the operation executes the simple table lookup:

```
dst = pLevels[src]
```

Even for this simple operation, `LUT` gives some performance advantage over straight C/C++. Take the simplest example, a null function for which the tables map any input value to itself. This code initializes the table:

```
for (i =0; i<len; i++)
{
    pValues[i] = i;
    pLevels[i] = i;
}
```

This Intel IPP call maps the source to the destination:

```
  ippiLUT_8u_C1R(pDst, dstStep, pDst, dstStep, size,
pValues, pLevels, 256);
```

This C/C++ loop does the same:

```
for (i =0; i<h; i++)
{
    for (j =0; j<w; j++)
    {
        *pTmp++ = pLevels[*pTmp];
    }
    pTmp+= dstStep-w;
}
```

The real usefulness of the LUT functions is in interpolating a result from a bigger table that is not complete. For example, to implement `mySin_16s`, initialize the tables like this:

```
float inc = 65535.0 / (len-1);
for (i =0; i<len; i++)
{
    float val = (float) i * inc - 32768.0;
    pValues[i] = (Ipp16s) val;
    pLevels[i] = (Ipp16s) 32768.0 *
                 ( sin(val / 32768.0 * IPP_PI) + 1.0 );
}
```

Notice that the input of sine is normalized from the range (-32768, 32767) to the range (-PI,PI), and the output is mapped from (-1.0,1.0) back to (-32768, 32767). Using these tables, the functions `LUT_Linear` and `LUT_Cubic` take the sine of any input array or image. The time required to calculate the result is constant, however complicated the function.

One further refinement of this method that is permitted by the LUT structures is to initialize the tables in a non-uniform way according to function curvature. That is, instead of incrementing the source values by a uniform amount, the code could, and should, increment them according to the expected inaccuracy of the linear or cubic approximation; perhaps using the second or third derivative. This would provide more accurate results without increasing the size of the table.

Further Reading

Documentation on the functions demonstrated in this chapter is contained in the signal-processing (Intel 2003, vol. 1) and image-processing (Intel 2003, vol. 2) volumes of the manual. The former contains signal-processing functions and the core library functions, such as `ippCoreGetCpuClocks`.

Chapter 5

Digital Filtering

This chapter explains the core signal processing functions in the Intel® Integrated Performance Primitives (Intel® IPP), while giving a small amount of background in signal processing. The first section explains filtering conceptually. This material is intended to provide a conceptual explanation of Fourier transforms and linear filters to those with limited digital signal processing (DSP) knowledge. The remainder of the chapter demonstrates most of those methods and concepts using Intel IPP functions.

The material in this chapter is limited to processing of one-dimensional signals. Intel IPP support for two-dimensional signals is limited primarily to images. Chapter 9 discusses filtering images in some detail.

Although audio processing is arguably the most common form of one-dimensional signal processing, this chapter is not dependent on audio as input. The signals, in general, are not required to be sounds or radio waves, except where a concrete example is more illustrative. For simplicity, the domains of the signals are often assumed to be time, although they could as easily be spatial signals. Chapter 6 discusses techniques for audio processing.

A Quick Course in Filtering

Digital filtering is a very big topic. This section attempts in a handful of pages to give you some intuition for the material that has filled dozens or hundreds of books, or at least the first few chapters of those books.

This section focuses on discrete and numerical methods, with little attention to the continuous functions. Furthermore, the tenor of this section is dictated by the implementation of the solution, and issues raised here are those encountered with general-purpose processors and high-level languages. Taking a software-oriented approach, the focus is almost exclusively digital, discrete, and algorithmic. For example, convolution of two signals is defined as:

$$y(n) = \sum x(t) * h(n-t)$$

However, the sigma summation form overlooks the realities of convolution in software, such as array lengths and temporary storage. Therefore, an effort is made to present such formulae rather in a code form:

```
for (n=0; n<sizeDst; n++)
    for (t=0; t<sizeSrc; t++)
     pDst[n] += pSrc[t] * pFilter[n-t]
```

The Idea of Filters

Filters take a series of inputs, manipulate them in some way without destroying all of the original information, and produce a series of outputs. This "some way" generally preserves most characteristics of the original data but removes others. Often it involves noise removal or information extraction. The inputs are often samples from some sensor or medium, such as audio from a microphone or CD player, or samples of a carrier wave from an antenna; however, regardless of the source and meaning, the time at which the samples are filtered is expressed as numerical entries in an array.

Figure 5.1 shows the input and output of a filter that removes some frequencies while preserving others. The original signal includes a low-frequency wave; that wave is removed from the filtered signal, leaving only two high-frequency waves.

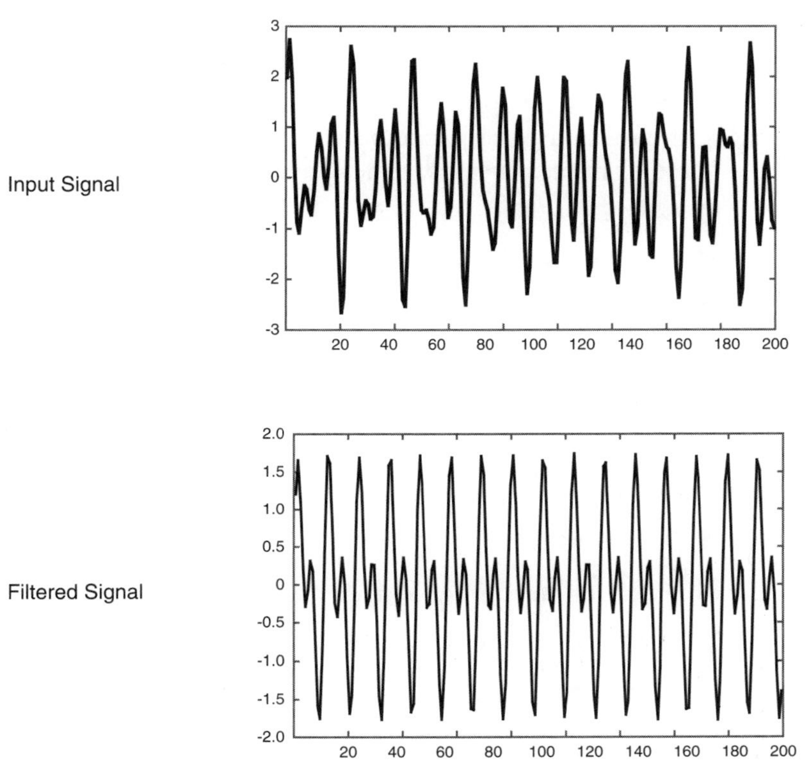

Figure 5.1 Input and Output of a Filter

The rest of this section identifies types of filters by the characteristics key to implementation and design of digital filters.

Linear vs. Nonlinear

A key distinction made between types of filters is linearity. If a filter is linear that means:

- Adding two inputs then filtering produces the same result as filtering then adding the two outputs: $F(x_1 + x_2) = F(x_1) + F(x_2)$.
- Multiplying the input by a constant then filtering produces the same result as filtering then multiplying the output by a constant: $F(ax_1) = aF(x_1)$.

If either of these formulae is ever not true, the filter is nonlinear. These two criteria can also be combined into one equation: $F(a_1 x_1 + a_2 x_2) = a_1 F(x_1) + a_2 F(x_2)$.

These formulae apply equally to scalar variables and signals. In most cases, the variable x_1 represents a signal or array of inputs.

Some examples of linear functions or systems are:

- F(x) = n x; F(x) = a
- F(x(t)) = average(x(t), x(t-1), x(t+1))
- F(x(t)) = x(t) + .5 x(t-1) + .5 x(t+1)
- Increase all values, for example, turn up the volume, by 50 percent.
- Attenuate signal by 50 percent at 60Hz (+/- 1Hz).

Examples of nonlinear filters include:

- F(x) = x+1, F(x) = x * x
- F(x(t)) = max(x(t), x(t-1), x(t+1))
- Add a 60-Hz wave to a signal
- Square the signal

There are many reasons why linearity is important. For one, while not all interesting operations are linear, linear filters are well explored, and most filter functions, including those in Intel IPP, perform linear filtering. Second, linear filters can be defined by a single input array, so a single function can perform any linear filter. By contrast, a nonlinear filter doesn't have a similar canonical form. Each function generally performs a specific nonlinear operation such as `max`, noted above as a nonlinear filter.

Time-Invariant vs. Time-Varying

Time-invariant filters are defined as systems for which shifting the input in time shifts the output by the same amount without otherwise changing the output. Here are some examples of time-invariant filters:

- All the linear and nonlinear filters mentioned above
- Delay the signal by three samples: F(x(t)) = x(t-3)

Here are two time-varying filters:

- Stretch signal to double the frequency
- Filters that change according to the input, or adaptive filters

Like linearity, time-invariance simplifies both study and implementation of filters. The core Intel IPP filter operations are time-invariant and linear, because linear filters can be expressed as an array, and time-invariant filters are those for which that array doesn't change in the life of the filter. Frequency-based filters are inherently time-invariant.

Causality, Latency, and Batch-Mode vs. Real-Time

Signal processing filters or operations have traditionally been classified as *causal* or *noncausal*. A causal function is one for which the output at time `n` only refers to inputs from time `n` or earlier. This literal causality derived from one-input, one-output DSP chips; in such chips, a filter that refers to future samples makes no sense. In practice, however, the trade-off is more fluid.

Generally, applications using DSP are either *real-time* or *batch-mode*. If the software system is taking input signals or chunks and producing outputs for immediate consumption, it might be thought of as a real-time system. Systems that are creating sound from or displaying the signal are examples of real-time systems. By contrast, systems that have the entire signal available at once and filter it, such as sound editing applications, are batch-mode.

Real-time systems are more dependent on *latency* than batch-mode systems. This is a question of both the delay from input to output and the synchronization with other elements. For example, if a system is performing frequency equalization, it might break the signal into component frequency bands, amplify or attenuate each sub-band, and recombine these frequency bands. Such a system would likely have a limit on acceptable variance of the delay from one band to the next.

Batch-mode systems have different constraints and more implementation options. One system that is generally batch-mode is a sound editor application. In such applications, an entire sound clip could be in memory at once. Any filtering done can be done on the whole signal, without breaking the signal up into smaller chunks or worrying too much about the amount of time to execute a filter.

The varying latency constraints dictate different sets of parameters and even choice of function. This might dictate the choice between convolution, finite impulse response filters, and frequency-based filtering.

The Frequency Domain and Fourier Transforms

The *Fourier transform* converts a signal indexed by time into a signal indexed by frequency. The inverse Fourier transform converts this signal back into the original time-based signal. The same information is contained in both the time-based and frequency-based versions of the signal, but the information is arranged differently.

One way to understand the operation of the Fourier transform is through the slightly more intuitive Fourier series. The idea of the Fourier series is that any periodic signal, and therefore any finite-length signal, can be expressed as the sum of sine and cosine waves of various frequencies. Figure 5.2 shows a square wave constructed in this way from sine waves.

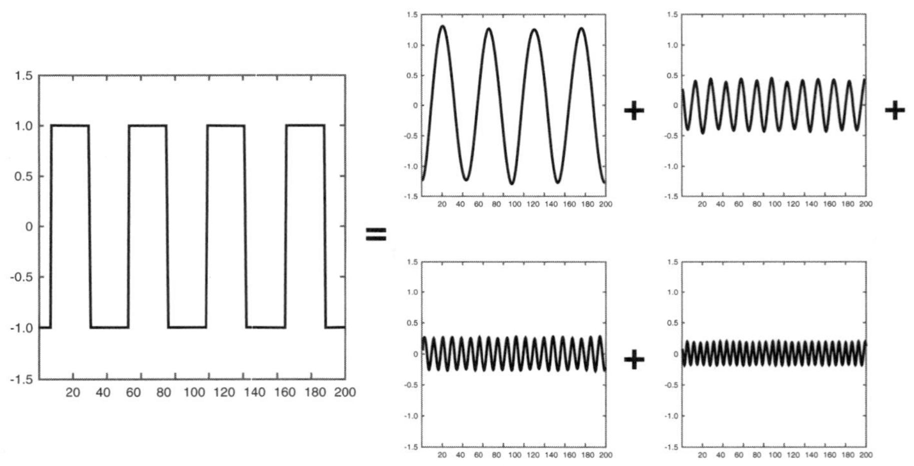

Figure 5.2 Fourier Series—Constructing a Signal from Sine Waves

The Fourier transform does essentially this. It calculates the set of sinusoids that best represent the original signal. For this reason the sinusoid is called the *basis function* of the Fourier Transform. A related transform, the *Discrete Cosine Transform* (DCT) , also uses sinusoids, but transforms can and do use square waves, triangle waves, and so on as their basis functions. The use of the sinusoid by the Fourier transform matches a typical physical or electrical oscillation and is therefore appropriate to break down frequency in audio and other physical systems.

Discrete Fourier Transform

The version of this transform that is relevant to software-based filtering is the ***Discrete Fourier Transform*** or DFT. The DFT is very similar to the Fourier series, in that it breaks a signal into a series of frequencies. Though there are several possible interpretations of "discrete", the DFT implemented in Intel IPP is discrete in both time and frequency. This DFT is defined as

$$F[n]=\frac{1}{N}\sum_{t=0}^{N-1}f[t]e^{-2\pi i(n/N)t}$$

which is equivalent to

$$F[n]=\frac{1}{N}\sum_{t=0}^{N-1}f[t]\cos(\frac{2\pi n}{N}t)-\frac{i}{N}\sum_{t=0}^{N-1}f[t]\sin(\frac{2\pi n}{N}t)$$

Here "i" is used to represent the square root of -1 rather than the electrical engineering convention, "j". You can use the DFT without comprehending these formulae directly. One way to gain some intuition for these formulae is to think of the signal f[t] as being "compared against" sinusoids of various frequencies by multiplying the signals together. One of the characteristics of this operation, often called correlation, is that two closely matching signals produce a high-magnitude product. So if the signal matches well, the product of the two signals and therefore the DFT ***coefficient*** for that frequency will be high; if it matches poorly, the product will be low.

Even if the input signal is exactly the frequency of a particular DFT component, the correlation will be low or zero if the input signal is shifted, or out of phase, relative to the sine or cosine wave. For this reason, the responses to both sine and cosine are calculated. The response to the cosine wave is the real part of the transform, and the response to the sine wave, which is shifted by one-fourth of a period relative to the cosine, is the imaginary part. The relationship between these responses at any single frequency component determines the shift or phase of that component. The sum of the squares of the two is the magnitude of the response at that frequency.

Referring back to the formulae, the constant factor 1/N is intended to force the magnitude of the result of the eventual inverse transform to be equal to that the original signal. To achieve this, the signal must be divided by N between the forward and inverse transform. The constant can therefore be applied on either the forward or inverse transforms, or a constant of `1/sqrt(N)` can be applied on both.

Fourier Transform Coefficients and Frequencies

Note that the frequency of each sinusoid is $2\pi n/N$. Therefore, since n is defined from 0 to N-1, the frequency ranges from 0 to 2π-$2\pi/N$. The first coefficient with a non-zero frequency has frequency $2\pi/N$. At frequency $2\pi/N$, there is one cycle per N samples; that is, there is one cycle through the whole signal. As the sample number increases to n = N/2, the frequency increases to π, which is one cycle every two samples. This is known as the *Nyquist rate*. A sinusoid of frequency higher than that rate is indistinguishable from some sinusoid of frequency lower than that rate.

Figure 5.3 shows this effect. The waves shown are the real parts of the inverse DFTs taken on spikes at two different Fourier coefficients; that is, they are the sinusoid-like sequences that have a response at a single frequency.

The real parts of the signals are identical and indistinguishable. The imaginary parts of these signals, not shown, are flipped versions of each other.

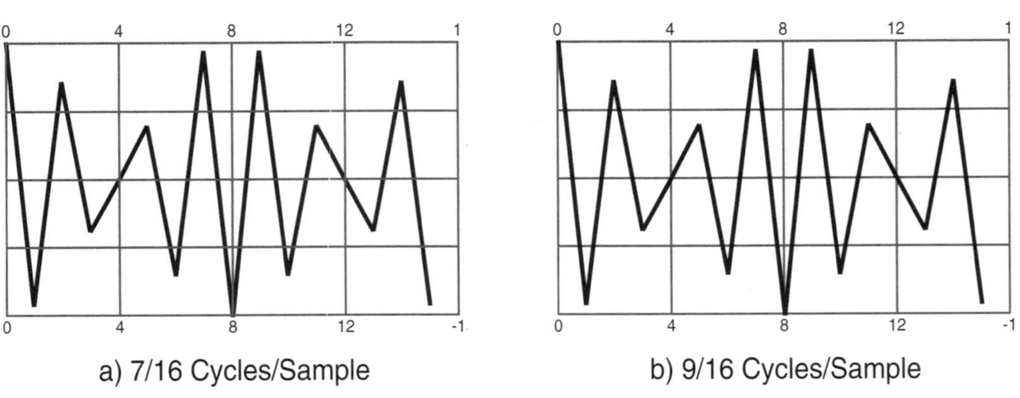

Figure 5.3 Sampled Sinusoids at Two Frequencies

It is important to understand the correlation between Fourier coefficients and particular frequencies. There are n cycles per N samples, or n/N cycles per sample. For a given sampling rate in samples per second, it is possible to calculate the frequency in cycles per second. If the sampling rate is S samples per second, and there are N samples, then the frequency for coefficient n is

S samples/second * n/N cycles/sample = S*n/N cycles/second

This equation is useful in correlating a particular frequency range to a range of Fourier coefficients, or vice-versa.

Fourier Transform Pairs

Figure 5.4 shows some potentially enlightening time-domain signals and their DFTs. For simplicity, the phase is ignored and only the magnitude of the signal is displayed.

The first graph shows the frequency response of a constant input. It shouldn't be surprising that this frequency response is nonzero only at zero frequency, since by definition the constant input does not cycle. This zero-frequency component is often referred to as the *DC coefficient* (direct current) . This is a reference to direct current, the constant kind of electricity. The other coefficients are occasionally referred to as the *AC coefficient* (alternating current) .

The DC coefficient is either the sum or the average of the entire signal, depending on the use of constants. Because of this, the DC component is often used in video or image coding, usually in conjunction with the Discrete Cosine Transform, to preview the encoded information without performing the inverse transform.

One might assume from the above explanation of sinusoid-to-frequency-coefficient connection that the transform of the sinusoid, the second pair in the figure, would be a single spike. A single spike in frequency actually transforms back to a real cosine wave summed with an imaginary sine wave; this fact can be seen from the formula above. The response of a real sine wave is actually two spikes of half the magnitude. The inverse transforms of these two spikes have the same real response, but the imaginary response is inverted. So the real response sums and the imaginary response cancels out, leaving a real sine wave.

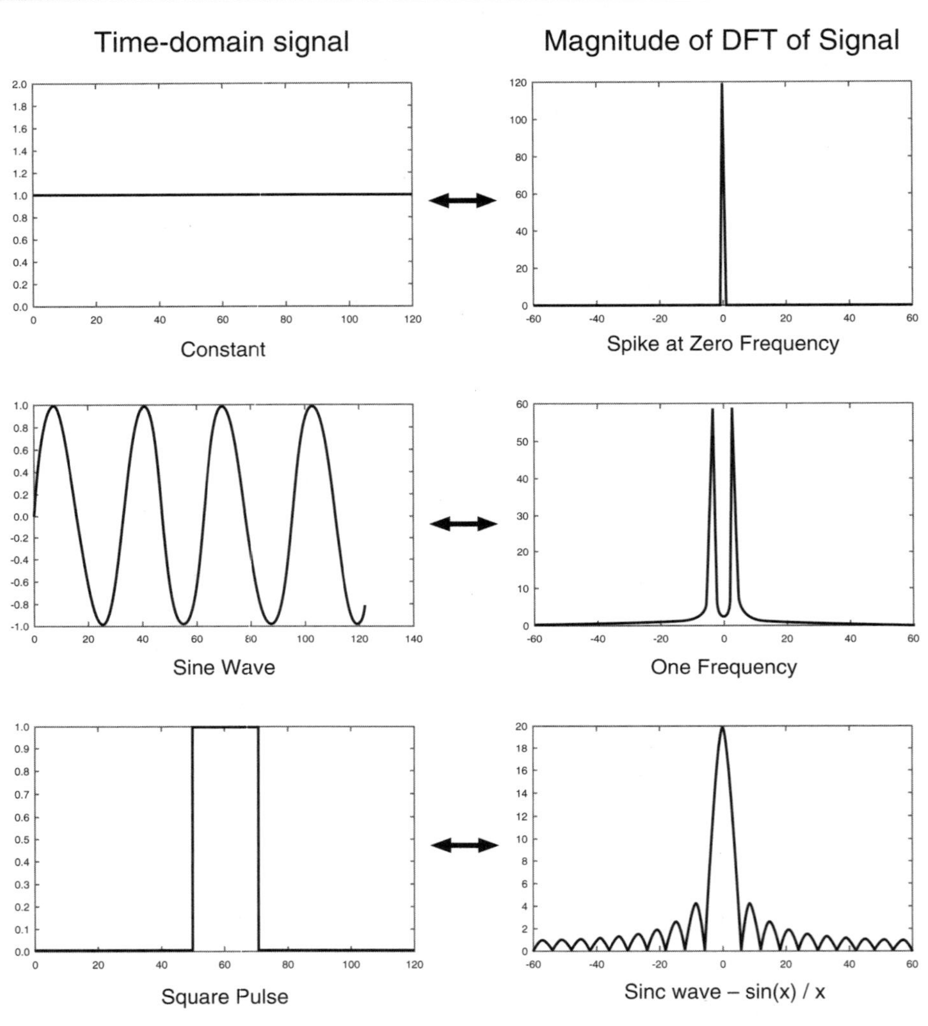

Figure 5.4 Some Signals and the Magnitude of Their DFTs[1]

[1] For display purposes, the low frequencies are in the middle, with positive frequencies to the right and "negative" frequencies, equivalent to frequencies between π and 2π, to the left. This tends to group the interesting features together. However, it does not match the DFT formula above and doesn't match the DFT function output. I'll use this shifted display in this section, but the graphs in the next section display the unmodified code output.

Fourier Transform Properties

To understand the following sections a little better, it is important to be aware of certain characteristics of the Fourier transform.

Linearity

The Fourier Transform is a linear function. One effect of this function is that the time-domain signal can be interpreted as the sum of several independent frequency components. If each single spike transforms to a sine wave, then several spikes transform to the sum of the corresponding sine waves.

Reciprocity

The Fourier transform is reversible. It is possible to reconstruct the original signal from the information in the Fourier coefficients. If it weren't possible, the DFT wouldn't be useful for filtering, only for analysis.

The inverse DFT is almost identical to the DFT. Look closely for the changed sign:

$$F[n] = \frac{1}{N}\sum_{t=0}^{N-1} f[t]e^{2\pi i(n/N)t}$$

which changes the expanded version to:

$$F[n] = \frac{1}{N}\sum_{t=0}^{N-1} f[t]\cos(\frac{2\pi n}{N}t) + \frac{i}{N}\sum_{t=0}^{N-1} f[t]\sin(\frac{2\pi n}{N}t)$$

Because the formulation is so similar, almost all the properties of the Fourier transform are true of the inverse FT.[2]

Symmetry

The Fourier transform has a number of useful symmetry properties. These properties are summarized in Table 5.1.

---

[2] Undoubtedly, true enlightenment lies in intuitively understanding why calculating the frequencies of the frequency-domain representation brings you back to the time domain.

Table 5.1 Symmetry of Pairs for the Fourier Transform

Time Domain	Frequency Domain
Real and symmetric	Real and symmetric
Real and antisymmetric	Imaginary and antisymmetric
Real	Conjugate symmetric or hermitian
Symmetric	Symmetric
Antisymmetric	Antisymmetric

A conjugate symmetric or hermitian signal is one for which the real component is symmetric and the imaginary component is antisymmetric

Since the transform is linear, the real-to-conjugate-symmetric pair can actually be derived from the previous two pairs. Any signal is the sum of a symmetric component and an antisymmetric component, so a real signal would transform to a real-and-symmetric component summed with an imaginary-and-antisymmetric component. That is, it would transform to a conjugate symmetric signal.

Convolution

Signal multiplication in the frequency domain is equivalent to *convolution* in the time domain for continuous signals or discrete signals of infinite length. In other words, if X_1=DFT(x_1) and X_2=DFT(x_2), then `DFTInv(X1 * X2) = Convolve(x1, x2)`. The proof of this Convolution Theorem of Fourier Transforms is outside of the scope of this book, but the discrete version is important to designing and analyzing time-domain filters. This is explained below, in the section "Convolution Revisited".

Continuous convolution is defined as

$$\mathbf{y}(n) = \int_{i=-\infty}^{\infty} x_1(i) * x_2(n-i)$$

That is, signal x_2 is flipped and shifted by `n` relative to signal x_1; the integral of that product is the convolution. The definition for the discrete version is in a later section.

Filtering in the Frequency Domain

A reversible transform that breaks a signal down into its component frequencies is all that's necessary to construct a frequency-based filter. The only remaining step is to manipulate, usually by multiplication, the frequency coefficients of a particular signal. Then the inverse transform of the result is the filtered signal. And because the transform in this case is linear, only the frequencies corresponding to the modified coefficients are affected.

Figure 5.5 shows an ideal operation of this sort.

Classifying Filters

Filters are often classified as "pass" or "stop", meaning that they either attenuate a frequency range or attenuate all but that range. This is generally modified with "low", "band", or "high", indicating that the range is the low end of the frequency spectrum, the high end, or a contiguous range of frequencies in the middle. For example, a *high-pass* filter tries to remove all but a specified range of high frequencies, while a *band-stop* filter tries to eliminate a range of frequencies. A band-stop filter is often referred to as a "notch" filter, particularly when the band in question is narrow, such as the one in Figure 5.5.

Time-Domain Filters

Frequency-domain filtering is conceptually simple and intuitive. Time-domain filtering, on the other hand, can be mathematically simple but generally has less-than-intuitive results. The frequency domain filtering described above is a simple multiplication to enhance or attenuate certain frequencies. In the time domain, that simple element-by-element multiplication with a frequency spectrum becomes a convolution with a signal. The filter that was designed to modify the frequencies becomes an almost random sequence of filter coefficients, usually some cousin of the *sinc* function pictured in Figure 5.4.

Take, for example, the frequency-domain notch filter in Figure 5.6 and the inverse DFT of that filter in Figure 5.7. The former is multiplied by the DFT of the input signal and will obviously remove or attenuate a small frequency range from the signal. But it's not nearly so obvious that convolving by the latter will produce a mathematically equivalent result.

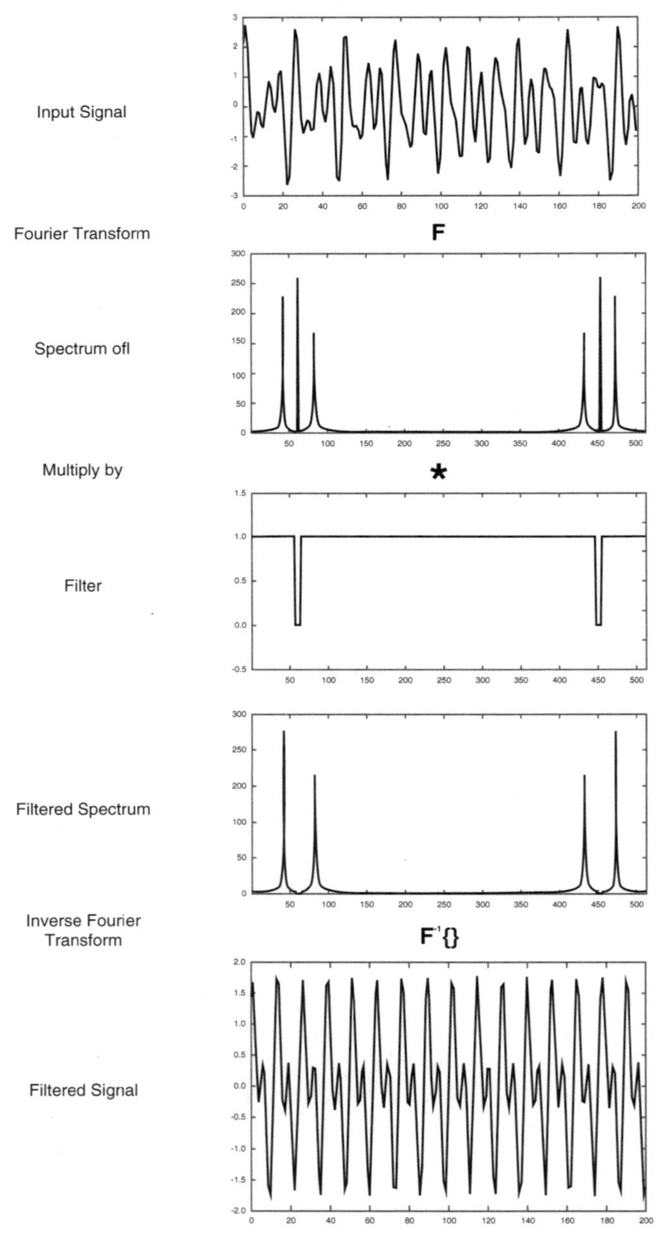

Figure 5.5 Band-Stop Filter in the Frequency Domain

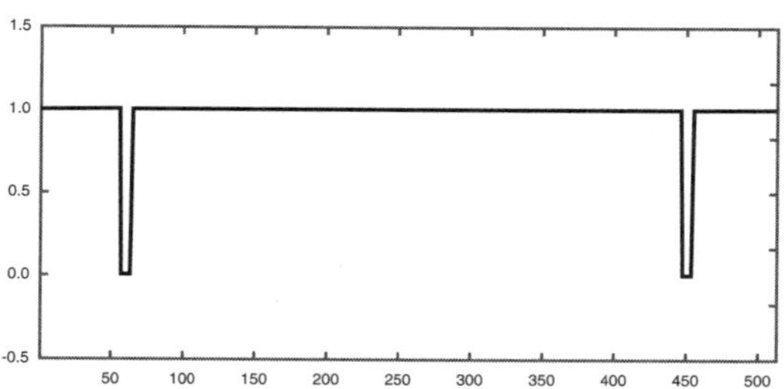

Figure 5.6 The Notch Filter from Figure 5.5

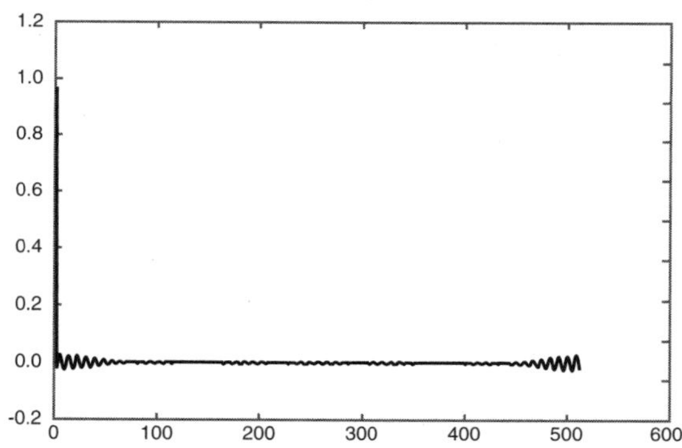

Figure 5.7 The Notch Filter in the Time Domain

Here is a relatively simple example of filtering in the time domain, a weighted averaging function:

```
for (i=1; i<len-1; i++)
    out[i] = .25 * in[i-1] + .5 * in[i] + .25 * in[i+1];
```

Each element is set to a weighted average of its neighbors. Examining the corner-case inputs gives one a feel for the effect this function will have on a signal. For example, an unchanging signal will remain unmodified by this filter, while a very-high-frequency signal alternating 1, -1, 1, -1, and so on will be reduced to 0. Intuitively, then, this is likely a low-pass filter.

In imaging, this function is a filter called a “blur”, and it reduces the detail and softens the edges of an image. If an audio signal is filtered this way, high pitches are reduced significantly, mid-range pitches are reduced slightly, and low pitches are relatively unaffected.

This sum-of-products operation can instead be put in the form of a convolution; it's easy to see that this operation is both linear and time-invariant. The three constant coefficients, .25, .5, and .25, are convolved with the signal `in`. Code using such a convolution might look like:

```
filter = { .25, .5, .25 };
convolve( in, out, filter, len);
```

Recall that convolution in the time domain is equivalent to multiplication in the frequency domain. So the effect of this convolution can be seen by looking at the product of the DFT of the array `in` and the DFT of the array `filter`. Figure 5.8 shows that DFT, and we can see that this is in fact a low-pass filter, albeit a rather inexact one.

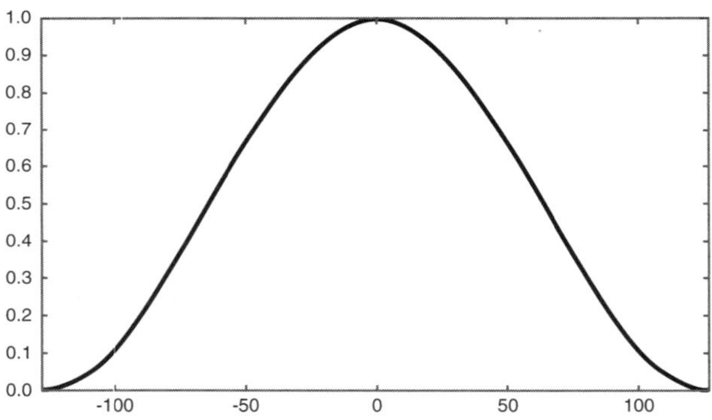

Figure 5.8 The Frequency Response of the Filter {.25, .5, .25}

Note also that this filter is symmetric. As indicated above, a real, symmetric filter has a real, symmetric frequency response. This can be a desirable quality in a filter, particularly in a real-time or synchronization situation, since it means that the delay is linear to the frequency and easy to calculate.

Convolution Revisited

With continuous convolution for infinite signals, time-domain convolution is exactly equivalent to frequency-domain multiplication. However, for finite signals this equivalency is not exact at the ends of the signal.

As in continuous convolution, discrete convolution `y[n]` is calculated by flipping signal x_2 and shifting it by `n` relative to signal x_1. The overlapping elements of the two signals are then multiplied together. The formula is as follows:

$$y[n] = \sum_{i=0}^{n-1} x_1[i] * x_2[n-i]$$

The signals $x_1[n]$ and $x_2[n]$ are zero for n less than zero or greater than the signal length. The sum of the products is the value y[n].

The edge effects are unfortunately not clear from formula. The code in Figure 5.9 implements this formula for two signals, `pSig1` and `pSig2`.

```
for (i=0; i< (len1+len2-1); i++) {
    pDst[i] = 0;
    for (j=0; j<len2; j++)  {
        if ((i-j >= 0) && (i-j < len1))
            pDst[i] += (pSig2[j] * pSig1[i-j]);
    }
}
```

Figure 5.9 Code for Convolution

Looking at the C/C++ code, it's apparent that the result of the operation is a signal `y` that is `length(`x_1`) + length(`x_2`) - 1` elements long. The result of convolution is longer than either of the original signals. Most applications require a filtered signal of the same length as the unfiltered. It should also be obvious that this convolution result, being of different length, cannot possibly be mathematically identical to the DFT-based result. These issues are generally handled in one of two ways:

- The extra data can be saved and used in filtering the next block of data. Between the extra data from the previous block of filtering and the data passed to the next block, the block can be filtered exactly. This saved data is called the delay line.

- Instead of linear convolution, *cyclic convolution* can be used. Cyclic convolution is mathematically identical to multiplication in the DFT domain.

When the former method is used, it is usually referred to as a *Finite Impulse Response* (FIR) filter. This method is used when the signal is part of a longer stream of data, as is true in real-time processing. For example, if the signal and filter were 256 elements long, and the full signal were a

10-second audio clip, the size of the total signal could be so much longer than the filter as to be almost infinite. In that case, the edge effects will be negligible.

The latter might be appropriate for finite signals or batch mode operation. In this case, the signal is treated as if it wraps around itself to simulate the extra data that does not exist beyond the ends of the signal. A simple cyclic convolution routine is implemented below.

```
// pSig1 is the reference signal; its length is
// equal to or longer than that of pSig2
for (i=0; i< len1; i++)
{
    pDst[i] = 0;
    for (j=0; j<len2; j++)
    {
        ind = i-j;
        if (ind < 0) ind+= len1;
        else if (ind >= len1) ind-=len1;
        pDst[i] += (pSig2[j] * pSig1[ind]);
    }
}
```

Figure 5.10 Code for Cyclic Convolution

Filtering in Intel IPP

The one-dimensional functions in Intel IPP concentrate in the following areas:

- Arithmetic
- Filtering
- Analysis
- Coding

The arithmetic functions are applied in Chapter 4, though they are not the focus of that chapter. Chapter 6 does some analysis on audio signals. Chapter 7 discusses audio coding. This section explains the filtering functions in Intel IPP, as well as the signal generation and Fourier transform functions.

This section draws heavily on functions covered in the three core chapters of the signal processing portion of the manual (Intel 2003, vol. 1). The Signal Generation subsection maps to the "Vector Initialization" chapter. The Frequency Domain Filtering subsection maps to the "Transform" chapter. The remaining sections rely on the "Filtering" chapter.

Signal Generation

The examples in the following sections rely heavily on artificial input data. This data is generated using several Intel IPP signal generation functions. One of these is the `ippsVectorJaehne` function.

For visualization purposes, it is often valuable to have a single signal that spans multiple frequencies. For this reason Intel IPP supplies a function that generates a "Jaehne" waveform. This function implements the equation

$$\sin(0.5\pi n^2/len)$$

This generated signal looks like a sine wave in a hurry. The "instantaneous frequency" is 0.5πn/len. The signal starts at zero frequency and increases in frequency until it hits the Nyquist rate just as it reaches n = len-1. Figure 5.11 shows this signal and the magnitude of its DFT. As the figure shows, the signal has a fairly even distribution across the frequency spectrum. For longer lengths, the gaps in the frequency coverage are relatively small. However, the oscillation near the edges of the frequencies covered, known as ringing, does not diminish.

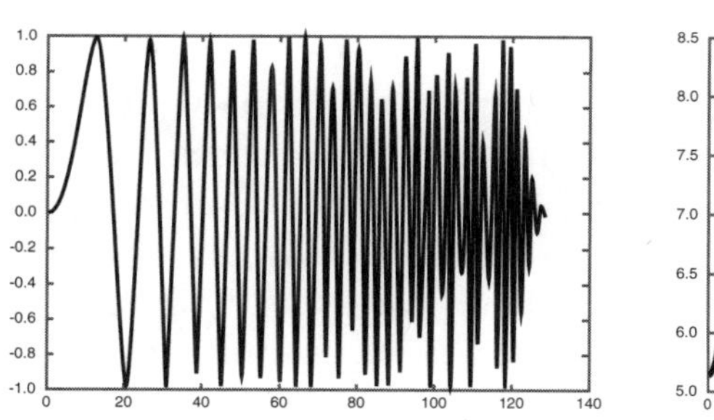

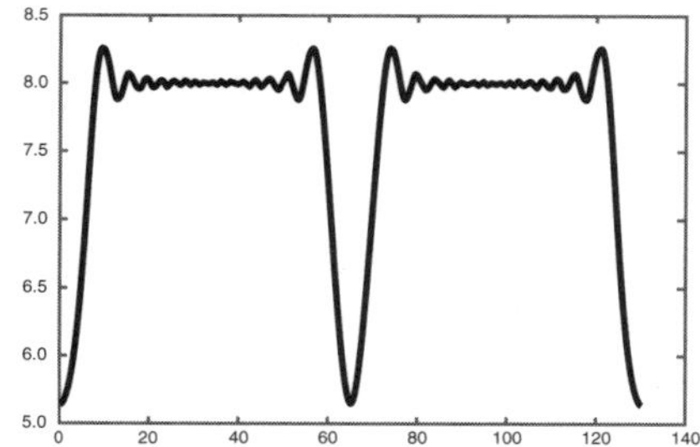

Figure 5.11 The Jaehne Signal and the Magnitude of its Frequency Response

The following call generates a Jaehne signal of length `len` and magnitude 1.0:

```
ippsVectorJaehne_32f( pSrc, len, 1.0 );
```

There are other signal generation functions, such as sinusoid generators, that are useful in testing filters. There are also random number generators that are useful in simulating noise and are used in adaptive filters. The Intel IPP generation functions are summarized in Table 5.2.

Table 5.2 Signal Generation Functions in Intel® Integrated Performance Primitives (Intel® IPP)

Function name	Description
`ippsTone_Direct`	Generate a sinusoid
`ippsTriangle_Direct`	Generate a triangle wave
`ippsRandGaussInitAlloc`, `ippsRandUniformInitAlloc`	Initialize State for random number generation
`ippsRandGauss`, `ippsRandUniform`, `ippsRandGauss_Direct`, `ippsRandUniform_Direct`	Generate a sequence of random numbers with a Gaussian (normal) or uniform distribution
`ippsVectorJaehne`	Generate a Jaehne signal
`ippsVectorRamp`	Generate a linearly increasing or decreasing ramp

Frequency Domain Filtering

Frequency-domain filtering with Intel IPP uses either the `ippsFFT` family or the `ippsDFT` family of functions. Both perform the Fourier transform, but the `ippsFFT` functions dictate that only the *Fast Fourier Transform* (FFT) algorithm be used. The FFT is a commonly used optimized algorithm for the transform, but it is only defined for signals with lengths that are for powers of two. The DFT functions in Intel IPP are not restricted to powers of two, but internally use the FFT algorithm in those cases.

Executing the FFT

Most of the naming conventions for Fourier transforms in Intel IPP are detailed in Chapter 2. Because of the symmetry properties of the DFT, there are special memory-efficient layouts for the input and output arrays. Table 5.3 shows the five FFT and DFT memory layouts supported.

Table 5.3 `ipps` Fourier Transform Memory Layouts

Code	Meaning	Layout	Size
`R`	Real	$R_0R_1R_2 \ldots R_{N-1}$	N
`C`	Complex	$R_0I_0R_1I_1 \ldots R_{N-1}I_{N-1}$	2N
`CCS`	Complex Conjugate-Symmetric	$R_0 0 R_1I_1 \ldots R_{N/2} 0$	N+2
`Pack`	Packed Real-Complex	$R_0R_1I_1 \ldots R_{N/2}$	N
`Perm`	Permuted Real-Complex	$R_0R_{N/2}R_1I_1 \ldots R_{N/2-1}I_{N/2-1}$	N

The layout code "R_n" represents the real component of element n; "I_n" represents the imaginary component of element n. Size is the number of values required to represent an N-element sequence.

The last three memory layouts represent an attempt to optimize the transform for the common case in which the input is real. As noted earlier in the explanation of Fourier transforms, when the input is real, the output is conjugate-symmetric. In this case, it is unnecessary to make that half of the signal explicit. The CCS format takes advantage of this by only returning elements 0 through N/2.

The CCS output is two elements larger than the input. Since conjugate symmetric data has a zero imaginary component for the first and middle, two other formats are provided, both equal in size to the input. Pack and Perm formats remove the two zeros by packing and reordering the data, respectively. The downside of these formats is that the data is no longer valid complex data; therefore, functions that operate on complex numbers have to be used with care, or can't be used at all.

Figure 5.12 is an example of calling the FFT function `ippsFFTFwd_RToCCS_32f`. This code produces results similar to those in Figure 5.11.

```
void myFFT_RToC_32f32fc(Ipp32f* pSrc, Ipp32fc*pDst, int
      order)
{
    IppsFFTSpec_R_32f *pFFTSpec;
      ippsFFTInitAlloc_R_32f( &pFFTSpec, order,
         IPP_FFT_DIV_INV_BY_N, ippAlgHintFast );
      ippsFFTFwd_RToCCS_32f(pSrc, (Ipp32f*)pDst,
         pFFTSpec, 0 );
    ippsConjCcs_32fc_I(pDst, 1<<order);
    ippsFFTFree_R_32f(pFFTSpec);
}
...
      Ipp32f* pSrc = ippsMalloc_32f(len);
      Ipp32f* pDstMag = ippsMalloc_32f(len);
      Ipp32fc* pDst = ippsMalloc_32fc(len);
      ippsVectorJaehne_32f( pSrc, 1<<order, 1 );
      myFFT_RToC_32f32fc(pSrc, pDst, order);
      ippsMagnitude_32fc(pDst, pDstMag, 1<<order);
...
```

Figure 5.12 Calculating the Magnitude of the FFT of a `VectorJaehne`

The function defined in Figure 5.12, `FFT_RToC`, is a potentially valuable function that cannot be found in the Intel IPP API. It takes a real input and produces the unabbreviated complex output. However, the inverse function, `FFT_CToR`, is not usually valid, since a complex input will have a real output only if the input is also conjugate-symmetric. For this reason, the `RToCCS` and `CCSToR` flavors exist in Intel IPP but the `RToC` and `CToR` flavors do not.

The function `FFTInitAlloc` allocates and initializes a specification structure to contain the tables needed for executing an optimized Fourier transform, then sets the variable `pFFTSpec` to point to it. Note the following:

- The memory containing these tables is dynamically allocated and must later be freed by `ippsFFTFree_R_32f`.
- There are numerous flavors of the initialization function. This version deals with FFTs whose input array is real (hence the "`_R`") and 32-bit floating point ("`_32f`"). For each there is a corresponding function to release the memory.
- The same `spec` structure is used for both forward and inverse transforms.

- The variable `order` is the $\log_2$ of the signal length. As noted earlier, the FFT is defined only for powers of two, so this order is an integer. The DFT function group, shown just below, handles lengths that aren't powers of two.
- Since the order of the data and the operation is embedded in the `pFFTSpec` structure, it will not later be passed into the function `ippsFFTFwd` or `ippsFFTInv`.
- The third argument determines how the constant factor will be handled. Without a constant factor, FFTInv(FFTFwd(x)) will be N*x. `IPP_FFT_DIV_INV_BY_N` indicates that the constant factor will be divided out on the inverse FFT.
- The last argument advises the library whether to use the fastest, most accurate, or best overall version. The effect of this flag is platform-dependent.

The forward FFT is performed by this call:

```
ippsFFTFwd_RToCCS_32f(pSrc, (Ipp32f*)pDst,
   pFFTSpec, 0 );
```

For simplicity, `0` is passed in as the temporary buffer space; this tells Intel IPP to allocate the buffer. Most often, optimized code should allocate a single buffer of a size indicated by `ippsFFTGetBufSize`, and keep that buffer and the `FFTSpec` structure through multiple calls of the FFT. In this case, the buffer is allocated and freed by `FFTFwd`, and the `spec` structure is allocated and freed by `myFFT_RToC`.

After the FFT creates a CCS-format output, the `ippsConjCcs` function expands the abbreviated form into a full complex representation. This converts the array

R_0	0	R_1	I_1	...	$R_{N/2}$	0

into

R_0	0	R_1	I_1	...	$R_{N/2}$	0	$R_{N/2-1}$	$-I_{N/2-1}$	...	R_1	$-I_1$

While many signal manipulations can be done directly on the CCS-format data, others, such as displaying the signal, are better done on the expanded form.

Calling the DFT

The family of functions ippsDFT is almost identical to the FFT functions above, except that DFT functions can operate on any size, not just powers of two. Figure 5.13 below shows how to call ippsDFT. Note that, other than the conversion from "order" to "len" and the text replacement of "FFT" with "DFT", this function is almost identical to myFFT_RToC. The only exception is the enumerated value IPP_FFT_DIV_INV_BY_N, which is used even though the function called is DFT.

```
void myDFT_RToC_32f32fc(Ipp32f* pSrc, Ipp32fc*pDst, int
    len)
{
    IppsDFTSpec_R_32f *pDFTSpec;
    ippsDFTInitAlloc_R_32f( &pDFTSpec, len,
        IPP_FFT_DIV_INV_BY_N, ippAlgHintFast );
    ippsDFTFwd_RToCCS_32f(pSrc, (Ipp32f*)pDst, pDFTSpec,
        0 );
    ippsConjCcs_32fc_I(pDst, len);
    ippsDFTFree_R_32f(pDFTSpec);
}
```

Figure 5.13 A Function to Calculate the DFT of a Vector

As noted above, the implementation of DFT in Intel IPP will use the FFT if the length of the signal is a power of two. In code that might be used for signals that are and aren't powers of two, the DFT can be called without concern for degraded performance. For this reason, the actual performance advantage of using FFT functions directly is quite small and is due only to the removal of a single branch. However, where code size is a concern, using the FFT may still make sense, as the Fourier transform functions have a fairly large memory footprint.

Wrapping the Fourier Transform Efficiently

Initializing the specification structures and buffers for the DFT is tedious work and can lead to inefficiencies in the calling code. Ideally, each specification structure should be created only once, and a single buffer should persist through multiple DFT calls. Furthermore, the code that allocates these structures should be coded only once.

Figure 5.14 demonstrates a class that keeps track of specification structures and memory buffers. While it covers only a few data types, the classes therein can easily be expanded to cover every type supported by Intel IPP.

The `FTSpec` class wraps the Intel IPP Fourier transform specification structures. It supports a linked list of `FTSpec` objects with a pointer to another object of its class, and supports self-identification with the `Matches` method. The constructor allocates the appropriate specification structure according to its arguments.

The key `FTWrap` methods are `GetSpec_`, `ResizeBuf_`, and `FT`. The `GetSpec_` private function searches through the linked list of specification objects looking for an `FTSpec` that matches the parameters provided. If one is found, that one is used. Otherwise, a new structure is allocated and added to the list. Using this method, each identical structure is allocated only once, then saved and reused.

The `ResizeBuf_` method maintains the buffer pointed to by `pBuffer_`. Each time a transform is executed, it checks first to see if the buffer is large enough to accommodate that operation. If not, the buffer is reallocated. This single buffer is saved and reused from transform to transform, and only requires a limited number of reallocations.

The overloaded `FT` method performs the Fourier transform for a particular data type. After acquiring a specification structure and ensuring that the buffer is of sufficient size, the function calls some flavor of `ippsDFT`. If it is not uniquely determined by the inputs, the function takes a flag `fwd` that indicates whether the forward or inverse transform is needed.

```
class FTSpec
{
private:
    int flag_;
    IppHintAlgorithm hint_;
    int type_;
    int len_;
public:
    FTSpec* pNext;
    void* pSpec;

    FTSpec(int len, FTType type, int flag, IppHintAlgorithm
        hint);
    ~FTSpec();
    int Matches(int len, FTType type, int flag,
        IppHintAlgorithm hint);
};

class FTWrap
```

```
{
    private:
        int mDFTCount_;

        IppHintAlgorithm hint_;
        int flag_;

        Ipp8u* pBuffer_;
        int bufSize_;

        void* GetSpec_(int len, FTType type);
        void ResizeBuf_(int size);

        FTSpec* pFirstSpec_;

    public:
        FTWrap();
        FTWrap(int flag, IppHintAlgorithm hint);
        ~FTWrap();

        IppStatus FT(const Ipp32f* pSrc, Ipp32fc* pDst,
            int len);
        IppStatus FT(const Ipp32fc* pSrc, Ipp32f* pDst,
            int len);
        IppStatus FT(const Ipp32fc* pSrc, Ipp32fc* pDst,
            int len, int fwd);
    …

};

FTSpec::FTSpec(int len, FTType type, int flag,
    IppHintAlgorithm hint) :
    flag_(flag), hint_(hint), type_(type), len_(len)
{
    switch (type)
    {
    case FT16s16sc:
        ippsDFTInitAlloc_R_16s((IppsDFTSpec_R_16s**)&pSpec,
            len, flag, hint);
        break;
    case FT16sc16sc:
        ippsDFTInitAlloc_C_16sc(
            (IppsDFTSpec_C_16sc**)&pSpec, len, flag, hint);
        break;
    case FT32f32fc:
        ippsDFTInitAlloc_R_32f((IppsDFTSpec_R_32f**)&pSpec,
            len, flag, hint);
        break;
    case FT32fc32fc:
        ippsDFTInitAlloc_C_32fc(
```

```
            (IppsDFTSpec_C_32fc**)&pSpec, len, flag, hint);
        break;
    case FT64f64fc:
        ippsDFTInitAlloc_R_64f((IppsDFTSpec_R_64f**)&pSpec,
            len, flag, hint);
        break;
    case FT64fc64fc:
        ippsDFTInitAlloc_C_64fc(
            (IppsDFTSpec_C_64fc**)&pSpec, len, flag, hint);
        break;
    }
}

void* FTWrap::GetSpec_(int len, FTType type)
{
    FTSpec* pNode = pFirstSpec_;
    while (pNode)
    {
        if (pNode->Matches(len, type, flag_, hint_))
            return (void*)pNode->pSpec;
        pNode = pNode->pNext;
    }
    pNode = new FTSpec(len, type, flag_, hint_);
    pNode->pNext = pFirstSpec_;
    pFirstSpec_ = pNode;
    return pNode->pSpec;
}

void FTWrap::ResizeBuf_(int size)
{
    if (pBuffer_) ippsFree(pBuffer_);
    pBuffer_ = ippsMalloc_8u(size);
    bufSize_ = size;
}

IppStatus FTWrap::FT(const Ipp32f* pSrc, Ipp32fc* pDst,
    int len)
{
    IppStatus st;
    void *pSpec = GetSpec_(len,FT32f32fc);
    int bufSize;
    ippsDFTGetBufSize_R_32f((IppsDFTSpec_R_32f*)pSpec,
        &bufSize);
    if (bufSize_ < bufSize) ResizeBuf_(bufSize);
    st = ippsDFTFwd_RToCCS_32f(pSrc, (Ipp32f*)pDst,
        (IppsDFTSpec_R_32f*)pSpec, pBuffer_);
    return st;
}
```

Figure 5.14 Definition and Methods for the FTSpec and FTWrap Classes

Filtering With FFT

As noted previously, a reversible linear transform enables frequency-domain filtering such as in Figure 5.5. Figure 5.15 lists code that uses `ippsFFT` to perform a frequency-domain filter.

```
// Set the filter to ones in the low-frequency half of
// the spectrum
void myMakeCCSFilter_32fc(Ipp32fc** pFilter, int len)
{
    *pFilter = (Ipp32fc*)ippsMalloc_32f(len+2);
    Ipp32fc one = {1.0, 0.0};
    ippsZero_32fc( *pFilter, len/2+1 );
    ippsSet_32fc(one, *pFilter, len/4);
}

void myFilter_32f(Ipp32f* pSrc, Ipp32fc* pFilterCCS,
      Ipp32f*pDst, int order)
{
    IppsFFTSpec_R_32f *pFFTSpec;
    Ipp32fc *pTmp =
        (Ipp32fc*)ippsMalloc_32f((1<<order)+2);
    ippsFFTInitAlloc_R_32f( &pFFTSpec, order,
        IPP_FFT_DIV_INV_BY_N, ippAlgHintFast );
    ippsFFTFwd_RToCCS_32f(pSrc, (Ipp32f*)pTmp, pFFTSpec,
        0 );
    ippsMul_32fc_I(pFilterCCS, pTmp, (1<<(order-1)) + 1);
    ippsFFTInv_CCSToR_32f((Ipp32f*)pTmp, pDst, pFFTSpec,
        0 );
    ippsFree(pFFTSpec);
}

myMakeCCSFilter_32fc(&pFilter, 1<<order);
myFilter_32f(pSrc, pFilter, pDst, order);
spView2_32f( pSrc, 1<<order, pDst, 1<<order,"G: Source;"
    "B: Dest", 1 );
```

Figure 5.15 Code for a Simple Frequency-Domain Filter

This code differs from the earlier example in the filter generation. The function `myMakeCCSFilter_32f` creates a simple low-pass filter that removes half of the frequencies.

These lines set the first half of `pFilter` to one, and the rest to zero:

```
Ipp32fc one = {1.0, 0.0};
ippsZero_32fc( *pFilter, len/2+1 );
ippsSet_32fc(one, *pFilter, len/4);
```

The length of the filter is `len/2+1`, where `len` is the length of the original time-domain signal. This filter is abbreviated from a full filter of length `len` because it will be multiplied against a compressed complex-conjugate-symmetric (CCS) signal, so it is, in fact, only half of the filter.

This CCS format actually simplifies the filter construction by forcing the creation of a symmetric filter, since the CCS format can represent only symmetric signals. A nonsymmetric frequency filter would be complex when transformed to the time domain, and would therefore produce a complex output for the system. Care must be taken when not working with CCS format.

Figure 5.16 compares this half filter with an expanded filter. Array a) is the filter created by `MakeCCSFilter` that will be multiplied against a CCS signal. Array b) is the expansion of this filter, created with `ippsConjCcs_32fc`, which should be used when multiplying against a full complex signal.

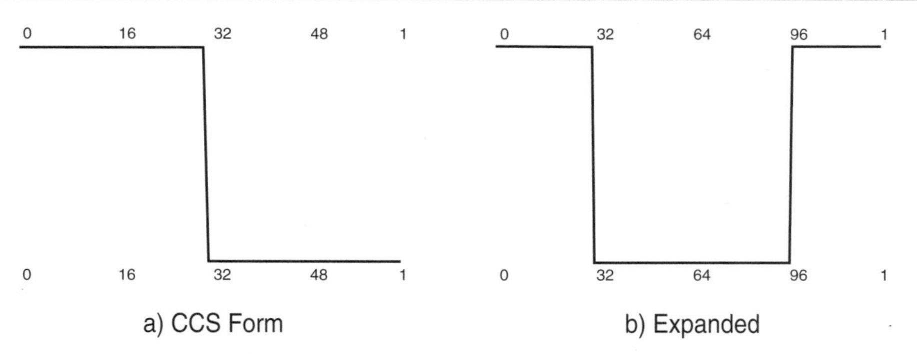

Figure 5.16 Frequency Domain Filters

Since the cutoff point is N/4, this filter should remove any frequencies over

$$S*n/N = S*N/4/N = S/4.$$

That is, any frequencies more than one-fourth the sampling rate, or more than one cycle every four samples, should be removed. Take a look at the source and destination signals as graphed in Figure 5.17. Note that the original, in gray, increases the speed of its oscillation toward the left of the graph, but the filtered signal, in black, does not. After filtering, there are no frequency components in the signals with a period less than four samples.

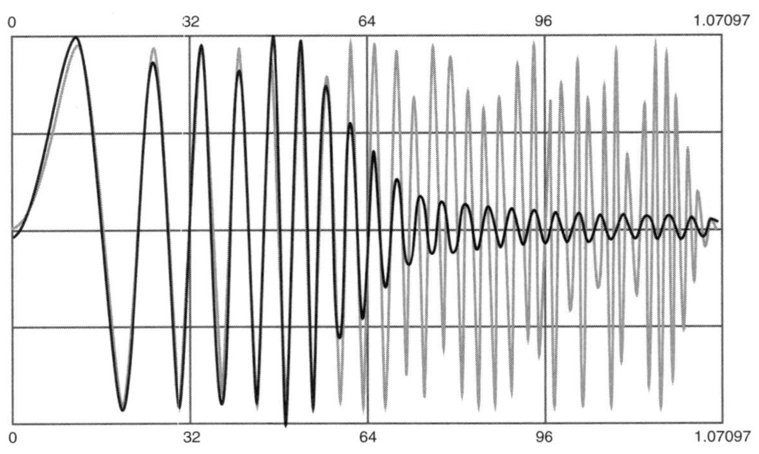

Figure 5.17 Source and Destination for FFT-Based Filter

Time Domain Filtering

A good introduction to time-domain filtering in Intel IPP is to implement the simple example that opened the Time-Domain Filters section earlier in this chapter. That example applied a filter `{ 0.25, 0.5, 0.25 }` against an input signal. Figure 5.18 shows an implementation of that filter using the FIR functions in Intel IPP.

```
void myFilterA_32f(Ipp32f* pSrc, Ipp32f*pDst, int len)
{
    // Low-pass filter:
    Ipp32f taps[] = { 0.25f, 0.5f, 0.25f };
    Ipp32f delayLine[] = { 0.0f, 0.0f, 0.0f };
    IppsFIRState_32f *pFIRState;

    ippsFIRInitAlloc_32f( &pFIRState, taps, 3,
        delayLine );
    ippsFIR_32f(pSrc, pDst, len, pFIRState );
    ippsFIRFree_32f(pFIRState);
}
```

Figure 5.18 A Simple Time-Domain Filter Using `ippsFIR`

The first step is to create a short, real, symmetric filter of length 3. The elements of the filter, called *taps*, are placed in the array `taps`.

The delay line is then initialized. For most FIR functions, the delay line must be the same length as the filter, although in some cases Intel IPP requires the array to be longer for efficiency. The delay line holds the historical samples, in reverse order. That is, if the source data starts at time `t`, then the element `delayLine[0]` is the source data from time `t-1`, `delayLine[1]` is from time `t-2`, and so on.

When using the `InitAlloc` protocol for `FIR`, filling the delay line array with zeros is actually unnecessary. If `ippsFIRInitAlloc_32f` is passed a zero for that argument, it automatically sets the delay line in `pFIRState` to all zeros.

The actual filtering is done by `ippsFIR_32f`, which performs `len` iterations of filtering the source and placing the result in the destination. During each iteration, one value is taken from `pSrc[n]` and placed in the delay line. Then the dot product of the filter and the delay line is taken, and the result written to `pDst[n]`. At all times, `pFIRState` holds the last `tapslen` samples in its internal delay line. In this case, there are three samples.

The results of passing this function a 128-point Jaehne signal are shown in Figure 5.19. The low frequencies are relatively untouched, while the highest frequency elements are reduced almost to nothing. It doesn't take too much imagination to see that the frequencies of this signal have been modified as if by multiplication by the filter in Figure 5.8.

In practice, this filter is unlikely to be useful because of the gradual fall-off. Filters of short lengths are unable to represent abrupt transitions in the frequency domain.

Comparing Intel IPP filter types

FIR is just one of the Intel IPP time-domain filter functions. You can group the filters into five subclasses: convolution, correlation, FIR, LMS, and IIR. Within each class, there are flavors for data type and calling convention. Table 5.4 is a quick explanation of these classes.

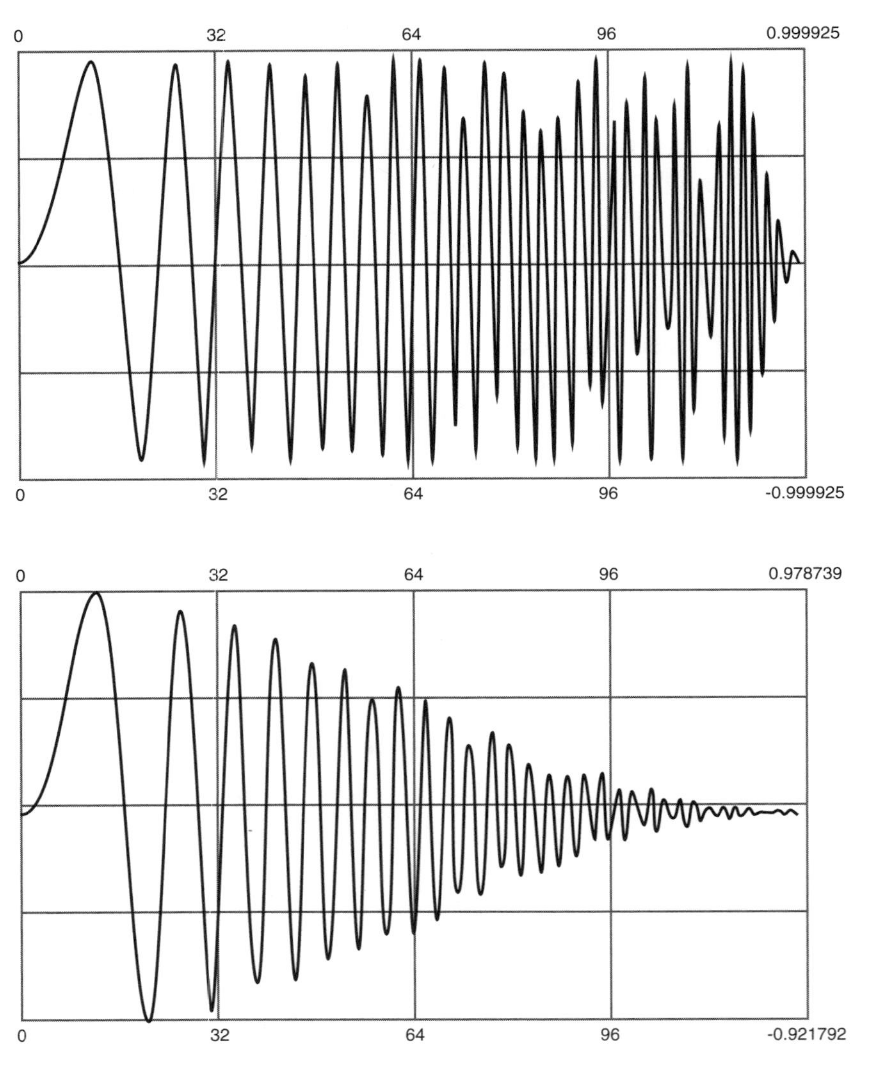

Figure 5.19 Source and Destination for FIR Filter `{0.25, 0.5, 0.25}`.

Table 5.4 Time-Domain Filter Functions in Intel® Integrated Performance Primitives (Intel® IPP)

Class	Description
Convolution	Convolve two signals of any length; resulting length is len1+len2-1
Correlation	Convolution without reversing either signal
FIR	Apply a finite impulse response filter to a signal; different from convolution mostly in setup, how edges are handled, and output length (which is equal to input length)
LMS	Adaptive FIR: Apply an FIR, but adapt the filter taps each filter cycle
IIR	Apply an infinite impulse response filter; like an FIR applied twice each cycle – once on the input history and once on the output history. IIR filters tend to be shorter but more complicated and less stable than FIR filters

This section demonstrates the distinctions between these filter types, and provides some sense of when each type is useful.

Convolution. Two types of convolution are supported in Intel IPP, linear and cyclic, but cyclic convolution is only supported for limited number of sizes and types. The functions `ippsConv_*` perform linear convolution while `ippsConvCyclic*` functions perform cyclic convolution. Table 5.5 lists these functions.

Table 5.5 Convolution Functions in Intel® Integrated Performance Primitives (Intel® IPP)

Function name	Description
`ippsConv_[32f|64f]`	Linear convolution of two `Ipp32f` or `Ipp64f` signals
`ippsConv_16s_Sfs`	Linear convolution of two `Ipp16s` signals with output scaling
`IppsConvCyclic*_16s_Sfs`	Fixed-size cyclic convolution of `Ipp16s` signals

Figure 5.20 below uses `ippsConv` to convolve two signals that have been initialized with `ippsTriangle`.

```
Ipp16s* pSrc1 = ippsMalloc_16s(len1);
Ipp16s* pSrc2 = ippsMalloc_16s(len2);
Ipp16s* pDst = ippsMalloc_16s(len1+len2-1);
float phase=3.141592654f;
ippsTriangle_Direct_16s(pSrc1, len1, 256.0f, 2.0/len1,
   0.0f, &phase);
ippsAddC_16s_I(256, pSrc1, len1);
phase=0.0;
ippsTriangle_Direct_16s(pSrc2, len2, 256.0f, 2.0/len2,
   0.0f, &phase);
ippsAddC_16s_I(256, pSrc2, len2);
ippsConv_16s_Sfs(pSrc1, len1, pSrc2, len2, pDst, 8);
```

Figure 5.20 `ippsConv` Called on Two Offset Triangle Waves

The allocation functions are included to highlight the sizes. The array `pDst` must be as long as the two signals would be together if overlapping by just one sample; that is, `len1+len2-1`.

The sources are two triangle functions, one with phase 0.0 starting at a peak, and the other with phase pi starting at a trough. The triangle waves are symmetric around 0, so the range is initially -256 to 256. However, the results are more obvious if both signals are exclusively positive, so 256 is added to each signal. Also note that the phase is passed as a pointer and the new phase returned at that location, so that a subsequent call of `ippsTriangle` can generate more samples in the same sequence.

The convolution is performed by `ippsConv_16s`. Previous examples have used floating-point data for simplicity, but in order to demonstrate the use of scaling, all these arrays are `Ipp16s`.

When a nonzero scaling factor is passed to `ippsConv`, the operation is performed in such a way that the data is not lost during the process, and the result is divided by $2^{scalefactor}$ before it's returned.

There are several ways to estimate the scale factor needed. In this case, with 15 data bits, excluding the sign bit, the maximum scale factor that could be required is

$$\log_2(\max(pSrc1) * \max(pSrc2) * \min(len1,len2)) - 15 \text{ bits} =$$

$$\log_2(\max(pSrc1)) + \log_2(\max(pSrc2)) + \log_2(\min(len1,len2)) - 15 =$$

$$\log_2(512) + \log_2(512) + \log_2(64) - 15 =$$

$$9 + 9 + 6 - 15 = 9$$

A scale factor of 8 proved to be the factor required for these two signals. The maximum value of the output was 17,404, so a scale factor of 7 would have resulted a maximum value greater than 32,767, and the function would have had to clamp the result.

The triangle-wave sources and the result of the convolution are graphed in Figure 5.21.

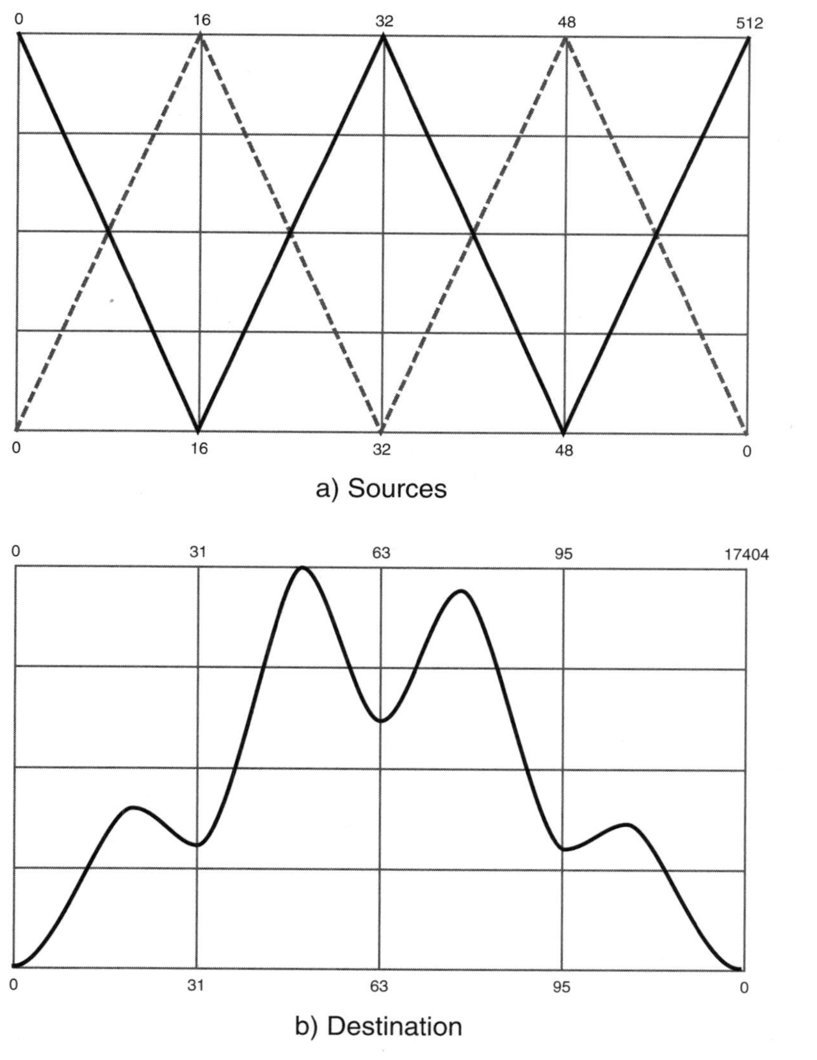

Figure 5.21 Convolution of Two Triangle Waves

Convolution and FIR filters are mathematically interchangeable. The code sample shown in Figure 5.22 demonstrates a filter from above implemented using ippConv.

```
void myFilterA_32f(Ipp32f* pSrc, Ipp32f*pDst, int len)
{
    Ipp32f taps[] = { 0.25f, 0.5f, 0.25f };
    ippsConv_32f(pSrc, len, taps, 3, pDst);
}
```

Figure 5.22 A Simple Time-Domain Filter Using Intel® Integrated Performance Primitivies (Intel® IPP)

This code has almost exactly the same result as the FIR in Figure 5.18. The only difference is that the pDst in this case is two elements longer. If these two elements are ignored, the results are identical.

Finally, Figure 5.23 implements the useful myConvCyclic_32f function using linear convolution.

```
int myConvCyclic_32f(const Ipp32f* pSrc1, int lenSrc1,
    const Ipp32f* pSrc2, int lenSrc2, Ipp32f* pDst,
      Ipp32f* pBuffer)
{
    Ipp32f* pTmp;
      if (pBuffer == 0) pTmp =
         ippsMalloc_32f(lenSrc1+lenSrc2-1);
      else pTmp = pBuffer;
      int lenmx = (lenSrc1 > lenSrc2 ? lenSrc1 :
      lenSrc2);
    ippsConv_32f(pSrc1, lenSrc1, pSrc2, lenSrc2, pTmp);
    ippsCopy_32f(pTmp, pDst, lenmx);
    ippsAdd_32f_I(pTmp+lenmx, pDst, lenSrc1+lenSrc2-1-
      lenmx);
    if (pBuffer == 0) ippsFree(pTmp);
    return 0;
}
```

Figure 5.23 A ConvCyclic Function Implemented with ippsConv

Cyclic convolution is clearly defined for equal-length signals. For unequal length signals, it is generally assumed that the result should be the greater of the two lengths. After the maximum length calculation is made, the first lenmx elements of the convolution result are copied from the temporary buffer to the destination using ippsCopy. Then the remaining data from the convolution result is added element-by-element to the start of the output buffer using `ippsAdd`.

Compare the result in Figure 5.24 with that in Figure 5.21. For one, it's shorter. For another, the curve consists of two large humps instead of one large hump and two half-height ones. In fact, this result is the other result with the two ends wrapped around each other and added together.

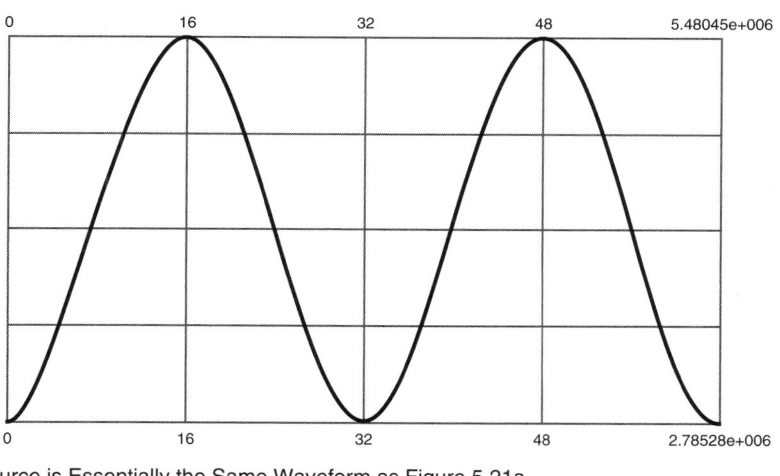

Figure 5.24 Result of a Cyclic Convolution.

Correlation is mathematically the same as convolution, but the second signal is not flipped. The input signals are shifted and multiplied element-by-element in their original order. The other fundamental differences between it and convolution are:

- As a consequence of the missing flip, when the signals are different, the operation is no longer commutative; that is, the order of arguments affects the outcome of the operation.
- Correlation is divided into two explicit flavors, autocorrelation and cross-correlation. Autocorrelation is the correlation of one signal with itself; cross-correlation is the correlation between two signals.
- Correlation is more commonly used in analysis than in filtering.

Due to these fundamental differences, the functions supporting correlation differ slightly from those supporting convolution. The differences in the implementation are:

- In an attempt to make all elements of a correlation output approximately even and not drop off near the ends of the signal, correlation functions often support normalization. Intel IPP supports two types of normalization, biased and unbiased. Biased normalization divides the output by the total length of the source signal. Unbiased normalization divides each output value by the number of elements of overlap between the sources for that value.
- In Intel IPP, correlation functions take as an argument a length for the destination, and the result is only calculated and output to that length.
- Intel IPP cross-correlation functions also take as an argument the offset (called `lowlag`) of the correlation result from the logical beginning of the output

Table 5.6 lists the Intel IPP correlation functions.

Table 5.6 Correlation Functions in Intel® Integrated Performance Primitives (Intel® IPP)

Function name	Description
`ippsCrossCorr_*`	Unnormalized correlation of two signals
`ippsCrossCorr_NormA_*`	Normalized but biased correlation of two signals; normalized by `1/srcLen`
`ippsCrossCorr_NormB_*`	Normalized, unbiased correlation of two signals; normalized by `1/(srcLen-n)`
`ippsAutoCorr_*`	Unnormalized autocorrelation
`ippsAutoCorr_NormA_*`	Normalized but biased autocorrelation
`ippsAutoCorr_NormB_*`	Normalized, unbiased autocorrelation

Figure 5.25 demonstrates correlation with unbiased normalization on an audio signal. This code uses a class `WaveFile` to load a `.wav` file from disk. This class, which is defined and explained in Chapter 6, loads the header when `Open` is called, then reads the file into memory when `ReadAsShort` is called.

To avoid scaling, the code segment converts the input wave file to floating point with `ippsConvert_16s32f`.

```
wave.Open(filename);
int len = wave.GetNumSamples();
Ipp16s* pSrc = ippsMalloc_16s(len);
int sampcount = wave.ReadAsShort(len, pSrc);

Ipp32f* pSrc32f = ippsMalloc_32f(len);
Ipp32f* pDst32f = ippsMalloc_32f(len*2);

ippsConvert_16s32f(pSrc, pSrc32f, len);

Ipp32f mean;
ippsMean_32f(pSrc32f,len, &mean, ippAlgHintFast);
ippsSubC_32f_I(mean, pSrc32f, len);

ippsAutoCorr_NormB_32f(pSrc32f, len, pDst32f,len);
```

Figure 5.25 Autocorrelating a Signal

Neither `ippsAutoCorr_32f` nor `ippsAutoCorr_NormA_32f` produces an output of consistent magnitude. Both output signals decrease significantly near the end of the signal. However, as shown in Figure 5.26, `ippsAutoCorr_NormB_32f` produces a nicely stable output. The stability is improved by normalizing the source data around zero before the autocorrelation, by subtracting the mean with `ippsMean` and `ippsSubC`.

The result of autocorrelation can be used to pick out key cyclic information, such as a beat frequency. Cross-correlation is often used for pattern matching.

FIR. The finite-impulse response filter is the core function for filtering. An example of one flavor of FIR is above. Table 5.7 lists the other flavors of FIR. Adaptive versions of FIR are covered in the next section.

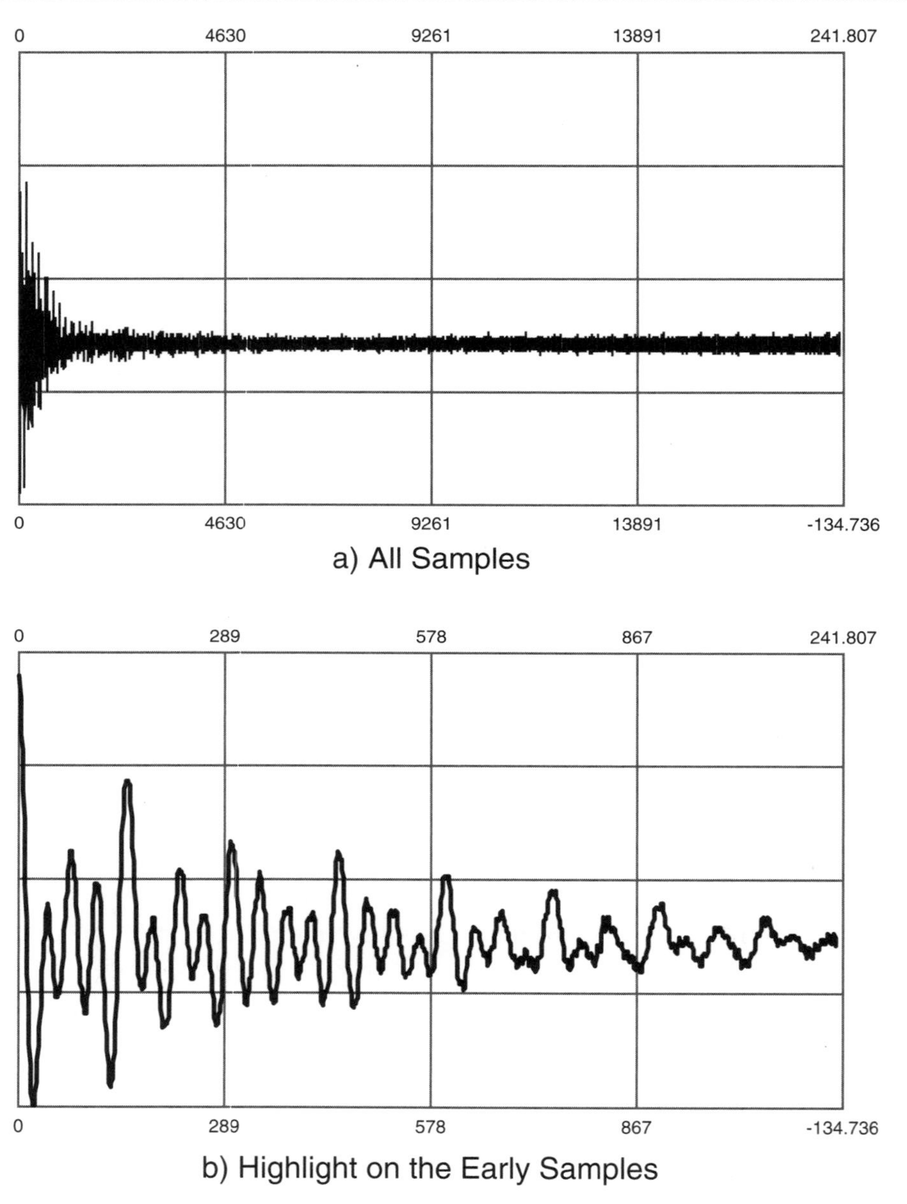

Figure 5.26 Autocorrelation of an Audio Signal

Table 5.7 FIR Functions in Intel® Integrated Performance Primitives (Intel® IPP)

Function name	Description
`ippsFIR_*`	FIR, requires Init
`ippsFIROne_*`	FIR, one input sample, requires Init
`ippsFIR_Direct_*`	FIR, no Init
`ippsFIROne_Direct_*`	FIR, one input sample, no Init
`ippsFIRMR_Direct_*`	FIR and resample, no Init

The distinctions among the first four FIR types from this table are best demonstrated with an example. The code in Figure 5.27 lists four implementations of a `myFilter*_32f` function. All of them perform the same operation using a different Intel IPP function.

The two functions `myFilter1_32f` and `myFilter3_32f` first perform the same initialization steps. The resulting `IppsFIRState_32f` structures are interchangeable. In the execution, `Filter3` calls `ippsFIROne_32f` once per sample in a loop, while for `Filter1` the loop is inside the `ippsFIR_32f` function.

This same relationship holds between the functions `myFilter2_32f` and `myFilter4_32f`, which use the multiple-sample and one-sample versions of the `Direct` FIRs. These two contrast with `Filter1` and `Filter3` in that the `Direct` versions of the FIR require no initialization and keep the state in arrays rather than a specification structure.

Note that in `myFilter2_32f` and `myFilter4_32f` that the delay line is allocated `2*tapslen` elements instead of the usual `tapslen`. The reason for this is that the delay line also serves as a buffer in the `Direct` versions of FIR. All input values are copied there so that the convolution operation can be done on contiguous data. As a result, this taps array must be twice the size of the taps, large enough to hold `tapslen` new input samples and `tapslen` previous input samples.

```
// Uses ippsFIR_32f
void myFilter1_32f(Ipp32f* pSrc, Ipp32f*pDst, int len,
      Ipp32f* pTaps, int tapslen)
{
    Ipp32f* pDelayLine = ippsMalloc_32f(tapslen);
    ippsZero_32f(pDelayLine,tapslen);
    IppsFIRState_32f *pFIRState;
      ippsFIRInitAlloc_32f( &pFIRState, pTaps, tapslen,
            pDelayLine );
    ippsFIR_32f(pSrc, pDst, len, pFIRState );
    ippsFIRFree_32f(pFIRState);
```

```
    ippsFree(pDelayLine);
}

// Uses ippsFIR_Direct_32f
void myFilter2_32f(Ipp32f* pSrc, Ipp32f*pDst, int len,
      Ipp32f* pTaps, int tapslen)
{
    Ipp32f* pDelayLine = ippsMalloc_32f(tapslen*2);
    ippsZero_32f(pDelayLine,tapslen*2);
    int index = 0;
      ippsFIR_Direct_32f(pSrc, pDst, len, pTaps, tapslen,
            pDelayLine, &index );
    ippsFree(pDelayLine);
}

// Uses ippsFIROne_32f
void myFilter3_32f(Ipp32f* pSrc, Ipp32f*pDst, int len,
      Ipp32f* pTaps, int tapslen)
{
    Ipp32f* pDelayLine = ippsMalloc_32f(tapslen);
    ippsZero_32f(pDelayLine,tapslen);
    IppsFIRState_32f *pFIRState;
      ippsFIRInitAlloc_32f( &pFIRState, pTaps, tapslen,
            pDelayLine );
    for (int i=0; i<len; i++)
      ippsFIROne_32f(pSrc[i], pDst+i, pFIRState );
    ippsFIRFree_32f(pFIRState);
}

// Uses ippsFIROne_Direct_32f
void myFilter4_32f(Ipp32f* pSrc, Ipp32f*pDst, int len,
      Ipp32f* pTaps, int tapslen)
{
    Ipp32f* pDelayLine = ippsMalloc_32f(tapslen*2);
    ippsZero_32f(pDelayLine,tapslen*2);
    int index = 0;
    for (int i=0; i<len; i++)
            ippsFIROne_Direct_32f(pSrc[i], pDst+i, pTaps,
                  tapslen, pDelayLine, &index );
    ippsFree(pDelayLine);
}
```

Figure 5.27 Four Equivalent Functions Using Different Flavors of `ippsFIR`

These functions use floating-point taps and data. Floating-point data is easier because of the greater dynamic range. Floating-point taps are much more conducive to filter design than integral taps. For this reason, both integral and floating-point taps are supported for FIR when the input samples are integers. Functions like `FIR32s_16s` use `Ipp32s` taps on `Ipp16s` data, and provide a scale factor for the taps that's applied during the operation. Functions like `FIR32f_16s` instead use floating-point taps on integral data, which is much more flexible and convenient.

The last set of FIR functions in the table is the `FIRMR` group. These functions *upsample* the signal before the applying FIR by adding `upFactor-1` zeros between each pair of samples, then *downsample* the result after the FIR by deleting `downFactor-1` out of every `downFactor` samples. These filters are demonstrated on audio samples in Chapter 6.

The imaging subset of functions in Intel IPP provides a number of fixed-kernel filters, many of which support one-dimensional operation. Those kernels that are supported are just a few taps long, but they execute very quickly. See Chapter 9 for a discussion of these filters.

FIRLMS. Intel IPP supports a set of filter functions that modify the filter taps even as they filter a signal. The modification is done to try to make a filter that produces a target output for a given input. These filter functions are known as adaptive filters.

The particular type of adaptive filters in Intel IPP use the *least mean squared* (LMS) adaptation method. These functions modify the taps at each step in order to minimize the mean squared error between the filter output and a provided target output. The function also provides the filter result, which is useful in a real-time system that is trying to adapt to new signal characteristics even as it filters the signal. Table 5.8 lists the LMS filters in Intel IPP.

Adaptive filters have several applications. One use of LMS filters is to create a model for an unknown "black box" system with an FIR filter. The algorithm to do this passes a series of random numbers through the black box system to obtain a series of output values. Then it calls the LMS function, using those output values as the target values for the same random inputs. The idea is to develop a filter to produce the same outputs for those random inputs. Over time, the filter is likely to approximate the black box, if the black box can be approximated with a linear filter.

Table 5.8 Adaptive FIR Functions in Intel® Integrated Performance Primitives (Intel® IPP)

Function name	Description
ippsFIRLMS_*	FIR and filter adaptation, requires Init
ippsFIRLMSOne_Direct_*	FIR and filter adaptation, one sample, no Init
ippsFIRLMSMRPutVal_*	Prepares for FIRLMSMROne
ippsFIRLMSMROne_*	FIR and resample, prepares for FIRLMSMRUpdateTaps
ippsFIRLMSMROneVal_*	Same as FIRLMSMRPutVal then FIRLMSMROne
ippsFIRLMSMRUpdateTaps_*	Filter adaptation after FIRLMSMROne or FIRLMSMROneVal

Figure 5.28 is an example of using LMS filters to approximate a black box filter.

```
IppsRandUniState_32f* pStateRand;
ippsRandUniformInitAlloc_32f(&pStateRand, -1.0, 1.0, 23);

IppsFIRState_32f* pStateBB;
myBlackBoxInitAlloc_32f(&pStateBB, tapslen);

IppsFIRLMSState_32f* pStateLMS;
ippsFIRLMSInitAlloc_32f(&pStateLMS, pTapsLMS, tapslen,
      pDelayLine, 0);

int index=0;
float mu = 1.0/10.0/(float)tapslen;
Ipp32f resBB, resLMS, samp;
for (int i=0; i<4; i++)
{
    for (int j=0; j<3000; j++)
    {
      ippsRandUniform_32f(&samp, 1, pStateRand);
      ippsFIROne_32f(samp, &resBB, pStateBB);
            ippsFIRLMS_32f(&samp, &resBB, &resLMS, 1, mu,
               pStateLMS);
    }
    ippsFIRLMSGetTaps_32f(pStateLMS, pTapsLMS);
    spView_32f( pTapsLMS, tapslen, "Taps for LMS", 0 );
}
ippsFIRGetTaps_32f(pStateBB, pTapsBB);
spView_32f( pTapsBB, tapslen, "Taps for Black Box", 1 );
```

Figure 5.28 Modeling an Unknown System with an Adaptive Filter

The first step is initialization. The call to the function `ippsRandUniformInitAlloc_32f` creates the state for a uniformly-distributed random number generator. This generator produces numbers between -1 and 1; argument 23 is the seed. Then the call to function `myBlackBoxInitAlloc_32f` creates an `ippsFIRState_32f` structure for an unknown filter of length `tapslen`. Finally, the function call to `ippsFIRLMSInitAlloc_32f` initializes the LMS filter; for convenience, this filter also has the length `tapslen`, although in a real situation the length of the black box filter would not be known. The taps and delay line are in `pTapsLMS` and `pDelayLine`, respectively, and are both allocated and initialized elsewhere.

To save memory and reduce complexity, the code uses the one-sample versions of each of these functions. That means that the only storage needed, besides that for the `State` structures, is for the output of each of the three functions. In the inner loop, one call generates a single random number, the next adds the random value `samp` to the input stream and filters it with the black box filter, and the last filters the same value with the LMS filter and adapts the filter.

The argument `mu` sets the rate of adaptation. If the rate is too high, the adaptation can quickly become unstable and produce garbage results. A good rule of thumb for `mu` is that it should be in the range

$$0 < mu < \frac{1}{10NP}$$

The variable `P` is the power of the input. It can be approximated by the average of the squared values of some number of inputs:

$$P \approx \frac{1}{1+M} \sum_{n=0}^{M} x[n] * x[n]$$

Since the random input values are between -1.0 and 1.0, the power can't be greater than 1. So `mu` in this case is set to 1/(10 * N).

The code uses a nested loop so that the results can be displayed every 3,000 cycles. These results, shown in Figure 5.29, show a gradual convergence to a filter very similar to the black-box filter. The black box filter, revealed in that figure, is a Gaussian function.

In this code, the termination criterion is arbitrary, chosen by hand according to a visual similarity between the adapted filter and the "unknown" filter. Where such a criterion is necessary, it should generally be based on convergence. Every few samples, the filter should be checked to see how much change has taken place. When the change over a time period has diminished below a threshold, the adaptation can be declared a success and ended. It is also possible to decrease `mu` over time according to this criterion to converge more accurately.

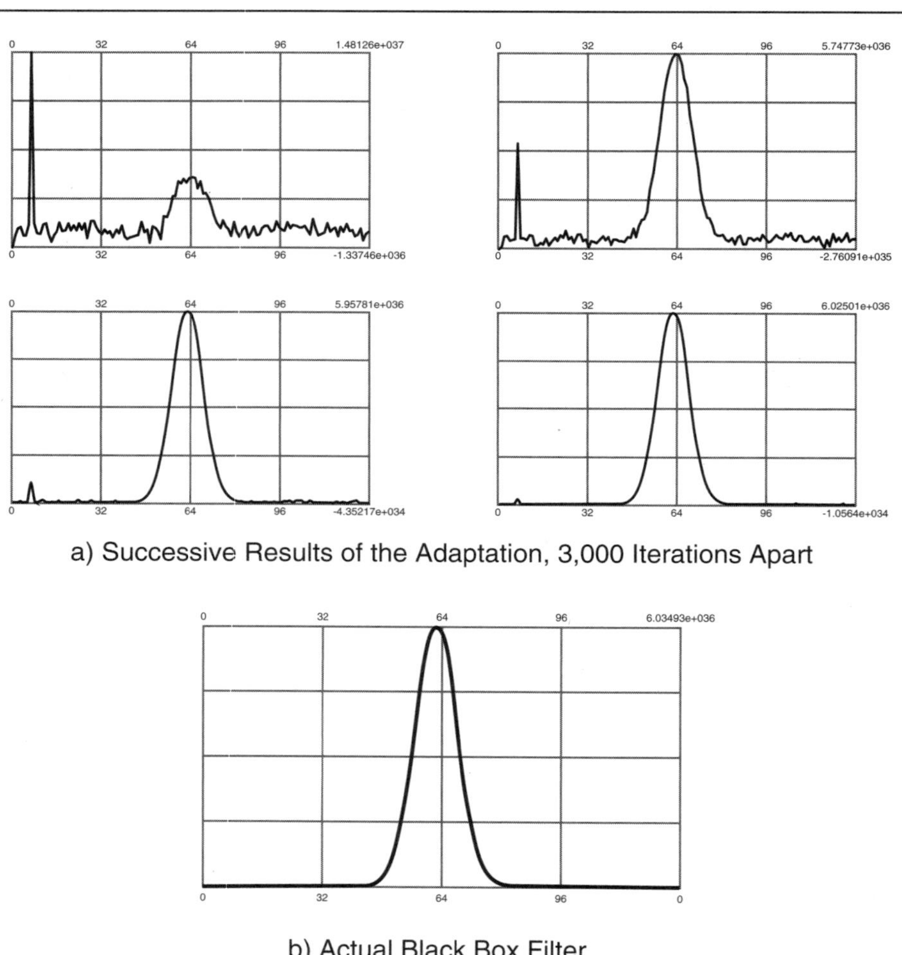

a) Successive Results of the Adaptation, 3,000 Iterations Apart

b) Actual Black Box Filter

Figure 5.29 LMS Adaptation of an FIR Filter to Match a Black Box Filter

Other Topics

This is not a complete coverage of Intel IPP filtering and not nearly complete coverage of the vast area of filtering. Intel IPP includes several other filtering functions and functions applicable to filtering. Chief among these are *infinite impulse response* (IIR) filters, windowing, filter design functions, and nonlinear filters.

Infinite Impulse Response Filters

The finite impulse response filter is only one of the two major types of linear filters. The other is the infinite impulse response (IIR) filter. IIR filters have an "infinite" response in the sense that at each step, the history of filter outputs is included in the filter operation.

IIR filters can be specified in two ways. The basic version of IIR takes as input two filters concatenated together. One set of taps is applied to the last `len` inputs, the other to the last `len` outputs.

The other version takes an array of *biquad* filters. Each biquad is a six-tap filter, three of which are applied to inputs and three applied to outputs. The filters are cascaded so that the output of each feeds into the next. Figure 5.30 compares this topology with the single-filter version.

IIR filters are demonstrated in the next chapter.

Windowing

By taking the inverse Fourier transform of a frequency envelope, you can generate a time-domain FIR filter. When convolved with a signal, that filter should have the same effect as the multiplication in the frequency domain. This simple method, while effective, is not optimal. Because of the sinusoidal nature of the signals, the abrupt, square filter in Figure 5.5 generates an awkwardly large filter in the time domain. This filter does not decay rapidly enough to produce a compact FIR filter. This filter ends abruptly at the edges rather than tapering off.

One way to counter this effect is by applying a *windowing* function. Such functions smooth the filters by multiplying them by a triangular or bell-shaped curve.

Figure 5.31 shows two FIR filters, before and after application of a Blackman window, and the result of applying these filters to a Jaehne signal. Both result in some *ringing*, the term for the overshoot of the filtered result. However, the ringing in the first is much worse, exceeding the ideal 1.0 result by 1.32 as compared to 1.19 for the windowed version.

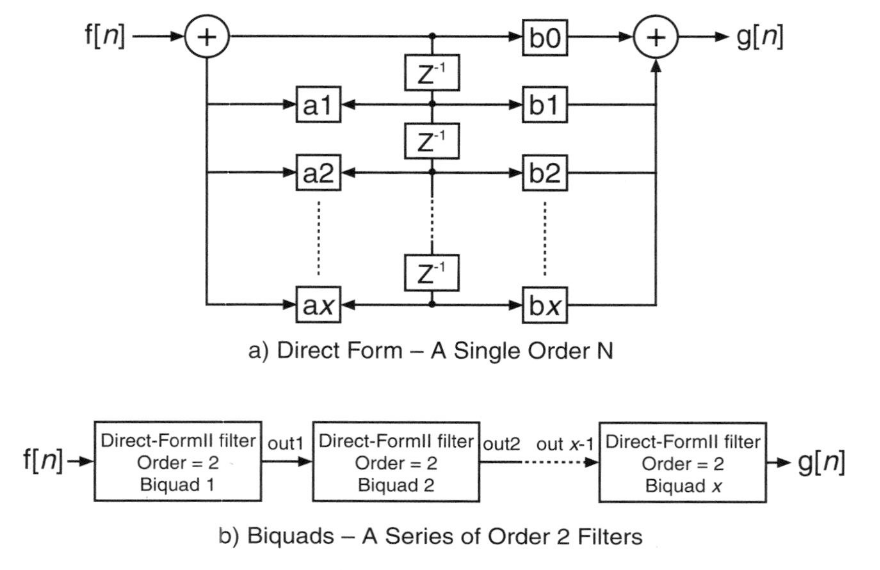

Figure 5.30 Two Topologies for IIR Filters

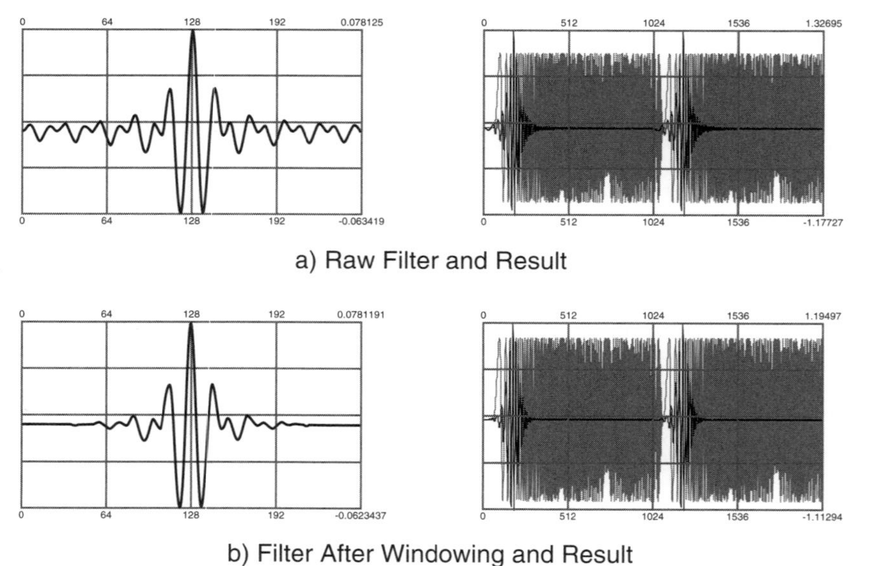

a) Raw Filter and Result
b) Filter After Windowing and Result

Figure 5.31 Two Filters in the Frequency Domain

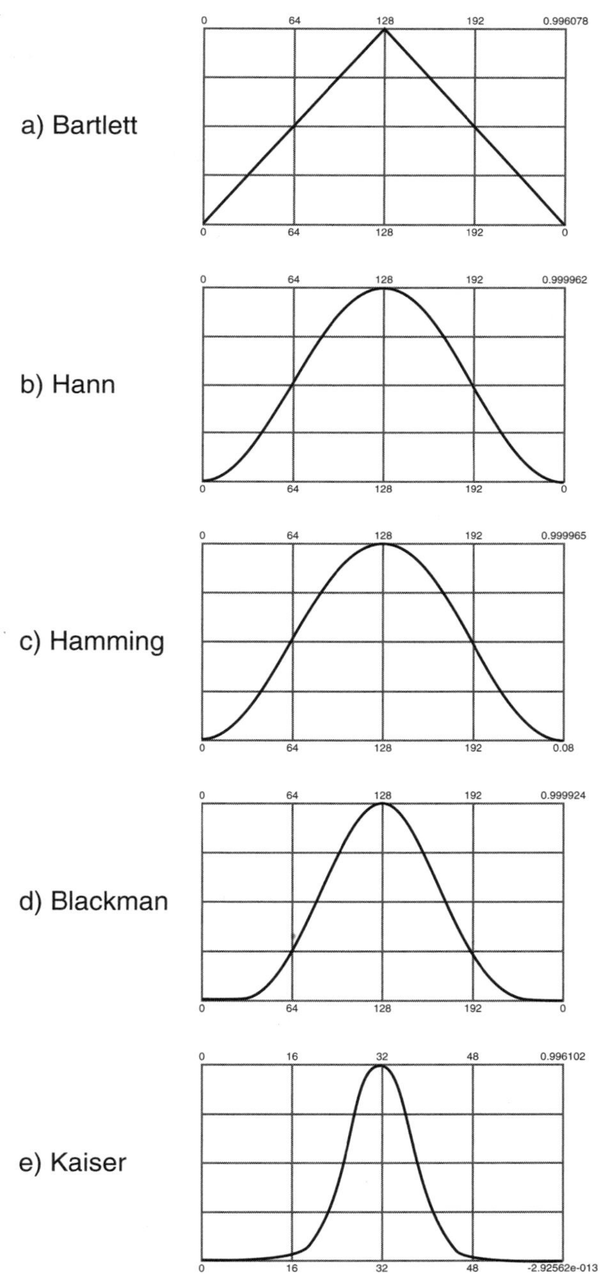

Figure 5.32 Five Windowing Functions

The windowing functions all operate on the principle that the center of the filter should be left untouched, but the surrounding elements should be attenuated according to their distance from the center of the filter. The Bartlett window is a simple triangle pulse. The Blackman, Hann, and Hamming windows are functions of sinusoids. The Kaiser window is based on the Bessel function. All of the windows are shown in Figure 5.32.

Filter Design

In addition to providing tools for building filters from the ground up, Intel IPP contains complete filter design functions that generate filters of requested lengths for requested frequency parameters. These functions are listed in Table 5.9.

Table 5.9 Filter Generation Functions in Intel® Integrated Performance Primitives (Intel® IPP)

Function name	Description
`ippsFIRGenLowpass_*`	Generate an FIR filter that blocks frequencies above a cutoff frequency
`ippsFIRGenHighpass_*`	Generate an FIR filter that blocks frequencies below a cutoff frequency
`ippsFIRGenBandpass_*`	Generate an FIR filter that blocks frequencies outside of a frequency range
`ippsFIRGenBandstop_*`	Generate an FIR filter that blocks frequencies inside of a frequency range

Nonlinear Filters

The Intel IPP supports only a limited set of nonlinear filters. These are listed in Table 5.10. The usual frequency domain analysis doesn't apply to these filters.

Table 5.10 Non-Linear Filters in Intel® Integrated Performance Primitives (Intel® IPP)

Function name	Description
`ippsFilterMedian_*`	Set output to the median value in the neighborhood of each element
`ippiFilterMin_*`	Set output to the minimum value in the neighborhood of each element
`ippiFilterMax_*`	Set output to the maximum value in the neighborhood of each element

Further Reading

Discrete Systems and Signal Processing (Strum and Kirk 1989) is a good introductory text for signal processing. *Signals and Systems* (Oppenheim and Willsky 1983) is a thorough signal-processing book with an emphasis on analog but some digital material. *Discrete-Time Signal Processing* (Oppenheim and Schafer 1989) covers material very similar to that in this chapter and the next, and has a nice level of detail. *The Fourier Transform and Its Applications* (Bracewell 1986) is a great book on the Fourier transform, but there is very little emphasis on the discrete version.

Discrete Signal Processing using MATLAB (Ingle and Proakis, 2000) is an excellent bridge between the more theoretical works above and practical software signal processing solutions. Each algorithm within is implemented in Matlab, so the methods have been reliably "reduced to practice," as it were.

While not technically reading material, the program `ippsdemo.exe` that comes with Intel IPP is an excellent tool for experimenting with Intel IPP signal processing functionality. With it, you can generate, filter, window, and transform signals using underlying Intel IPP functions.

Chapter 6

Audio Processing

The previous chapter introduced digital signal processing techniques and Intel® Integrated Performance Primitives (Intel® IPP) functions, particularly for filtering. This chapter expands on that discussion by providing interesting and useful applications in audio processing. These applications can be broadly classified into audio generation, audio analysis, and audio manipulation.

The examples also demonstrate how additional Intel IPP signal processing functions can be used.

Audio sources

Each of the examples in this chapter requires test signals to demonstrate the technique. This section explains how audio signals can be generated or acquired efficiently with Intel IPP functions.

Generating Audio

Intel IPP has a range of signal generation operations. The functions of some, like `ippsSet` and `ippsZero`, are obvious. Other functions, such as `ippsSignalJaehne`, have been described in previous chapters and will be used here. The remaining signal generation functions are described below.

Generating Triangle Waves

The function ippsTriangle generates a regularly repeating wave of alternating increasing and decreasing lines.

```
IppStatus ippsTriangle_Direct_32f(Ipp32f* pDst, int
   len, float magn, float rfreq, float asym, float*
   pPhase);
```

The period is determined by the rfreq argument. The magnitude is set by the magn argument, which determines the maximum value of the wave. The slopes are determined by the asym argument, which determines where in the wave cycle the peak occurs. The value ranges from π to $-\pi$, both of which are saw-tooth waves. If zero, a symmetric triangle wave will be generated.

Generating Tones

The function ippsTone generates a sinusoid with frequency rfreq in cycles-per-sample and shifted from a cosine wave by pPhase radians. Since there are numerous ways to implement this function of varying accuracies, the function also takes an algorithm hint.

```
IppStatus ippsTone_Direct_32f(Ipp32f* pDst, int len,
   float magn, float rfreq, float* pPhase,
   IppHintAlgorithm hint);
```

In contrast, the function ippsSin calculates the sine of each element of a vector. In fact, ippsTone can be implemented by generating a sequence with ippsRamp then calling ippsSin on the result.

Generating Arbitrary Functions

The function ippsRamp is particularly valuable in creating mathematic functions. It generates linearly increasing or decreasing data starting at offset and increasing each element by slope.

```
IppStatus ippsVectorRamp_32f(Ipp32f* pDst, int len,
   float offset, float slope);
```

Take for example the function y=sin(ax). This function can be implemented for x between 0 and 9 by first generating a ramp from 0 to 9, then multiplying the entire ramp by the constant a with ippsMul, then calling ippsSin on the result. Or in this case you can generate the function more efficiently by creating a ramp from 0 to 9*a, on which you call ippsSin.

Generating Random Data

Intel IPP includes two types of random number generation functions. The function ippsRandUniform generates uniformly distributed random numbers within a range of values. The function ippsRandGauss generates values with a Gaussian or normal distribution with a certain mean and standard deviation.

Generating Touch Tones

The tones generated by every touch-tone phone are actually the sum of two tones of different frequencies. These tones are referred to as ***Dual Tone Multi-Frequency*** (DTMF) tones. Figure 6.1 shows the two frequencies in hertz used to create the sound for each button on the phone.

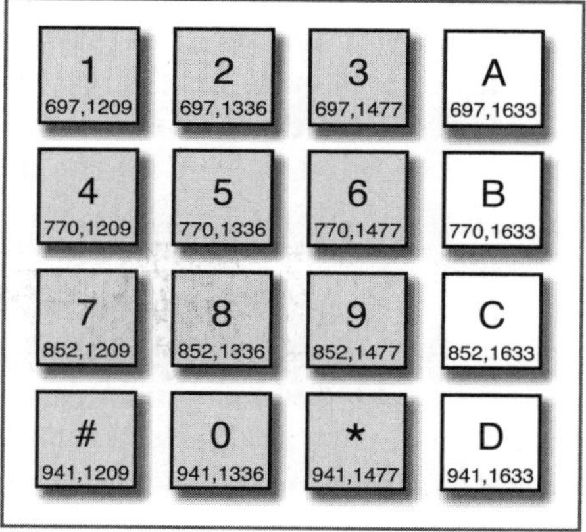

Figure 6.1 A Touchpad and Associated Touch-Tone Frequencies

Note the pattern in the frequencies. The first frequency in the pair is the same across each row and the second frequency is the same down each column. Even though the pad has 16 buttons, only eight distinct frequencies are generated.

The right-most column with buttons labeled A, B, C, and D, is not found on touch-tone phones, but is part of the specification.

This is a good example of calculating frequencies for several reasons. For one, the frequency of the tones is specified in cycles per second rather than in cycles per element. This makes an additional calculation necessary. Second, the results will be familiar if played. Finally, playing the result into a telephone receiver will demonstrate conclusively whether the system produced the correct tones. Playing tones into the phone receiver will dial the telephone.

The code in Figure 6.2 uses `ippsTone` to generate these frequencies. The function `myMakeTone_16s` will generate a tone of length `len` and magnitude `mag` in the array `pDst`. Calculating the frequency requires both the character code; 0 to 9, A to D, *, or #; and the sampling rate. The frequency in cycles per second divided by the sampling rate in samples per second equals the frequency in cycles per sample. The frequency in Intel IPP generation functions is in cycles per sample.

The tone generation functions require that the frequency in cycles per sample be less than or equal to the Nyquist rate, 0.5. Tones at frequencies greater than 0.5 cycles per sample appear to have a frequency below 0.5. Since `ippsTone` generates an error for these values, `myMakeTone` checks to see if the sampling rate is at least equal to twice the maximum frequency in samples per second.

The frequencies of the touch tones are in the array `codeList`. The index is determined by cycling through the array looking for the character in `code`. Using that index, the frequency for the first call is calculated by:

```
(float)codeList[index].freq1/(float)samplesPerSec
```

The first call to `ippsTone_Direct` generates the first of the pair of tones into `pDst` directly. The second generates a tone of the second frequency into `pTmp` that is then added to `pDst` using an in-place add.

The magnitude `mag` is treated as a maximum value, so the magnitude passed to each tone generation call is half of that.

```
const int mapSize = 16;
struct CodeMap { char code; int freq1; int freq2; }
      codeList[mapSize] = {
     '1',  697, 1209, '2', 697, 1336,
     '3', 697, 1477, 'A', 697, 1633,
     '4',  770, 1209, '5', 770, 1336,
     '6', 770, 1477, 'B', 770, 1633,
     '7',  852, 1209, '8', 852, 1336,
     '9', 852, 1477, 'C', 852, 1633,
     '*',  941, 1209, '0', 941, 1336,
     '#', 941, 1477, 'D', 941, 1633 };
```

```
int myMakeTone_16s(Ipp16s* pDst, int len, char code,
      int mag, int samplesPerSec)
{
     // Sampling rate must be twice the
     // highest frequency
     if (samplesPerSec < (1633*2)) return -1;

     int index = -1, i;
     for (i=0; i<mapSize; i++)
         if (code == codeList[i].code)
         {
             index = i; break;
         }
     if (index == -1) return -1;

     Ipp16s* pTmp = ippsMalloc_16s(len);
     float phase = 0;
     ippsTone_Direct_16s(pDst, len, mag/2,
         (float)codeList[index].freq1/(float)samplesPerSec,
         &phase, ippAlgHintNone);
     phase = 0;
     ippsTone_Direct_16s(pTmp, len, mag/2,
         (float)codeList[index].freq2/(float)samplesPerSec,
         &phase, ippAlgHintNone);
     ippsAdd_16s_I(pTmp, pDst, len);
     ippsFree(pTmp);

     return 0;
}
…

     char pNumber[numSize+1] = "2345678";
     Ipp16s *pDial = ippsMalloc_16s(totSamps);
     Ipp16s* pTmp = pDial;
     ippsZero_16s(pDial, totSamps);
     for (i=0; i<numSize; i++)
     {
         myMakeTone_16s(pTmp, toneSamps, pNumber[i],
             16384, sampleRate);
         pTmp += toneSamps + gapSamps;
     }
…
```

Figure 6.2 Generating DTMF Tones with `ippsTone`

The results are more familiar when heard than when graphed, but Figure 6.3 shows the tones generated for the sequence "2345678" and a close-up of the tone for "1".

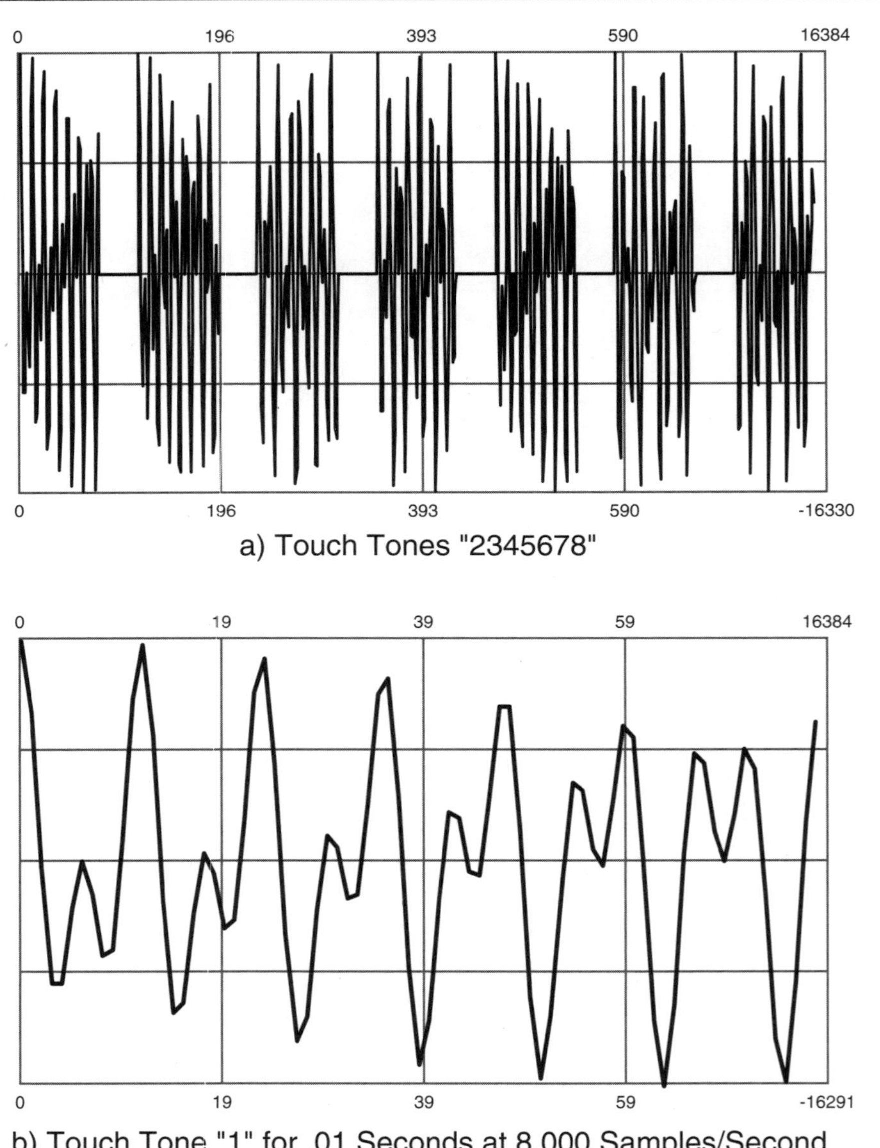

Figure 6.3 Tones Generated

Wave Audio

Artificial audio tends to be too random or not random enough. It's generally more interesting to work on real audio, even if the signals are short and simple in nature. Most examples in this chapter use samples containing whistling or counting.

The audio samples used are loaded from wave files. The code examples depend on two classes to read, interpret, play, and write these wave files. These classes load only *pulse-code modulation* (PCM) wave files. PCM files contain uncompressed 16-bit data, the same format that is used for CD audio. Chapter 7 shows how Intel IPP code can be used to decode other audio formats.

Class `WaveFile` contains the file I/O and the logic that interprets the header. The definition of this class is in Figure 6.4. The `Open` method opens the file, reads the header, and closes it. If the header indicates that the file is not a wave file, or is a wave file of a format not supported by this class, it returns `-1`.

The `ReadAsShort` method reads the data from the file into the `pSamples` array up to a maximum of `numElem` elements. If the data in the file has fewer than 16 bits per element, the function converts that data to 16-bit.

The method `WriteAs` writes the data from the `pSamples` array into the specified file. The class must have previously opened a valid wave file, since it uses the header of the previous file as the header of the new file.

The `Play` methods play a wave file directly from disk.

```
class WaveFile
{
private:
     int SampleRate;
     int BitsPerSample;
     int BytesPerSample;
     int ShiftBits;
     int NumChannels;
     int NumSamples;
     int DataLength;
     int BytesPerElem;

     int isValid_;
     char* pHead_;
     char* pFilename_;
     int hSize_;

public:
```

```
    WaveFile() : isValid_(0), pHead_(0), pFilename_(0) { }
    ~WaveFile();

    int Open(const char* pFilename);

    int GetSampleBits() const { return BitsPerSample; }
    int GetSampleBytes() const { return BytesPerSample; }
    int GetNumChannels() const { return NumChannels; }
    int GetNumSamples() const { return NumSamples; }
    int GetElemBytes() const { return BytesPerElem; }
    int GetSampleRate() const { return SampleRate; }

    int WriteAs(const short* pSamples,
                const char* pFilename);

    int ReadAsShort(short* pSamples, int numElem) const;

    int Play();
    static int Play(const char* filename);
};
```

Figure 6.4 Declaration of the `WaveFile` Class

The other class used to load and manipulate wave files is `WaveMem`, declared in Figure 6.5. The `WaveMem` class is designed to allow editing and playback of data from a wave file. It can either be used to create a new wave file, using the `InitAlloc` and `Set` functions, or it can interface with a `WaveFile` class instance to read existing wave data into memory. The `GetShortBuffer` methods allow direct access to the data array. This function returns data compatible with Intel IPP functions that operate on `Ipp16s` data.

The examples in this chapter use the `ReadFromFile`, `GetShortBuffer`, and `Play` functions.

```
class WaveMem
{
    private:
        int bitsPerSample_;
        int bytesPerSample_;
        int samplesPerSec_;
        int nChannels_;

        int len_;

        unsigned char* pBuffer_;
        int bufSize_;
```

```
    int playReady_;
    int memReady_;

public:
    WaveMem() : playReady_(0), memReady_(0),
        pBuffer_(0) {}
    ~WaveMem() { Free(); }

    int Init(int bitsPerSample, int samplesPerSec,
             int nChannels);
    int Alloc(int len);
    int Free();
    int InitAlloc(int len, int bitsPerSample,
                  int samplesPerSec, int nChannels)
    {
        if (!Init(bitsPerSample, samplesPerSec,
                  nChannels))
            return Alloc(len);
        else return -1;
    }

    int CopySettings(const WaveMem* pWaveMem);

    // length in elements
    int Set(short* pSamples);
    int Set(char* pSamples);

    void SetBitsPerSample(int bitsPerSample)
    {
        bitsPerSample_ = bitsPerSample;
        bytesPerSample_ = (bitsPerSample+7)/8;
        playReady_ = 0; memReady_ = 0;
    }
    void SetSamplesPerSec(int samplesPerSec)
    {
        samplesPerSec_ = samplesPerSec;
        playReady_ = 0; memReady_ = 0;
    }
    void SetNumChannels(int nChannels)
    {
        nChannels_ = nChannels;
        playReady_ = 0; memReady_ = 0;
    }

    int GetSamplesPerSec() const
        { return samplesPerSec_; }
    int GetNumChannels() const
        { return nChannels_; }
    int GetBitsPerSample() const
```

```
        { return bitsPerSample_; }

    int GetLen() const { return len_;}
    const short* GetShortBuffer() const;
    short* GetShortBuffer();
    int ReadFromFile(const WaveFile* pWaveFile);
    int WriteToFile(WaveFile* pWaveFile);

    int Play(int wait = 1);
};
```

Figure 6.5 Declaration of the `WaveMem` Class

Although not required for the samples in this chapter, a class `WaveStream` that loads the data one chunk at a time would be valuable in real situations.

Audio Analysis

In Chapter 5, the focus of signal processing techniques was filtering for noise removal and frequency-band separation. Signal processing techniques can also be applied to extracting information from signals. This section demonstrates methods of signal analysis, either by inspection or by automated calculation. It introduces several functions that can be performed on audio signals to make information easier to extract.

Phase and Shift

The discrete Fourier transform produces a complex output even if the input signal is real. Interpreting these complex values isn't simple, which is why Chapter 5 largely glossed over it. That discussion presented a simplified discussion of the frequency domain by focusing entirely on the magnitude of the frequency response and largely ignoring the phase of that response. When a filter is real and symmetric in one domain, that filter is also real and symmetric in the other. Since the filters presented were real in both domains, they had a phase of zero, and the simplification held. This approach is reasonable for some frequency filtering tasks, but there are also exciting applications that use phase.

The complex values are more intuitive when they are presented in a phase-magnitude format. The magnitude is then the response of the transform at each frequency, and the phase is the shift or delay of that frequency. To illustrate this, the code in Figure 6.6 generates several tones of different phases then prints the real, imaginary, magnitude, and phase components of the Fourier transform.

```
float phase=0.0;
int freq=2000;
FTWrap ft(IPP_FFT_DIV_FWD_BY_N, ippAlgHintNone);

for (; phase<IPP_PI; phase+=0.5)
{
    ippsTone_Direct_32f(pSrc, len, 16384.0,
        (float)freq/len, &phase, ippAlgHintNone);
    ft.FT(pSrc, pDst, len);
    ippsCartToPolar_32fc(pDst, pMag, pPhase, len);
    printf("%.2f,%.2f,%.2f,%.2f\n",
            pDst[freq].re, pDst[freq].im,
            pMag[freq], pPhase[freq]);
}
```

Figure 6.6 Code to Calculate and Analyze the Fourier Transforms of Tones

Table 6.1 lists the values of the first coefficient for the Fourier transforms of the tones generated by the code in Figure 6.6. Since the input is a pure sine wave, the output is a spike at the frequency of the wave. The magnitude of the spike is half the magnitude of the wave because this is actually only one of the two symmetric spikes. The phase of the spike is the same as the `phase` argument to `ippsTone`, which shifts the generated signal. Note that as the input phase changes, it affects the ratio between the real and imaginary components of the Fourier transform coefficient but does not change the magnitude.

Another illustrative example is the Jaehne signal. As previously explained, the Jaehne signal spans the possible frequencies, increasing from zero frequency to the Nyquist rate, one-half the sampling rate. In audio terms, this signal is called a "chirp" and is used as a test signal.

Since each frequency is represented in this signal, and the magnitude of the Fourier transform is mostly uniform, it stands to reason that there is some other information that determines the order of those frequencies. That information is the phase.

Table 6.1 Fourier Transforms for Tones of Various Phases

phase passed to `ippsTone`	Real	Imaginary	Magnitude	Phase
`0.0`	8192.00	1.76	8192.00	0.00
`0.5`	7186.62	3932.10	8192.00	0.50
`1.0`	4418.73	6898.09	8192.00	1.00
`1.5`	567.16	8172.34	8192.00	1.50
`2.0`	-3423.51	7442.34	8192.00	2.00
`2.5`	-6574.56	4887.12	8192.00	2.50
`3.0`	-8113.22	1133.35	8192.00	3.00

The code in Figure 6.7 generates a Jaehne signal, plays it, and displays the phase and magnitude of the Fourier transform.

The predominant data type in this example is Ipp16s, because that is a common and playable audio type, and it is efficient to manipulate. However, the routine that performs the Fourier transform, `myViewFT_16s`, converts it first to `Ipp32f` to avoid scaling and dynamic range issues.

After converting the data to `Ipp32f`, the function calculates the Fourier transform using the `FTWrap` class, then expands it with `ippsConjCcs`. Because both the phase and magnitude are needed, the most efficient function to convert this complex data is with `ippsCartToPolar`.

```
int main(int argc, char* argv[])
{
    int len;
    int sampRate = 44100;
    float duration = 1.0f;
    len = (int)sampRate*duration;

    WaveMem wm;
    wm.InitAlloc(len, 16, sampRate, 1);

    ippsVectorJaehne_16s(wm.GetShortBuffer(), len, 16384);

    spView_16s(wm.GetShortBuffer(), len/32, "Signal Start",
            0);

    myViewFT_16s(wm.GetShortBuffer(), len, 1);

    return 0;
}
```

```
int myViewFT_16s(Ipp16s* pSrc, int len, int isModal)
{
    FTWrap ft;
    Ipp32f *pSrc32f = ippsMalloc_32f(len);
    Ipp32fc *pDst = ippsMalloc_32fc(len);
    Ipp32f *pMag = ippsMalloc_32f(len);
    Ipp32f *pPhase = ippsMalloc_32f(len);

    ippsConvert_16s32f(pSrc, pSrc32f, len);

    ft.FT(pSrc32f, pDst, len);
    ippsConjCcs_32fc_I(pDst, len);
    ippsCartToPolar_32fc(pDst, pMag, pPhase, len);

    spView_32f(pPhase, len/64, "Phase", 0);
    Ipp32f offset=0.0;

    // Simple unwrapping algorithm
    for (int i=1; i<len; i++)
    {
        if ((pPhase[i] - offset - pPhase[i-1]) > 3)
            offset+=3.141592654*2;
        pPhase[i] -= offset;
    }

    spView_32f(pPhase, len/64, "'Unwrapped' Phase", 0);
    spView_32f(pMag, len, "Magnitude", isModal);

    ippsFree(pSrc32f);
    ippsFree(pDst);
    ippsFree(pMag);
    ippsFree(pPhase);

    return  0;
}
```

Figure 6.7 Code to Analyze Jaehne (Chirp) Signal

Figure 6.8 a), b), and c) show the generated signal and results of the conversion to phase-magnitude representation. Graph a) shows the first few hundred samples of the Jaehne signal; almost every frequency is represented equally, and the higher frequencies are later in the signal. Graph b) shows the distribution of magnitude across the frequency spectrum.

The phase as shown in c) and d) represents a continuously decreasing shift that is concealed by a particular characteristic of the phase. If the phase is $x + 2\pi n$, where n is an integer, it has the same effect as a phase of x. The function `PolarToCart` cannot distinguish between actual phases of $\pi/2$ and $5\pi/2$, so it assumes that the phase is between $-\pi$ and π. As a result, instead of a continuous curve, graph c) is sawtooth-like.

The segment in Figure 6.7 "unwraps" the phase to get the continuously decreasing graph in Figure 6.8 d). Unwrapping is the process of attempting to determine the actual phase by assuming that the phase is continuous. If the curve is continuous, large discontinuities are interpreted as a jump to the other extreme. To unwrap these jumps, the code subtracts 2π for every previous loop. This process of unwrapping produces a much more interesting graph that clearly validates the unwrapping method and shows that the phase does decrease with frequency.

The reason the phase is decreasing with frequency is that the higher frequencies occur later in the time domain signal. A negative shift in those frequencies would move them from the origin to that location. Because the frequency increases continuously in the time domain, the phase graph should reasonably show a phase that is continuously decreasing. Each frequency is represented, but is increasingly shifted or delayed from the start of the signal.

The Short-Time Fourier Transform

The Fourier transform as formulated in Chapter 5 is not well suited to analysis on most audio signals. For signals of a few seconds or longer, several instances of a particular frequency can occur from different sources or, from the analysis perspective, with different meanings. A Fourier transform over the entire signal blurs and conceals the effects of these individual sound elements. For these signals the *short-time Fourier transform* (STFT)) is usually more appropriate.

The STFT takes a Fourier transform on a windows portion of the signal instead of the entire signal at once. An abrupt boundary to the STFT window would cause undesirable aliasing effects. For this reason, a windowing function is applied to the signal in the time domain that smoothes these edges. While different windowing functions are possible, the Hanning window has a particular characteristic that allows easy reconstruction of overlapping transformed blocks into the original signal. See the discussion under Spectral Manipulation, below.

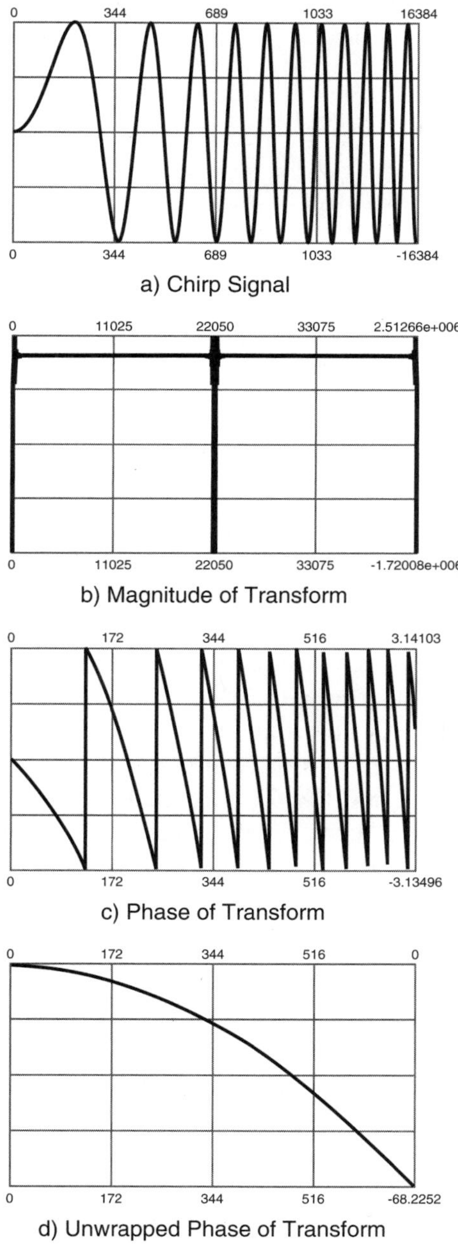

Figure 6.8 Chirp and its Fourier Transform

The STFT, implemented with Intel IPP, is listed in Figure 6.9.

```
IppStatus mySTFFTFwd_RToC_32f32fc(Ipp32f* pSrc, Ipp32fc* pDst,
      int order, IppsFFTSpec_R_32f* pSpec, Ipp32f* pBuffer)
{
    IppStatus st;
    st  = ippsWinHann_32f(pSrc, pBuffer, 1<<order);
    if (st < 0) return st;
    st = ippsFFTFwd_RToCCS_32f(pBuffer,
           (Ipp32f*)pDst, pSpec, 0);
    if (st < 0) return st;

    st = ippsConjCcs_32fc_I(pDst, 1<<order);
    if (st < 0) return st;

    return st;
}
```

Figure 6.9 Short-Time Fourier Transform

The function `mySTFFT` performs an STFT on the input signal using the FFT. The FFT specification structure `pSpec` must be initialized before calling to perform an FFT of the correct order. A temporary buffer of size 2^{order} `(1<<order)` must also be allocated and passed to the function. The allocation of this structure and the temporary buffer are placed outside of this function for efficiency, since they can be reused for each of the repeated calls to this function.

The Hanning window is applied before the FFT using the function `ippsWinHann`. Then the function calls the FFT, the output of which is in the compact CCS form. Finally, the output is expanded to a full complex representation with `ippsConjCcs`. The full complex representation isn't always necessary for analysis or manipulation, so it may be possible to skip this step.

This transform is invertible using a second Hanning window and an inverse FFT. The full code for the inverse transform is listed in Figure 6.26. The next section illustrates a use of this transform for signal analysis.

Spectral Analysis

The purpose of the STFT is to analyze long signals without blurring the information. The usual approach is to take a series of transforms, sliding the window a fixed increment between each one. These windows usually overlap in case information lies across a boundary. The results of a series of STFTs taken on a signal are referred to as a spectrogram of that signal.

The code in Figure 6.10 calculates a series of transforms on a signal at regular intervals and puts the results in a single two-dimensional array.

```
IppStatus mySpectrum_32f(Ipp32f* pSrc, Ipp32f* pDstMag,
      Ipp32f* pDstPhase, int len, int resolution, int ftLen)
{
     IppStatus st;
     Ipp32fc* pDst = ippsMalloc_32fc(ftLen);
     int i;

     int order, tlen = ftLen;
     for (order=-1; tlen>0; tlen>>=1) order++;

     IppsFFTSpec_R_32f* pSpec;
     st = ippsFFTInitAlloc_R_32f(&pSpec, order,
         IPP_FFT_DIV_INV_BY_N, ippAlgHintNone);
     if (st < 0) return st;

     Ipp32f * pBuffer = ippsMalloc_32f(ftLen);

     for (i=0; i<(len/resolution-3); i++)
     {
         st = mySTFFTFwd_RToC_32f32fc(pSrc+i*resolution,
             pDst, order, pSpec, pBuffer);
         if (st < 0) return st;
         st = ippsCartToPolar_32fc(pDst, pDstMag+i*ftLen,
             pDstPhase+i*ftLen, ftLen);
         if (st < 0) return st;
     }
     st = ippsFFTFree_R_32f(pSpec);
     return ippStsOk;
}
```

Figure 6.10 Calculating the Spectrogram

In each step, the inner loop code takes an STFT of length `ftLen`. Between two consecutive transforms, the pointer to the source is incremented by `resolution`. The increment will almost always be less than the transform length to allow the transforms to overlap.

The result of the transform is converted from complex values to a phase-magnitude representation.

An image of the magnitude output of this function, using an increment of 64 and a transform size of 256, is shown in Figure 6.11.

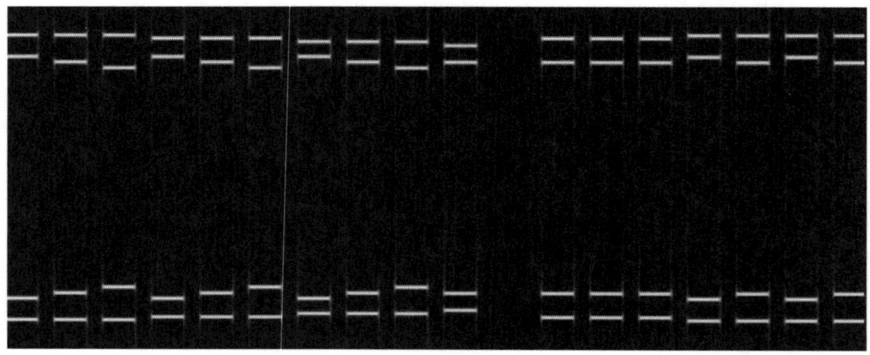

Figure 6.11 Spectrogram of DTMF Tones String "1234567890 5551212"

This image is very clear compared with the time-domain graph of similar data in Figure 6.3. The two frequencies in each tone are clearly visible, as is the progression of the higher and lower tones. There are a number of ways of handling this data in software, depending on the application. In this case, the spectrogram is more powerful than is probably warranted by the application, so a simple maximum value taken on the spectral values could determine what tones the data contained.

Note that despite the windowing function, there are still aliasing effects at the start and the end of the tones. At those locations, due to the abrupt edges of the tones, there is some response at every frequency. This effect can be heard in the signal as a popping sound. Adding windowing to the function that generates the DTMF tones would prevent this popping.

The function `myViewSpectrum`, which is not listed, generates and displays the graph in Figure 6.11. This function is presented as an imaging example in Chapter 9.

This discussion has focused on this spectrograph as M individual transforms on blocks of length N, partly because the FFT, DFT, and windowing functions in Intel IPP are well suited to the STFT-based model. It is also possible to think of it as a bank of N filters; each filter is tuned to a particular frequency. Of the output generated by these filters, M samples are kept. The filter bank model can be implemented using the multi-rate filters in Intel IPP. These multi-rate filters upsample, filter, and downsample in one call. If the down-sample factor is set to the block length, the multi-rate filter will calculate M samples out of the total output signal.

Goertzel Transform

Some situations require a more targeted transform than the full Fourier transform. In some cases, only a single frequency is needed. In those cases, the Fourier transform can be inefficient compared to a filter bank or transform that calculates the response at only one or a few frequencies. The Goertzel transform performs the Fourier transform at one frequency.

The code in Figure 6.12 uses this transform to detect DTMF tones in an audio signal. This is a good application for the Goertzel transform, since finding DTMF tones requires that only eight frequencies be checked.

This algorithm has two parts. The first part checks all eight frequencies to find coefficients that are over the threshold. To do this, it calls the Goertzel transform on a sliding window of data; this window is `ftLen` long, and each step shifts the window by `ftRes`, the resolution. The frequency passed to the `ippsGoertz` function is the frequency divided by the sampling rate.

The `scalefactor`, a constant 8 here, has been pre-calculated to ensure that the result of the call to `ippsGoertz` is less than the maximum value held in an `Ipp16s` variable, $2^{15} - 1$. This value is based on the maximum response of a pure DTMF tone, which was on the order of 2^{23}.

The routine then determines if the square of the magnitude of the response is greater than the square of the threshold. If so, the corresponding value in the `pF1` or `pF2` array is set to 1.

The second portion finds discontinuities in the pF1 and pF2 arrays that indicate the start of a tone. A tone is considered to have begun if both of the component tones are greater than the threshold, and at least one of the two tones wasn't greater than threshold the last time it was checked.

```
// A perfect match will have a transform result of around
// mag1*mag2*toneLen/4.
// If the minimum tone length, in samples, is minToneLen *
//      samplesPerSec,
// then the threshold is minMag*minToneLen*samplesPerSec

float thresh = minMag * (float)(ftLen - ftRes)/4.0;
float thresh2 = thresh * thresh;
const int scaleFactor = 8;

// Compensate for the scale factor in the threshold
thresh2 /= 65536.0f;
int pF1Last[4], pF2Last[4];
int pF1[4] = {0,0,0,0}, pF2[4] = {0,0,0,0};
Ipp16sc res;
float t;
int i,j, ci=0;

for (j=0; j<=len-ftLen; j+=ftRes)
{
    // Find frequency responses over threshold
    for (i=0; i<4; i++)
    {
        pF1Last[i] = pF1[i];
        pF2Last[i] = pF2[i];

        float freq = (float)pFreqs1[i]/(float)samplesPerSec;
        ippsGoertz_16s_Sfs(pSrc + j, ftLen, &res, freq,
            scaleFactor);
        t = ((float)res.re*(float)res.re +
            (float)res.im*(float)res.im);
        pF1[i] = t > thresh2;

        freq = (float)pFreqs2[i]/(float)samplesPerSec;
        ippsGoertz_16s_Sfs(pSrc + j, ftLen, &res, freq,
            scaleFactor);
        t = ((float)res.re*(float)res.re +
            (float)res.im*(float)res.im);
        pF2[i] = t > thresh2;
    }

    // Find discontinuities in thresholds
    for (i=0; i<16; i++)
```

```
        if (((pF1[i/4] > pF1Last[i/4]) && pF2[i%4]) ||
            (pF1[i/4] && (pF2[i%4] > pF2Last[i%4])))
        {
            code[ci++] = codeList[i].code;
            if (ci > codelen) return ci;
        }
}
```

Figure 6.12 Using the Goertzel Transform to Detect DTMF Tones

This method works for a broad range of tone lengths and sample rates, but is still potentially fragile. In particular, it depends on two difficult calculations, the determination of the threshold value and the determination of the length of the Fourier transform. The former is based on a preset minimum magnitude for the tones; the latter uses a preset minimum tone length. However, the Goertzel transform is not the cause of this fragility.

Cepstrum

The cepstrum[1] is a method that has been long used to estimate a spectral envelope for a signal. It is based on the idea that a signal can be modeled as the convolution of two components, the spectral envelope and a filter. Sometimes the original signal is the data, and the filter is the noise. In speech recognition, the spectral envelope is roughly the excitation by the vocal chords, and must be separated from the speech information created by the mouth and tongue.

Figure 6.13 shows the process of calculating the real cepstrum. A windowing function is often applied to the signal before the first FFT.

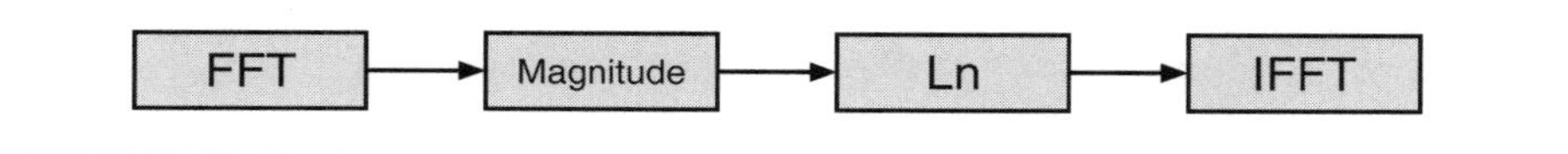

Figure 6.13 Real Cepstrum Calculation

[1] "Cepstrum" is "spectrum" with the first four characters reversed. Using the same whimsical convention, the elements of the cepstrum are sometimes referred to as quefrencies.

The model is that the input to this system is the convolution of two pieces of information that need to be separated, or

y' = convolution(f, y)

Once in the time domain, this is expressed as

Y' = F * Y

When the logarithm is taken, the product becomes a sum, and the following holds:

log(Y') = log(F) + log(Y)

Implementing the Cepstrum

The code in Figure 6.13 calculates this real cepstrum.

```
IppStatus myCepstrum_R_32f(Ipp32f* pSrc, Ipp32f* pDst, int len,
      FTWrap *pFTWrap, Ipp32f* pBuffer)
{
     Ipp32fc* pFT;
     Ipp32f* pMag;
     int bufFlag = (pBuffer == 0);

     if (bufFlag)
     {
         pFT = ippsMalloc_32fc(len/2+1);
         pMag = ippsMalloc_32f(len/2+1);
     }
     else
     {
         pFT = (Ipp32fc*)pBuffer;
         pMag = (Ipp32f*)pBuffer + len+2;
     }

     pFTWrap->FT(pSrc, pFT, len);
     ippsMagnitude_32fc(pFT, pMag, len/2+1);
     ippsAddC_32f_I(0.00001, pMag, len/2+1);
     ippsLn_32f_A11(pMag, pMag, len/2+1);
     ippsRealToCplx_32f(pMag, 0, pFT, len/2+1);
     pFTWrap->FT(pFT, pDst, len);
```

```
    if (bufFlag)
    {
        ippsFree(pFT);
        ippsFree(pMag);
    }
    return ippStsOk;
}
```

Figure 6.14 Calculating the Real Cepstrum

The routine requires temporary storage of size 3*(len/2+1) `float` elements. If the `myCepstrum` function is to be called repeatedly, it is efficient to allocate this buffer once, outside of the function. Otherwise, the buffer will be allocated and freed automatically.

For efficiency in both execution and development time, this routine makes use of the wrapper `FTWrap`, introduced in Chapter 5. This `FTWrap` is also allocated outside of the function so that it will persist.

After the FFT, the magnitude is taken, making this a real rather than complex cepstrum. To decrease the likelihood of passing an invalid value to the natural logarithm function `ippsLn`, a small value (0.00001) is added to each element in the signal. The function `ippsRealToCplx` then interleaves the real magnitude signal with zeros. This call takes advantage of the fact that if the pointer to the imaginary data is zero, then the imaginary components of the output are set to zero. Finally, this real signal is transformed back into the time domain using the `FTWrap` class.

Calculating the Spectral Envelope

A common operation based on the cepstrum is calculation of the spectral envelope. Due to the symmetry of the Fourier transform, dropping later samples in the time-domain samples performs a low-pass filter on the frequency coefficients. Therefore, zeroing out the high end of the cepstrum coefficients results in a smoothed curve for the frequency response. Figure 6.15 compares this curve, called the spectral envelope, with the unfiltered log of the spectrum. The spectral envelope is more likely to provide high-level information about the signal than the unmodified spectrum.

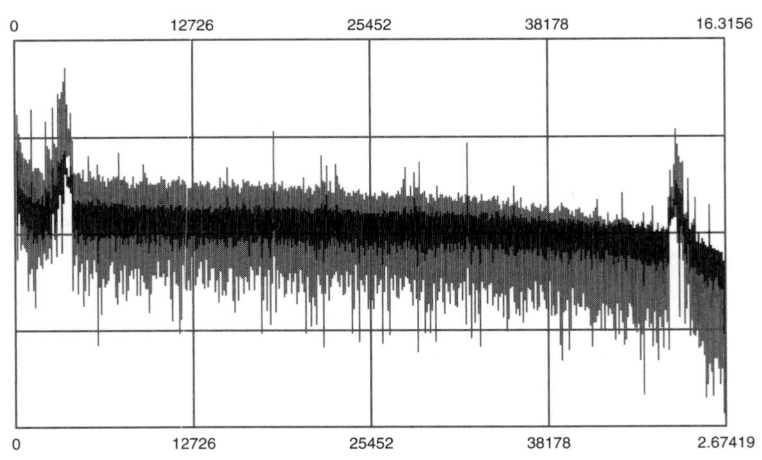

Figure 6.15 Log-Spectrum and Spectral Envelope of a Signal

This curve is generated by the code in Figure 6.16. After calculating the cepstrum with the `myCepstrum` function from Figure 6.14, the function zeros out the coefficients with indices greater than the parameter `cutoff`; in this code, `len/4` is used for that cutoff. The complete Fourier transform of that signal is the spectral envelope. Since this is a complex signal in the frequency domain, `ippsMagnitude` is called before the signal is displayed.

```
IppStatus mySpecEnv_32f(Ipp32f* pSrc, Ipp32fc* pDst, int len,
      int cutoff, FTWrap* pFTWrap, Ipp32f* pBuffer)
{
     Ipp32f* pCepstrum;
     int bufFlag = (pBuffer == 0);
     if (bufFlag) pBuffer =
         ippsMalloc_32f(myGetSpecEnvBufSize_32f(len));
     pCepstrum = pBuffer;

     myCepstrum_R_32f(pSrc, pCepstrum, len, pFTWrap,
             pBuffer+len);
     ippsZero_32f(pCepstrum+cutoff, len-cutoff);
     pFTWrap->FT(pCepstrum, pDst, len);
     ippsConjCcs_32fc_I(pDst, len);

     if (bufFlag) ippsFree(pCepstrum);
     return ippStsOk;
}
```

```
...
    mySpecEnv_32f(pSignal, pSpecEnv, len, len/4,
        &ftWrap, pBuffer);
    ippsMagnitude_32fc(pSpecEnv, pSpecEnvMag, len);
    spView2_32f(pSpecMag, len/2, pSpecEnvMag, len/2,
        "Spectral Envelope and Spectrum", 1);
...
```

Figure 6.16 Calculating the Spectral Envelope

Fundamental Pitch Calculation with Cepstrum

One application of the cepstrum and spectral envelope is to calculate the fundamental pitch of a signal. The fundamental pitch is the underlying frequency of the signal, with the information removed. In a sung tune, it is the tune rather than the words.

The code in Figure 6.17 performs a simple fundamental pitch calculation. The loop is the portion of this code that estimates the fundamental pitch block-by-block. After converting the data to `Ipp32f`, the loop calls the spectral envelope function from Figure 6.16. The magnitude of the complex result should then contain the frequency information. Frequencies below the value `minFreq` are ignored. The highest value above that point, as determined by the function `ippsMaxIndx`, is considered to be the fundamental pitch.

```
int i, len, step = 2048, minFreq=200;
WaveFile wf;
if (wf.Open("..\\..\\sounds\\tuneless2.wav")) return -1;

WaveMem wm;
wm.ReadFromFile(&wf);

len = wm.GetLen();
minFreq = (float)minFreq * (float)step /
        (float)wf.GetSampleRate();

FTWrap ftWrap;
Ipp32f* pSignal = ippsMalloc_32f(step);

Ipp32fc* pSpecEnv = ippsMalloc_32fc(step);
Ipp32f* pSpecEnvMag = ippsMalloc_32f(step);

int* pMax = ippsMalloc_32s(len/step);
Ipp32f* pMax32f = ippsMalloc_32f(len/step);
```

```
Ipp32f dummy;

Ipp32f* pBuffer =
        ippsMalloc_32f(myGetSpecEnvBufSize_32f(step));

for (i=0; i<len-step; i+=step)
{
    ippsConvert_16s32f(wm.GetShortBuffer()+i, pSignal,
              step);

    mySpecEnv_32f(pSignal, pSpecEnv, step, step/4,
              &ftWrap, pBuffer);
    ippsMagnitude_32fc(pSpecEnv, pSpecEnvMag, step);

    ippsMaxIndx_32f(pSpecEnvMag+minFreq,
              step-minFreq*2, &dummy, pMax+i/step);
    pMax[i/step] += minFreq;
}

ippsConvert_32s32f(pMax, pMax32f, len/step);
spView_32f(pMax32f, len/step,
      "Fundamental frequency estimate", 1);
```

Figure 6.17 Estimating the Fundamental Pitch with the Spectral Envelope

After calculating the pitch for each of 48 blocks, the code plots the results. Running this code on a simple signal produces the graph in Figure 6.18. The actual frequencies are equal to this frequency multiplied by the sampling rate over the block size.

Using the values in the `pMax` array, you can test the accuracy of this calculation by constructing a series of tones at the same frequency.

The code in Figure 6.19 first converts the frequency into cycles-per-sample, the unit used by `ippsTone`. Then it finds the maximum absolute value of the signal within that block, so the tone can match the original in volume. The result is a set of tones that, when played, sounds roughly the same as the original signal.

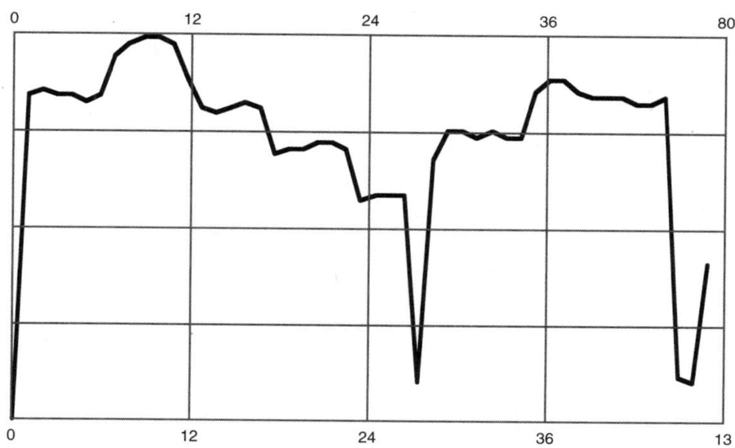

Figure 6.18 Fundamental Pitch for "London Bridge Is Falling Down"

```
for (i=0; i<len-step; i+=step)
{
    float freq = (float)pMax[i/step]/(float)step;
    ippsAbs_16s_I(wm.GetShortBuffer()+i, step);
    ippsMax_16s(wm.GetShortBuffer()+i, step, &mag);
    IppStatus st =
        ippsTone_Direct_16s(wm.GetShortBuffer()+i,
        step, mag, freq, &phase, ippAlgHintNone);
}
```

Figure 6.19 Artificially Generating a Signal with the Same Fundamental Frequency

Audio Manipulation

The methods in the previous section are very useful in guiding signal manipulation, or providing an appropriate domain in which to add effects or make modifications. This section uses these methods to modify signals to create effects and perform conversions.

Echoes with Infinite Impulse Response Filters

Infinite Impulse Response (IIR) filters are described briefly in the previous chapter. They are feedback filters for which the calculation of each output sample uses both input samples and previous output samples. The filter response is considered to be infinite because each output sample can be affected by every previous input, no matter how distant.

IIR filters are generally used because they can have very short filters and therefore require less computation. The drawbacks are a more difficult design and numerical stability.

There are N taps multiplied against input samples, and another N taps multiplied against the previous output samples. The taps are laid out as shown in Figure 6.20, and they are applied to the signal as follows:

$$A_0 * y_t = \sum_{n=0}^{N} x_{t-n} * B_n - \sum_{n=1}^{N} y_{t-n} * A_n$$

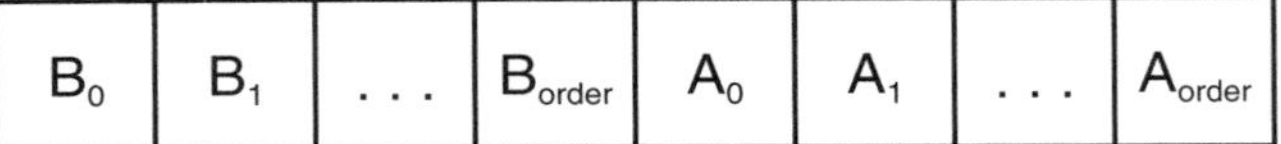

Figure 6.20 Filter Tap Layout for IIR

> ***Note*** A_0 is ostensibly the inverse gain of the filter, but in practice Intel IPP treats this value as 1. The value need only be nonzero.

The code in Figure 6.21 uses the function `ippsIIR` to create an echo effect. In this case, the IIR filter is used just to take advantage of the feedback mechanism.

The function `myEchoInitAlloc_32f` creates the filter and passes it to `ippsIIRInitAlloc_32f` to generate the IIR state structure. The filter created has three nonzero taps. Tap B_0 is 1.0 so that the input passes through unmodified. Tap A_0 is 1.0 so that there is no gain on the signal. Tap A_{delay} is the tap that creates the echo. It adds an attenuated version of the signal delayed by `delay` samples. The constant value 0.3 is used for the echo, which produces a pleasing echo.

```
IppStatus myEchoInitAlloc_32f(IppsIIRState_32f** pState,
      int len, int delay)
{
     int tapsLen = 2*(len+1);
     Ipp32f* pTaps = ippsMalloc_32f(tapsLen);
     Ipp32f* pATaps = pTaps + len+1;
     ippsZero_32f(pTaps, tapsLen);

     pTaps[0] = 1.0f;
     pATaps[0] = 1.0f;
     if ((delay <= len) && (delay > 0)) pATaps[delay-1]=0.3f;
     IppStatus st = ippsIIRInitAlloc_32f(pState, pTaps, len, 0);
     ippsFree(pTaps);
     return st;
}

int main(int argc, char* argv[])
{
     IppsIIRState_32f* pState;

     int len, filterLen;
     Ipp32f *pSignal, delay = 0.1;

     WaveFile wf;
     if (wf.Open("c:\\mm\\sounds\\onetoten.wav")) return -1;

     WaveMem wm;
     wm.ReadFromFile(&wf);
     wm.Play(0);

     len = wm.GetLen();
     pSignal = ippsMalloc_32f(len);
     ippsConvert_16s32f(wm.GetShortBuffer(), pSignal, len);

     spView_32f(pSignal+8000, 8000, "Source", 0);

     filterLen = (int) wf.GetSampleRate() * delay;
     myEchoInitAlloc_32f(&pState, filterLen,
             (int)wf.GetSampleRate() * delay);

     IppStatus st = ippsIIR_32f_I(pSignal, len, pState);

     spView_32f(pSignal+8000, 8000, "Filtered", 1);

     ippsConvert_32f16s_Sfs(pSignal, wm.GetShortBuffer(), len,
             ippRndNear, 0);

     wm.Play(0);
```

```
    ippsFree(pSignal);

    return 0;
}
```

Figure 6.21 Code Using IIR to Create an Echo

This is a fun and illustrative example of IIR, but is arguably not a proper use of the function. The IIR function in Intel IPP does not check to see which taps are equal to zero, so it can perform unnecessary operations. An IIR filter this sparse could be implemented with multiply and add functions, which would almost certainly be more efficient. A more interesting application that could also be done with IIR is an echo using a frequency-specific acoustic model.

Resampling with Multi-Rate FIR

The Intel IPP provides a class of functions that support simultaneous resampling and filtering. This allows intelligent conversion of audio data from one sampling rate to another. Each function performs this operation in three steps: upsampling, filtering, and downsampling.

Upsampling is the process of lengthening a signal by inserting samples. One or more zeros are inserted between each pair of samples. If the sampling factor is M, then M-1 zeros are inserted. Since these values are initialized to zero, the sampling operation is usually followed by a filter operation. The filter operation can interpolate between each pair of samples to set reasonable values, or calculate the value based on a broader range of samples.

Downsampling is the process of shortening a signal by dropping samples. If the sampling factor is N then N-1 samples are dropped out of each N sample in the signal. Only each Nth sample is copied to the new array. It is also usually preceded by application of a filter so that the information contained in the dropped samples isn't completely lost.

There can be efficiency advantages to performing these operations at the same time. Since the algorithm can assume that certain samples will be dropped, it does not have to calculate those samples. In practice, though, it can be more efficient to calculate all samples in a signal rather than adding a conditional expression in an inner loop.

Figure 6.22 illustrates a multi-rate filter with an upsampling factor of two and a downsampling factor of three. The filter used, with taps {0.5, 1.0, 0.5}, performs a linear interpolation between each pair of samples. That filter leaves old samples intact while calculating new samples as the average of the two surrounding values.

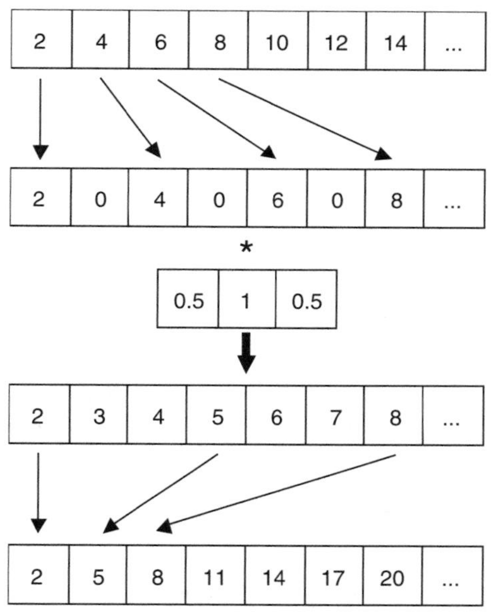

Figure 6.22 Illustration of a Multi-rate FIR

The Intel IPP function that implements this operation is `ippsFIRMR`. The code in Figure 6.23 uses `ippsFIRMR` to change the sampling rate of an audio sample from its current rate to 8,000 samples per second.

To perform this change, the upsampling factor should be the sampling rate of the destination, and the downsampling factor should be the sampling rate of the source. However, for a sampling rate change from 44,100 to 8,000, the operation is slow even when optimized. The multi-rate FIR is not designed for sampling rates that large and takes several seconds to process a 5-second clip. For this reason, the code above assumes that both rates are divisible by 100. The right way to do this is to calculate the greatest common factor between the two sampling rates, assuming that they are not mutually prime. In the case of 44,100 and 8,000, 100 actually is the greatest common factor.

The filter created performs a linear interpolation on the upsampled signal. In this signal, each pair of data samples will be separated by `upSample - 1` zeros. The input data samples pass unmodified, multiplied by the 1.0 value at `pTaps[upSample-1]`. All other zeros are replaced by a weighted average of the two nearest values. To avoid amplifying or attenuating the signal, each pair of taps that are `upSample` samples apart sum to 1.0.

Take, for example, a zero offset by n from a sample. If this data lies at `pData[x+n]`, will be changed according to:

```
pData[x+n] = (1.0 - n/upSample) * pData[x] +
      n/upSample * pData[x+upSample]
```

The `numIters` argument passed to `ippsFIRMR` is neither the length of the source nor that of the destination. The input array size is `numIters * downFactor` and the output is `numIters * upFactor`. In this case, the `numIters` argument is set to the input size divided by the downsampling factor. This argument can be difficult for large sizes, since this formula will likely produce a fractional result and not all of the input will be processed into the output.

The trickiest argument to `ippsFIRMR` is `upPhase`, which determines how many zeros are inserted before the first source value. Since the filter designed in this example has its center at `pTaps[upSample]`, an `upPhase` value of one will shift the input so that the first valid output sample will equal the first input sample. This alignment is more noticeable for smaller sampling rates, such as those illustrated in Figure 6.22, than with the large rates in this example.

The delay line length, as defined in the manual, is `(tapsLen + upFactor - 1) / upFactor`.

```
int len, filterLen, delayLen, i;
Ipp32f* pTaps;
Ipp16s* pDelayLine;

WaveFile wf;
if (wf.Open("..\\..\\sounds\\onetoten.wav")) return -1;

WaveMem wm, wmd;
wm.ReadFromFile(&wf);
wm.Play(0);
```

```
len = wm.GetLen();

wmd.CopySettings(&wm);
wmd.SetSamplesPerSec(8000);
int upSample = wmd.GetSamplesPerSec()/100,
    downSample = wm.GetSamplesPerSec()/100;
wmd.Alloc(len*upSample/downSample);

int offset = 8500, viewLen = 200;
spView_16s(wm.GetShortBuffer()+offset, viewLen,
           "Source", 0);

// Create Linear interpolation filter
filterLen = upSample*2-1;
pTaps = ippsMalloc_32f(filterLen);
ippsVectorRamp_32f(pTaps, upSample,
    1.0/upSample, 1.0/upSample);
ippsVectorRamp_32f(pTaps+upSample-1, upSample,
    1.0, -1.0/upSample);
spView_32f(pTaps, filterLen, "Filter", 0);

// Set up delay line
delayLen = (filterLen+upSample-1)/upSample;
pDelayLine = ippsMalloc_16s(delayLen);
ippsZero_16s(pDelayLine, delayLen);

ippsFIRMR32f_Direct_16s_Sfs(
    wm.GetShortBuffer(), wmd.GetShortBuffer(),
    len/downSample, pTaps, filterLen,
    upSample, 1, downSample, 0, pDelayLine, 0);

spView_16s(wmd.GetShortBuffer()+ offset*upSample/downSample,
   viewLen*upSample/downSample, "Destination", 1);

wmd.Play(0);

ippsFree(pTaps);
ippsFree(pDelayLine);

return 0;
```

Figure 6.23 Code to Resample an Input Signal with FIRMR

Signal a) in Figure 6.24 is rough as an artifact of the original sound capture. The card captured the audio at 22,050 Hz then upsampled to 44,100 Hz by duplicating samples. The result is a visible and audible stairstep.

When the filter of signal b) is applied, conceptually a far longer signal is created by inserting 79 linearly interpolated samples between each pair of source values. Then, one out of 441 samples is retained and copied into the destination.

The resulting signal is shown in c). Other than the smoothing, the signal looks very similar. Note that, due to the lower sampling rate, the segment shown is 36 samples long in contrast to the original 200.

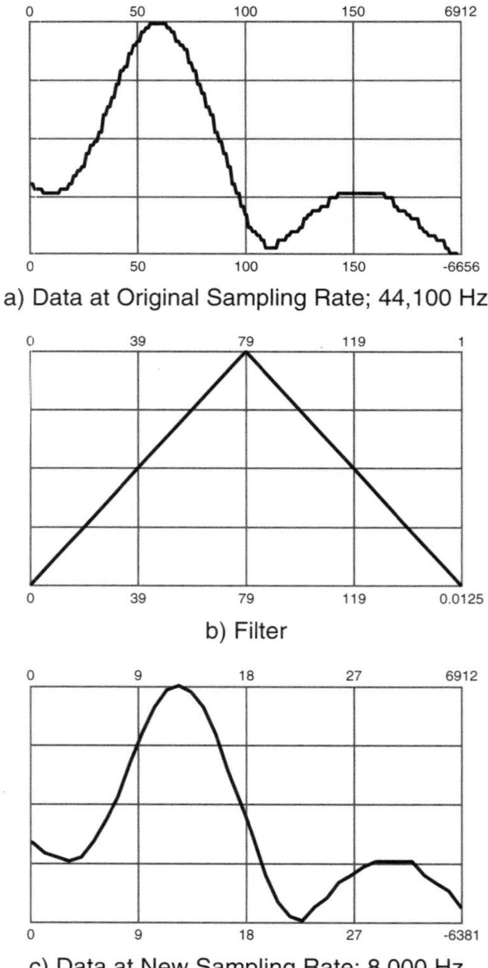

Figure 6.24 Results of Resampling with `FIRMR`

Spectral Manipulation

The Spectral Analysis section introduced the spectrogram, a two-dimensional time-frequency representation of a signal. That section focused on analysis of the signal through this representation, which made obvious frequency characteristics that changed over time. This section will show how to reconstruct the signal from this representation, so that the transform can be used to manipulate the signal as well.

Because of the particular formulation of the short-time Fourier transform, the operation is reversible. This is due to a property of the windowing function used. When the Hanning window is applied twice on overlapping sequences, it is possible to reconstruct the original signal.

This property is illustrated in Figure 6.25. On the left are four sequences of squared Hanning windows. Each of these windows is shifted by one-fourth of the width of the window from the last. The sum of these windows is on the right; in steady state, this sum is constant. From this you can conclude that multiplying overlapping segments of a signal by a Hanning window twice, then summing these segments, produces the original signal multiplied by a constant.

Therefore, the appropriate inverse of the STFT in Figure 6.9 is an FFT followed by a Hanning window. In using this STFT to create and reconstruct from a spectrograph, the width of the transform must be four times the shift between windows. This shift is sometimes referred to as the resolution in time.

The code in Figure 6.26 implements this inverse transform and uses it in a waveform-reconstruction function. The function `myWaveform_32f` takes a spectrogram divided into two arrays, the magnitude and the phase, and returns the reconstructed signal. The other arguments are the length of the reconstructed signal, and the resolution in time. The size of the Fourier transform is assumed to be four times this resolution.

The spectrogram is a two-dimensional array, equal in size to the Fourier transform size multiplied by the number of time slices, or `dstLen/resolution`. The number of elements in the array is therefore four times the destination length.

After initializing the specification structure `pSpec` for the appropriate size of FFT, the function starts the inner loop. For each `ftLen` elements, this loop merges the magnitude and phase into a single complex array, inverts the STFT, and adds the result to a sliding location in the destination array.

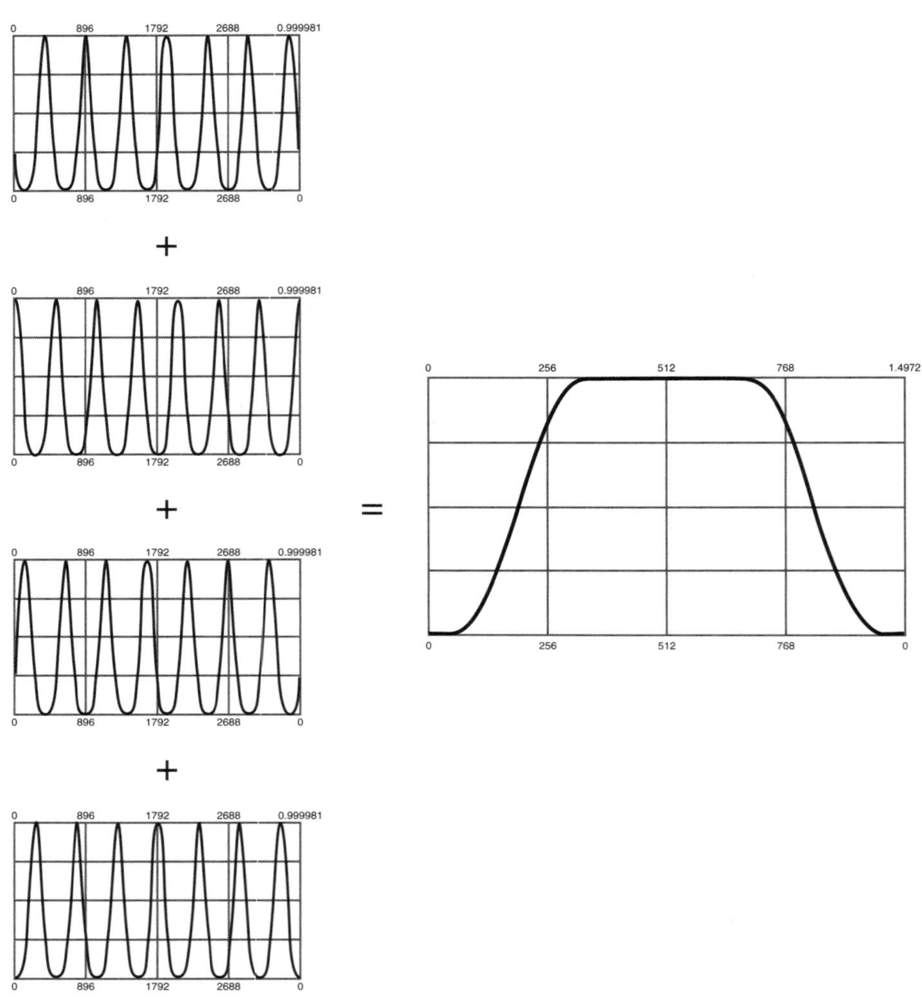

Figure 6.25 Four Sequences of Squared Hanning Windows and Their Sum

In the last stage, the code calculates the constant offset for the Hanning window of the current `FTLen`. The final array is divided by this constant so that the result has the same magnitude as the source.

```
IppStatus mySTFFTInv_CToR_32fc32f(Ipp32fc* pSrc, Ipp32f* pDst,
      int order, IppsFFTSpec_R_32f* pSpec)
{
     IppStatus st;

     st = ippsFFTInv_CCSToR_32f((Ipp32f*)pSrc, pDst,
             pSpec, 0);

     st = ippsWinHann_32f_I(pDst, 1<<order);
     if (st < 0) return st;
     return st;
}

IppStatus myWaveform_32f(Ipp32f* pSrcMag, Ipp32f* pSrcPhase,
      Ipp32f* pDst, int dstLen, int resolution)
{
     int ftLen = resolution*4;

     int order, tlen = ftLen;
     for (order=-1; tlen>0; tlen>>=1) order++;

     IppStatus st;
     Ipp32fc* pSrcTmp = ippsMalloc_32fc(ftLen);
     Ipp32f* pDstTmp = ippsMalloc_32f(ftLen);
     int i;
     ippsZero_32f(pDst, dstLen);
     IppsFFTSpec_R_32f* pSpec;
     st = ippsFFTInitAlloc_R_32f(&pSpec, order,
             IPP_FFT_DIV_INV_BY_N, ippAlgHintNone);
     if (st < 0) return st;

     for (i=0; i<dstLen/resolution; i++)
     {
         st = ippsPolarToCart_32fc(pSrcMag+i*ftLen,
                 pSrcPhase+i*ftLen, pSrcTmp, ftLen);
         if (st < 0) return st;
         st = mySTFFTInv_CToR_32fc32f(pSrcTmp, pDstTmp,
                 order, pSpec);
         if (st < 0) return st;
         st = ippsAdd_32f_I(pDstTmp, pDst+i*resolution,
                 ftLen);
         if (st < 0) return st;
     }
     st = ippsFFTFree_R_32f(pSpec);

     // Re-normalize Hanning constant factor
     ippsSet_32f(1.0f, pDstTmp, ftLen);
     ippsWinHann_32f_I(pDstTmp, ftLen);
```

```
    ippsWinHann_32f_I(pDstTmp, ftLen);
    ippsAdd_32f_I(pDstTmp+ftLen/2, pDstTmp, ftLen/4);
    ippsAdd_32f_I(pDstTmp+3*ftLen/4, pDstTmp, ftLen/4);
    ippsAdd_32f_I(pDstTmp+ftLen/4, pDstTmp, ftLen/4);

    spView_32f(pDstTmp, ftLen, "Hanning", 0);
    ippsDivC_32f_I(pDstTmp[0], pDst, dstLen);

    ippsFree(pSrcTmp);
    ippsFree(pDstTmp);

    return ippStsOk;
}
```

Figure 6.26 Code Reconstructing a Signal from its Spectrogram

Because it is possible to reverse the calculation of this spectrum, it is useful to perform modifications in the spectral domain. When the waveform is reconstructed from the spectrum, these modifications are reflected in the final product. This permits manipulation of the signal similar to that in Chapter 5, but over a longer timeframe.

The next section uses this transform to stretch a signal in time.

Signal Stretching

Changing the length of a signal normally affects the frequencies of the signal. Adding samples to a signal, for example by repeating each sample, without changing the playback sampling rate lowers the frequency of the sample. Stretching a signal to a longer length while avoiding this effect is more complicated than just adding samples.

Signal stretching using the spectrogram functions is performed in three steps:

1. Calculate the spectrogram using the source resolution
2. Scale the phase of each sample by the ratio of destination resolution to source resolution
3. Reconstruct the waveform using the destination resolution

Figure 6.27 illustrates the difference between source and destination resolutions.

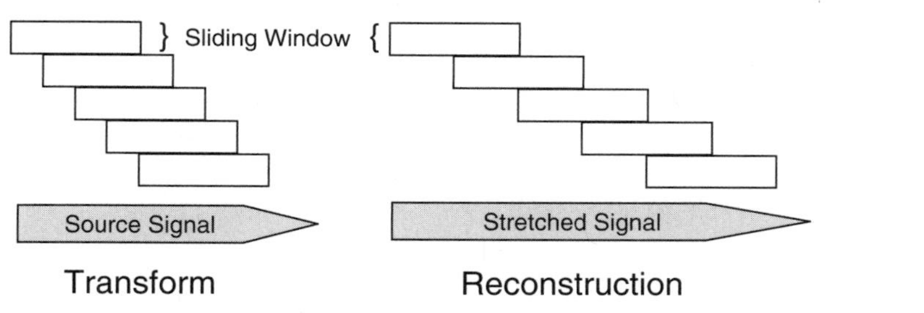

Figure 6.27 Windows for Signal Stretching

The phase adjustment in step 2 is made on the actual, unwrapped phase of the signal. When the ratio of resolutions is integral, the phase adjustment is easy to perform. Assuming the phase is p and the actual phase is $2\pi n + p$, multiplying the phase by an integer r will have the same effect on the actual phase: $2\pi nr + rp \equiv rp$. The function `myStretch_32f` in Figure 6.28 performs stretching by an integral factor. This code also demonstrates how the spectrum creation and reconstruction code from Figure 6.10 and Figure 6.26 can be used.

```
IppStatus myStretch_32f(Ipp32f* pSrcPhase, int srcRes,
    Ipp32f* pDstPhase, int dstRes, int fLen, int tLen)
{
    int i;

    for (i=0; i<tLen; i++)
    {
        int offset = i*fLen;
        ippsMulC_32f(pSrcPhase+offset,
            (float)dstRes/(float)srcRes,
            pDstPhase+offset, fLen);
    }

    return ippStsOk;
}
...
    int len = wm.GetLen();
    int srcRes = 128, dstRes = 512;
    int ftSize = dstRes*4;
    int specLen = len/srcRes*ftSize;
    int dstLen = len * (dstRes/srcRes);

    mySpectrum_32f(pSignal, pMag, pPhase, len, srcRes,
```

```
        ftSize);

    myStretch_32f(pPhase, srcRes, pDstPhase, dstRes, ftSize,
        specLen/ftSize);

    myWaveform_32f(pMag, pDstPhase, pSignal, dstLen, dstRes,
        ftSize);
```

Figure 6.28 Code to Stretch an Audio Signal in Time

If the phase is not an integer, this formula no longer holds, and an effort must be made to determine the actual phase. This is done by unwrapping the phase in a manner conceptually similar to that in Figure 6.7.

Faux Stereo

A monaural signal can be converted to a virtual stereo signal by manipulating the relative frequencies of the left and right channels. The input signal is multiplied by one factor per channel. The factor is a function of the angle between the simulated sound source and straight ahead. Assuming that the sound source angle is less than +/- 45°, the functions are:

$$S_{left} = (\cos(\theta) - \sin(\theta))\, S_{mono}$$

$$S_{right} = (\sin(\theta) + \cos(\theta))\, S_{mono}$$

At the extremes, +/- 45°, one channel is exactly the input signal and the other is zero.

The code in Figure 6.29 makes this calculation. The function `myWMStereo` calculates a stereo signal wrapped in a `WaveMem` from a mono signal and an array of angles.

This function needs a temporary buffer to hold the intermediate results, since the calculation is done in `Ipp32f` but the input and output data is in `Ipp16s`. For this reason, the operation is done on `bufSize` elements at a time. This attempts to balance the cost of memory usage with the cost of call overhead. For the most efficiency, the number of calls to `ippsMalloc` should be reduced to one, allocating enough memory for all temporary arrays. That wouldn't be very clean, though.

The function `ippsSinCos` calculates both the sine and cosine of an array of inputs. The arrays `pSin` and `pCos` first capture the result of the `ippsSinCos` call, then hold the product of those sines and cosines and the mono input signal. The left channel is the difference between these arrays, and the right is their sum. After these arrays are converted back to `Ipp16s`, the two signals pTmpDstL and pTmpDstR are interleaved into the destination using the function ippsRealToCplx, as shown in Chapter 4.

The last code section repeats each of these stages in case the input array isn't an integer multiple of the buffer size.

```
IppStatus myWMStereo(const WaveMem &wm, WaveMem &wms,
      Ipp32f* pAngle)
{
    int i, len = wm.GetLen();

    wms.CopySettings(&wm);
    wms.SetNumChannels(2);
    wms.Alloc(len);

    static int bufSize = 4096;

    Ipp32f* pSin = ippsMalloc_32f(bufSize);
    Ipp32f* pCos = ippsMalloc_32f(bufSize);
    Ipp32f* pTmp = ippsMalloc_32f(bufSize);
    Ipp16s* pTmpDstL = ippsMalloc_16s(bufSize);
    Ipp16s* pTmpDstR = ippsMalloc_16s(bufSize);

    for (i=0; i<len-bufSize; i+=bufSize)
    {
        ippsConvert_16s32f(wm.GetShortBuffer()+i, pTmp,
                 bufSize);

        ippsSinCos_32f_A11(pAngle+i, pSin, pCos, bufSize);
        ippsMul_32f_I(pTmp, pSin, bufSize);
        ippsMul_32f_I(pTmp, pCos, bufSize);

        ippsSub_32f(pCos, pSin, pTmp, bufSize);
        ippsConvert_32f16s_Sfs(pTmp, pTmpDstL, bufSize,
                 ippRndNear, 0);
        ippsAdd_32f(pCos, pSin, pTmp, bufSize);
        ippsConvert_32f16s_Sfs(pTmp, pTmpDstR, bufSize,
                 ippRndNear, 0);

        ippsRealToCplx_16s(pTmpDstL, pTmpDstR,
            (Ipp16sc*)wms.GetShortBuffer()+i, bufSize);
    }

    ippsConvert_16s32f(wm.GetShortBuffer()+i, pTmp, len-i);

    ippsSinCos_32f_A11(pAngle+i, pSin, pCos, len-i);
    ippsMul_32f_I(pTmp, pSin, len-i);
    ippsMul_32f_I(pTmp, pCos, len-i);
```

```
    ippsSub_32f(pCos, pSin, pTmp, len-i);
    ippsConvert_32f16s_Sfs(pTmp, pTmpDstL, len-i, ippRndNear,
            0);
    ippsAdd_32f(pCos, pSin, pTmp, len-i);
    ippsConvert_32f16s_Sfs(pTmp, pTmpDstR, len-i, ippRndNear,
            0);

    ippsRealToCplx_16s(pTmpDstL, pTmpDstR,
        (Ipp16sc*)wms.GetShortBuffer()+i, len-i);

    ippsFree(pSin);
    ippsFree(pCos);
    ippsFree(pTmp);
    ippsFree(pTmpDstL);
    ippsFree(pTmpDstR);

    return ippStsNoErr;
}
```

Figure 6.29 Code to Convert Mono Audio to Faux Stereo

Figure 6.30 shows the result when an array of the constant value 10,000 is used as the audio input. The first graph shows the angle used to calculate the stereo signal; the second shows the two channels of the output signal. The absolute value of the two channels is the important value.

At higher frequencies, the psychoacoustics are more complicated. At those frequencies, manipulating the phase is necessary to create the illusion of a stereo signal. See the two works cited below for more details.

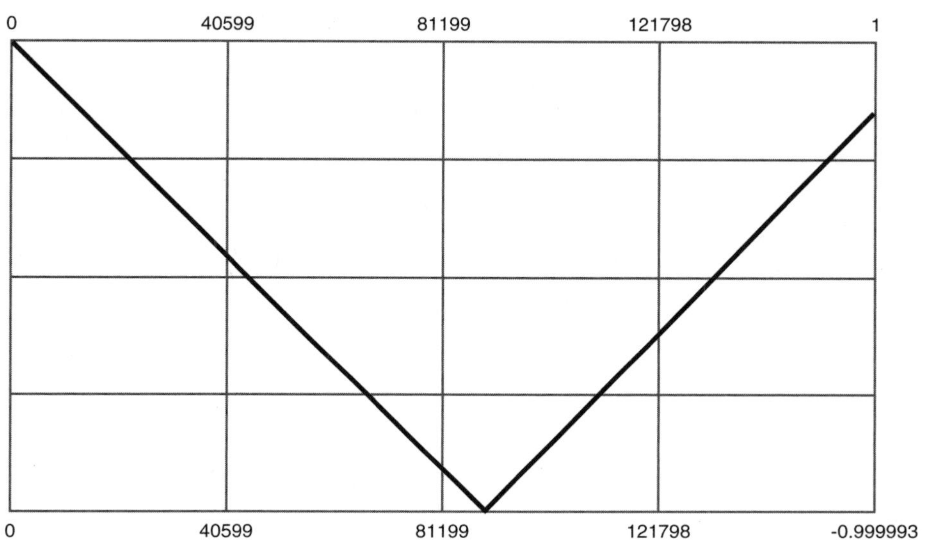

a) Angle of Audio Source from Straight Ahead

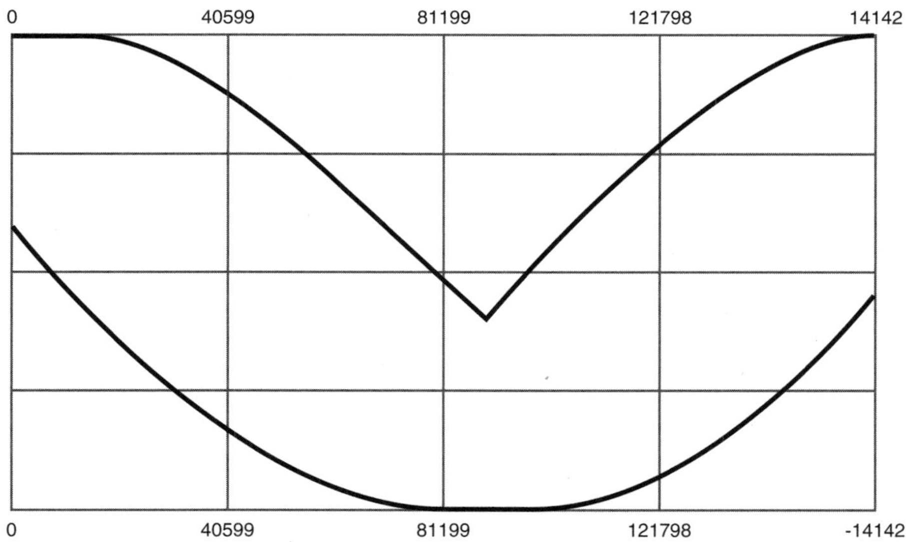

b) Weighting of Audio Source Left and Right Channels (*10,000)

Figure 6.30 Results of Mono Audio to Faux Stereo Conversion

Further Reading

DAFX (Zolzer 2002) inspired many of the examples in this chapter. If you are looking for solutions for audio analysis or manipulation, including more detail on many of the methods in this chapter, it is extremely useful. It also contains dozens of interesting and fun audio processing experiments. Most algorithms are implemented in Matlab[†].

The Computer Music Tutorial (Roads 1995) is a very large work containing descriptions of a range of topics of interest to a software developer in digital sound or music. Topics include audio formats, signal processing, signal analysis, and effects generation.

Chapter 7

Audio Coding

Audio data is usually coded to reduce its size. Raw digital audio is large for today's storage and bandwidth. Compact disc audio has 16 bits per sample in stereo at 44,100 samples per second, which is over 10 megabytes of data per minute. In portable audio, there is always a call to put more audio on smaller devices, so compression is essential, particularly when compressed audio is reasonably about one-tenth the size of uncompressed audio. In networked audio, the persistent need to reduce the amount of bandwidth per stream leads to the same conclusion.

The Intel® Integrated Performance Primitives (Intel® IPP) library supports audio *codecs* (encoder/decoders) in general, but has a particular focus on two popular open coding standards: MP3 and AAC. MP3 is the most advanced audio format from MPEG-1, and AAC is the Advanced Audio Coding format MPEG-2. MPEG-4 AAC is supported to the extent that it is an expansion of MPEG-2.

Some formats have little or no support. In particular, Intel IPP does not provide samples for the popular but proprietary RealAudio† and Windows Media† formats. Some modules in Intel IPP may still be applicable to implementations of these formats.

Audio Coding Basics

As with lossless coding, much of the compression in audio is from redundancy. To this end, both AAC and MP3 utilize stereo coding, in which the right and left channels, often varying together, are also coded together.

Also, when the data is transformed into the frequency domain, it is usually the case that there are sets of frequencies, particularly high frequencies, that have little data in them and may even be zero.

The other source of compression is perceptibility. Psychoacoustic research demonstrates that strong signals mask weaker signals of nearby frequencies in the human ear. The ear has resolution of as little as 100 hertz for low frequencies and as much as 4 kilohertz for high frequencies. As a result, much of the data in frequency bands surrounding high-volume bands can be sparsely encoded without introducing noticeable errors. The quantization step does this by reducing the number of data levels.

When the information in the data has been reduced sufficiently, the reduced information is turned into a reduced bit count using variable-length coding, usually *Huffman coding*. The idea is that the more-frequent data elements are encoded with fewer bits than the less-frequent elements. After quantization, the rate of some codes, particularly -1, 0, and 1, is very high, and these codes can be represented with very few bits. Also, sequences of zeros can be encoded together.

Figure 7.1 shows how these blocks are put together in an encoder and decoder. The filter bank transforms data between the time domain and the frequency domain. Once the data is in the frequency domain, the encoder can determine which bands should be encoded fully and which can be compressed more. The quantization block then differentially reduces the amount of information by frequency band. Good quantization for audio is exponential. Finally, variable-length coding exploits the redundancy in the quantized codes.

MP3 and AAC are implemented with feedback loop around the quantization that controls the data rate. At each step, the encoder adjusts the amount of quantization according to the projected data rate after the coefficients are variable-length coded. Two loops try to balance data rate and noise by decreasing the quantization where noticeable noise is introduced and increasing it elsewhere.

Though many other operations are required to encode or decode an audio stream, these high-level blocks represent the codec and the most expensive parts of the coding. Quantization is frequently nonlinear, and nonlinear quantization is expensive. The filter bank is also a time-intensive operation. And, since the variable-length coding is a bit-by-bit operation, software implementations of it are difficult and expensive.

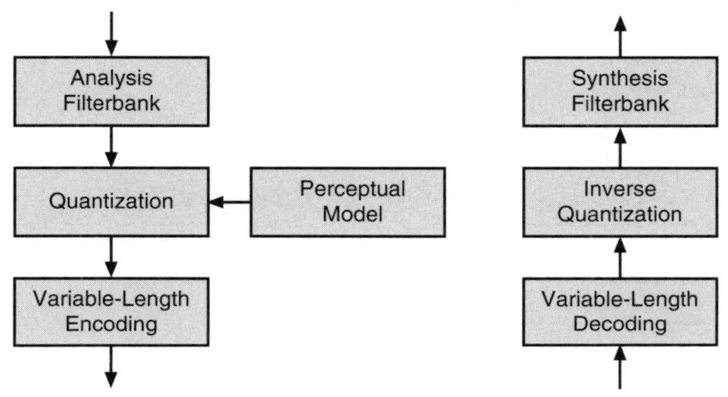

Figure 7.1 High-Level Diagram of Audio Coding

MP3

Perhaps the most popular audio compression format is MPEG-1 Layer 3, commonly known as MP3. It is the third layer of the audio part of the international MPEG (Motion Picture Experts Group) standard. However, an MPEG-1 Layer 3 codec is not precisely equivalent to an MP3 codec, since the former implies support for layers 1 and 2 as well.

MP3 Codec Components

Figure 7.2 is a detailed diagram of the blocks in a software MP3 codec. The blocks are explained one-by-one in the order they take place in the decoder.

Huffman Encoding and Decoding

The variable-length code in MP3 is a Huffman code. There are several preset options for the Huffman coding tables.

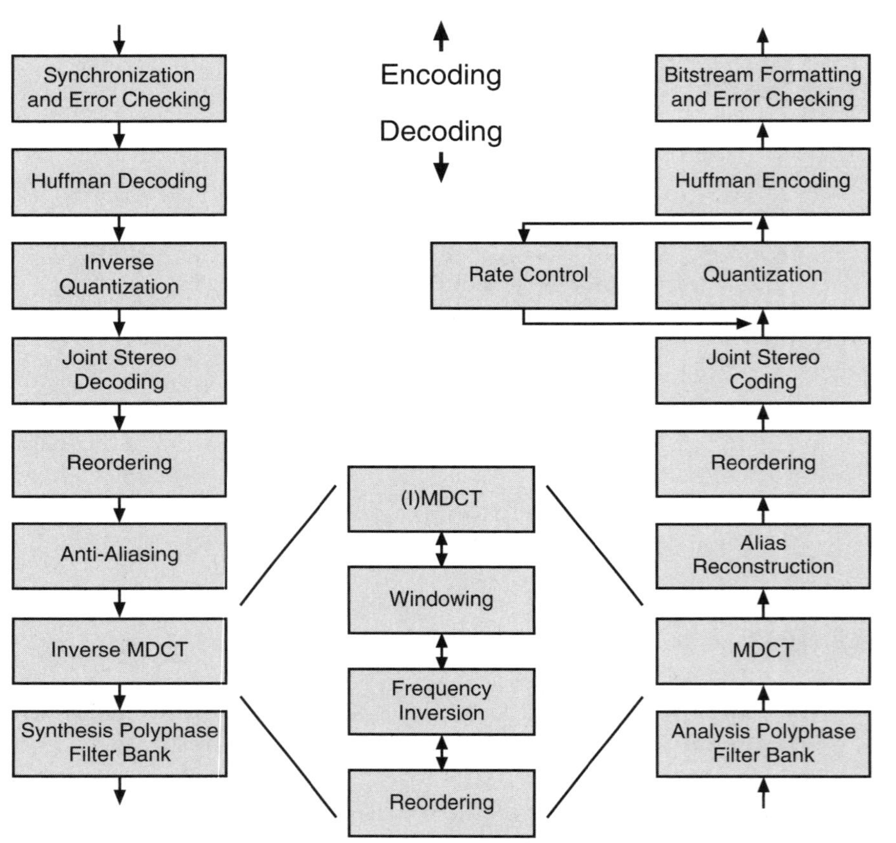

Figure 7.2 Components for MP3 Codec

Each block of coefficients is divided into three regions: zeros, "count1", and "big values". The statistics of each dictate the Huffman tables. The first, containing the highest-frequency coefficients, is all zeros and isn't coded at all. The second contains only the values 0 and ±1, so needs only a very simple Huffman table. The third, containing the remaining values, is further divided into three sub-regions. This permits three separate tables to accommodate the statistics of smaller frequency ranges.

A decoder typically spends about five percent of its time in the Huffman decoding stage. Huffman encoding is more expensive.

Quantization and Inverse Quantization

The *quantization* step reduces the amount of information in each coefficient in an intelligent way. It allows less important coefficients to be reduced to a coarse-grained set of levels without introducing perceptible noise. To achieve this, the determination of importance is based on perceptual models. The idea is to set the quantization level so that the resulting noise is below the threshold of perception. Generally, greater energy in a frequency band allows higher quantization in the surrounding bands for some time period around the energy peak.

On the encoding side, adjusting the quality to match a certain bit rate is quite complicated. It can be done with nested loops to iterate between increasing the global scale to control the bit rate and decreasing some individual scales to reduce perceptible noise below threshold.

Because of the nonlinear distribution of intensity of audio data, the quantization in MP3 is exponential. On the forward quantization, the encoder applies global and local scale factors before raising the data to the three-fourths power. The inverse operation in the decoder raises the data to four-thirds power before inverting the scale operation.

Since the sign must be preserved and the output must be real, the formula for the forward exponential is:

$$\text{sign}(s[i]) * \text{abs}(s[i])^{3/4}$$

The global scale factor is very useful in rate control. The frequency-band-specific scale factors determine the noise shaping factors and are determined by the perceptual analysis.

The nonlinear quantization and inverse quantization can be very expensive. Over a third of the decode time is likely to be this single step.

Reordering

On the encoding side, coefficients in short blocks and transitional blocks need to be reordered after the filter bank to match the high-frequency-first order used by the Huffman encoding. On the decoding side, the coefficients for those blocks must be reordered back into the short and transitional blocks. A reordering step between the transform and filter bank are both described below.

Joint-Stereo Coding and Decoding

MP3 has four modes that determine how many channels there are and how they are encoded relative to each other. They are: ***single-channel***, ***dual-channel*** (two unrelated channels), ***stereo***, and ***joint stereo***. Joint stereo coding uses the redundancy between the left and right channels to compress the signal further than the two channels could be compressed independently.

The stereo processing block performs the necessary processing to convert a stereo signal into separate left/right stereo signals. There are two modes of stereo redundancy coding in MP3: middle/side stereo coding (MS-stereo) and intensity stereo coding.

Intensity stereo coding codes the sum of the left and right channels rather than all the information for some bands. The left-right breakdown is conveyed only in differing scale factors for the left and right channels, one per band.

The middle/side coding method converts a left and right channel into a joint coding channel (middle) and a difference-coding channel (side). The formulae for decoding are:

$$left = \frac{(middle + side)}{\sqrt{2}}$$

$$right = \frac{(middle - side)}{\sqrt{2}}$$

For encoding the formulae are:

$$middle = \frac{(left + right)}{\sqrt{2}}$$

$$side = \frac{(left - right)}{\sqrt{2}}$$

Anti-Aliasing

The forward frequency transform includes an alias reduction for long blocks to reduce artifacts from overlapping windows. In the decoder, this aliasing information must be added back in to get an accurate result. The alias transform consists of eight butterfly calculations for each sub-band.

MDCT

The main distinguishing characteristic between MPEG-1 layer-3 audio and the other layers of MPEG-1 audio is the *modified discrete cosine transform* (MDCT) . The MDCT is used to generate a finer-grained frequency resolution to exploit additional redundancy. It breaks down the post-filter-bank signal by calculating a frequency transform on a block of samples from each of 32 subbands. The two sizes of blocks in MP3 are: 12-element short blocks and the 36-element long blocks. In the steady state, half of the samples encoded or decoded are old samples that overlap with the previous block, so these blocks usually represent 6 and 18 new samples, respectively. In the transition between short and long blocks the coding still uses 12-element and 36-element blocks but can use 6, 18, or 24 new samples each stage. The MDCT component and a few others generally require separate versions for each block size.

To smooth the reconstruction of the overlapping blocks, the inverse MDCT window function is applied. This function is either a sine window or the Kaiser-Bessel derived window.

Between the MDCT and filter bank stages, the data is often reordered. A software MDCT naturally is most efficient if the 12 or 36 elements from a sub-band are contiguous. However, most filter bank implementations are more efficient if all 32 samples from a given time are contiguous.

The MDCT represents only a small percentage of the total computation time in MP3.

Frequency Inversion

The decoder must compensate for frequency inversions in the synthesis polyphase filter bank. Every odd time sample of every odd subband is multiplied by –1.

Analysis and Synthesis Filter Banks

The most expensive and most distinguishing step in the coding is the *polyphase filter bank*. The filter bank calculates a filter on 512 samples of the input, of which 32 are new. For each new 32-sample block input, the forward filter produces one sample for each of 32 sub-bands.

For reference, the synthesis filter bank is

$$s_t[i] = \sum_{k=0}^{63} M_{ik} \sum_{j=0}^{7} C[k+64j] \times x[k+64j]$$

where M_{ik} is

$$M_{ik} = \cos\left[\frac{(2 \times i + 1) \times (k - 16) \times \pi}{64}\right]$$

By analyzing these equations carefully, it is possible to perform this calculation with a windowing operation followed by a cosine transform.

Almost half of the time required to decode an MP3 stream is spent in the filter bank calculation.

MP3 in Intel® Integrated Performance Primitives (Intel® IPP)

Intel IPP has two sets of functions supporting MP3, a specific set and a general one. This section presents the general, broadly applicable set. The functions for MP3 in this group are almost the same as the functions for AAC. For example, the same scaling functions perform quantization for both codecs.

The specific set, most of which have `_MP3` in the name, are part of a specific integer-based encoder and decoder. The fit in any other encoder or decoder is awkward. For example, the function `ippsMDCTInv_MP3_32s` operates on 32 sub-bands of 18 samples each in Q5.26 fixed-point, performs 32 separate inverse MDCTs, and returns the results as Q7.24 fixed-point. This integer-only set of functions is intended to support a small, resource-light codec, and the entire set is tied to data structures `IppMP3FrameHeader` and `IppMP3SideInfo`.

In addition, floating-point encoder and decoder samples use the general audio coding functions. In Intel IPP 4.0, the encoder supports mono and stereo, but not joint stereo mode; the decoder supports mono, stereo, and joint stereo modes, but not dual channel mode. Neither supports variable bit rates.

The following code examples are taken from those samples. Most are from the decoder because it is more carefully optimized, and therefore includes more Intel IPP calls. Many of the techniques and functions could be reapplied to the encoder.

The inner loop of this example is listed in Figure 7.11. Almost all of the calls to Intel IPP are embedded in the major blocks, such as the functions `Huffmancodebits`, `Dequant`, `IMDCT` and `SubBandSynth`. The functions `ReadMainData` and `GetScaleFactors` extract the side information from the bit stream.

```
// restores actual scalefactors to the values extracted
// from the bitstream. Four scalefactors in DC->si_globGain
// (beginning at an offset of 210)
// are restored to the DC->ScaleFactor vector.
ippsCalcSF_16s32f((short*)DC->si_globGain, 210,
    (float*)DC->ScaleFactor, 4);
ReadMainData(DC);

main_data_bits = (DC->MainData.pCurrent_dword -
    DC->MainData.pBuffer)*32 + (32 - DC->MainData.nBit_offset);

for (gr = 0; gr < DC->header.id+1; gr++) {
    for (ch = 0; ch < DC->stereo; ch++) {
        // detect start point
        DC->MainData.pCurrent_dword = DC->MainData.pBuffer +
            (main_data_bits >> 5);
        DC->MainData.nBit_offset = 32 - (main_data_bits % 32);
        main_data_bits += DC->si_part23Len[gr][ch];

        DC->part2_start = (DC->MainData.pCurrent_dword -
            DC->MainData.pBuffer)*32 + 32 -
            DC->MainData.nBit_offset;

        if (DC->header.id)
            GetScaleFactors(DC, gr, ch);
        else
            GetScaleFactors_LSF(DC, ch);

        Huffmancodebits(DC, gr, ch);
        Dequant(DC, gr, ch);
    }

    if (DC->header.mode == 0x01 )
        JointStereo(DC);

    for (ch = 0; ch < DC->stereo; ch++) {
        Reordering(DC, gr, ch);
        Antialiasing(DC, gr, ch);
        IMDCT(DC, gr, ch);
        SubBandSynth(DC, gr, ch);
```

```
    }

    // combines the data from all channels in the working
    // array after the SubBandSynth phase into one joined
    // vector.
    ippsJoin_32f16s_D2L( (const float**)pSampl, DC->stereo,
        576, DC->outsamples + gr*576*DC->stereo);
}
```

Figure 7.3 MP3 Sample Decoder Main Loop

Huffman Encoding and Decoding

Not all variable-length codes in MP3 are general enough to use reusable functions. Therefore, the Huffman encoding stage requires a mix of somewhat general coding functions and MP3-specific ones. For example, one of the coding regions does not use Huffman explicitly, but encodes a block of four samples using one or two noncontiguous bits.

The MP3 sample includes the hard-coded Huffman tables and uses a mix of Intel IPP functions and custom code. Figure 7.4 lists the sections that use these functions.

The first of the three segments initializes Intel IPP Huffman tables. The sample includes fixed, statically defined MP3 Huffman tables in the `ptable` field of elements of the array `huff_table`. For each of these tables the code first calculates the memory required to hold each internal-format table. Then it allocates the memory with the `malloc` function and builds the table with the function `ippsBuildHDT`. The result is put in the `phuftable` field of elements of the same array. Keeping an array of these internal-format tables is a necessary approach.

The decoding is done in two stages. The second segment above decodes the three "big values" subregions. If the table contains an escape code, the implementation uses the MP3-specific function `DecodeVLC_MP3ESCBlock`; otherwise, it uses the `DecodeVLC_Block` function. Each call of these functions decodes an entire subregion at once, but won't read more than a 576-element block.

The region after "big values" is "count1" which contains only values -1, 0, or 1. The function `DecodeVLC` decodes one four-element code at a time. By comparing the bit-stream offset in the input with the offset in the output, the loop keeps track of the number of bits read. Each code is encoded as one bit initially; if the code bit is nonzero, a sign bit will immediately follow. The code segment above extracts this bit by hand using the function `Getbits`.

The loop continues to decode until there are no bits remaining or until it has read 576 elements. When the segment runs out of bits, the remaining codes are assumed to be zero.

```
// Initialize internal Intel IPP Huffman tables all at once
for(i = 1; i < 34; i++) {
    if (huff_table[i].ptable) {
        ippsGetSizeHDT_32s (huff_table[i].ptable,
            phufBuffer, 1 << 16, &hufsize);
        huff_table[i].phuftable = (int*)malloc(hufsize);
        ippsBuildHDT_32s( huff_table[i].ptable,
            huff_table[i].phuftable, hufsize);
    }

...

// Three regions in the big values section
for (j = 0; j < 3; j++) {
    idx = DC->si_pTableSelect[gr][ch][j];
    ptable = DC->huff_table[idx].phuftable;
    linbits = DC->huff_table[idx].linbits;
    if (idx) {
        if (linbits == 0) {
            ippsDecodeVLC_Block_32s( &BS->pCurrent_dword,
                (unsigned int*)&(BS->nBit_offset), ptable,
                (reg[j]-i)/2, &(*DC->smpl_xs)[ch][i]);
        } else {
            ippsDecodeVLC_MP3ESCBlock_32s(
                &BS->pCurrent_dword,
                (unsigned int*)&(BS->nBit_offset),
                ptable, (reg[j]-i)/2, linbits,
                &(*DC->smpl_xs)[ch][i]);
        }
        i = reg[j];
}

...

while ( (nbits > 0) && ((i+4) <= 576)) {

bt = BS->nBit_offset; // store count of bits

    // decodes huffman-coded values from the bitstream
    // pBS with ptable as the huffman table
```

```
// the &(BS->iBitOffset) indicates the number of unread
// bits in the bitstream's current word
// the decoded value is written to t.i
ippsDecodeVLC_32s( &BS->pCurrent_dword,
    (unsigned int*)&BS->nBit_offset,
    DC->huff_table[idx].phuftable, &(t.i));

// Calculate number of bits remaining
bt -= BS->nBit_offset;
sign = (bt >> 31);
nbits -= (bt + (32 & sign));

v = t.v;

if (v) {
    nbits--;
    if (Getbits(BS, 1))
        v = -v;
}

w = t.w;
...
```

Figure 7.4 Portion of the Huffman Decoder in MP3 Sample

The encoder works similarly. The big values region is coded with the `ippsEncodeVLC_Block` and `ippsEncodeVLC_MP3ESCBlock` functions. Encoding of the count1 region is done by hand, since it can be done with about a dozen lines of code.

The function `ippsHuffmanCountBits` is a key part of the quantization loop, used for rate control.

Quantization

The functions `ippsPow34` and `ippsPow43` perform the nonlinear portion of the quantization and inverse quantization, respectively. The functions either work entirely within 32-bit floating point or can convert the frequency band to or from a 16-bit signed integer.

The scale portion of the quantization is divided into a two-step process. The function `ippsCalcSF_16s32f` calculates an array of the scale factor multipliers. For an array of scale factors `pSrc` and a constant `offset`, it calculates: $2^{1/4(pSrc[i] - offset)}$

If pSrc is global_gain and offset is 210, this is the global scale factor calculation. This global gain for the MP3 sample code was calculated for each channel in the main loop, Figure 7.11. This function can also calculate the band-specific scale factors with an offset of 0.

The function ippsMulC_32f_I is useful for applying a global scale factor. The function ippsApplySF is meant to apply scale factors band-by-band. It multiplies each of a series of contiguous blocks of varying lengths by a single array of scale factors. One of its arguments is an array listing the offsets of each block, which in this case are the spectral bands.

Figure 7.5 lists one branch of the inverse quantization function Dequant that uses each of these functions.

```
int Dequant(sDecoderContext* DC, int gr, int ch)
{
    float   xx;
    short   scl;
    int     count = DC->non_zero[ch];
    int     sfb;

    scl = -2-2*(short)DC->si_sfScale[gr][ch];
    xx    = DC->ScaleFactor[gr][ch];

    ippsPow43_16s32f ( (*DC->smpl_xs)[ch], (*DC->smpl_xr)[ch],
        576);

    if (DC->si_blockType[gr][ch] != 2 )
    {
        float tmp21[21];
        short sf_tmp[21];

        // Should use ippsMulC_16s_I:
        if (DC->si_preFlag[gr][ch] == 0)
        {
            for (sfb = 0; sfb < 21; sfb++)
                sf_tmp[sfb] = scl*DC->ScaleFactors[ch].l[sfb];
        } else {
            for (sfb = 0; sfb < 21; sfb++)
                sf_tmp[sfb] = scl*
                    (DC->ScaleFactors[ch].l[sfb]+pretab[sfb]);
        }

        ippsCalcSF_16s32f( sf_tmp, 0, tmp21, 21);

        // multiplies first 21 elements of scale-factor array
```

```
        // by global scale
        ippsMulC_32f_I( xx, tmp21, 21);

        ippsApplySF_32f_I( (*DC->smpl_xr)[ch], tmp21,
            sfBandIndex[DC->header.id]
                [DC->header.samplingFreq].l, 22);
    ...
}
```

Figure 7.5 Inverse Quantization in the MP3 Decoder Sample

MDCT

The Intel IPP function `ippsMDCT_32f` performs the MDCT on a block of samples, and the inverse MDCT is done by `ippsMDCTInv_32f`. The MDCT stage is generally more complicated than just these two functions. For one, because of the overlap between consecutive blocks, there is a windowing function applied after the inverse MDCT and before the forward MDCT. The frequency inversion step that inverts every other sample is also naturally combined with the MDCT block. Finally, the reordering of data described in the previous section is generally combined in the same block.

Figure 7.6 lists the code for forward windowing and MDCT for both 12-element short blocks and 36-element long blocks. Each has a specification structure allocated earlier.

The code needs to operate on three short blocks at a time. After windowing and transforming each block, the code sequence recombines them. The `ippsInterleave` function sorts the coefficients between blocks by frequency to make the variable-length coding more effective.

The function `ippsMul_32f_I` is the best for the windowing function and the frequency inversion. In fact, if the window is multiplied in advance by an alternating sequence of ones and zeros, both steps can be performed with one multiplication. The constant version of this function, `ippsMulC_32_I`, is useful for applying the constant scale factor that makes the MDCT gain-neutral.

```
    // MDCT for short blocks
    for(i = 0; i < 32; i++)
    {
        ippsMul_32f( in+6, pWindow, tmp_in, 12);
        ippsMul_32f( in+12, pWindow, tmp_in+12, 12);
        ippsMul_32f( in+18, pWindow, tmp_in+24, 12);

        ippsMDCTFwd_32f( tmp_in, tmp_out, pSpec12,
            pBuffer);
        ippsMDCTFwd_32f( tmp_in+12, tmp_out, pSpec12,
            pBuffer);
        ippsMDCTFwd_32f( tmp_in+24, tmp_out, pSpec12,
            pBuffer);

        ippsMulC_32f_I( 2.f/12, tmp_out, 18);
        ippsInterleave_32f(tmp_out2, 3, 6, out);

        in += 36;
        out += 18;
    }
...
    // MDCT for long blocks
    for(i = 0; i < 32; i++)
    {
        ippsMul_32f_I(in, &EC->mdct_win[block_type][j], 36);
        ippsMDCTFwd_32f( in, out, pSpec36, mdct_bfr);

        in += 36;
        out += 18;
    }
    ippsMulC_32f_I( 2.f/36, ptr_out, 576);
...
```

Figure 7.6 MDCT in the MP3 Encoder Sample

Filter Bank

The filter bank, interestingly, is also done with a careful combination of cosine transform and multiplication.

On the analysis or encode side, the data is arrayed in 64 circular buffers of 8 values, for efficiency. Each buffer contains the values necessary to calculate the inner sum:

$$\sum_{j=0}^{7} C_{ik}[j] \times x[j]$$

In each iteration, 32 new time samples replace the oldest values. This arrangement of memory is efficient for vectorization and therefore for Intel IPP use.

The cosine matrix coefficients have the following helpful properties:

- $M_i[k] = M_i[32-k]$ for k = 0..15
- $M_i[16] = 1$ for any i
- $M_i[48-k] = -M_i[48+k]$ for k = 1..15
- $M_i[48] = 0$ for any i

These properties allow the following simplification:

$$s_t[i] = \sum_{k=0}^{15} M_{ik} (\sum_{j=0}^{7} C[k+64j] \times x[k+64j] +$$

$$\sum_{j=0}^{7} C[(32-k)+64j] \times x[(32-k)+64j])) +$$

$$\sum_{k=0}^{15} M_{ik} (\sum_{j=0}^{7} C[(48-k)+64j] \times x[(48-k)+64j] -$$

$$\sum_{j=0}^{7} C[(48+k)+64j] \times x[(48-k)+64j]))$$

This simplification decreases the number of multiplications by half. More importantly, the inverse DCT implements this formula directly. It is well known that the DCT can be optimized with FFT and therefore implemented very efficiently. The resulting implementation, listed in Figure 7.11, is very efficient.

```
for(l = 0; l < 18; l++)
{
    even[ch] = (++even[ch] & 0x1);

    if (line[ch][even[ch]])
        line[ch][even[ch]]--;
    else
        line[ch][even[ch]] = 7;

    idx = line[ch][even[ch]];

    j   = 8 - idx;


    for(i = 0; i < 32; i++) {
        shft = ((31 - i) + (even[ch] << 5)) & 0x3f;
        EC->filter_bfr[ch][shft][idx] = input[i];
    }

    for(i = 0; i <= 16; i++) {
        shft = (i + (even[ch] << 5)) & 0x3f;
        tmp32[16 - i] = 0;

        for(k = 0; k < 8; k++)
        {
            tmp32[16 - i] +=
                Ccoef[i][j+k]*EC->filter_bfr[ch][shft][k];
        }
    }

    for(i = 17; i < 32; i++) {
        shft = (i + (even[ch] << 5)) & 0x3f;
        idx = i - 16;
        for(k = 0; k < 8; k++) {
            tmp32[idx] +=
                Ccoef[i][j+k]*EC->filter_bfr[ch][shft][k];
        }
    }

    j   = (8 - line[ch][((even[ch]+1) & 0x1)]) & 0x7;

    shft = (32 + (even[ch] << 5)) & 0x3f;
    for(k = 0; k < 8; k++) {
        tmp32[16] +=
            Ccoef[32][j+k]*EC->filter_bfr[ch][shft][k];
    }
```

```
        for(i = 33; i <= 47; i++) {
            shft = (i + (even[ch] << 5)) & 0x3f;
            idx = i-16;

            tmp32[idx] = 0;
            for(k = 0; k < 8; k++)
            {
                tmp32[idx] +=
                    Ccoef[i][j+k]*EC->filter_bfr[ch][shft][k];
            }
        }

        for(i = 49; i < 64; i++) {
            shft = (i + (even[ch] << 5)) & 0x3f;
            idx = 80 - i;

            for(k = 0; k < 8; k++) {
                tmp32[idx] -=
                    Ccoef[i][j+k]*EC->filter_bfr[ch][shft][k];
            }
        }

        tmp32[0] *= sqrtN;
        for(i = 1; i < 32;i++)
            tmp32[i] *= sqrtN2;

        sts = ippsDCTInv_32f(tmp32, output, EC->pDCTSpec,
            DCTBuffer);

        input  +=32;
        output += 32;
    }
```

Figure 7.7 Analysis Filter Bank Implemented with Inverse DCT

AAC

Since the definition of MP3 in 1991, there has been considerable research into better use of perceptual information in audio coding. Out of this research emerged MPEG-2 Advanced Audio Coding (AAC) . It offers a better compression ratio than MP3. With the sum of many small improvements, AAC reaches on average the same quality as MP3 at about 70 percent of the bit rate.

AAC vs. MP3

Many of the modules underwent modification, but here are the main improvements between MP3 and AAC:

- Simpler and more flexible filter bank
- Improved joint stereo coding
- Improved Huffman coding
- Temporal noise shaping
- Prediction
- Audio Transport

In AAC the transport is separate from the codec. The standard defines two transport types, *Audio Data Interchange Format* (ADIF) and *Audio Data Transport Stream* (ADTS). The former has a single header. Playback can only begin at the top of the stream, and it does not support variable data rates. The latter packs AAC data into frames with a header very similar to the MPEG-1 header format. It supports variable data rates and has header data embedded among the frame data between synchronization words.

Profiles

There are three profiles in AAC with differing levels of complexity. They are the *low complexity profile*, which has no prediction tool, limited TNS tool, the *scalable sampling rate profile*, which is similar but with an additional gain control block, and the *main profile*, which is less common and supports all compression blocks.

Implementing AAC

Each of the components in AAC is slightly different from its MP3 counterpart. However, they are similar enough for this section to merely highlight the changes between them and the impact on implementation.

Intel IPP contains enough functions to optimize the bulk, by time, of an AAC encoder and decoder. The most computationally intensive blocks of AAC encoder and decoder pipeline are covered by Intel IPP functionality. Intel IPP is most valuable in the filter bank, quantization, and Huffman coding.

Figure 7.8 shows a diagram of AAC coding, highlighting the main differences from MP3. This section explains the AAC blocks, with particular attention to changes, and the Intel IPP functions that support them in more detail.

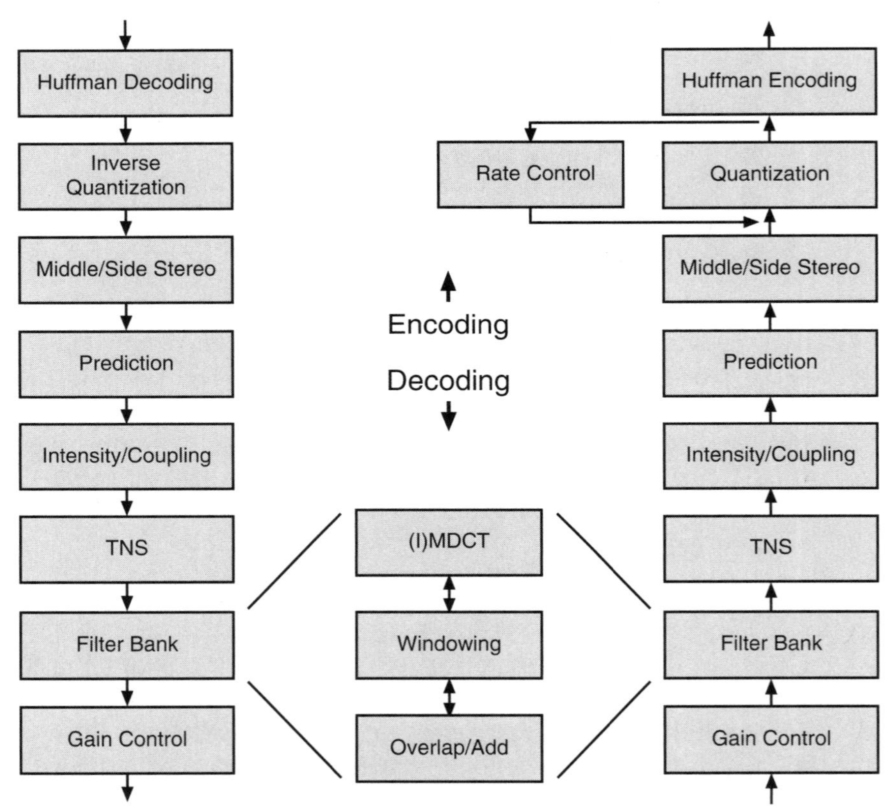

Figure 7.8 Components for AAC Encode and Decode

Huffman Coding

Intel IPP provides Huffman encoding and decoding functions for decoding blocks of coefficients. There is no translation performed for control codes, although the decoding functions extract control codes from the stream.

AAC Huffman coding is organized somewhat differently. It supports more modes for encoding and decoding, including coding of one, two, or four elements at a time. The functions supporting Huffman encoding for AAC are completely different from those for MP3. There are three encoding functions: `ippsEncodeBlock_1tuple_VLC`, which encodes a single element from the sequence, `ippsEncodeBlock_2tuple_VLC`, which encodes two elements and `ippsEncodeBlock_4tuple_VLC`, which encodes four. Figure 7.9 shows these functions in use.

```
for (sect_counter = 0;  sect_counter < pSectData->sect_num;
    sect_counter ++)
{
    sect_end += pSectData->sect_len[sect_counter];
    data_end  = pData->sfb_offset[sect_end];
    sect_cb   = pSectData->sect_cb[sect_counter];

    switch(cb_type[sect_cb])
    {
    case 0:
    case 1:
        ippsEncodeBlock_4tuple_VLC_16s(
            &pData->x_quant[data_begin],
            (data_end-data_begin),
            pData->pHuffTables->internal_huff_tables[sect_cb],
            &pBS->pCurrent_dword,&pBS->nBit_offset);
        break;
    case 2:
    case 3:
    case 4:
        ippsEncodeBlock_2tuple_VLC_16s(
            &pData->x_quant[data_begin],
            (data_end-data_begin),
            pData->pHuffTables->internal_huff_tables[sect_cb],
            &pBS->pCurrent_dword,&pBS->nBit_offset);
        break;
    }

    data_begin = data_end;
...
```

Figure 7.9 Huffman Encoding in AAC

The functions that support rate control by determining the final size of bit stream for each of these "tuples" are ippsCountBits_1tuple_VLC, ippsCountBits_2tuple_VLC, and ippsCountBits_4tuple_VLC. Both use the tables created by ippsBuildHET_VLC; be careful not to confuse this with ippsBuildHET.

The same decoding functions are used regardless of how the elements are grouped. For decoding, there is overlap with the MP3 functions. The function ippsDecodeVLC decodes one code, which may be one, two, or four elements. The function ippsDecodeVLC_Block decodes a code block using a non-escape Huffman table; the function ippsDecodeVLC_AACESCBlock decodes a block of codes from a table with escapes, which encode values greater than 15. Building the tables for AAC is the same as building them for MP3.

Quantization and Inverse Quantization

The quantization functions ippsPow34_32f, ippsPow43_16s32f, ippsCalcSF_16s32f, and ippsApplySF_32f_I are tailored exactly for use in AAC quantization. Figure 7.10 lists the function apply_scale_factors from the AAC decoder sample.

In this example, there are two branches. If the window is long, containing 36 samples, the entire window is scaled at once. If there are multiple short windows, three scaling vectors are applied, one for each window.

```
void
apply_scale_factors(sAACDecoderContext*DC,
    sIndividual_channel_stream* pStream)
{
    …
    if (pStream->is_window_long)
    {
        ippsPow43_16s32f(pStream->spectrum,
            DC->spectrum[DC->real_channel_num],LEN_SPECTRUM);
        ippsCalcSF_16s32f(pSFData->sf[0], SF_OFFSET, real_sf,
            pStream->ics_info.max_sfb);
        apply_offset_window = DC->apply_offset_long_window;
        ippsApplySF_32f_I(DC->spectrum[DC->real_channel_num],
            real_sf, apply_offset_window,
            pStream->ics_info.max_sfb);
    }
    else
    {

        ippsPow43_16s32f(pStream->spectrum,
```

```
                tmp_spectrum,LEN_SPECTRUM);
            for (real_w = 0, g = 0;
                 g < pStream->num_window_groups; g ++)
            {
                ippsCalcSF_16s32f(pSFData->sf[g], SF_OFFSET,
                    real_sf, pStream->ics_info.max_sfb);
                for (i = 0; i < pStream->ics_info.max_sfb+1; i++)
                {
                    real_short_apply_offset[i] =
                        DC->apply_offset_short_window[i]*
                        pStream->window_group_length[g];
                }
                ippsApplySF_32f_I(tmp_spectrum + real_w*128,
                    real_sf, real_short_apply_offset,
                    pStream->ics_info.max_sfb);
                real_w += pStream->window_group_length[g];
            }
            deinterleave(DC,pStream,tmp_spectrum,
                DC->spectrum[DC->real_channel_num]);

        }
    }
```

Figure 7.10 Scaling Code from AAC Decoder Sample

Mid/Side Stereo Coding

In AAC, the mid/side stereo coding is asymmetric. The formulae for decoding are:

$$left = middle + side$$

$$right = middle - side$$

The formulae for encoding are:

$$middle = \frac{(left + right)}{2}$$

$$side = \frac{(left - right)}{2}$$

Prediction

The new prediction module in AAC is only supported in the main profile. The module is used to represent stationary or semistationary parts of an audio signal. Instead of repeating such information for sequential windows, a simple repeat instruction can be passed.

Intensity / Coupling

Intensity implements generalized joint intensity stereo coding between both channels of a channel pair so that channel spectra can be shared across channel boundaries. It can perform a down-mix of one sound object into the stereo image.

Temporal Noise Shaping

Temporal noise shaping (TNS) is a new block in AAC intended to increase the quality of low-bit-rate audio, particularly speech. It controls the temporal shape of the quantization noise within each window of the transform by applying a filter to parts of the spectral data of each channel.

Filter bank

Instead of a two-stage filter bank, AAC has a single filter bank comprised of an MDCT and windowing. The windows, blocks, and options are akin to those in MP3. Figure 7.11 shows how the Intel IPP MDCT and multiplication can be combined into an AAC filter bank for long windows.

The last step in the filter bank is the addition of overlapping windowed segments.

```
if (DC->is_window_long[i])
{
    N = 2048;
    ippsMDCTInv_32f(DC->spectrum[i],DC->samples[i],
        DC->pIMDCTSpecLong,DC->pIMDCTBuffer);
    if (DC->window_sequence[i] ==
        ONLY_LONG_SEQUENCE)
    {
        if (DC->old_window_shape[i] == 0)
        {
            ippsMul_32f_I(DC->sin_long_wnd_table,
                DC->samples[i], N / 2);
        }
        else
        {
            ippsMul_32f_I(DC->KBD_long_wnd_table,
```

```
                    DC->samples[i], N / 2);
        }

        if (DC->window_shape[i] == 1)
        {
            ippsMul_32f_I(
                &DC->KBD_long_wnd_table[N / 2],
                &DC->samples[i][N / 2], N / 2);
        }
        else
        {
            ippsMul_32f_I(
                &DC->sin_long_wnd_table[N / 2],
                &DC->samples[i][N / 2], N / 2);
        }
    }
…

// Overlap-add
for (k = 0; k < N / 2; k++)
{
    DC->samples[i][k] +=
        DC->prev_samples[i][k + N / 2];
}
```

Figure 7.11 Filter Bank for AAC

Gain Control

Gain control reconstructs the time waveform through the gain control tool's filter bank. Only the SSR profile supports gain control.

Other Topics

Intel IPP supports other audio and speech codecs than those described here. There is some overlap in the Intel IPP functions that support these other codecs, but the samples showing how to implement each codec are separate. The other codecs supported in Intel IPP 4.0 are:

- AC-3 decoding
- Integer MP3
- MPEG-4 TwinVQ encoder and decoder
- Many speech coders: G.722, G.723, G.726, G.728, G.729, GSM/AMR and GSM/FR

Refer to the samples information and download page of the Intel IPP Web site (Intel 2003a) for further details and to download these samples.

Further Reading

Pan (1995) covers MP3 at the block level. Brandenburg, the creator of MP3, compares and contrasts MP3 and AAC, also at the block level (1999).

Chapter 8

Image Processing

The Intel® Integrated Performance Primitives (Intel® IPP) imaging functions are designed to hide within new or existing objects. Often, the arguments required to specify imaging operations or the code required to calculate those arguments can be tricky and involved. On the other hand, parameters and objects at the next level up can be clean and comprehensible. And many of the operations, such as calculating bounding boxes and handling edge effects, only need to be written once.

This chapter examines the imaging model, with a particular emphasis on wrapping image data and simple image functions in C++ objects. The key calculations for image allocation and parameterization are presented. The imaging functions follow a uniform set of conventions, facilitating both comprehension of the arguments and design of object layers.

Later chapters explain particular Intel IPP imaging functions in more detail. Chapter 9 demonstrates filtering and geometric functions. Chapter 10 covers functions for image and video coding, such as JPEG. Chapter 12 includes a section on computer vision functions.

Images in Intel® Integrated Performance Primitives (Intel® IPP)

This first section explains the model of images supported by Intel IPP functions, in particular, the parameters used to describe Intel IPP images. These parameters, along with the function descriptors, must specify the layout of the image in memory. Each function needs to be told or be able to calculate the location of the start of each row of the image, the width of those rows, the number of rows, and the size and data type of each pixel.

Particular issues that constrain the parameter scheme include:

- Alignment of memory for performance
- Operating on sub-images
- Functions with different source and destination sizes
- Functions with different origins for source and destination

This section begins to explain how that information is provided to Intel IPP functions and how the first two of these features are supported. Chapter 9 will explain in detail how the last two bullet points are handled in Intel IPP.

Image Definition and Rectangle of Interest

One of the design principles of Intel IPP was that redundancy in the function arguments should be kept at a minimum. Redundant arguments can conflict, and conflicting arguments lead to unpredictable or undefined behavior. This philosophy is reflected in the parameterization of images used in most Intel IPP imaging functions. A full image definition would be a pointer, size, memory stride, and rectangle. But most Intel IPP image functions take fewer than that, accepting only the arguments necessary to minimally specify how many pixels to process and where they are. A typical function is `Add`:

```
IppStatus ippiAdd_32f_C3R(
      const Ipp32f* pSrc1, int src1Step,
      const Ipp32f* pSrc2, int src2Step,
      Ipp32f* pDst, int dstStep,
      IppiSize roiSize);
```

In this argument list, each image is specified by a pointer that indicates the start of the data and a memory stride or "step" argument. A size for each image would be redundant, since all the function needs is the number of lines to process and the number of pixels per line. Instead of each image having a size, the size of the operation is specified once by the `roiSize` parameter. The rectangle from the two sources and written to the destination is the same size for each image, since each source pixel affects only one destination pixel, and vice-versa.[1] This region is called the *rectangle of interest* (ROI).

Most Intel IPP image functions, including `Add`, above, support ROIs. The ROI acts like a stencil; only data inside the ROI can be read or written. The ROI region is treated, in most cases, as an entire image. Each image must provide a rectangle of memory that is at least the size of the ROI.

The step parameter sets the number of bytes between successive lines in the image. Because it is individual for each image, the images may be larger than the ROI and still be part of the same operation. The step parameter then indicates to the function how wide the image actually is.

Note

> Sizes, offsets, and most other arguments are expressed in pixels, but step arguments are always in bytes. The most common customer support issue for Intel IPP, at least on `ippi` functions, is accidentally putting step in pixels. In particular, putting the image width for the step argument, while tempting, will usually result in an `ippStsStepErr` or a memory exception. The step in bytes is at least three times the width in pixels for an RGB image.
>
> It is essential that step be in bytes since the memory buffer width is not always an even number of pixels.

Figure 8.1 illustrates these arguments.

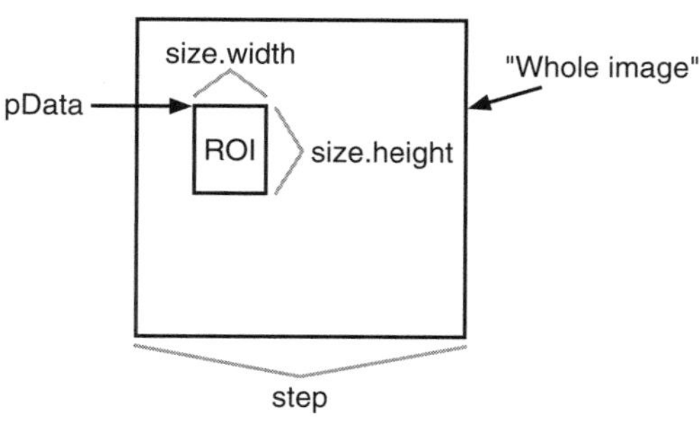

Figure 8.1 Parameters Defining an Image

[1] I refer to operations for which each pixel in the destination maps to one pixel in the source as "point" operations, in contrast to "neighborhood" operations such as filters.

If the ROI fills the entire image, then the `pData` pointer is set to the beginning of the image in memory, for example, `pDataStart`. The fields of the `size` structure are the size of the image. The `step` is the width times the number of channels[2] plus padding.

If the origin of the ROI is not the beginning of the image, then the `pData` argument needs to be calculated. To offset the pointer from the origin by `(xOffset, yOffset)` calculate:

```
pData = pDataStart + numChannels*xOffset + step*yOffset
```

This assumes one-byte pointers, such as an `Ipp8u*`. If the pointer is to a multiple-byte format, you need to divide the third term by the number of bytes per pixel per channel, since the compiler will interpret the number added to the pointer the same way as an index, as a quantity of elements, not bytes. This calculation recurs often in code using Intel IPP, and any image object using Intel IPP should include it.

The step parameter can also be used to pad the image for alignment. Due to cache and other memory concerns, most Intel architecture processors exhibit a significant performance benefit if every scan line starts on an 8-, 16-, or 32-byte boundary, depending on the processor. This alignment requires that the starting pointer of the image be aligned to such a boundary, but it also requires that the number of bytes in each line is a multiple of 8, 16, or 32. In order to force that alignment, most images require extra bytes on the end of each line to extend the width in bytes to the next boundary.

Figure 8.2 shows these parameters as they are used for alignment.

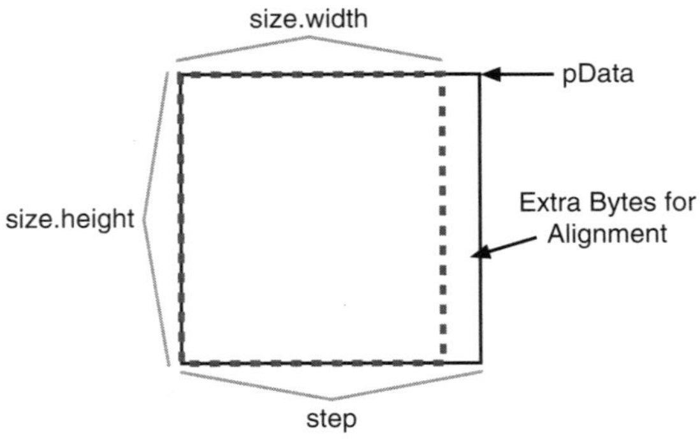

Figure 8.2 Image Parameters Used to Pad for Alignment

[2] See Chapter 2 for an explanation of channels and other IPP image options.

There are some exceptions to this parameterization of the image. Some functions take as arguments a size or even an explicit rectangle for each image. There are also some for which the ROI does not operate exactly like a stencil. Most of the exceptions are among the geometric operations. The assumption that the source and destination images are the same shape does not hold for geometric operations. Geometric operations and their parameters are discussed in Chapter 9.

Also, some functions don't take an ROI. These functions are not very common. They have no "R" in the name, and are generally fixed-size functions like `ippiDCT8x8`.

Allocation, Initialization, and Copying

Intel IPP has allocation functions just for images that make alignment easier. These functions take as arguments the width and height of the image in pixels and return the memory stride in bytes. The exact amount of memory allocated isn't known until after the call; then it can be calculated as

```
memSize = stride * size.height;
```

Copy functions follow this argument sequence, essentially the same as the `Add` function above:

- `pSrc, srcStride` - source data pointer and stride
- `pDst, dstStride` - destination data pointer and stride
- `size` - size of the operation
- other arguments, if any

Note that, as with `Add` and most other image functions, there is only one size and that size is the size of the rectangle copied. The function is not told whether either of the images is larger than the rectangle to be copied. There is no redundancy in the arguments, which means that there is less risk of providing incompatible arguments, but also means that there is no safety net. If the `size` argument exceeds the extent of the memory of either image, a memory exception could occur.

Figure 8.3 below shows the use of memory allocation and copy functions to copy several rectangles of varying sizes.

```
int main(int argc, char *argv[])
{
      IppiSize size = {320, 240};

      // Allocation and initialization
      int stride;
      Ipp8u* pSrc = ippiMalloc_8u_C3(size.width, size.height,
            &stride);
      ippiImageJaehne_8u_C3R(pSrc, stride, size);
      ipView_8u_C3R(pSrc, stride, size, "Source image", 0);
      int dstStride;
      Ipp8u* pDst = ippiMalloc_8u_C3(size.width, size.height,
            &dstStride);

      // Copy 1: Entire image
      ippiCopy_8u_C3R(pSrc, stride, pDst, dstStride, size);
      ipView_8u_C3R(pDst, dstStride, size, "Destination image
            1", 0);

      // Copy 2: Smaller ROI
      IppiSize ROISize = { size.width/2, size.height/2 };
      ippiCopy_8u_C3R(pSrc, stride, pDst, dstStride, ROISize);
      ipView_8u_C3R(pDst, dstStride, ROISize, "Destination
            image, small", 0);

      // Copy 3: Smaller ROI and offset source pointer
      IppiPoint srcOffset = { size.width/4, size.height/4 };
      ippiCopy_8u_C3R(pSrc + srcOffset.x*3 +
            srcOffset.y*stride, stride, pDst, dstStride,
            ROISize);
      ipView_8u_C3R(pDst, dstStride, ROISize, "Destination
            image, small & shifted", 1);

      return 0;
}
```

Figure 8.3 Simple Code for Allocating, Initializing, and Copying an Image

The code first allocates the source and destination images. The function `ippiMalloc_8u_C3` first sets the stride to the smallest multiple of 32 that is greater than `width*numChannels` or 320*3; in this case, the stride should be exactly 320*3 = 960. Then the function allocates `stride*height`, or 960*240, bytes, and returns the pointer to the data on the stack and the stride in the third argument.

If the memory allocation function were allocating pixels larger than one byte—for example, the function `ippiMalloc_32f_C3`, which allocates 32-bit floating-point pixels—then the function would set the stride to the smallest multiple of 32 that is greater than `width * numChannels * bytesPerChannel`, or `width*3*4`.

The `ImageJaehne` function allocates a convenient test image, which is shown in Figure 8.4. This image is interesting for several reasons:

- It contains many frequencies, just as the Jaehne vector does.
- The rapid alternation of light and dark is very sensitive to filters and geometric operations. Visible patterns are produced by most modifications.
- Like an easy jigsaw puzzle, the source location of a piece of the image can be determined from the shape and frequency of the waves.

Another reasonable option for test images is `ImageRamp`.

The first copy is a straightforward copy of the entire image. The result is identical to the original image, although as noted before, the size of memory could be different if the strides are different. This is most likely to happen when the memory for one image is allocated outside of Intel IPP.

The function `ipView_8u_C3R` is not a library function; rather, it is a simple tool that displays a single image in a dialog box. The call is shown in the source code listing because it indicates exactly what image has been displayed, when, and with what parameters. The images generated are those found in Figure 8.4 and subsequent figures.

The second copy is half the size in each dimension of the first copy. The result is placed in the same memory, starting at `pDst`. In fact, since the stride and the source pointer are the same, and only the size differs, the image section is placed in the exact location that held that corner previously. The result is image b), below. Note that the copy affects the lower-left corner rather than the upper-left corner because this is a bottom-up bitmap. The origin is in the lower left.

The third copy offsets the source pointer but not the destination. The source pointer is offset by (number of channels) * (X offset) + (stride) * (Y offset). In this case, the source is offset by one-fourth of the image so the center of the image is copied. Since the destination pointer is not offset, this information is copied into the corner of the destination image.

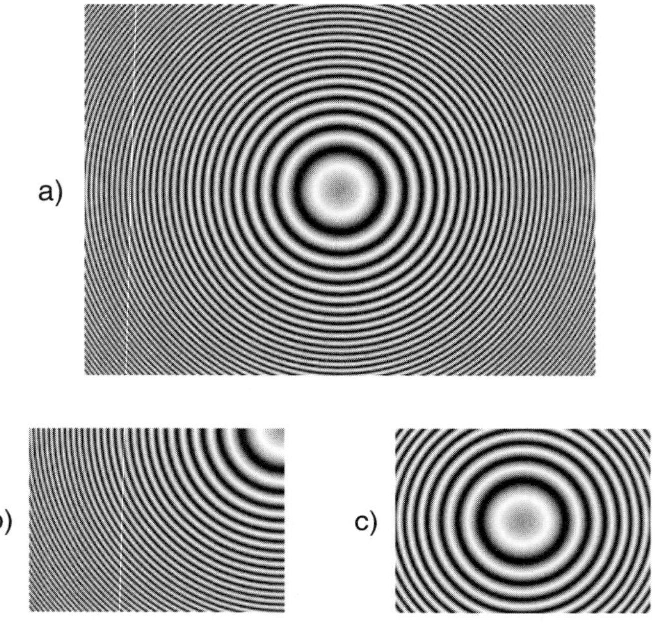

Figure 8.4 Images Generated by `ipView_8u_C3R` Tool

In addition to rectangles of interest, there are also *mask regions of interest* for which the region is set on a pixel-by-pixel basis. Certain image functions, those with the `M` descriptor, support these directly. Further explanation and a `Mask` class follow the `Image` object discussion.

Image Objects

The Intel IPP imaging functions are primitives, and as such, they take very raw arguments. These arguments often require more setup and calculation than `Copy` did above. The advantage of writing a higher-level layer on top of these primitives is that the layer can implement that complexity once, then hide it in an object with straightforward arguments. The Intel IPP interface was designed with the assumption that the primitives will be wrapped in such a higher-level layer, perhaps but not necessarily C++. The primitives are therefore agnostic to this layer, and so are as nonspecific as possible without sacrificing performance, reliability, or basic usability.

This and subsequent sections will demonstrate one way to wrap Intel IPP imaging functions in an object-oriented programming (OOP) framework. I expect that the reader will adapt these classes according to personal needs, or read the examples and adapt individual methods or equations to fit in existing image classes.

The `Image8u` Object

Figure 8.5 is the declaration of the `Image8u` object that encapsulates the Intel IPP image parameters for `Ipp8u` data. The goal of this object is to do the math required to manipulate pointers and image sizes. It produces exactly the arguments needed for Intel IPP functions, starting with the more-intuitive arguments that are passed to it. Ideally, this math should be invisible to both the caller and the later classes that implement image operations.

The class has four data members: the data pointer, the memory stride, the size of the image, and the number of channels. The number of channels should be one, three, or four. The names of these private data members, and those of all other private members, end in an underscore to differentiate them from arguments and local variables.

The member functions provide member data access, memory allocation, copying and cloning, and shifting and clipping for ROI. There are also member functions to load the image from a bitmap (.bmp) file and display the image on the screen. Each of these is described in more detail later.

```
class Image8u
{
private:
    Ipp8u* pData_;
    int stride_;
    IppiSize size_;
    int channelCount_;

public:
//  Constructors
    Image8u();
    Image8u(IppiSize size, int channelCount);
    Image8u(int w, int h, int channelCount);
    Image8u(const Image8u* pImage);
```

```
//  Destructor
    ~Image8u();

//  Initialization
    int InitAlloc(int w, int h, int channelCount);
    int InitAlloc(IppiSize size, int channelCount);
    int Alloc();
    void Free();

//  Accessors
    virtual IppiSize GetSize() const;
    virtual int GetStride() const;
    virtual const Ipp8u* GetConstData() const;
    virtual const Ipp8u* GetConstData(int x, int y) const;
    virtual Ipp8u* GetData() const;
    virtual Ipp8u* GetData(int x, int y) const;

    int GetChannelCount() const;

//  Copy Methods
    IppStatus CopyFrom_R(const Ipp8u* pSrcData, int srcW,
            int srcH, int srcStride, int dstX, int dstY);
    IppStatus CopyFrom(const Ipp8u* pSrcData, int srcStride);
    IppStatus CopyFrom_R(const Ipp8u* pSrcData,
            IppiSize srcSize, int srcStride,
            IppiPoint dstOffset);
    IppStatus CopyFrom(const Image8u* pSrcImage);
    IppStatus CopyFrom_R(const Image8u* pSrcImage,
            IppiSize srcSize, IppiPoint dstOffset);
    IppStatus CopyFrom_R(const Image8u* pSrcImage,
            int srcW, int srcH, int srcStride,
            int dstX, int dstY);

    IppStatus CopySettings(const Image8u* pImage);
    IppStatus Clone(const Image8u* pImage);

    // Utilities
    int View(int isModal=1) const;
    int View(const char* pTitle, int isModal) const;

    void Zero();
    int LoadBMP(const char* pFilename);
```

```
    virtual int CheckCompat(const Image8u* pImage) const;
    virtual IppiSize GetOverlap(IppiSize size) const;
    virtual IppiRect GetOverlap(IppiRect rect) const;
    virtual IppiRect GetOverlap(IppiRect rect1,
            IppiRect rect2) const;
    virtual IppiSize GetOverlap(const Image8u* pImage) const;
    virtual IppiRect GetOverlap(const Image8u* pImage,
            IppiPoint startIndex) const;

};
```

Figure 8.5 Class Declaration for `Image8u`

This class could be placed in a template in order to allow one set of code to handle multiple data types: `Image<8u>`, `Image<16s>`, and `Image<32f>`. Modifying this class here would complicate the class, so the `Image8u` class is kept as a single-type class. Hopefully, the extension to templates is obvious enough.

Figure 8.6 shows the implementations of the member functions for initialization and allocation of the image class. The basic protocol is as follows: if the data pointer `pData_` is nonzero, the image data can be assumed to have been allocated for the correct size; if it is zero, image data has not been allocated. When the image size is changed, the image is re-initialized and the data reallocated so that the image remains valid. The `Alloc`, `Free`, and other functions are public so a user of the class can control this directly.

Note that the stride variable is always set when `ippiMalloc` is called, even when the `CopySettings` method is invoked. Thus the stride may be different from that of a copied image that is otherwise identical. The stride can be considered a characteristic of the allocated memory rather than of the image, more like the data pointer than the image size.

```
Image8u::Image8u(int w, int h, int channelCount) : pData_(0)
{
    InitAlloc(w,h,channelCount);
}

Image8u::Image8u(IppiSize size, int channelCount) : pData_(0)
{
    InitAlloc(size.width,size.height,channelCount);
}
```

```
// Initialization

int Image8u::InitAlloc(int w, int h, int channelCount)
{
    Free();

    size_.width = w;
    size_.height = h;
    channelCount_ = channelCount;

    return Alloc();
}

int Image8u::Alloc()
{
    if (pData_) return 0;

    switch (channelCount_)
    {
    case 1:
        pData_ = ippiMalloc_8u_C1(size_.width,
          size_.height, &stride_);
        break;
    case 2:
        pData_ = ippiMalloc_8u_C2(size_.width,
          size_.height, &stride_);
        break;
    case 3:
        pData_ = ippiMalloc_8u_C3(size_.width,
          size_.height, &stride_);
        break;
    case 4:
        pData_ = ippiMalloc_8u_C4(size_.width,
          size_.height, &stride_);
        break;
    default:
        pData_ = 0;
        break;
    }
    return (pData_ == 0);
}

void Image8u::Free()
{
    if (pData_) ippiFree(pData_);
    pData_ = 0;
}

IppStatus Image8u::CopySettings(const Image8u* pImage)
```

```
{
    Free();

    channelCount_ = pImage->GetChannelCount();
    size_.height = pImage->GetSize().height;
    size_.width = pImage->GetSize().width;

    Alloc();

    return ippStsOk;
}

IppStatus Image8u::Clone(const Image8u* pImage)
{
    CopySettings(pImage);
    return CopyFrom(pImage);
}
```

Figure 8.6 Initialization and Allocation for `Image8u`

Figure 8.7 lists the code for the `CopyFrom_R` method. This method copies all or part of a data array into the current `Image8u` object (i.e. `this`). All the other copy methods in `Image8u` use this function to perform the actual copy after converting or supplying extra arguments.

The arguments `dstX` and `dstY` are the offsets of the beginning of the ROI from the origin of the destination image. The first call finds the data pointer to the beginning of the ROI using the very useful `GetData(x,y)` function, described below. Nothing indicates whether the source data pointer is the actual origin of a memory image; the source data pointer may have already been offset. The size of the ROI is calculated as the intersection of the source and destination sizes.

The switch statement checks the number of channels and calls the appropriate Intel IPP image copy function. Almost all Intel IPP functions support 1-channel, 3-channel, or 4-channel images exclusively, so any other channel count here results in an error. This function uses the `IppStatus` codes to report that error.

```
//  Copy Methods
IppStatus Image8u::CopyFrom_R(const Ipp8u* pSrcData, int srcW,
   int srcH, int srcStride, int dstX, int dstY )
{
   Ipp8u* pDstP = GetData(dstX, dstY);

   IppiSize roi;
   roi.width = IPP_MIN(srcW, GetSize().width-dstX);
   roi.height = IPP_MIN(srcH, GetSize().height-dstY);

   IppStatus st;

   switch (channelCount_)
   {
   case 1:
       st = ippiCopy_8u_C1R(pSrcData, srcStride, pDstP,
        GetStride(), roi);
       break;
   case 3:
       st = ippiCopy_8u_C3R(pSrcData, srcStride,
        pDstP, GetStride(), roi);
       break;
   case 4:
       st = ippiCopy_8u_C4R(pSrcData, srcStride,
        pDstP, GetStride(), roi);
       break;
   default:
       st = ippStsBadArgErr;
   break;
   }
   return st;
}
```

Figure 8.7 The `CopyFrom_R` Method of `Image8u`

Figure 8.8 illustrates the variables used in this function, as they would apply to a pair of images.

The code has no way to know where the start of the "whole" source image is, but it doesn't matter. It is sufficient to read and write `srcW` pixels, then skip `stride - srcW * channelCount_` bytes to the next scan line.

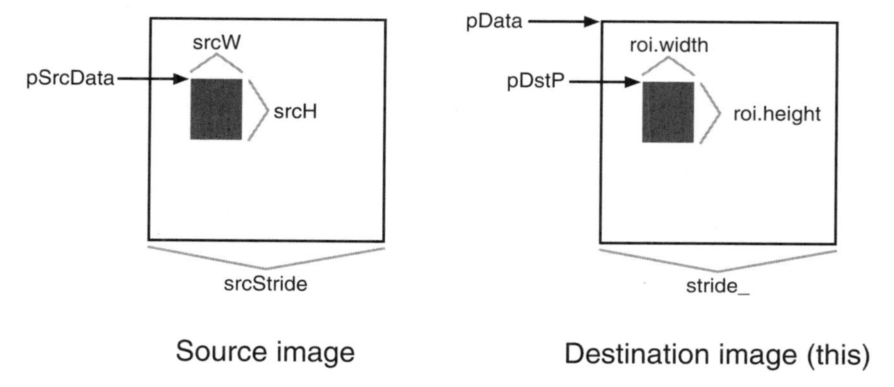

Figure 8.8 Illustration of Arguments for `Image8u::CopyFrom_R` Method

Note that the variables `roi.width` and `roi.height` are calculated in such a way that they won't exceed the boundaries of the source ROI or the destination image. The variable `pDstP` is also calculated by the function `GetData(x,y)`, which replaces the calculation:

```
pDst = GetData() + dstX * GetChannelCount() +
    dstY * GetStride();
```

This function, listed in Figure 8.9 with other accessor functions, provides a data pointer shifted to a particular pixel in the image.

This figure shows another useful function, `GetOverlap(rect)`. This function performs a sort of clipping, calculating the overlap between the current image and a rectangle. For the purposes of understanding the location of the rectangle, it assumes that the current image starts at (0,0), since there is no other starting offset information for the current image. Another overloaded member might be implemented that took an offset into the current image.

`IppiRect` contains four fields:

```
typedef struct {
    int x;
    int y;
    int width;
    int height;
} IppiRect;
```

These two functions can be used like this:

```
IppiRect rect = im.GetOverlap(roi);
IppiSize size = { rect.width, rect.height };
ippiFoo(im.GetData(rect.x, rect.y), im.GetStride(),
   size);
```

The definition for `Image8u` contains several other overloaded `GetData` functions and `GetOverlap` functions. These are omitted because, for the most part, they reformat the data then pass the results into the core functions in the figure.

```
IppiSize Image8u::GetSize() const { return size_; }

int Image8u::GetStride() const { return stride_; }

...

Ipp8u* Image8u::GetData() const { return pData_; }

Ipp8u* Image8u::GetData(int x, int y) const
{
    return pData_ + x*channelCount_ + y*stride_;
}

...

IppiRect Image8u::GetOverlap(IppiRect rect) const
{
    IppiRect oRect;
    oRect.x = IPP_MAX(0, rect.x);
    oRect.y = IPP_MAX(0, rect.y);
    oRect.width =
        IPP_MIN(GetSize().width, rect.width+rect.x);
    oRect.height =
        IPP_MIN(GetSize().height, rect.height+rect.y);
    return oRect;
}
...
```

Figure 8.9 Methods Supporting Data Access and ROI for `Image8u`

Two other class methods bear explanation. The function `View` opens up a dialog box, using the `ipView_8u` tool function described above. If the second argument is zero, the function launches a new thread for the box and return; otherwise, it waits until the box is closed.

The method `LoadBMP` loads a bitmap (`.bmp`) file into the image, setting the image parameters appropriately. The file and image formats of bitmap files are generally easy to adapt to the image format and Intel IPP image parameters. The function does not handle the versions of the format that are not easily adapted.

The `ROI` Class

The `Image8u` class above assumes a separately specified rectangle of interest, so it always provides access to the entire image. It should be possible to make an object that appears to be an image but also encapsulates the ROI concept. Deriving this ROI class from the image class makes it usable as an `Image8u`, but overriding some members automatically provides access to an ROI of the image rather than the entire image.

This class is not fully implemented here, since there are too many possible variants, but a sketch of this class is listed in Figure 8.10. This code overrides the `GetSize()` and `GetData()` methods so that instead of the image size and pointer, they return the size of the ROI and the start of the ROI, respectively. If the internal ROI is set, `GetData(x,y)` adds to the offset provided before passing on the call to the `GetData` of the parent class.

```
class ROI : public Image8u
{
private:
    int isROI_
    IppiRect roi_;
    ...

public:
    ROI();
    ROI(IppiSize size, int channelCount);
    ROI(const Image8u* pImage, IppiRect roi);
    ...

    virtual IppiSize GetSize() const;
    virtual const Ipp8u* GetConstData() const;
    virtual const Ipp8u* GetConstData(int x, int y) const;
    virtual Ipp8u* GetData();
    virtual Ipp8u* GetData(int x, int y);

    void SetROI(IppiRect roi);
    ...
```

```
};

//--------------------

void ROI::SetROI(IppiRect roi) { roi_ = roi; isROI_ = 1;}

IppiSize ROI::GetSize() const
{
    if (isROI_)
    {
        IppiSize size = { roi_.width, roi_.height };
        return size;
    }
    else
        return Image8u::GetSize();
}

Ipp8u* ROI::GetData()
{
    if (isROI_)
        return Image8u::GetData(roi_.x, roi_.y);
    else
        return Image8u::GetData();
}

Ipp8u* ROI::GetData(int x, int y)
{
    if(isROI_)
        return Image8u::GetData(roi_.x+x, roi_.y+y);
    else
        return Image8u::GetData(x,y);
}
```

Figure 8.10 Partial Interface for an ROI Class

There are numerous issues to consider. This class will work as specified for functions such as `Image8u::CopyFrom_R`, as long as those functions only use the accessor functions `GetSize` and `GetData`, but there are multiple interpretations for other functions. Think about the desired behavior of methods such as `CopySettings`, `Clone`, and `LoadBMP`. Should `LoadBMP` overwrite the size of the existing ROI, or try to read the image into it? In a thorough implementation, each of these methods should probably be overridden.

For some derived operations such as geometric transforms, the ROI is treated as the entire image, so the start of the ROI is the coordinate system origin. For example, `ippiRotate`, which performs rotation about the origin, rotates the image around the corner of the ROI rather than the image. This might or might not be the desired behavior. For region operations such as filters, the data outside the ROI is ignored even if it provides a perfect border. This is probably not the desired behavior, and motivates a second set of accessors that probes the actual extent of the data. See the discussion on borders in the filter section of Chapter 9 for more detail.

Finally, depending on planned use, the image memory might be handled differently. For example, memory management might improve if the ROI object wrapped the image data or `Ipp8u` object by holding a copy of it, instead of just inheriting the image data from its parent. Also, multiple ROIs could exist for a single image, which might require a scheme for memory management, perhaps in `Image8u` itself, that includes a use-count or list.

The `Mask` Class

Another type of region of interest is the mask region of interest. A mask is a way of specifying individually for each pixel whether an operation should be performed on that pixel. It is implemented as a separate image of zero and nonzero elements that acts as a stencil, much as rectangles of interest do. If the mask pixel is nonzero, the operation is performed on the analogous image pixel; otherwise, the pixel is skipped. Sometimes, the operation is simply not performed on the source pixel, and sometimes the result of the operation is not written to the destination.

The most prominent function group that supports mask is `ippiCopy` with the descriptor `M`. The masks supported by `Copy` are 8-bit and 1-channel, even if the data is another size or multiple-channel. That means that all three-color channels of an RGB image will be treated the same by an Intel IPP mask function.

Several functions can generate these masks. Chief among them is `ippiCompare`. This function compares two images or an image and a constant and produces an 8-bit, 1-channel result compatible with `ippiCopy_*_*MR` functions. For images with more than one channel, the compare condition is considered true only if the comparison is true for all channels of a pixel.

Figure 8.11 shows a wrapper class for use with the copy-with-mask functions that supports generation of mask using these comparison functions.

The Mask class is derived from the Image8u class because it is an image, though restricted to one channel, and should support the same functionality. The class adds Compare functions to generate the mask with one of several compare operations, and adds the CopyWithMask functionality that is the *raison d'être* of the Mask class.

The private Compare_ functions are called by the public versions after some limited conversion of arguments. In Compare_(image1, image2, op), the images are first checked for compatibility, in this case having the same number of channels, and the size of the overlapping area is found. The math has been implemented previously so these steps take only three calls. Then the proper Intel IPP function is called. The ippiCompare_8u_C*R functions take two images and return the mask in a third; they perform one of five comparison operations as specified by the last argument, an IppCmpOp enumeration.

Since both functions are thin wrappers for Intel IPP functions, CopyWithMask_R looks very similar to Compare. It also has the same order of operations: check compatibility, get overlap, and operate. The copy is performed by one of the Intel IPP functions matching ippiCopy_8u_C*MR.

```
class Mask : public Image8u
{
private:
    int Compare_(const Image8u* pSrc1,
        const Image8u* pSrc2, IppCmpOp op);
    int Compare_(const Image8u* pSrc,
        Ipp8u threshold, IppCmpOp op);
    int Compare_(const Image8u* pSrc,
        Ipp8u* pThresholds, IppCmpOp op);

protected:

public:
    Mask();
    Mask(IppiSize size, int channelCount);
    Mask(int w, int h, int channelCount);
    Mask(const Image8u* pImage);

    ~Mask();
```

```
    int CreateByCompare_GT(const Image8u* pSrc1,
         const Image8u* pSrc2);
    int CreateByCompare_GTE(const Image8u* pSrc1,
         const Image8u* pSrc2);
    int CreateByCompare_EQ(const Image8u* pSrc1,
         const Image8u* pSrc2);

    int CreateByCompare_GT(const Image8u* pSrc,
         Ipp8u pThreshold);
    int CreateByCompare_GTE(const Image8u* pSrc,
         Ipp8u pThreshold);
    int CreateByCompare_LT(const Image8u* pSrc,
         Ipp8u pThreshold);
    int CreateByCompare_EQ(const Image8u* pSrc,
         Ipp8u pThreshold);

    int CreateByCompare_GT(const Image8u* pSrc,
         Ipp8u* pThresholds);
    int CreateByCompare_GTE(const Image8u* pSrc,
         Ipp8u* pThresholds);
    int CreateByCompare_LT(const Image8u* pSrc,
         Ipp8u* pThresholds);
    int CreateByCompare_EQ(const Image8u* pSrc,
         Ipp8u* pThresholds);

    int CopyWithMask(const Image8u* pSrc, Image8u* pDst);
    int CopyWithMask_R(const Image8u* pSrc, IppiRect srcROI,
         Image8u* pDst, IppiPoint dstOffset);
};

//----------------------------

int Mask::Compare_(const Image8u* pSrc1, const Image8u* pSrc2,
    IppCmpOp op)
{
    int st;
    if (st = pSrc1->CheckCompat(pSrc2)) return st;

    int nChannels = pSrc1->GetChannelCount();

    IppiSize size = GetOverlap(pSrc1->GetOverlap(pSrc2));
```

```
    if (nChannels == 1)
         st = (int)ippiCompare_8u_C1R(
           pSrc1->GetConstData(), pSrc1->GetStride(),
           pSrc2->GetConstData(), pSrc2->GetStride(),
           GetData(), GetStride(),
           size, op);
    else if (nChannels == 3)
         st = (int)ippiCompare_8u_C3R(
           pSrc1->GetConstData(), pSrc1->GetStride(),
           pSrc2->GetConstData(), pSrc2->GetStride(),
           GetData(), GetStride(),
           size, op);
    else if (nChannels == 4)
         st = (int)ippiCompare_8u_C4R(
           pSrc1->GetConstData(), pSrc1->GetStride(),
           pSrc2->GetConstData(), pSrc2->GetStride(),
           GetData(), GetStride(),
           size, op);
    else st = -1;

    return st;
}

int Mask::CreateByCompare_GT(const Image8u* pSrc1, const
    Image8u* pSrc2)
{
    return Compare_(pSrc1, pSrc2, ippCmpGreater);
}
...

int Mask::CopyWithMask_R(const Image8u* pSrc, IppiRect srcROI,
           Image8u* pDst, IppiPoint dstOffset)
{
    int st;
    if (st = pDst->CheckCompat(pSrc)) return st;

    IppiRect rect = GetOverlap(
         pSrc->GetOverlap(pDst,dstOffset),srcROI);
    IppiSize size = {rect.width, rect.height};
    if (pSrc->GetChannelCount()==1)
         st = (int)ippiCopy_8u_C1MR(
           pSrc->GetConstData(rect.x, rect.y),
           pSrc->GetStride(),
           pDst->GetData(rect.x, rect.y),
           pDst->GetStride(), size,
           GetData(rect.x, rect.y), GetStride());
    else if (pSrc->GetChannelCount()==3)
         st = (int)ippiCopy_8u_C3MR(
           pSrc->GetConstData(rect.x, rect.y),
```

```
        pSrc->GetStride(),
        pDst->GetData(rect.x, rect.y),
        pDst->GetStride(), size,
        GetData(rect.x, rect.y), GetStride());
    else if (pSrc->GetChannelCount()==4)
        st = (int)ippiCopy_8u_C4MR(
        pSrc->GetConstData(rect.x, rect.y),
        pSrc->GetStride(),
        pDst->GetData(rect.x, rect.y),
        pDst->GetStride(), size,
        GetData(rect.x, rect.y), GetStride());
    else st = -1;
    return st;
}
```

Figure 8.11 Class `Mask` and Some Methods

Figure 8.12 shows how this class can be used. This code uses the compare-against-constant version of `CreateByCompare`. If all three channels of a pixel in `image` are greater than the constant, in this case 128, then the mask is set to ones; otherwise, it is set to zero. Performing a compare based on one channel of a three-channel image can be done by comparing the image against (val,0,0), (0,val,0), or (0,0,val).

```
    Image8u image;
    if (image.LoadBMP(argv[1]))
        return -1;
    image.View(argv[1],0);

    Mask m(&image);
    m.CreateByCompare_GT(&image, 128);
    m.View("Mask",0);

    Image8u dstImage;
    dstImage.CopySettings(&image);
    dstImage.Zero();

    m.CopyWithMask(&image, &dstImage);

    dstImage.View("Masked Image", 1);
    return 0;
```

Figure 8.12 Using Class `Mask`

Figure 8.13 shows the source image, the mask that is the result of the compare, and the result of the copy. The background of the final image is set to black by the `dstImage.Zero()` call. The `CopyWithMask` call does not touch those pixels.

a) Source Image

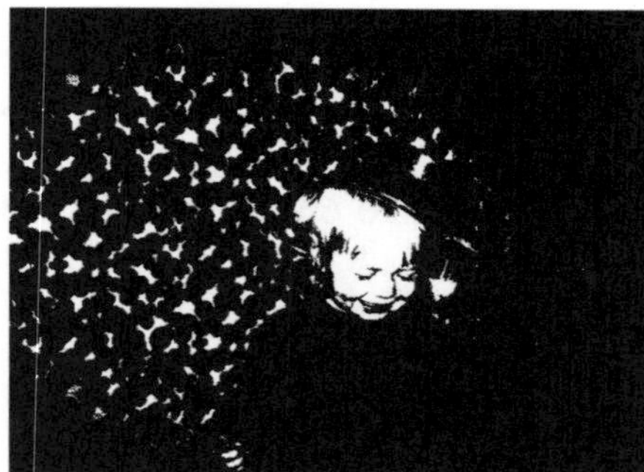

b) The Mask Resulting From `Compare`

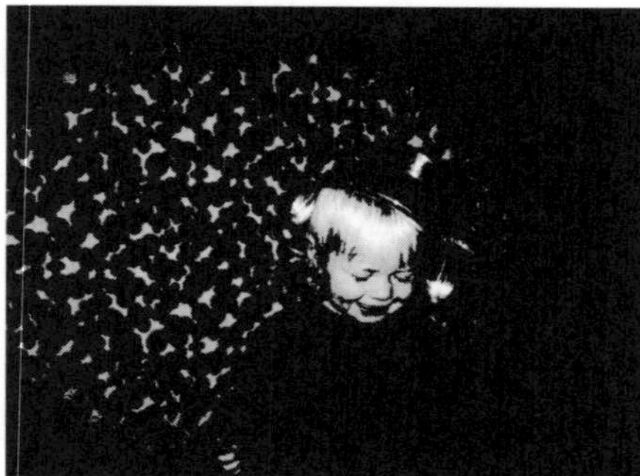

c) Result of `copywithmask`

Figure 8.13 Images Resulting from `Copy` and `Compare`

One possible extension to this class would be the `MaskedImage` class. Such a class could maintain both a masked version of the image and an unmasked one. The value is that the copy with mask need only be performed once and the result cached. In order to realize this class, the `GetData()` and `GetConstData()` methods could be modified so that any read or write to the image would be masked appropriately. A robust *and* efficient implementation would probably require a locking semaphore-like mechanism for the image data.

There are a few other functions that support the mask region of interest. The `Set` function supports mask, as does `Add` in some cases. Some computer vision functions also support masks.

Chapter 9

Image Filtering and Manipulation

The Intel® Integrated Performance Primitives (Intel® IPP) imaging function set covers the types of operations that are found in such imaging tools and applications as image and video editing, image and video compression, human-computer interface, and image analysis. Chief among these functions are those that filter images and those that transform them geometrically. This chapter explains these two major groups.

For each of these two function sets, the image model requires some expansion. The two sections in this chapter each start with an explanation of this expansion. Each section then contains several examples of classes that wrap Intel IPP functions and provide a number of key utility calculations.

The examples contained herein depend on the `Image8u` class developed in the previous chapter. The filter and transform classes take and return objects of that class and use the utilities that that image class provides.

Image Filtering

The same mathematical operations that produce filters in one-dimensional signals can be applied to two-dimensional images, generally by a simple expansion of the formula. Image filters can be designed and analyzed using the Fourier transform, and filters can be executed in the frequency domain or using convolution.

The differences in image filters are due to the nature of most images. The number of pixels in any dimension of a typical image is several hundred or a few thousand, in contrast to the hundreds of thousands of samples in even a short audio sample. Filters any larger than ten or twenty elements wide exhibit noticeable edge effects. As a result, filters for images tend to be smaller, at least in any one dimension

Further, frequency domain manipulation for sound is directly related to human perception of sound, but the same is not true for images. The frequency domain in which images are generally manipulated is frequency in space rather than frequency in time. While the sensors in the ear perceive temporal frequency directly, the sensors in the eye do not perceive spatial frequency at all; they measure an estimate of temporal frequency and interpret it as color. Perception of spatial frequency is a much higher-level phenomenon.

When an image filter manipulates images in the frequency domain, the results are not usually as directly correlated to the visual information as they are in audio. One consequence is that *ad hoc* filters are somewhat common in images. These filters are developed because they have intuitive results and obvious visual effects. The exact frequency domain effect is less relevant. Take, for example, the visual effect of the filter with taps { ¼, ½, ¼ } that was analyzed in Chapter 5. Its two-dimensional analog is:

$$\begin{bmatrix} \frac{1}{16} & \frac{1}{8} & \frac{1}{16} \\ \frac{1}{8} & \frac{1}{4} & \frac{1}{8} \\ \frac{1}{16} & \frac{1}{8} & \frac{1}{16} \end{bmatrix}$$

If it's not apparent, this filter is a weighted-average filter, the visual effect of which is to blur the image. The audio effect of a simple "blur" is not usually precise enough, but this blur operation models an image defocus well.

Rectangles of Interest and Borders

Image sizes, edges, and rectangles of interest (ROIs) are slightly more complicated for filter operations and other "neighborhood" operations. In contrast to "pixel" operations, for which each source pixel maps to one destination pixel and vice-versa, such functions use several source pixels to calculate each destination pixel. As described in Chapter 5, the trouble caused by the edges in the one-dimensional case is handled by circular convolution, artificial values in the delay line, and/or "infinitely" long signals. In the two-dimensional images, each of these has an analog.

Linear filtering in images is done by two-dimensional convolution, even if it is not referred to as such. Strictly, in convolution, a two-dimensional array of values, called a *kernel*, is flipped and passed over the two-dimensional image. At each pixel, every kernel element is multiplied against every corresponding neighborhood pixel. The sum of those products is the new pixel value. This two-dimensional convolution is exactly analogous to the one-dimensional convolution that is the core of one-dimensional linear filtering. Figure 9.1 illustrates a filter kernel, source image, and filter result.

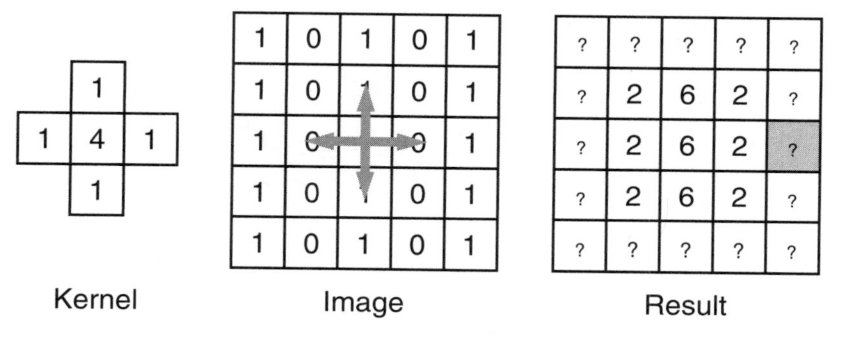

Figure 9.1 Illustration of an Image Filter

Not all filtering functions in Intel IPP flip the kernel. Frequently, it doesn't matter whether the kernel is flipped or not, since many image processing kernels are symmetric.

Many nonlinear filters depend on kernels, or at least kernel shapes, but the core operation of those filters is not convolution. Nonlinear functions in Intel IPP include `Min`, `Max`, `Median`, `Erode`, and `Dilate`.

From an implementation point of view, the tricky issue for image filters is the edge of the image. Look at the pixels filled with question marks in Figure 9.1. The reason those values are unknown is that they depend on unknown source data. Performing the convolution by hand, you can see that in the case of the highlighted pixel, the filter result is equal to 1*0 + 1*1 + 4*1 + 1*1 + 1**a pixel off the right side*. The question is how to interpret that pixel off the right side. Here are some considerations:

- The formula requires some value there, even if it is zero.
- The quality at the edge suffers noticeably if the values are zero, as can be seen in Figure 9.2.
- The performance of the code suffers noticeably if the edge is a special case.

Given these considerations, it is essential to address the edge of the image somehow.

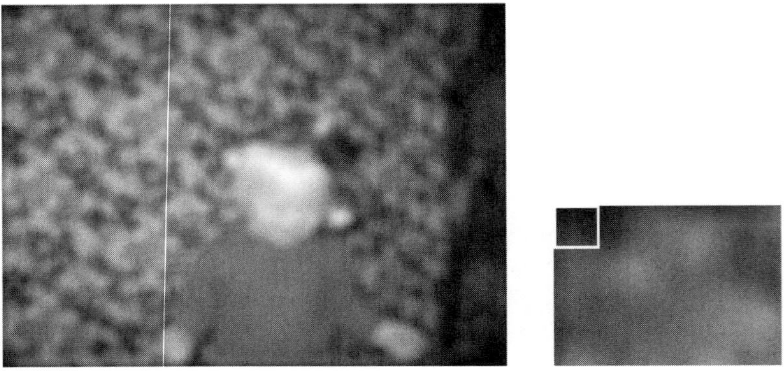

Figure 9.2 Filtering Effects at the Edge of the Image

There is one remaining filter parameter, the kernel anchor. What the illustration in Figure 9.1 does not show is that the *anchor* of the kernel, the point at which the filter result is written, may be shifted off the center. Some filter implementations allow the location of the anchor to be anywhere within the kernel. The anchor determines the offset of the output data and affects how much border is needed and where.

In Figure 9.3, the kernel is illustrated in two positions in an image, with the anchor, highlighted, placed slightly off-center. The dashed rectangle represents the data generated by the filter and its location relative to the source data. As long as the anchor is within the destination image, source data is needed everywhere the kernel touches. The actual size of the source image needed is a function only of the kernel size, but the anchor determines both the location of the destination data relative to the source data and the offset of the source data relative to the `pSrc` pointer.

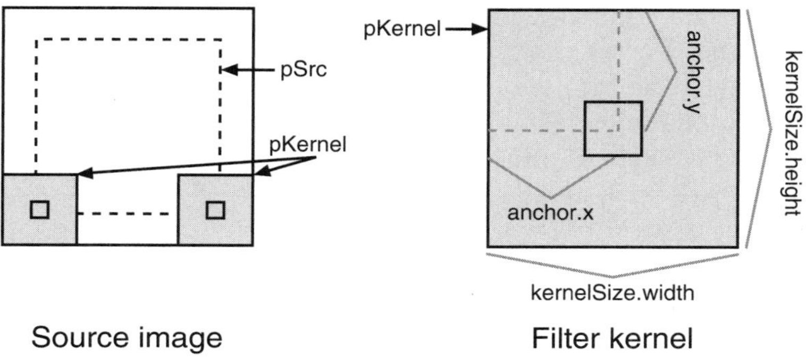

Figure 9.3 Illustration of Relationship of Kernel, Border, and Anchor in Intel® Integrated Performance Primitives (Intel® IPP)

Figure 9.3 also introduces the parameters that Intel IPP uses to parameterize the images and filter kernel. Here is a prototype for a typical filter function:

```
IppStatus ippiFilter_8u_C3R(
      const Ipp8u* pSrc, int srcStep,
      Ipp8u* pDst, int dstStep,
      IppiSize dstSize,
      const Ipp32s* pKernel, IppiSize kernelSize,
      IppiPoint anchor, int divisor);
```

The first four arguments, specifying the two images, are standard Intel IPP image arguments. But note that the next argument, the size, specifies the destination size rather than the source and destination size. In the case of most Intel IPP filter operations, the destination is smaller than the source; it contains only the pixels that are far enough inside the source image that the kernel overlaps entirely with the source image.

The pointer to the source data, `pSrc`, is offset into the image as shown in Figure 9.3 and Figure 9.4. As an example, take a case in which `pSrc` represents the origin (0,0). For a function in which the filter is not flipped, such as `ippiFixedFilter`, the source image data must extend from `(-anchor.x,-anchor.y)` to `(dstSize.width + kernelSize.width - anchor.x - 1, dstSize.height + kernelSize.height - anchor.y - 1)`. That entire rectangle must lie within a valid memory space or a memory fault will occur.

For a function that does flip the kernel, such as convolution, the source image data must extend from (kernelSize.width - anchor.x - 1, kernelSize.height - anchor.y - 1) to (dstSize.width + anchor.x, dstSize.height + anchor.y).

The kernel itself is an array of length kernelSize.width * kernelSize.height containing the filter taps. The x and y fields of anchor range from 0 to kernelSize.width-1 and from 0 to kernelSize.height-1, respectively.

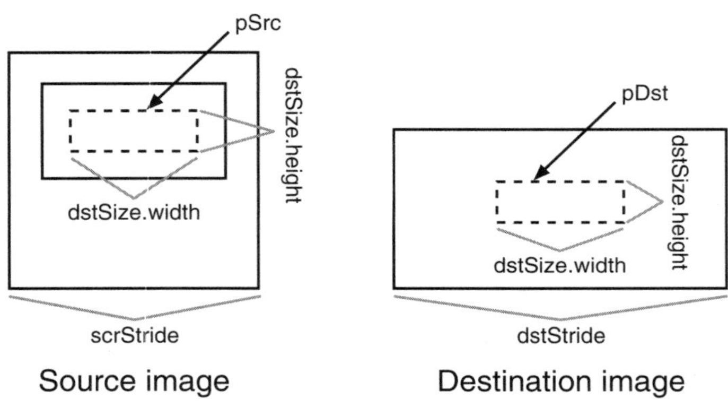

Figure 9.4 ROI for Neighborhood Operations

Because the acceptability of having a filtered image that is smaller than the source is application-dependent, the source image may need to be extended before the filter function is called. The data that is added around the edges is called the *border*, and there are several methods of generating the data to fill that area.

Handling this border properly can be challenging. You must calculate the offsets, create a larger image, generate the border data, and manipulate the source and destination ROIs, if any. Creating a bordered image usually requires the allocation of a new image and copying the original data into the right place. Fortunately, the logic for creating borders need only be developed once and encapsulated in a class from which all filter operations can be derived.

`Filter` Class

The `Filter` class is an abstract class that encapsulates ROI and relative-size calculations and border generation. The declaration of this class is in Figure 9.5.

Functions are available to read the kernel size and anchor position, but potentially useful methods for setting the kernel size and anchor position must be omitted from this abstract class. If they were included, it would restrict the usefulness of the class as a parent, since many filtering functions take only a limited range of sizes or don't allow the anchor to be set. For those functions, `GetAnchor` will return the constant anchor, the center of the kernel, and `GetKernelSize` will return the constant size, likely either `{3,3}` or `{5,5}`.

The most important member functions in `Filter` are `MakeBorderImage`, which fills `pBorderIm` with the image plus a border sufficient for the filter operation; and `Go`, which prepares the arguments for and calls the `Go_` pure-virtual function. The definitions of these two functions are explained below, as are the definitions of the ROI functions.

```
class Filter
{
private:
    int borderMode_;
    int borderVal_;

    IppiRect srcROI_;
    IppiRect dstROI_;

    int isSrcROI_, isDstROI_;…

    IppiSize GetDestSize_(IppiRect srcROI) const;

protected:
    virtual int Go_(const Ipp8u* pSrc, int srcStep,
         Ipp8u* pDst, int dstStep,
         IppiSize dstROISize, int nChannels) = 0;

public:
    Filter();
    ~Filter();

    enum { NONE, VAL, REFLECT, REPEAT, WRAP };
    void SetBorderMode(int type);
```

```
    void SetBorderVal(int val) { borderVal_ = val; }
    int GetBorderMode() const;

    void SetSrcROI(IppiRect srcROI);
    void ClearSrcROI() {isSrcROI_ = 0;}
    void SetDestROI(IppiRect dstROI);
    void ClearDestROI() {isDstROI_ = 0;}

    virtual int GetXMinBorder() const;
    virtual int GetXMaxBorder() const;
    virtual int GetYMinBorder() const;
    virtual int GetYMaxBorder() const;

    virtual IppiSize GetKernelSize() const = 0;
    virtual IppiPoint GetAnchor() const = 0;

    virtual IppiRect GetFullSrcRect(IppiRect srcRect) const;

    virtual IppiRect GetDestRect(IppiRect srcSize) const;
    virtual IppiSize GetDestSize(IppiSize srcSize) const;
    virtual IppiSize GetDestSize() const;

    virtual IppiRect GetSrcRect(IppiRect dstSize) const;
    virtual IppiSize GetSrcSize(IppiSize dstSize) const;
    virtual IppiSize GetSrcSize() const;

    int MakeBorderImage(const Image8u* pSrc,
            Image8u* pBorderIm, int borderMode) const;

    int Go(const Image8u*pSrc, Image8u* pDst);
};
```

Figure 9.5 Class Declaration for `Filter`

Calculating ROI

Before any border creation or filtering occurs, a memory block of the appropriate size to contain the new image must be created. The first step is to calculate the size of the expected image. Figure 9.6 lists the functions that facilitate this.

The method `GetSrcRect` calculates the rectangular boundary of the source image based on the boundary of the destination image and the kernel size and anchor point. The function supports users trying to produce a destination image of a certain size, most likely the same size as the source, and want to pad the source accordingly. The results of this function will likely be used to allocate an image with border of the correct size for a particular source image.

The core equations are these four lines:

```
xMin = dstRect.x - GetXMinBorder();
yMin = dstRect.y - GetYMinBorder();
xMax = dstRect.x + dstRect.width + GetXMaxBorder();
yMax = dstRect.y + dstRect.height + GetYMaxBorder();
```

Those functions calculate the border size using the anchor and kernel size. Compare these equations against the variables illustrated in Figure 9.3.

The subsequent lines support a source and destination ROI by calculating the region of overlap between the source ROI if any, destination ROI if any, and borders. An additional static function `Filter::GetOverlap (IppiRect, IppiRect)` would make this operation easier, but the code is clear and short nevertheless.

The function `GetDstRect` performs the inverse operation, calculating the boundary of the destination from the boundary of the source. It supports a mode of operation in which the code creates a destination image as big as possible using the existing pixels in the source. The dashed rectangle in Figure 9.3 gives an idea of how the size of this destination image is calculated from the kernel and source image sizes.

```
int Filter::GetXMinBorder() const
    { return GetAnchor().x; }
int Filter::GetXMaxBorder() const
    { return GetKernelSize().width - GetAnchor().x - 1; }
int Filter::GetYMinBorder() const
    { return GetAnchor().y; }
int Filter::GetYMaxBorder() const
    { return GetKernelSize().height - GetAnchor().y - 1; }

IppiRect Filter::GetSrcRect(IppiRect dstRect) const
{
    int xMin, yMin, xMax, yMax;

    xMin = dstRect.x - GetXMinBorder();
    yMin = dstRect.y - GetYMinBorder();
    xMax = dstRect.x + dstRect.width + GetXMaxBorder();
    yMax = dstRect.y + dstRect.height + GetYMaxBorder();

    if (isDstROI_)
    {
```

```
        xMin = IPP_MAX(xMin, dstROI_.x);
        yMin = IPP_MAX(yMin, dstROI_.y);
        xMax = IPP_MIN(xMax, dstROI_.x + dstROI_.width);
        yMax = IPP_MIN(yMax, dstROI_.y + dstROI_.height);
    }

    if (isSrcROI_)
    {
        xMin = IPP_MAX(xMin, srcROI_.x);
        yMin = IPP_MAX(xMin, srcROI_.y);
        xMax = IPP_MIN(xMax, srcROI_.x + srcROI_.width);
        yMax = IPP_MIN(yMax, srcROI_.y + srcROI_.height);
    }

    IppiRect srcRect;
    srcRect.x = xMin;
    srcRect.y = yMin;
    srcRect.width = xMax - xMin;
    srcRect.height = yMax - yMin;

    return srcRect;
}
```

Figure 9.6 Methods of Class `Filter` Designed to Facilitate Borders

Calculating the Border

The "meatiest" function in the abstract class `Filter` is `MakeBorderImage`. This function creates a new image that is a copy of a provided source image with an outside border added. This operation is independent of any particular filter function, so it is possible to put it here in the parent class. It uses the characteristics of the child class, primarily kernel size and anchor point, to calculate the size of the new image, the "border image", and the placement of the source image within it.

This function supports four types of borders:

- VAL—fill the border with a single constant
- REPEAT—fill the border by copying the outermost row or column
- WRAP—fill the border with data from the opposite side of the image
- REFLECT—flip the outermost rows or column and fill the border with them

The source for `MakeBorderImage` is listed in Figure 9.7.

```
int Filter::MakeBorderImage(const Image8u* pSrc,
      Image8u* pBorderIm, int borderMode) const
{
// Argument checking
// Initialization / ROI Handling
// Allocation of pBorderIm
...
    int xMin = GetXMinBorder(), yMin = GetYMinBorder();
    if (borderMode == VAL)
    {
         Ipp8u border3[3] = { borderVal_, borderVal_,
          borderVal_ };
         Ipp8u border4[4] = { borderVal_, borderVal_,
          borderVal_, borderVal_ };

         if (nChannels == 1)
          st = ippiCopyConstBorder_8u_C1R(
            pSData, sStride, sSize,
            pBData, bStride, bSize,
            yMin, xMin, borderVal_);
         else if (nChannels == 3)
          st = ippiCopyConstBorder_8u_C3R(
            pSData, sStride, sSize,
            pBData, bStride, bSize,
            yMin, xMin, border3);
         else if (nChannels == 4)
          st = ippiCopyConstBorder_8u_C4R(
            pSData, sStride, sSize,
            pBData, bStride, bSize,
            yMin, xMin, border4);
    }
    else if (borderMode == REPEAT)
    {
         if (nChannels == 1)
          ippiCopyReplicateBorder_8u_C1R(
            pSData, sStride, sSize,
            pBData, bStride, bSize,
            yMin, xMin);
         else if (nChannels == 3)
          ippiCopyReplicateBorder_8u_C3R(
            pSData, sStride, sSize,
            pBData, bStride, bSize,
            yMin, xMin);
         else if (nChannels == 4)
          ippiCopyReplicateBorder_8u_C4R(
```

```
            pSData, sStride, sSize,
            pBData, bStride, bSize,
            yMin, xMin);
    }
    else
    {
        int i;
        int xmin = GetXMinBorder(), xmax = GetXMaxBorder();
        int ymin = GetYMinBorder(), ymax = GetYMaxBorder();
        int w = pSrc->GetSize().width;
            int h = pSrc->GetSize().height;

        pBorderIm->Zero();
        pBorderIm->CopyFrom_R(
                pSrc->GetConstData(), w,h,
                pSrc->GetStride(),xmin,ymin);

        if (borderMode == REFLECT)
        {
          for (i=0; i<ymin; i++)
            pBorderIm->CopyFrom_R(
              pSrc->GetConstData(0, i+1),
              w,1, pSrc->GetStride(),
              xmin,ymin-i-1);
          for (i=0; i<ymax; i++)
            pBorderIm->CopyFrom_R(
              pSrc->GetConstData(0, h-1 - i-1),
              w,1, pSrc->GetStride(),
              xmin,h+ymin-1 + i+1);
          for (i=0; i<xmin; i++)
            pBorderIm->CopyFrom_R(
              pSrc->GetConstData(i+1,0),
              1,h, pSrc->GetStride(),
              xmin-i-1,ymin);
          for (i=0; i<xmax; i++)
            pBorderIm->CopyFrom_R(
              pSrc->GetConstData(w-1 - i-1,0),
              1,h, pSrc->GetStride(),
              w+xmin-1 + i+1,ymin);
        }
        else if (borderMode == WRAP)
        {
          pBorderIm->CopyFrom_R(pSrc->GetConstData(0, 0),
            w,ymax, pSrc->GetStride(),min,h+ymin);
          pBorderIm->CopyFrom_R(pSrc->GetConstData(0,h-ymin),
            w,ymin, pSrc->GetStride(), xmin,0);
          pBorderIm->CopyFrom_R(pSrc->GetConstData(0, 0),
            xmax,h, pSrc->GetStride(), w+xmin,ymin);
          pBorderIm->CopyFrom_R(pSrc->GetConstData(w-xmin,0),
            xmin,h, pSrc->GetStride(), 0,ymin);
```

```
        }
    }

    return 0;
}
```

Figure 9.7 `Filter` Member Function `MakeBorderImage`

Intel IPP has two functions to create borders automatically: `ippiCopyConstBorder` and `ippiCopyReplicateBorder`. These correspond to the border modes VAL and REPEAT of `MakeBorderImage`. As a result, these two border modes do not require much work, and the function merely passes on the arguments to the border functions.

Note Some care is necessary when passing arguments to the Intel IPP border functions. Intel IPP uniformly uses the order (horizontal, vertical) for coordinate pairs such as (x,y) and sizes such as (width, height). However, the border functions use the reverse order, taking `yBorder` and `xBorder` in that order.

One other note is that the manual uses "top" to mean "vertical start", but the point (0,0) may not be at the top of an image. Right-side-up DIBs, for example, have their origins in the lower-left corner.

The other two border options, REFLECT and WRAP, are implemented by calls to `Image8u::CopyFrom_R`. REFLECT requires one copy per border column or row, because the rows and columns appear in the opposite order in the border. This is implemented by using an ROI of (width,1) or (1,height).

The WRAP code requires four copies and no loops. It copies four blocks, left, right, top, and bottom of sizes `(leftborderwidth, height)`, `(rightborderwidth, height)`, `(width, topborderheight)`, and `(width, bottomborderheight)`, respectively.

Border images resulting from these options are shown in Figure 9.8.

Note that the corners of REFLECT and WRAP are black because none of the four copies in the `MakeBorderImage` function copy to that area. For completeness, those corners should be extensions of the interior images. Those borders could be created with four additional copies, for WRAP, or four more loops of copies, for REFLECT. Filling the corner border is necessary for achieving the best quality destination image if the filter is square or rectangular, but not if it is a cross.

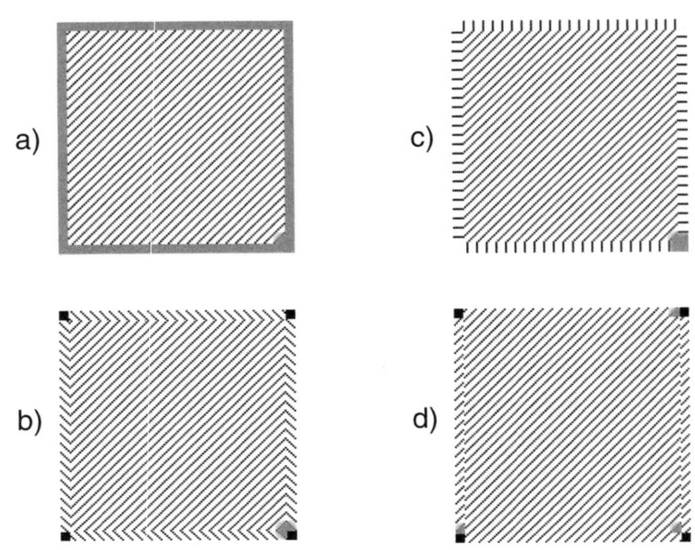

Figure 9.8 Four Border Modes Demonstrated

Empirically, REFLECT produces good results. Adding a REPEAT border also results in nice destination images, though when a blur filter is applied to such an image, the edges stand out as not blurry enough. For many real images, WRAP produces inferior results, particularly in blur filters. The benefit of WRAP is mathematical, because filtering with a WRAP border is the same as a circular convolution, which is the same as a simple frequency-domain filter. That is, taking the Fourier transform of an image and a filter, then taking their product, then inverting the transform on that product mimics a circular convolution.

Filtering the Image

The pure virtual class `Filter` doesn't perform any filtering. The function `Go` prepares the arguments in an Intel IPP-like form and passes them to `Go_`, a pure-virtual function that should be implemented by any child class. The `Go` function is listed in Figure 9.9.

The `Go` method can be called with the `Filter` object in no-border mode if the border has been created explicitly or isn't needed. In that case, it calculates the actual destination size then calls `Go_` with arguments based on the source image argument. When `Go` is called in any other border mode, it first creates a temporary border image of the appropriate size using MakeBorderImage. Then it calls Go_ using arguments based on that temporary image.

```
int Filter::Go(const Image8u*pSrc, Image8u* pDst)
{
    int nChannels = pSrc->GetChannelCount();
    if (nChannels != pDst->GetChannelCount()) return -1;

    IppiSize dstSize =
    {
         IPP_MIN(pSrc->GetSize().width, pDst->GetSize().width),
         IPP_MIN(pSrc->GetSize().height, pDst->GetSize().height)
    };

    if (borderMode_ == NONE)
    {
         dstSize.width =
           IPP_MIN(pSrc->GetSize().width-GetXMinBorder(),
              pDst->GetSize().width);
         dstSize.height =
           IPP_MIN(pSrc->GetSize().height-GetYMinBorder(),
              pDst->GetSize().height);
         return Go_(pSrc->GetConstData(
              GetXMinBorder(),GetYMinBorder()),
           pSrc->GetStride(),
           pDst->GetData(), pDst->GetStride(),
           pDst->GetSize(), nChannels);
    }
    else
    {
         Image8u tmp;
         MakeBorderImage(pSrc, &tmp, borderMode_);
         return Go_(
           tmp.GetConstData(GetXMinBorder(),GetYMinBorder()),
           tmp.GetStride(),
           pDst->GetData(), pDst->GetStride(),
           pDst->GetSize(), nChannels);
    }
}
```

Figure 9.9 The Filter Method Go

Filters and Tiling

Some images are either too large or unwieldy to load directly into memory, or would be too unwieldy to do so. One technique employed to manipulate such large images is to break the image up into smaller pieces, called tiles. The tiles, frequently square and having sizes between 64 x 64 and 256 x 256, are presumably stored on disk until needed. The tiles are laid out in memory as if they were full images to allow the tiling engine to load them and operate on them individually. Figure 9.10 shows such a tiled image.

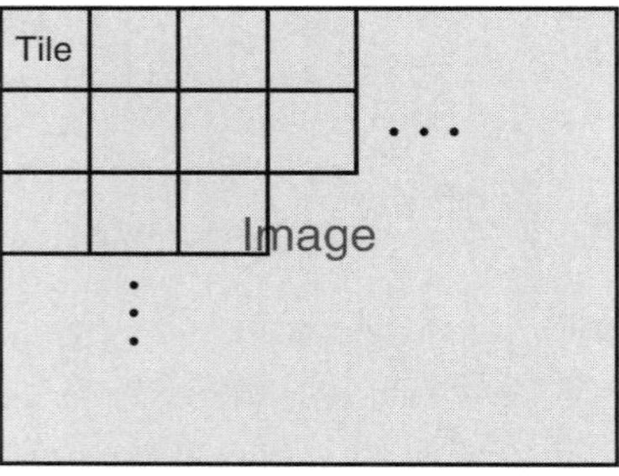

Figure 9.10 Illustration of a Tiled Image

Careful tile access improves the performance by minimizing the number of times a given image portion needs to be brought from memory, by trying to ensure that each tile is used as much as possible while in memory. Likewise, if the tile access is implemented correctly, the tile should be accessed from the cache, and the number of times that is gets loaded into the cache should be minimized.

The issues arising from filtering a tiled image and the strategy for resolving them are almost identical to those for any image border. A source image of size (tileW, tileH) is available, and a destination image of the same size should be generated by the application of a filter. In this case, the data outside the image is available, unless the tile is at the edge of the full image, but the data is not in memory contiguous with that of the tile. Using one of the above border modes ignores the information available.

To support this mode, the `Filter` class could quite reasonably support a further method to handle borders named `TILING`. A separate method `MakeBorderImageTiling` would be required to support this new border version, since it would have to take as input up to eight other tiles.[1] This method would calculate the offsets of the relevant data within the each tile, then perform a copy nearly identical to that in the WRAP border mode.

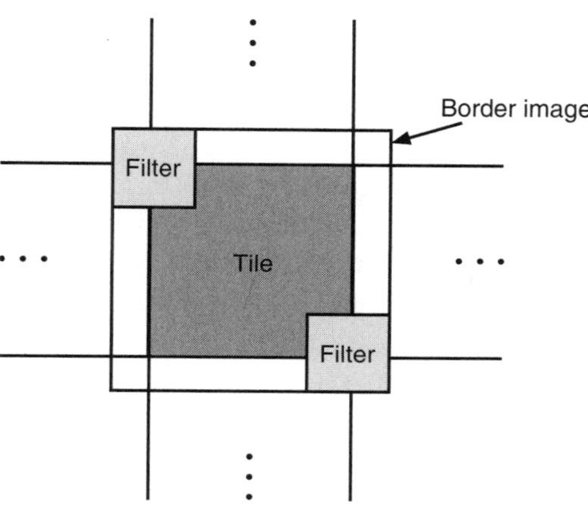

Figure 9.11 Illustration of an Image with Border Constructed From Multiple Tiles

General Filters

With the `Filter` class in place, it is much easier to wrap Intel IPP filter functions in a few easy-to-use classes. Sizes, borders, and regions of interest require no further attention. Only the protected `Go_` function and the accessor functions for the particular arguments for the Intel IPP filter functions need to be implemented.

The most general filter functions are `ippiFilter` and `ippiFilter32f`. These functions take a filter kernel of arbitrary size and content and apply it to any image. The two functions can be wrapped in a single `GeneralFilter` class.

[1] Supporting filter kernels larger than twice the tile size would require a larger number of tiles, or require that the tiles be aggregated into a larger block. This is a corner case that would require additional logic or additional copies.

GeneralFilter *Class*

There are two groups of general filter functions. ippiFilter functions take Ipp8u or Ipp16s data and filter it with a kernel of Ipp32s values, or take Ipp32f data and filter it with an Ipp32f kernel. ippiFilter32f functions take Ipp8u or Ipp16s data and filter it with an Ipp32f kernel. In this implementation, one class supports both, though it could just as easily be split into two classes.

Both of these functions allow arbitrary sizes of kernels and can take an anchor anywhere within the kernel, so the class needs SetKernel and SetAnchor functions and kernel_ and anchor_ members.

Designing filters with only integers is very difficult. At the very least, since all nonzero taps are equal to or greater than one, the filter will amplify the signal as it filters it. For this reason, the ippiFilter functions that take integral kernel taps as arguments also take a divisor argument. During the operation, each of the taps is divided by that divisor. So this class needs a function to set the divisor.

The interface declaration and part of the implementation for the GeneralFilter class is listed in Figure 9.12.

The flag isKernel32f allows GeneralFilter to wrap both Ipp32f and Ipp32s filters. If this flag is set, the filter acts as an Ipp32f filter. An Ipp32s filter uses the pKernel32s array to hold the data; an Ipp32f filter uses the pKernel32f_ pointer. Private functions Alloc32f_ and Alloc32s_ allocate the memory for the kernel.

The kernel data is set by the overloaded SetKernel function. The kernel array is taken in the same format as is taken by the Intel IPP functions, so the data is just copied element-by-element into the local array. The version of SetKernel that takes 32s data also takes the divisor to be passed on to ippiFilter.

The anchor is optional. If it is not set, as indicated by the flag isAnchorSet_, the center of the filter will be used in the Intel IPP call and returned by GetKernel.

The code for Go_ is straightforward. Between the variables set by the SetKernel and SetAnchor functions and those passed by the Filter::Go function, all the arguments to Filter or Filter32f are prepared in advance for use with an Intel IPP function. All that remains is to call the right version of Filter according to the number of channels and kernel data type, ippiFilter[32f]_8u_C1R, ippiFilter[32f]_8u_C3R, or ippiFilter[32f]_8u_C4R.

This particular function does not support the ippiFilter[32f]_8u_AC4R functions that would skip the alpha channel and process only the other three.

An additional flag that determined whether to or not to skip the alpha channel would allow support of the AC4 version of the function.

```
class GeneralFilter : public Filter
{
private:
    IppiSize size_;
    GeneralFilterType type_;

    int isKernel32f_;
    Ipp32f* pKernel32f_;
    Ipp32s* pKernel32s_;
    int divisor_;
    IppiSize kernelSize_;

    int isAnchorSet_;
    IppiPoint anchor_;

    void Alloc32f_(IppiSize kernelSize);
    void Alloc32s_(IppiSize kernelSize);

protected:
    virtual int Go_(const Ipp8u* pSrc, int srcStep,
        Ipp8u* pDst, int dstStep,
        IppiSize dstROISize, int nChannels);


public:
    GeneralFilter();
    ~GeneralFilter();

    void SetAnchor(IppiPoint anchor);
      …
    void SetKernel(const Ipp32s* pKernel, IppiSize
        kernelSize, int divisor);
    void SetKernel(const Ipp32f* pKernel, IppiSize
        kernelSize);

      …
};

// ----------------------

int GeneralFilter::Go_(const Ipp8u* pSrc, int srcStep,
    Ipp8u* pDst, int dstStep,
    IppiSize dstROISize, int nChannels)
```

```
{
    IppStatus st;
    if (isKernel32f_)
    {
        if (nChannels == 1)
          st = ippiFilter32f_8u_C1R(pSrc, srcStep,
             pDst, dstStep, dstROISize,
             pKernel32f_, kernelSize_, anchor_);
        else if (nChannels == 3)
          ...
    }
    else
    {
        if (nChannels == 1)
          st = ippiFilter_8u_C1R(pSrc, srcStep,
             pDst, dstStep, dstROISize,
             pKernel32s_, kernelSize_, anchor_,
             divisor_);
        else if (nChannels == 3)
          ...
    }
    return (int)st;
}
```

Figure 9.12 `GeneralFilter` Class and Member Function `Go`

`GeneralFilter` *Usage*

Writing code using this filter is easy. The difficulty is in determining or designing the filter needed. Figure 9.13 demonstrates how to construct and use a filter that blurs to a source image. First it loads the image from a file. Then it displays it with `Image8u::View`. Then it creates a 5 x 5 filter that approximates a Gaussian blur, and uses it as the kernel to create a `GeneralFilter` object. Then it allocates a destination image and filters the source image into it.

```
    Image8u image;
    if (image.LoadBMP(argv[1])) return -1;
    image.View(argv[1],0);

    Ipp32f pKernel[25] = { 1, 4, 6, 4, 1,
                4, 16, 24, 16, 4,
                6, 24, 36, 24, 6,
                4, 16, 24, 16, 4,
                1, 4, 6, 4, 1 };
    for (int i=0; i<25; i++) pKernel[i] /= 256.0;
```

```
GeneralFilter f;
f.SetKernel(pKernel, 5,5);
f.SetBorderMode(f.REFLECT);

Image8u filteredImage(image.GetSize(),
     image.GetChannelCount());
f.Go(&image, &filteredImage);
filteredImage.View("Filtered", 1);
```

Figure 9.13 Using `GeneralFilter` to Blur an Image

By setting the border mode of the filter to REFLECT, the code segment directs the filter to automatically generate a temporary border image. This temporary image created by the `Filter` class is convenient but can be dangerously inefficient. Each call to `Go` with a border mode other than NONE causes the function to allocate and initialize a new border image. The concern is the time spent in the memory allocation. Memory copies are quick, but memory allocation is very slow.

This is the reason that the `filter::GetBorderImage` method is public. Reusing the same image array is perfectly reasonable, even if the data changes. The time to process multiple images or video frames with different data but the same image size would be perfectly reasonable if reusing the border image memory. It would be very poor if the border image were reallocated each frame.

In fact, a nice optimization of `GetBorderImage` would be to determine whether the memory required by source and border exceeds the current size of the border image, and reallocate the border image only if so. After successive uses, the border image eventually would not need to be reallocated. However, with video and many other applications, it's just as likely that all the images will all be the same size.

No sub-image ROI has been applied, so `Filter::MakeBorderImage`, when called, automatically ensures that the destination image is the same size as the source. Assuming this, the image `filteredImage` is created with size `image.size`. It would be more error tolerant to allocate an image of size `f.GetDestSize(image.size)` for the destination.

Figure 9.14 shows the result of the `image.View()` and `filteredImage.View()` calls.

a) Source Image

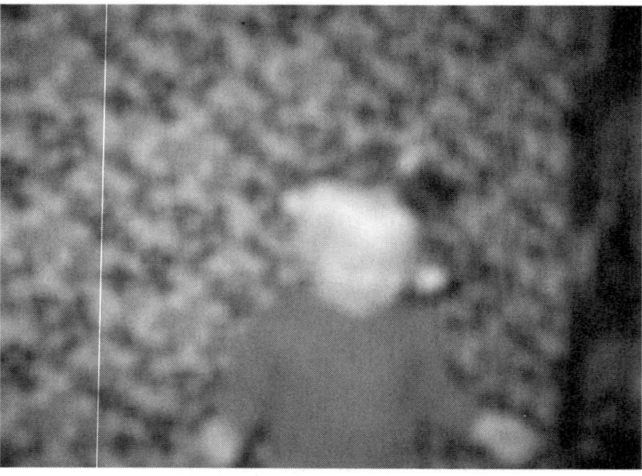

b) Blurred Image

Figure 9.14 Results of Filtering with a `GeneralFilter` Blur

Fixed Filters

Designing a filter kernel to perform a particular task is not always necessary. A number of standard kernels can be found in image-processing books that perform blurs, edge detection, gradient calculations, and so on. Intel IPP has a convenient set of functions implementing these "fixed filters" with predefined kernels.

These functions are implemented this way for performance as well as convenience. For this reason, the kernels they implement tend to be important and frequent, but they also tend to lend themselves to easy optimization.

Figure 9.15 lists the declaration and part of the implementation of a `FixedFilter` class that can wrap this large group of functions. The function `Init` sets the filter type, anchor, and size. The fixed filters in Intel IPP, by their nature, accept only a certain range of sizes. The complete list of sizes is 3 x 3, 5 x 5, 1 x 3, 1 x 5, 3 x 1, and 5 x 1, but most kernels support only a subset of these sizes. The `Init` function takes any size but only functions for sizes in this list. It also does not check whether the particular fixed filter function to be called accepts that size of kernel; the imaging volume of the Intel IPP manual has a table showing which functions take which sizes.

The two arrays, `pAnchors_` and `pMaskSizes_`, map each kernel size to the Intel IPP code for that size and the corresponding fixed anchor locations. For example, `pMaskSizes_[3][3]` is equal to the constant `ippMskSize3x3`, and `pAnchors_[3][3]` is equal to the point (1,1).

This class uses a shorthand method for calling the filter function. Since all current fixed filter functions have the same prototype, it is possible to define a type `FilterFn` that holds a pointer to an Intel IPP fixed filter pointer. This new type allows the creation of a separate `SetFilterFn_` method that converts the arguments provided to `Init` into a function pointer that can later be used to call the Intel IPP function without further conversion. The member variable `pFilterFn_` holds this function pointer. This method is not entirely portable since the declaration is explicitly `_stdcall`, but it does make the code more readable.

The implementation of `SetFilterFn_` in Figure 9.15 supports only two types of filters, median and Gaussian. The latter has been discussed previously. The former is a nonlinear filter, sometimes used for noise removal, that sets each pixel to the median value of a neighborhood around it.

Because of a peculiarity of `ippiFilterMedian` functions, three functions take disjoint sets of sizes: `ippiFilterMedianHoriz` takes sizes 3 x 1 and 5 x 1; `ippiFilterMedianVert` takes 1 x 3 and 1 x 5; and `ippiFilterMedianCross` takes 3 x 3 and 5 x 5. Because they take non-overlapping size arguments, the size uniquely determines which function should be called, and they are treated here as one function.

Note that there is no C4 version of these median filters, so the AC4 versions are used. The alpha channel is skipped, presumably because the result of a median filter on an alpha channel is inconsistent with the result on RGB data.

The `ippiFilterGauss` function is less complicated, and the code setting the function pointer for `FixedFilterType GAUSS` takes only a handful of lines.

Many other fixed filter functions are not included in this example. With the exception of mask size, they all take the same arguments, so adding them to the `FixedFilterType` enumeration and the `Go` method is almost trivial.

```
class FixedFilter : public Filter
{
public:
    typedef enum {NONE, GAUSS, MEDIAN} FixedFilterType;

private:
    IppiSize size_;
    FixedFilterType type_;

    static IppiPoint pAnchors_[6][6];
    static int pMaskSizes_[6][6];

    typedef IppStatus _stdcall FilterFn (
         const Ipp8u* pSrc, int srcStep,
         Ipp8u* pDst,int dstStep,
         IppiSize dstRoiSize,
         IppiMaskSize mask);
    FilterFn* pFilterFn_;

    int FixedFilter::SetFilterFn_(int nChannels);

protected:
    virtual int Go_(const Ipp8u* pSrc, int srcStep,
         Ipp8u* pDst, int dstStep,
         IppiSize dstROISize, int nChannels);

public:
    FixedFilter();
    ~FixedFilter();

    int Init(FixedFilterType type, int width, int height);

    virtual IppiSize GetKernelSize() const;
    virtual IppiPoint GetAnchor() const;
};
```

```
//---------------------------

int FixedFilter::SetFilterFn_(int nChannels)
{
    IppiMaskSize maskSize (IppiMaskSize) =
         (pMaskSizes_[size_.height][size_.width]);
    if (type_ == MEDIAN)
    {
         if ((maskSize == ippMskSize3x3) ||
           (maskSize == ippMskSize5x5))
         {
           if (nChannels == 1)
             pFilterFn_ = ippiFilterMedianCross_8u_C1R;
           else if (nChannels == 3)
             pFilterFn_ = ippiFilterMedianCross_8u_C3R;
           else if (nChannels == 4)
             pFilterFn_ = ippiFilterMedianCross_8u_AC4R;
         }
         if ((maskSize == ippMskSize3x1) ||
           (maskSize == ippMskSize5x1))
         {
           if (nChannels == 1)
             pFilterFn_ = ippiFilterMedianHoriz_8u_C1R;
           else if (nChannels == 3)
             pFilterFn_ = ippiFilterMedianHoriz_8u_C3R;
           else if (nChannels == 4)
             pFilterFn_ = ippiFilterMedianHoriz_8u_AC4R;
         }
         if ((maskSize == ippMskSize1x3) ||
           (maskSize == ippMskSize1x5))
         {
           if (nChannels == 1) pFilterFn_ =
             ippiFilterMedianVert_8u_C1R;
           else if (nChannels == 3) pFilterFn_ =
             ippiFilterMedianVert_8u_C3R;
           else if (nChannels == 4) pFilterFn_ =
             ippiFilterMedianVert_8u_AC4R;
         }
    }
    else if (type_ == GAUSS)
    {
         if (nChannels == 1)
          pFilterFn_ = ippiFilterGauss_8u_C1R;
         else if (nChannels == 3)
          pFilterFn_ = ippiFilterGauss_8u_C3R;
         else if (nChannels == 4)
```

```
            pFilterFn_ = ippiFilterGauss_8u_C4R;
        }
        else
        {
            return -1;
        }
        return 0;
}

int FixedFilter::Go_(const Ipp8u* pSrc, int srcStep,
    Ipp8u* pDst, int dstStep, IppiSize dstROISize,
    int nChannels)
{
    IppiMaskSize maskSize =
        (IppiMaskSize) pMaskSizes_[size_.height][size_.width];

    if (SetFilterFn_(nChannels)) return -1;

    return (int)pFilterFn_(pSrc, srcStep,
        pDst, dstStep, dstROISize, maskSize);
}
```

Figure 9.15 Class FixedFilter and Some Methods

Figure 9.16 shows code similar to that previously shown for GeneralFilter that performs a 5 x 1 horizontal median filter using a constant gray border. Figure 9.17 contains the output of this code, an image smeared from side to side.

```
    Image8u image;
    if (image.LoadBMP(argv[1]))
        return -1;
    image.View(argv[1],0);

    FixedFilter f;
    f.Init(FixedFilter::MEDIAN, 5,1);

    f.SetBorderVal(128);
    f.SetBorderMode(FixedFilter.VAL);

    Image8u filteredImage(image.GetSize(),
        image.GetChannelCount());
    f.Go(&image, &filteredImage);
    filteredImage.View("Filtered", 1);
    return 0;
```

Figure 9.16 Using the FixedFilter Class

Figure 9.17 Result of `FixedFilter::Go` with Filter Type `MEDIAN`

Convolution

In addition to convolution between a filter kernel and an image, Intel IPP also supports convolution between two images. While mathematically the same as filtering, convolution has several key differences in the interface and implementation:

- Convolution takes place between two images, so each image has a size and a stride and neither has an anchor.
- Both images are the same type, in this case 8u, instead of 32s or 32f.
- The size of the result can either be the minimal size, of the area of total overlap (`ippiConvValid`), or the maximal size, of the area of any overlap (`ippiConvFull`).
- No image data is assumed to exist before the source pointer or after the provided size.

Because of these differences, a convolution class can't be derived from the `Filter` class above. However, the interface and implementation, listed in Figure 9.18, should be pretty familiar.

The function GetDestSize has a simple calculation to perform. Since these classes also support regions of interest for both sources, the width and height of the ROIs are used if present. Then, the destination size is determined. For ConvFull, the size of the destination image is one less than the sum of the sizes:

```
dstSize.width = w1 + w2 - 1;
dstSize.height = h1 + h2 -1;
```

For ConvValid, the size of the destination image is one more than the difference between the sizes:

```
dstSize.width = IPP_MAX(w1,w2) - IPP_MIN(w1,w2) + 1;
dstSize.height = IPP_MAX(h1,h2) - IPP_MIN(h1,h2) + 1;
```

```
class ConvFilter
{
private:
    // Support Rectangle of Interest for each image
    IppiRect src1ROI_, src2ROI_;
    int isSrc1ROI_, isSrc2ROI_;

public:
    ConvFilter();
    ~ConvFilter();

    void SetSrc1ROI(IppiRect src1ROI)
        { src1ROI_ = src1ROI; isSrc1ROI_ = 1; }
    void ClearSrc1ROI()
        { isSrc1ROI_ = 0; }
    void SetSrc2ROI(IppiRect src2ROI)
        { src2ROI_ = src2ROI; isSrc2ROI_ = 1; }
    void ClearSrc2ROI()
        { isSrc2ROI_ = 0; }

    enum { FULL, VALID };
    IppiSize GetDestSize(IppiSize src1Size, IppiSize src2Size,
        int type);

    int Go(const Image8u* pSrc1, const Image8u* pSrc2,
        Image8u* pDst, int type, int divisor);
};

//----------------

IppiSize ConvFilter::GetDestSize(IppiSize src1Size,
    IppiSize src2Size, int type)
{
    IppiSize dstSize = {0,0};
```

```
    int w1, w2, h1, h2;

    if (isSrc1ROI_)
         { w1 = src1ROI_.width; h1 = src1ROI_.height; }
    else
         { w1 = src1Size.width; h1 = src1Size.height; }

    if (isSrc2ROI_)
         { w2 = src2ROI_.width; h2 = src2ROI_.height; }
    else
         { w2 = src2Size.width; h2 = src2Size.height; }

    if (type == FULL)
    {
         dstSize.width = w1 + w2 - 1;
         dstSize.height = h1 + h2 -1;
    }
    else if (type == VALID)
    {
         dstSize.width = IPP_MAX(w1,w2) - IPP_MIN(w1,w2) + 1;
         dstSize.height = IPP_MAX(h1,h2) - IPP_MIN(h1,h2) + 1;
    }

    return dstSize;
}

int ConvFilter::Go(const Image8u* pSrc1, const Image8u* pSrc2,
    Image8u* pDst, int type, int divisor)
{
    int nChannels = pSrc1->GetChannelCount();
    if ((nChannels != pSrc2->GetChannelCount()) ||
         (nChannels != pDst->GetChannelCount()))
         return -1;

    typedef IppStatus _stdcall ConvFn(
         const Ipp8u* pSrc1,int src1Step, IppiSize src1Size,
         const Ipp8u* pSrc2,int src2Step, IppiSize src2Size,
         Ipp8u* pDst,int dstStep, int divisor);
    ConvFn *pConvFn;

    if (type == FULL)
    {
         if (nChannels == 1)
          pConvFn = ippiConvFull_8u_C1R;
         else if (nChannels == 3)
          pConvFn = ippiConvFull_8u_C3R;
         else if (nChannels == 4)
```

```
            pConvFn = ippiConvFull_8u_AC4R;
    }
    else if (type == VALID)
    {
        if (nChannels == 1)
            pConvFn = ippiConvValid_8u_C1R;
        else if (nChannels == 3)
            pConvFn = ippiConvValid_8u_C3R;
        else if (nChannels == 4)
            pConvFn = ippiConvValid_8u_AC4R;
    }

    Ipp8u const* pSrcData1, *pSrcData2;
    IppiSize src1Size, src2Size;

    if (isSrc1ROI_)
    {
        pSrcData1 =
          pSrc1->GetConstData(src1ROI_.x, src1ROI_.y);
        src1Size.width =
          IPP_MIN(pSrc1->GetSize().width-src1ROI_.x,
            src1ROI_.width);
        src1Size.height =
          IPP_MIN(pSrc1->GetSize().height-src1ROI_.y,
            src1ROI_.height);
    }
    else
    {
        pSrcData1 = pSrc1->GetConstData();
        src1Size = pSrc1->GetSize();
    }

    if (isSrc2ROI_)
    {
        pSrcData2 =
          pSrc2->GetConstData(src2ROI_.x, src2ROI_.y);
        src2Size.width =
          IPP_MIN(pSrc2->GetSize().width - src2ROI_.x,
            src2ROI_.width);
        src2Size.height =
          IPP_MIN(pSrc2->GetSize().height - src2ROI_.y,
            src2ROI_.height);
    }
    else
    {
        pSrcData2 = pSrc2->GetConstData();
        src2Size = pSrc2->GetSize();
    }
```

```
    return (int) pConvFn(pSrcData1,pSrc1->GetStride(),src1Size,
        pSrcData1,pSrc2->GetStride(),src2Size,
        pDst->GetData(), pDst->GetStride(), divisor);
}
```

Figure 9.18 `ConvFilter` Class Definition and Some Methods

These formulae are illustrated in Figure 9.19.

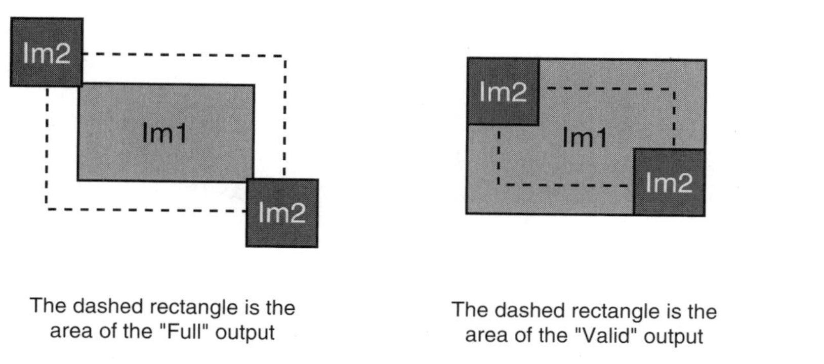
Im2
Im1
Im2
The dashed rectangle is the area of the "Full" output
Im2
Im1
Im2
The dashed rectangle is the area of the "Valid" output

Figure 9.19 Destination Rectangles for Convolution

This class is used in a method similar to the filters in the previous sections. Convolving two images together usually does not produce an interesting result, so one of the "images" is generally a filter.

Other Filter Functions

There are several other groups of filters in Intel IPP that are not represented in the previous three classes. They are each covered briefly in the sections that follow.

Separable Filters

Some filters can be decomposed into the convolution of a horizontal filter and a vertical filter. In these cases, the number of operations can be significantly reduced if the operation takes place in two stages: `ippiFilterColumn` and `ippiFilterRow`. Gaussian filters have this property.

For example, a 5 x 5 filter with this property could be reduced to two 5 x 1 filters, with roughly a 2.5x decrease in number of operations. Since the execution time for two-dimensional filters is proportional to the product of the dimensions and a separable filter's execution time is proportional to the sum of the dimensions, the larger the filter, the greater the gain.

These functions can also be used to perform one-dimensional filtering on two-dimensional data.

Box Filters

The term "box filter" has more than one meaning, but `ippiBoxFilter` is an averaging filter of arbitrary size. It has the same result as a filter with a kernel of all ones and divisor of the number of elements in the kernel. The result is a broadly blurred image.

Nonlinear Filters

There are several nonlinear filters that support kernels of arbitrary size. The functions `ippiMin` and `ippiMax` set each pixel to the minimum or maximum values in a neighborhood around it. `ippiFilterMedian` is like the fixed-filter median, but with an arbitrary size.

Frequency Domain Filters

The frequency domain analysis in the previous chapters applies to images. The `ippiFFT` function has a structure and argument format similar to `ippsFFT`, with an analogous symmetric output format. In some cases, frequency domain filters are valuable in images, though as noted in the introduction, frequency information isn't quite as interesting in images as it is in audio signals.

Geometric Transforms

Geometric transforms constitute a large and important segment of image operations. Any function that changes the size, shape, or orientation of the image or order of the pixels can be grouped under this broad classification. Because of the resulting differences between the source and destination images, geometric operations in Intel IPP take a larger number of more complicated arguments than other operations. This section explains the conventions of the geometric transforms in Intel IPP and demonstrates several functions of the complete set that it supports.

Geometric Transform Conventions

Because the size and shape of the source can be different from that of the destination, the usual image parameterization has to be broadened for geometric operations. In addition to starting pointer and memory stride, these operations take a size argument for each image. In most cases, this size argument is embedded within a full `IppiRect` structure and indicates not the size of the image but the location and extent of the rectangle of interest.

The math employed by the transform operations uses two coordinate systems, the source image coordinate system and the destination. Both systems have an origin (0,0) that is defined by the data pointer. The two coordinate systems are related by the geometric transform.

The source ROI is relative to the source origin, of course, and the destination ROI is relative to the destination origin. Conceptually, the source image is masked by the source ROI first, then transformed into the destination space, and then masked again by the destination ROI before being written into the destination image.[2]

Figure 9.20 is an illustration of a 45-degree rotation with an ROI for both source and destination, with the image parameters noted. The prototype of the Intel IPP function that performs this operation is:

```
IppStatus ippiRotate_8u_C3R(const Ipp8u* pSrc,
    IppiSize srcSize, int srcStep, IppiRect srcROI,
    Ipp8u* pDst, int dstStep, IppiRect dstROI,
    double angle, double xShift, double yShift,
    int interpolation);
```

---

[2] The `Resize` function behaves in a slightly simpler manner. Please see the section on `Resize` for details.

The `xShift` and `yShift` arguments, not shown in this diagram, are the number of pixels needed to move the source ROI after the transformation is applied. The `dstSize` in the figure is not passed into `ippiRotate`, though it is used in some operations, and the `dstROI` must not extend outside of the actual memory allocated.

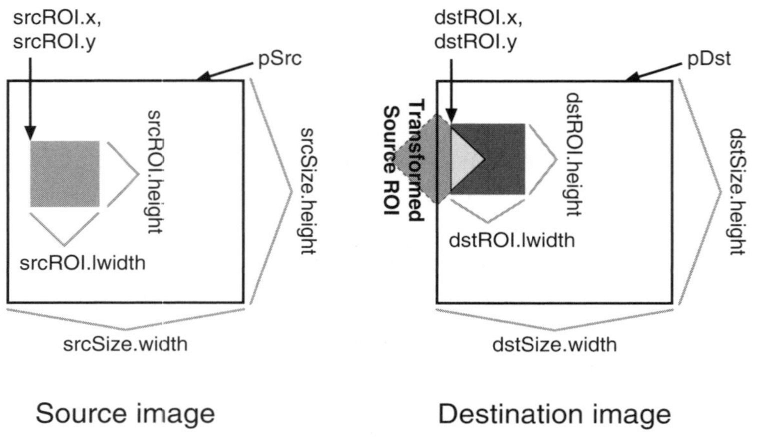

Figure 9.20 ROI for Geometric Operations

In the final image, the bold right triangle that indicates the overlap of the two regions is where the data is written. It is as if the source ROI is a rectangular stencil that is rotated and placed on top of the destination ROI stencil. The area inside both stencils is the only place in which the data is written.

In reality, most geometric operations are implemented backward. Each destination pixel must be filled, and several destination pixels may map to a single source pixel. So, after determining that a pixel is within the area to be written, the operation calculates the location in the source from which the pixel should be pulled. Figure 9.21 illustrates this inverse transform.

In most cases, the location in the source from which the data is to be drawn, indicated as (x', y') in the diagram, does not lie exactly on a source pixel. Intel IPP supports several forms of *interpolation* to calculate the value. The nearest neighbor method chooses the pixel that is closest to (x', y'). Linear interpolation takes a weighted average of the four surrounding pixels. Cubic interpolation fits a second-order curve to the data to calculate the (x', y') value. Super-sampling interpolation averages over a wider range of pixels and is suitable for resizing images to a much smaller size, such as when creating a thumbnail image.

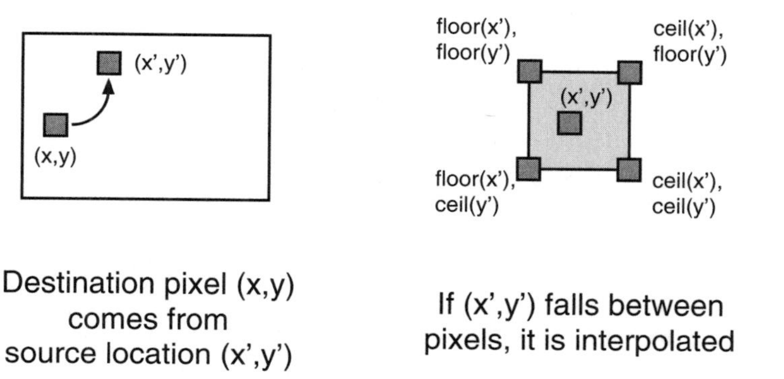

Figure 9.21 Geometric Operations Implemented as Inverse Transforms

Figure 9-22 is an example of a 90-degree rotation that shows some of these arguments in action. This code was used to display the results of the short-time Fourier transform in the example in Chapter 6.

```
int myViewSpectrum_32f(Ipp32f* pSrc, int len, int ftSize)
{
    IppiSize imgSize = { ftSize, len/ftSize };
    IppiRect imgRect = { 0.0, 0.0, ftSize, len/ftSize };

    IppiSize imgSizeRot = { len/ftSize, ftSize };
    IppiRect imgRectRot = { 0.0, 0.0, len/ftSize, ftSize };

    int imgStep, imgStepRot;
    Ipp8u* pImg = ippiMalloc_8u_C1(imgSize.width,
         imgSize.height, &imgStep);
    Ipp8u* pImgRot = ippiMalloc_8u_C1(imgSizeRot.width,
         imgSizeRot.height, &imgStepRot);

    Ipp32f max;
    ippsMax_32f(pSrc, len, &max);
    ippiScale_32f8u_C1R(pSrc, ftSize*sizeof(Ipp32f), pImg,
         imgStep, imgSize, 0.0, max);

    IppStatus st;
    st = ippiRotate_8u_C1R(pImg, imgSize, imgStep, imgRect,
```

```
        pImgRot, imgStepRot, imgRectRot, 90.0, 0.0, ftSize-1,
        IPPI_INTER_NN);

    ipView_8u_C1R(pImgRot, imgStepRot, imgSizeRot,
            "STFT Spectrum", 1);

    return  0;
}
```

Figure 9.22 Rotation by 90 Degrees to View the Short-Time Fourier Transform Spectrum

This function takes a two-dimensional `Ipp32f` array, formats it for viewing, and displays it. Unfortunately, the axes of the input are swapped relative to the desired orientation, so after converting the data to `Ipp8u`, the function needs to rotate it by 90 degrees.

The rotation parameters of interest are the sizes and shifts. Since the size of the source is `{ftSize, len/ftSize}`, the size of the destination is, as expected, `{len/ftSize, ftSize}` in order to hold the rotated image. The ROI rectangles encompass the entire image for both the source and destination images. The step arguments and memory pointers are set by `ippiMalloc`. The trickiest part is keeping all the interesting data in the right place in the destination, and that's what the shifts do.

The rotate function rotates the image around the origin. A 90-degree clockwise rotation will put the entire destination image below the origin, as shown in Figure 9.23. From this diagram, it should be obvious that moving the data so that it starts at (0,0) requires no horizontal shift and a vertical shift of `sourceSize.width-1`. In this case, that means that `yShift` should be `ftSize-1`.

The math was easy in this example because the angle was 90 degrees, and it was possible to visualize the necessary parameters. However, in the general case, it would be nice if the calculation required to keep the destination data visible were encapsulated in a few classes. This is particularly necessary for the more complicated geometric functions such as `ippiWarpPerspective`. The following examples do exactly that, one class per function group.

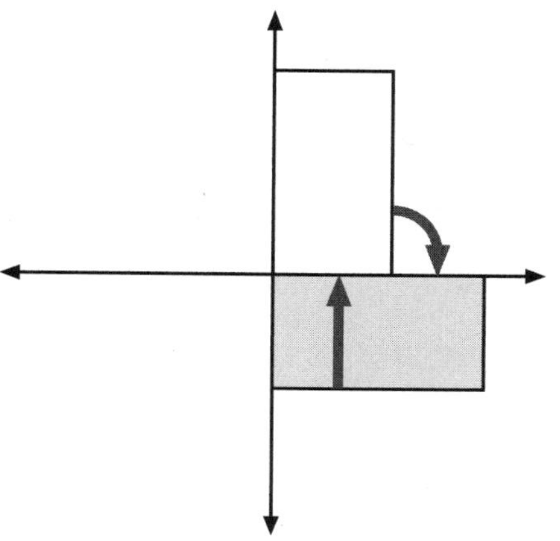

Figure 9.23 A 90-Degree Rotation and Shift

Resizing

The resizing functions change an image from one size to another. The pixels in the first image are either stretched by duplication or interpolation, or they are compressed by dropping or interpolation. A single resize operation can stretch the image in one direction and compress it in the other.

The function `ippiResize` operates in a slightly different way than the other geometric functions do in Figure 9.20. The origin of the source image coordinate system is defined to be the start of the rectangle of interest rather than the data pointer, and since the destination ROI is only a size not a rectangle, the destination data always starts at the data pointer and origin. As a result, in contrast to the rotation example above, the data does not require shifting to align the origins. The origins of the source and destination are automatically aligned, so the earliest data from the source ROI is placed in the earliest location in the destination ROI.

The code in Figure 9.24 is the declaration and part of the definition of a class that encapsulates Intel IPP resizing functions. This class encapsulates two types of resize functions: `ippiResize` and `ippiResizeCenter`. The former resizes using (0,0) as the focus of expansion or contraction; the latter uses `(xCenter,yCenter)` as this point. In this class, if the center is set, the `ResizeCenter` function is called.

Note that the class takes an `IppiRect` for the destination ROI argument, but the Intel IPP resize functions only take an `IppiSize`. The fields of the rectangle are used in two ways. The size of the rectangle is passed to the Intel IPP function. The start of the rectangle is used to offset the data pointer in this expression: `pDst->GetData(dstXOffset_, dstYOffset_)`.

```
class Resize
{
private:
    double xFactor_, yFactor_;
    int interp_;
    IppiRect srcROI_;
    IppiSize dstROI_;
    int dstXOffset_, dstYOffset_;
    int isSrcROI_, isDstROI_;

    double xCenter_, yCenter_;
    int isCenter_;

public:
    Resize();
    ~Resize();

    enum { NN, LINEAR, CUBIC, SUPERSAMPLE };
    void SetInterpType(int type);
    int GetInterpType() const;

    void SetFactors(double xFactor, double yFactor);
    void SetFactors(IppiSize srcSize, IppiSize dstSize);

    void SetSrcROI(IppiRect srcROI);
    void ClearSrcROI() {isSrcROI_ = 0;}
    void SetDestROI(IppiRect dstROI);
    void ClearDestROI() {isDstROI_ = 0;}

    void SetCenter(double xCenter, double yCenter);
    void ClearCenter() { isCenter_ = 0; }

    IppiSize GetDestSize(IppiSize srcSize) const;
    IppiSize GetDestSize() const;
    IppiSize GetSrcSize(IppiSize dstSize) const;
    IppiSize GetSrcSize() const;

    int Go(const Image8u*pSrc, Image8u* pDst);
};
```

```
//---------------------

IppiSize Resize::GetDestSize(IppiSize srcSize) const
{
    IppiSize dstSize;
    if (isSrcROI_)
    {
         dstSize.width = IPP_MIN(srcSize.width-srcROI_.x,
           srcROI_.width) * xFactor_;
         dstSize.height = IPP_MIN(srcSize.height-srcROI_.x,
           srcROI_.height) * yFactor_;
    }
    else
    {
         dstSize.width =
           (int)((double)srcSize.width * xFactor_);
         dstSize.height =
           (int)((double)srcSize.height * yFactor_);
    }

    return dstSize;
}

int Resize::Go(const Image8u*pSrc, Image8u* pDst)
{
    int channelCount = pSrc->GetChannelCount();
    if (channelCount != pDst->GetChannelCount()) return -1;

    if (!isDstROI_) {
         dstXOffset_ = dstYOffset_ = 0;
         dstROI_.width = pDst->GetSize().width;
         dstROI_.height = pDst->GetSize().height;
    }
    if (!isSrcROI_) {
         srcROI_.x = srcROI_.y = 0;
         srcROI_.width = pSrc->GetSize().width;
         srcROI_.height = pSrc->GetSize().height;
    }

    IppStatus st;
    if (isCenter_)
    {
         if (channelCount == 1)
           st = ippiResizeCenter_8u_C1R( pSrc->GetConstData(),
              pSrc->GetSize(), pSrc->GetStride(), srcROI_,
              pDst->GetData(dstXOffset_, dstYOffset_),
```

```
                pDst->GetStride(), dstROI_,
                xFactor_, yFactor_, xCenter_, yCenter_,
                interp_);
        else if (channelCount == 3)
          st = ippiResizeCenter_8u_C3R( pSrc->GetConstData(),
                pSrc->GetSize(), pSrc->GetStride(), srcROI_,
                pDst->GetData(dstXOffset_, dstYOffset_),
                pDst->GetStride(), dstROI_,
                xFactor_, yFactor_, xCenter_, yCenter_,
                interp_);
        else if (channelCount == 4)
          st = ippiResizeCenter_8u_C4R( pSrc->GetConstData(),
                pSrc->GetSize(), pSrc->GetStride(), srcROI_,
                pDst->GetData(dstXOffset_, dstYOffset_),
                pDst->GetStride(), dstROI_,
                xFactor_, yFactor_, xCenter_, yCenter_,
                interp_);
        else return -1;
    }
    else
    {
        if (channelCount == 1)
          st = ippiResize_8u_C1R( pSrc->GetConstData(),
                pSrc->GetSize(), pSrc->GetStride(), srcROI_,
                pDst->GetData(dstXOffset_, dstYOffset_),
                pDst->GetStride(), dstROI_,
                xFactor_, yFactor_, interp_);
        else if (channelCount == 3)
          st = ippiResize_8u_C3R( pSrc->GetConstData(),
                pSrc->GetSize(), pSrc->GetStride(), srcROI_,
                pDst->GetData(dstXOffset_, dstYOffset_),
                pDst->GetStride(), dstROI_,
                xFactor_, yFactor_, interp_);
        else if (channelCount == 4)
          st = ippiResize_8u_C4R( pSrc->GetConstData(),
                pSrc->GetSize(), pSrc->GetStride(), srcROI_,
                pDst->GetData(dstXOffset_, dstYOffset_),
                pDst->GetStride(), dstROI_,
                xFactor_, yFactor_, interp_);
        else return -1;
    }

    return ((int)st);
}
```

Figure 9.24 Resize Class and Some Methods

This class makes resizing images trivial. The code in Figure 9.25, which is very similar to the code that called the filter classes, resizes a source image by (2.0,0.5).

```
Resize r;
r.SetInterpType(Resize::LINEAR);
r.SetFactors(2.0, 0.5);
IppiSize newSize = r.GetDestSize(image.GetSize());

bigImage.InitAlloc(newSize, image.GetChannelCount());

r.Go(&image, &bigImage);
bigImage.View("Big image", 1);
```

Figure 9.25 Using the `Resize` Class

The result of this resize operation is shown in Figure 9.26.

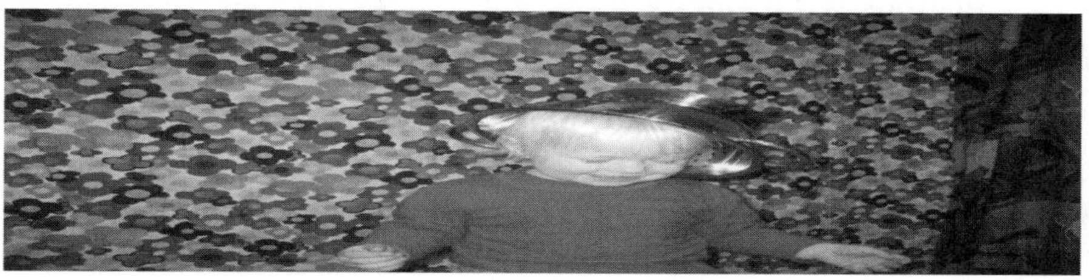

Figure 9.26 Result of `Resize::Go` with Factors (1.5, 0.5)

There is another resize function, `ippiResizeShift`. This function is designed for tiled images and uses a different pair of "factors" specially calculated by another function `ippiGetResizeFract`. It is necessary because of the simpler ROI handling in resize that was explained above.

Rotation

The rotation functions in Intel IPP are general and powerful but not user friendly. A user-friendly rotation would automatically resize and reallocate the destination image and make sure that all data from the source is captured in the destination. As noted in Figure 9.23, even a 90-degree rotation will produce an entirely invisible image if not shifted correctly.

The biggest problem is determining the location of the image after the rotation takes place, then correcting it with a shift. The goal of this section's `Rotate` class will be to place exactly this functionality in a wrapper around the Intel IPP classes.

The functions for rotation are summarized in Table 9.1.

Table 9.1 Rotation Functions in Intel® Integrated Performance Primitives (Intel® IPP)

Function name	Description
`ippiRotate`	Rotate an image around (0,0)
`ippiRotateCenter`	Rotate an image around (xCenter, yCenter)
`ippiGetRotateShift`, `ippiAddRotateShift`	Paired with `ippiRotate`, perform the same function as `ippiRotateCenter`
`ippiGetRotateQuad`	Calculate the four corners of the destination image
`ippiGetRotateBound`	Calculate the bounding box of the destination image

When used correctly, functions like `ippiGetRotateBound` make it relatively easy to resize and shift the destination to get a full image.

Figure 9.27 lists the `Rotate` class, which supports all the features of the Intel IPP rotate functions, including source and destination ROI, arbitrary center, and multiple interpolation types.

The functions `SetAngleDegrees` and `SetAngleRadians` set the member variable `angle_`. `SetAngleRadians` must first convert the angle, since `ippiRotate` takes its angle in degrees.

The method `GetDestSize_` uses `GetRotateBound` to calculate the top-most, bottom-most, left-most, and right-most extremes of the destination data. These values are returned in an array of type `double[2][2]` rather than an `IppiRect` structure because the bounding box is not usually integral. The values of the bounding box must first be rounded outward to account for interpolated and smoothed pixels; then they represent the most extreme pixels in each direction. Their differences plus one are the width and height of the transformed data.

If a center has been set with the `SetCenter` method, the call to `GetRotateShift` is made to avoid rounding error; in theory, it shouldn't change the outcome of the function. In fact, as it is currently implemented, with automatic output shifting every time, rotation should have exactly the same effect regardless of the center. This functionality is largely for demonstration and future potential.

The Go method that performs the rotation should be very familiar, since it is nearly identical to the equivalent Resize method. The main difference is the addition of these three lines:

```
ippiGetRotateBound(srcROI_, bound, angle_, xShift,
    yShift);
xShift -= bound[0][0];
yShift -= bound[0][1];
```

These lines determine the location of the start of the bounding box, and shift it to the origin. These shifts are then passed into the rotation functions as the shifts along the x-axis and y-axis. As a result, the rotated data is nicely framed within the destination image. The call to ippiGetRotateShift immediately preceding these lines should have no effect, since whatever shift is caused by rotation around a different center should be exactly removed by the subtraction of the bounding box origin.

This automatic shifting is convenient for retaining all the image data. If the goal of the rotation is something other than the visually best results, a slightly different formulation might be necessary. Replacing the automatic shift with a requested shift, "Rotate::SetAutoShift()", would meet that need.

The shifting specified by arguments to ippiRotate does not affect either origin or ROI. As a result, an ROI specified in the destination in the lower half of the image always captures the lower half of the result.

It might seem that the shift arguments passed to ippiRotate are redundant, since the starting x and y coordinates of the data are specified in the IppiRect. In fact, the ROI origin could be used for this purpose, but since the coordinate system origin remains at the data pointer, the data pointer would have to be shifted as well. This additional shift is awkward and inconvenient and, most importantly, since no fields of the IppiRect can be negative, it frequently produces invalid results. This potentially negative result prevents three-fourths of shifts from taking place and necessitates the "extra" shift arguments.

```
class Rotate
{
private:
    double angle_;
    int interp_;
    IppiRect srcROI_;
    IppiRect dstROI_;
```

```
    int isSrcROI_, isDstROI_;

    double xCenter_, yCenter_;
    int isCenter_;
//  double xShift_, yShift_;

    IppiSize GetDestSize_(IppiRect roi) const;

public:
    Rotate();
    ~Rotate();

    enum { NN, LINEAR, CUBIC };
    void SetInterpType(int type);
    int GetInterpType() const;
    void SetSmoothMode(int smoothFlag);

    void SetAngleRadians(double angle);
    void SetAngleDegrees(double angle);

    void SetSrcROI(IppiRect srcROI);
    void ClearSrcROI() {isSrcROI_ = 0;}
    void SetDestROI(IppiRect dstROI);
    void ClearDestROI() {isDstROI_ = 0;}

    void SetCenter(double xCenter, double yCenter);
    void ClearCenter() { isCenter_ = 0; }

    IppiSize GetDestSize(IppiSize srcSize) const;
    IppiSize GetDestSize() const;

    int Go(const Image8u*pSrc, Image8u* pDst);
};

//-------------

IppiSize Rotate::GetDestSize_(IppiRect srcROI) const
{
    double bound[2][2];
    double xShift = 0.0, yShift = 0.0;
    IppiSize dstSize = {0,0};

    if (isCenter_)
        ippiGetRotateShift(xCenter_, yCenter_, angle_,
          &xShift, &yShift);
    ippiGetRotateBound(srcROI, bound, angle_,
        xShift, yShift);

    dstSize.width = (int)(bound[1][0]+0.5) -
                  (int)(bound[0][0]-0.5) + 1.0;
```

```
    dstSize.height = (int)(bound[1][1]+0.5) -
                   (int)(bound[0][1]-0.5) + 1.0;

    if (isDstROI_)
    {
         if (dstSize.width > (dstROI_.width + dstROI_.x))
          dstSize.width = dstROI_.width +dstROI_.x;
         if (dstSize.height > (dstROI_.height + dstROI_.y))
          dstSize.height = dstROI_.height + dstROI_.y;
    }
    return dstSize;
}

int Rotate::Go(const Image8u*pSrc, Image8u* pDst)
{
    IppStatus st;

    double xShift=0.0, yShift=0.0;
    double bound[2][2];

    int channelCount = pSrc->GetChannelCount();
    if (channelCount != pDst->GetChannelCount()) return -1;

    if (!isDstROI_) {
         dstROI_.x = dstROI_.y = 0;
         dstROI_.width = pDst->GetSize().width;
         dstROI_.height = pDst->GetSize().height;
    }
    if (!isSrcROI_) {
         srcROI_.x = srcROI_.y = 0;
         srcROI_.width = pSrc->GetSize().width;
         srcROI_.height = pSrc->GetSize().height;
    }

    if (isCenter_)
         ippiGetRotateShift(xCenter_, yCenter_, angle_,
          &xShift, &yShift);
    ippiGetRotateBound(srcROI_, bound, angle_, xShift, yShift);
    xShift -= bound[0][0];
    yShift -= bound[0][1];

    if (channelCount == 1)
         st = ippiRotate_8u_C1R(pSrc->GetConstData(),
          pSrc->GetSize(), pSrc->GetStride(), srcROI_,
          pDst->GetData(), pDst->GetStride(), dstROI_,
          angle_, xShift, yShift, interp_);
    else if (channelCount == 3)
```

```
        st = ippiRotate_8u_C3R(pSrc->GetConstData(),
         pSrc->GetSize(), pSrc->GetStride(), srcROI_,
         pDst->GetData(), pDst->GetStride(), dstROI_,
         angle_, xShift, yShift, interp_);
    else if (channelCount == 4)
        st = ippiRotate_8u_C4R(pSrc->GetConstData(),
         pSrc->GetSize(), pSrc->GetStride(), srcROI_,
         pDst->GetData(), pDst->GetStride(), dstROI_,
         angle_, xShift, yShift, interp_);
    else return -1;

    return ((int)st);
}
```

Figure 9.27 `Rotate` Class and Some Methods

The code in Figure 9.28 puts this class to the test and demonstrates the behavior of ROIs. The first rotation has no region of interest, so the entire image is rotated. The result is shown in Figure 9.29a.

The second rotation has a source but not a destination region of interest. It is able to write anywhere in the destination, but only reads the upper-right quadrant of the source image. The result is a rotated rectangle, and the automatic shifting in the `Resize` class moves the result to the corner.

The third rotation uses the same destination image. The destination ROI asks like a stencil and only the upper-right corner of the result is written. As noted previously, the shift parameters do not effect the destination ROI. The image in Figure 9.29b contains both of these results.

```
    Rotate r;
    r.SetInterpType(Rotate::LINEAR);
    r.SetSmoothMode(1);
    r.SetAngleDegrees(482.0);

    IppiSize dstSize = r.GetDestSize(image.GetSize());
    rotImage.InitAlloc(dstSize, image.GetChannelCount());
    rotImage.Zero();
    r.Go(&image, &rotImage);
    rotImage.View("Rotated image", 0);

    rotImage.Zero();

    IppiRect srcROI = {
        image.GetSize().width/2,image.GetSize().height/2,
        image.GetSize().width/2,image.GetSize().height/2
    };
```

```
IppiRect srcROIFull = { 0, 0,
    image.GetSize().width, image.GetSize().height };
r.SetSrcROI(srcROI);
r.SetCenter(150.0, 150.0);
r.Go(&image, &rotImage);

IppiRect dstROI = {
    rotImage.GetSize().width/2,rotImage.GetSize().height/2,
    rotImage.GetSize().width/2,rotImage.GetSize().height/2
};

r.SetSrcROI(srcROIFull);
r.SetDestROI(dstROI);
r.Go(&image, &rotImage);

rotImage.View("Rotated image with two different ROIs", 1);

return 0;
```

Figure 9.28 Using the `Rotate` Class

Figure 9.29c shows what would happen if this line were removed from the `Rotate::Go` function:

```
ippiGetRotateBound(srcROI_, bound, angle_,
    xShift, yShift);
```

and these lines replaced it:

```
IppiRect tmpROI = {0,0,pSrc->GetSize().width,
    pSrc->GetSize().height};
ippiGetRotateBound(tmpROI, bound, angle_,
    xShift, yShift);
```

With this modification, the auto-shift ignores the source ROI, and the rotated data is written exactly where it would have been written if the source ROI were the entire image. You can see that the pieces fit together nicely.

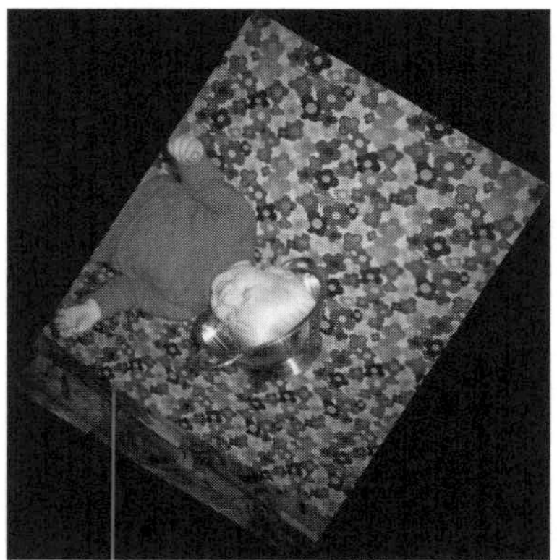

a) Rotate Without ROI

b) Two Rotations, One with Source ROI, One with Destination ROI

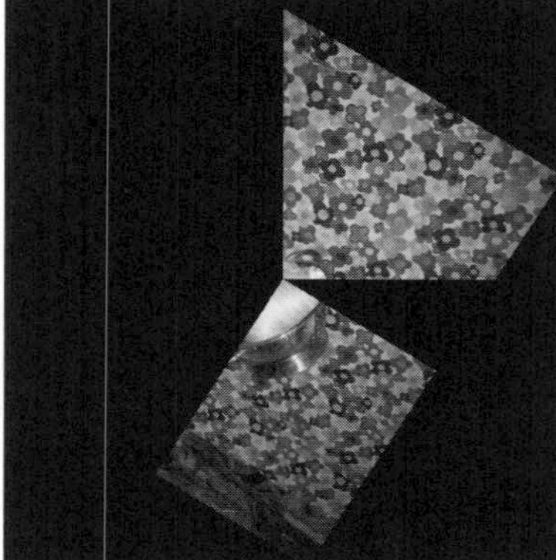

c) Rotations and ROIs in b), but Shift Ignores Source ROI

Figure 9.29 Rotation Results

Affine Transform

Rotation and resizing operations are subsets of the general affine transform. The affine transform is a general two-dimensional transform that preserves parallel lines. This transform is expressed as

```
xd = coeff[0][0] * xs + coeff[0][1] * ys + coeff[0][2]
yd = coeff[1][0] * xs + coeff[1][1] * ys + coeff[1][2]
```

The pair `(xs,ys)` is a point in the source image and `(xd,yd)` is a point in the destination image.[3] This calculation is general enough to shear, resize, and shift an image; in fact, each set of coefficients can be broken down into shears, size changes, and shifts. Rotation is also an affine operation and can be represented as a series of shears.

One of the main advantages of the affine transform is that several affine transforms can be combined into a single operation. When expressed in matrix form, the transforms are multiplied together to form a single matrix representing the final operation. These matrices must be kept in order for this multiplication since such operations are not commutative.

Since the implementation for affine transforms in Intel IPP is comparable in performance to rotation, the only advantage that `ippiRotate` has is simplicity. A good wrapper should take care of that.

Figure 9.30 lists a sample wrapper for the Intel IPP function that performs affine transforms, `ippiWarpAffine`. This wrapper allows a user to set the affine transform directly or assemble it as a series of shears, size changes, and rotations.

Presenting the affine transform C/C++ expression above as an equation, this affine transform can be described as:

$$x' = a_{00} * x + a_{01} * y + a_{02}$$

$$y' = a_{10} * x + a_{11} * y + a_{12}$$

[3] As noted earlier, the transforms work best if executed backward, so when implemented the equations are inverted to create expressions `xs = fx(xd,yd)` and `ys = fy(xd,yd)`. The goal is to have an expression for each destination pixel in the form `pDst[yd][xd] = pSrc[ys][xs] = pSrc[fy(xd,yd)][fx(xd,yd)]`.

Alternatively, it can be expressed in matrix form:

$$\begin{bmatrix} x' \\ y' \\ 1 \end{bmatrix} = \begin{bmatrix} a_{00} & a_{01} & a_{02} \\ a_{10} & a_{11} & a_{12} \\ 0 & 0 & 1 \end{bmatrix} \bullet \begin{bmatrix} x \\ y \\ 1 \end{bmatrix}$$

In the `Affine` class, calling individual functions `AddRotate`, `AddShear`, `AddResize`, and `AddAffine` causes the affine transform matrix to be premultiplied by the matrix describing that operation. For coding convenience and generality, these functions convert the specific arguments, such as rotation angles, into transform matrices to pass into `AddAffine`, which then does the work. `AddRotate` calls `AddAffine` with the rotation matrix:

$$\begin{bmatrix} \cos(\theta) & \sin(\theta) & 0 \\ -\sin(\theta) & \cos(\theta) & 0 \\ 0 & 0 & 1 \end{bmatrix}$$

`AddShear` calls `AddAffine` with the shear matrix:

$$\begin{bmatrix} 1 & xFactor & 0 \\ yFactor & 1 & 0 \\ 0 & 0 & 1 \end{bmatrix}$$

`AddResize` calls `AddAffine` with the resize matrix:

$$\begin{bmatrix} xFactor & 0 & 0 \\ 0 & yFactor & 0 \\ 0 & 0 & 1 \end{bmatrix}$$

The function `AddAffine` performs the matrix multiplication between the new matrix and the old transform matrix, with the new matrix first. The result replaces the old transform matrix.

It would also be possible to create another set of functions that place the operation at the front of the list, conceptually performing it before the rest of the transforms. Such a function would post-multiply by the new matrix each time.

The `Go` method uses the `ippiAffineBound` function to calculate the shift necessary to align the origins and to keep the transformed image in the destination area. These shifts in the x and y directions are added to the coefficients at [0][2] and [1][2], which are named a_{02} and a_{12} in the formula above.

Like the `Rotate` class, this class does not have an `AddShift` function because shifting is used to preserve the entire destination image. However, the matrix-based mechanism would support it quite naturally, as a multiplication by the matrix:

$$\begin{bmatrix} 1 & 0 & xshift \\ 0 & 1 & yshift \\ 0 & 0 & 1 \end{bmatrix}$$

While the automatic shifting is operating, the shift is removed regardless of its location in the sequence of operations. Because all the operations are linear, a shift added anywhere in the sequence does not affect any final coefficients except the shifts.[4]

Also unnecessary but done for cleanliness is the last operation in `Go` that restores the shift coefficients to their user-set state. This isn't necessary in the current implementation, but might be necessary if the auto-shifting were removed. Regardless, it is unclean to make that modification to the filter at all, since it prevents `Go` from being a `const` function.

```
class Affine
{
private:
    double angle_;
    int interp_;
    IppiRect srcROI_;
    IppiRect dstROI_;
```

[4] To confirm this, examine the formulation of the matrix multiplication in the `AddAffine` method. The shift coefficients are only used in calculating the shift coefficients (0,2) and (1,2). The other coefficients have no terms containing those coefficients in their formulae.

```
    int isSrcROI_, isDstROI_;

    double pCoeffs_[2][3];
    IppiSize GetDestSize_(IppiRect roi) const;

public:
    Affine();
    ~Affine();

    enum { NN, LINEAR, CUBIC };
    void SetInterpType(int type);
    int GetInterpType() const;
    void SetSmoothMode(int smoothFlag);

    void SetSrcROI(IppiRect srcROI);
    void ClearSrcROI() {isSrcROI_ = 0;}
    void SetDestROI(IppiRect dstROI);
    void ClearDestROI() {isDstROI_ = 0;}

    void Reset();
    void AddRotate(double degrees);
    void AddShear(double xShear, double yShear);
    void AddResize(double xFactor, double yFactor);
    void AddAffine(const double pCoeffs[2][3]);
    void SetAffine(const double pCoeffs[2][3]);

    IppiSize GetDestSize(IppiSize srcSize) const;
    IppiSize GetDestSize() const;

    int Go(const Image8u*pSrc, Image8u* pDst);
};

//------------------------

void Affine::AddRotate(double degrees)
{
    double s, c;

    degrees = degrees * IPP_PI / 180.0;
    ippsSinCos_64f_A50(&degrees, &s, &c, 1);

    double pCoeffs[2][3] = { { c, s, 0.0},
                             {-s, c, 0.0} };

    AddAffine(pCoeffs);
}

void Affine::AddShear(double xShear, double yShear)
{
    double pCoeffs[2][3] = { { 1.0, xShear, 0.0},
                             {yShear, 1.0, 0.0} };
```

```
    AddAffine(pCoeffs);
}

void Affine::AddResize(double xFactor, double yFactor)
{
    double pCoeffs[2][3] = { { xFactor, 0.0, 0.0},
                              {0.0, yFactor, 0.0} };
    AddAffine(pCoeffs);
}

void Affine::AddAffine(const double pCoeffs[2][3])
{
    double s00, s01, s02, s10, s11, s12;
    double d00, d01, d02, d10, d11, d12;

    s00 = pCoeffs[0][0]; s10 = pCoeffs[1][0];
    s01 = pCoeffs[0][1]; s11 = pCoeffs[1][1];
    s02 = pCoeffs[0][2]; s12 = pCoeffs[1][2];

    d00 = pCoeffs_[0][0]; d10 = pCoeffs_[1][0];
    d01 = pCoeffs_[0][1]; d11 = pCoeffs_[1][1];
    d02 = pCoeffs_[0][2]; d12 = pCoeffs_[1][2];

    //                    [x]
    //                    [y]
    //                    [1]
    //            [00 01 02]
    //            [10 11 12]
    //            [-  -   1]
    //     [00 01 02]
    //     [10 11 12]
    //     [-  -   1]

    pCoeffs_[0][0] = s00 * d00 + s01 * d10;
    pCoeffs_[1][0] = s10 * d00 + s11 * d10;

    pCoeffs_[0][1] = s00 * d01 + s01 * d11;
    pCoeffs_[1][1] = s10 * d01 + s11 * d11;

    pCoeffs_[0][2] = s00 * d02 + s01 * d12 + s02;
    pCoeffs_[1][2] = s10 * d02 + s11 * d12 + s12;
}

int Affine::Go(const Image8u*pSrc, Image8u* pDst)
{
    IppStatus st;
```

```
    double xShift=0.0, yShift=0.0;
    double bound[2][2];

    int channelCount = pSrc->GetChannelCount();
    if (channelCount != pDst->GetChannelCount()) return -1;

    if (!isDstROI_) {
         dstROI_.x = dstROI_.y = 0;
         dstROI_.width = pDst->GetSize().width;
         dstROI_.height = pDst->GetSize().height;
    }
    if (!isSrcROI_) {
         srcROI_.x = srcROI_.y = 0;
         srcROI_.width = pSrc->GetSize().width;
         srcROI_.height = pSrc->GetSize().height;
    }

    ippiGetAffineBound(srcROI_, bound, pCoeffs_);
    pCoeffs_[0][2] -= bound[0][0];
    pCoeffs_[1][2] -= bound[0][1];

    if (channelCount == 1)
         st = ippiWarpAffine_8u_C1R(pSrc->GetConstData(),
           pSrc->GetSize(), pSrc->GetStride(), srcROI_,
           pDst->GetData(), pDst->GetStride(), dstROI_,
           pCoeffs_, interp_);
    else if (channelCount == 3)
         st = ippiWarpAffine_8u_C3R(pSrc->GetConstData(),
           pSrc->GetSize(), pSrc->GetStride(), srcROI_,
           pDst->GetData(), pDst->GetStride(), dstROI_,
           pCoeffs_, interp_);
    else if (channelCount == 4)
         st = ippiWarpAffine_8u_C4R(pSrc->GetConstData(),
           pSrc->GetSize(), pSrc->GetStride(), srcROI_,
           pDst->GetData(), pDst->GetStride(), dstROI_,
           pCoeffs_, interp_);
    else return -1;

    pCoeffs_[0][2] += bound[0][0];
    pCoeffs_[1][2] += bound[0][1];

    return ((int)st);
}
```

Figure 9.30 `Affine` Class and Some Methods

Using class `Affine` is as easy as previous classes, but more fun because the class is more powerful. The code in Figure 9.31 performs a rotation and resize on the image before displaying it.

```
Affine r;
r.SetInterpType(Affine::LINEAR);
r.SetSmoothMode(1);
r.AddRotate(45.0);
r.AddResize(1.5, .75);

IppiSize dstSize = r.GetDestSize(image.GetSize());
newImage.InitAlloc(dstSize, image.GetChannelCount());
newImage.Zero();
r.Go(&image, &newImage);
newImage.View("Altered Image", 1);
```

Figure 9.31 Using the `Affine` Class

The result is displayed in Figure 9.32. Note that the data is exactly contained within the new image, thanks to `ippiGetAffineBound`.

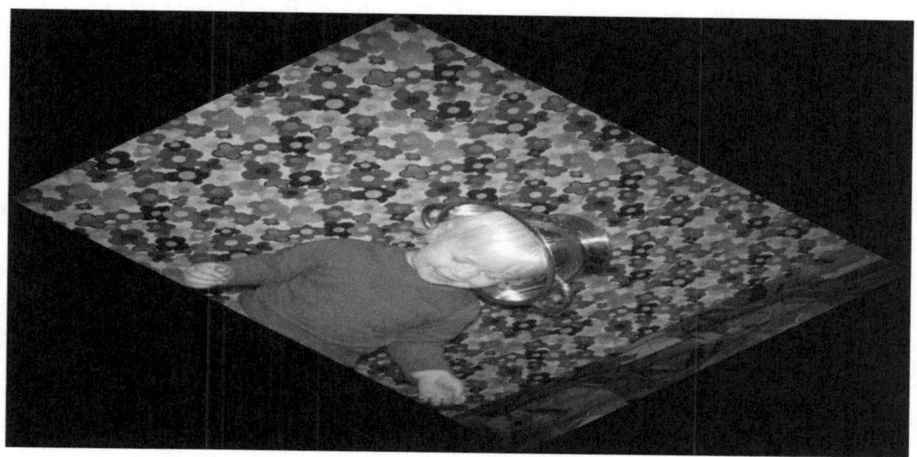

Figure 9.32 Result of `AddRotate(45)` and `AddResize(1.5, .75)`

Geometric Transforms and Tiling

Geometric operations present a real challenge for tiled images. Unlike other operations, no one-to-one mapping between source and destination tiles exists. Furthermore, the neighborhood that contributes to a destination tile isn't reliably regular—that is, it is neither rectangular nor a fixed size as it is with filtering. However, the Intel IPP functions have enough parameters that you can still operate on an image block-by-block.

Just as with other operations for tiled image, to implement a geometric operation, call the operation on every source tile that is appropriate. The first difference is that for each source block, you need to call the geometric function once for every destination block that it will overlap. The next difference is that you need to trick the geometric function into believing that the tile you pass is a piece of a much larger image that is contained in memory, rather than a complete image itself or a tile.

Assume the following pseudocode for performing geometric operations for tiling:

```
For each tile in source
    For each tile in destination
        Op(pSrc, srcROI, srcSize, pDst, dstROI, …)
```

Instead of passing the start of the tile as the source pointer into the geometric function, pass a pointer to where the start of the image *would be if the image were contiguous in memory rather than tiled*. The way to calculate this is to subtract the total offset in elements from the start of the image:

```
pSrc = pTile - numChannels*xOff - step*yOff
```

The `(xOff,yOff)` offsets are the coordinates of the tile in the image. For a multi-byte pixel, the third term becomes `(step/bpp)*yOff` because of the way the compiler handles pointer math. The `Image8u` object will calculate the right data if you use the expression `image.GetData(-xOff, -yOff)`.

The ROI of the image is a rectangle starting where the tile is supposed to start in the larger image. The size is the size of the tile. A rectangle for the above would be `{xOff, yOff, w, h}`.

The size of the image must be at least the offset plus the size of the tile; that is, an image big enough to contain that tile. However, the stride used must be the actual stride of the smaller image or tile, not the imaginary larger image. The same calculation is done for the destination, if tiled.

Figure 9.33 shows this operation. The `rotateTile` function tricks the `Rotate` function into believing that the tile is located at `srcOff` in an image of dimensions `(srcOff.x+w, srcOff.y+h)`. It then rotates as much of it as will fit into the destination, which is treated similarly.

In this example, the code using the `rotateTile` function loads an image from memory into the object `image`, and then treats that object as a tile in a larger image and rotates it nine times into the destination. It passes the same image to `rotateTile` each time, but to a different location for that tile. The code does not simulate a tiled image for the destination, but uses a larger image to capture the result.

```
int rotateTile(Image8u* pSrc, IppiPoint srcOff,
               Image8u* pDst, IppiPoint dstOff,
               double angle, int interp)
{
    int sw = pSrc->GetSize().width;
    int sh = pSrc->GetSize().height;
    int dw = pDst->GetSize().width;
    int dh = pDst->GetSize().height;

    IppiRect srcROI = { srcOff.x, srcOff.y, sw, sh };
    IppiSize srcSize = { srcOff.x+sw, srcOff.y+sh };
    IppiRect dstROI = { dstOff.x, dstOff.y, dw, dh };

    IppStatus st = ippiRotate_8u_C3R(
        pSrc->GetData(-srcOff.x, -srcOff.y),
        srcSize, pSrc->GetStride(), srcROI,
        pDst->GetData(-dstOff.x, -dstOff.y),
        pDst->GetStride(), dstROI,
        angle, 0, 0, interp);

    return st;
}

int main(int argc, char* argv[])
{
    Image8u image;
    if (image.LoadBMP(argv[1]))
        return -1;
    image.View(argv[1],0);
    int h=image.GetSize().height;
    int w=image.GetSize().width;
    Image8u rotImage;
    rotImage.InitAlloc(w*3, h*3, image.GetChannelCount());
```

```
    for (int i=0; i<3; i++)
        for (int j=0; j<3; j++)
        {
          IppiPoint srcOff = {w*i, h*j};
          IppiPoint dstOff = {0,0};
          rotateTile(&image, srcOff, &rotImage, dstOff, 10.0,
            IPPI_INTER_LINEAR | IPPI_SMOOTH_EDGE);
        }

    rotImage.View("Rotated image", 1);

    return 0;
}
```

Figure 9.33 Using Negative Offsets to Rotate a Tile

The output of this code is shown in Figure 9.34. The rotations interpret the source image as a tile at `(w*i, h*j)` for `i` equal to 0, 1, and 2 and `j` equal to 0, 1, and 2. The result is in a single image, but could easily have been into nine different destination tiles that had to be collected into a single image.

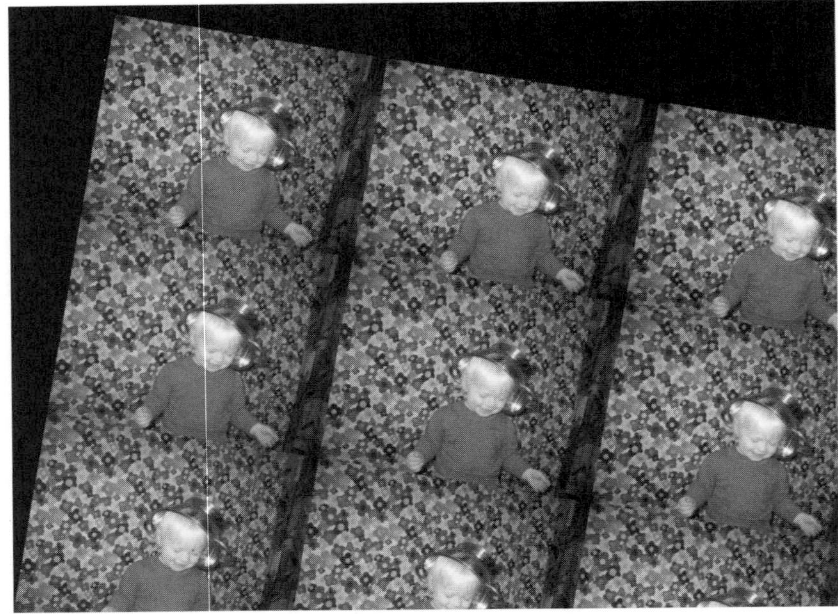

Figure 9.34 Result of Rotations in Figure 9.33

Iterating through the tiles shouldn't be done exhaustively. It is more efficient to consider only those tiles in the source that actually contribute and tiles in the destination that will contain new data. You can calculate a bounding rectangle in the source by using one of the `ippiGetXXXBound` functions. You can calculate the bounds of the tiles in the destination by transforming each corner of the source image into the destination image space, as in the examples above.

Other Transforms in Intel® Integrated Performance Primitives (Intel® IPP)

The preceding discussion covered only about half of the transforms in the Intel IPP API. The remaining transforms are briefly explained below.

Perspective Transform

In the same way the affine transform can be considered the general two-dimensional transform, the perspective transform can be considered the general three-dimensional transform. Properly applied, this transform can represent a projection of an image onto a plane of arbitrary orientation. It has more degrees of freedom than the affine transform, but looks similar:

$$\begin{bmatrix} x' \\ y' \\ n \end{bmatrix} = \begin{bmatrix} a_{00} & a_{01} & a_{02} \\ a_{10} & a_{11} & a_{12} \\ a_{20} & a_{21} & 1 \end{bmatrix} \bullet \begin{bmatrix} x \\ y \\ 1 \end{bmatrix}$$

This matrix multiplication is followed by normalization to (x'/n, y'/n, 1). This normalization is the nonlinear operation that enables the perspective effects that give the image a three-dimensional appearance.

An interesting `Perspective` class would thus include such functions as `AddXRotate()`, `AddYRotate()` and `AddZShift()`. These functions would require a matrix-oriented projection model and would themselves benefit from Intel IPP matrix operations. See Chapter 11 for a discussion on matrices and graphics.

Remap

The remap function is a completely general geometric transform. It takes a destination-to-source map the same size as the destination image. Each pixel has a corresponding floating-point (x,y) coordinate pair. The operation calculates the value at that location according to the interpolation mode and sets the destination pixel to that value. The remap function is most useful in morphing or exciting video effects, for which the other geometric transforms aren't flexible enough.

Shear

Shear is less useful and interesting than the other transforms, but it is included in the Intel IPP set because it can be performed efficiently. The support functions include `ippiGetShearQuad` and `ippiGetShearBound`.

Bilinear Transform

The bilinear warp can be useful for some projections or as an approximation of the perspective transform for some computer vision tasks. The transform can be expressed as

$$x' = c_{00} * x * y + c_{01} * x + c_{02} * y + c_{03}$$

$$y' = c_{10} * x * y + c_{11} * x + c_{12} * y + c_{13}$$

`Back` *Functions*

In addition to the usual forward-transform parameterization, it is possible in many cases to specify the transform with the reverse-transform coefficients. Since most operations are implemented this way, this method is, if anything, a little more efficient. Mainly, these functions are useful as direct replacements for reverse transform functions that are already implemented.

The functions that operate in this mode are `ippiWarpAffineBack`, `ippiWarpPerspectiveBack`, and `ippiWarpBilinearBack`.

Transform Calculation Functions

In many cases, a transform is dictated not by the coefficients but by the shapes or sizes of the source and destination. The coefficients may not be available. For these cases, Intel IPP has three functions that calculate the transform coefficient from bounding quadrangles. The functions that perform this calculation are `ippiGetAffineTransform`, `ippiGetPerspectiveTransform`, and `ippiGetBilinearTransform`.

Further Reading

The Pocket Handbook of Image Processing Algorithms in C (Myler 1993) is a nifty little reference for image-processing algorithms and filters. *Handbook of Image Processing Operators* (Klette 1994) is a good text for image-processing filters and machine-vision heuristics. *Fundamentals of Digital Image Processing* (Jain 1989) is one of the most prominent image-processing books. It is oriented on mathematics and signal processing rather than software implementation, but it is very comprehensive.

Geometric algorithms tend to be covered well in more graphics-oriented books, such as *Mathematical Elements for Computer Graphics* (Rogers 1990).

The Intel Integrated Performance Primitives 4.0 has a few image-processing examples that are worth investigating, including one sample that helps with the mathematics of tiling and one demo that allows you to play with various Intel IPP operations and see the results.

Chapter 10

JPEG and MPEG

This chapter is a brief introduction to video compression and decompression algorithms and their Intel® Integrated Performance Primitives (Intel® IPP)-based implementations, in particular, the popular JPEG and MPEG-2 formats. This chapter aims to demystify the Intel IPP options and philosophy for coding these algorithms and to give a few representative examples of coding in each area.

Overview of Coding

Image and video encoders and decoders, in software called *codecs*, are intended to compress their media for storage or transmission. Raw images are quite large; with present technology, raw digital video is almost unworkable. Moreover, working with these media uncompressed, except for capture and display, is completely unnecessary and inefficient with processors as they are. It is faster to read compressed video from disk and decompress it than it would be to read uncompressed video.

Most compression is based on taking advantage of redundancy and predictability in data to reduce the amount of information necessary to represent it. Two common techniques are run-length coding, which converts runs of data into run-lengths and values, and variable-length coding, which converts data of fixed bit lengths into variable bit lengths according to popularity. Huffman coding and arithmetic coding are examples of variable-length coding.

Another source of compression is perceptibility. Obviously, for some kinds of data, such as text and binary executables, compression must be lossless. A compression method that sometimes changed an "a" to an "A" would not be acceptable. Stand-alone Huffman coding is exactly reversible. However, it is possible to compress media information in a way that is not exactly reversible but is virtually undetectable. Such methods are called *lossy*. This means that the output is not guaranteed to be exactly the same. However, in many cases the loss can be imperceptible or have manageable visual effect. Just as with audio coding, the compression algorithm transforms the data into spaces in which information can be removed while minimizing the perceptible impact to the media.

Most media compression is done using transform-based coding methods. Such methods convert the position-based information into frequency-based or position/frequency-based information. The compression benefit is that important information becomes concentrated in fewer values. Then the coder can represent the more-important information with more bits and the less-important information with fewer bits. The perception model dictates the importance of information, but generally higher-frequency information is considered less important.

Figure 10.1 shows the framework of a transform-based encoding and decoding scheme.

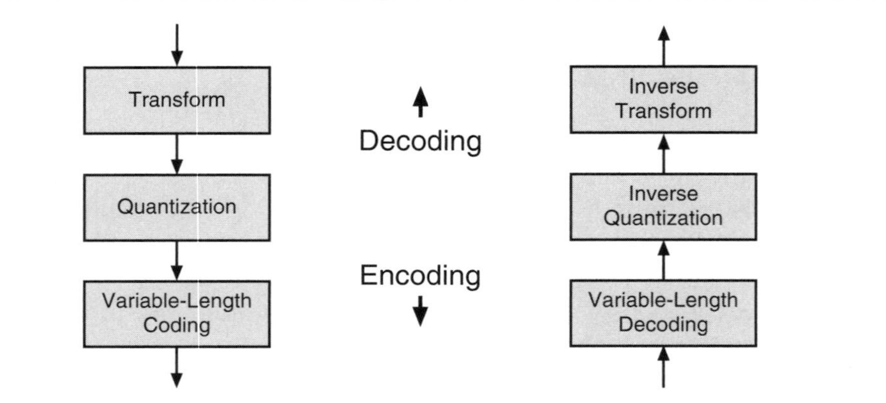

Figure 10.1 Simple Diagram of Transform-Based Image Coding

Compression schemes for video usually try to take advantage of a second source of redundancy, repetition between frames of video. The coder either encodes raw frames of video or encodes the difference, often compensated for motion, between successive frames.

Coding in Intel® Integrated Performance Primitives (Intel® IPP)

The Intel IPP support of image and video compression takes several forms. Intel IPP provides portions of codecs and includes samples that are partial codecs for several compression algorithms. In particular, it includes:

- General functions such as transforms and arithmetic operations that are applicable across one or more compression algorithms.
- Specific functions such as Huffman coding for JPEG that you can think of as "codec slices". At present, Intel IPP provides such functions for MPEG-1, MPEG-2, MPEG-4, DV, H.263, and H.264.
- Sample encoders and decoders of several major video and imaging standards, including JPEG, JPEG-2000, MPEG-2, and MPEG-4.

The subsequent sections will explain each of these elements for three algorithms, JPEG, JPEG-2000, and MPEG-2. The explanation includes all three of the above categories of support, leaning heavily on examples from the codec samples.

JPEG

JPEG is a widely used standard for image compression. The term is an acronym that stands for the Joint Photographic Experts Group, the body that designed the specification. JPEG is a powerful and effective compression technique that has been around for over a decade. It has gained popularity because of its effectiveness, because it is an international standard, and because a baseline JPEG codec can be built without using proprietary algorithms.

The primary JPEG version, *sequential lossy compression* or *sequential DCT-based compression*, follows the standard structure of the transform-based coder: transform, quantize, variable-length code. But JPEG is divided into four sub-codecs, listed here:

- *Sequential-lossy or sequential-DCT-based*. As noted, this version is transform-based. It used uses *Discrete Cosine Transform* or DCT. Images in this sub-codec are decoded all at once.
- *Sequential-lossless*. This mode of operation is lossless, so the size of the image is reduced without causing a loss of data. It is not transform based, but calculates differences between adjacent pixels to reduce the entropy of the encoded data.
- *Progressive-lossy or progressive-DCT-based*. Progressive images are encoded in such a way that it is possible to retrieve a low-resolution version of the image. The image is encoded in parts, with low frequencies and high-order bits first.
- *Hierarchical*. Like progressive images, hierarchical images are encoded in such a way that it is possible to retrieve a low-resolution version of the image. The image is encoded as a low-resolution image first followed by a series of refining difference images.

JPEG Codec Components

Figure 10.2 illustrates the major components of a software JPEG codec for the sequential DCT-based mode of operation. It demonstrates both the components within the JPEG standard and the additional components necessary to encode or decode a typical JPEG bitstream. Each component is described in detail below.

One component that is not shown is the file format parser. JPEG itself does not define a file format. The most commonly used is the *JPEG File Interchange Format* or JFIF, though JPEG-TIFF and FlashPix[†] are also used. JFIF is a simple file format that attaches a short header to the bit stream of a single encoded JPEG image. The data can be extracted from the file with little parsing of the header.

Since JFIF is so common, several of these components assume the JFIF format. In addition to providing organization to a JPEG file, JFIF specifies the color space and subsampling.

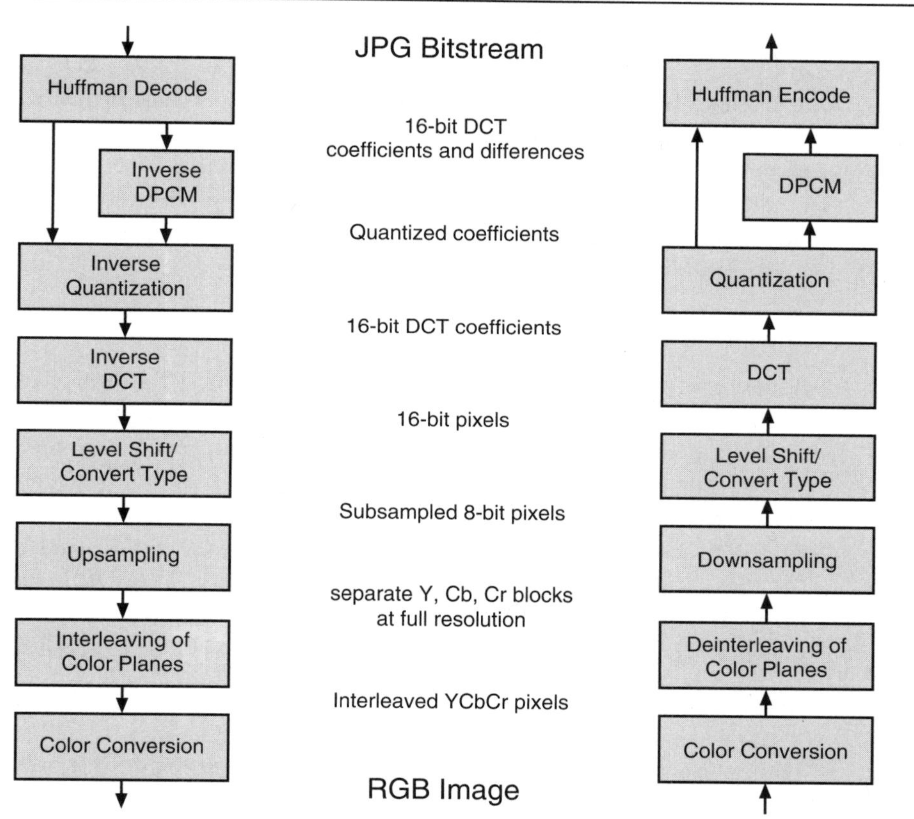

Figure 10.2 Components of a DCT-Based Sequential JPEG Implementation in Software

Variable-Length Coding

The first stage of decoding a JPEG image is decoding the information that is packed into a stream of bits. This stream is composed of data and control codes. The decoder interprets the sequence of bits as a series of variable-length codes then determines which parts are data and which are control codes.

The values extracted from the Huffman decoder block are coefficients resulting from the DCT of the encoder. The coefficients are encoded in zig-zag order, and are only encoded until the last nonzero coefficient. The Huffman decoder generally reconstructs the 8 x 8 blocks in the original order then outputs a set of 8 x 8 blocks of coefficients.

These blocks are grouped into a set of fewer than ten blocks called a *minimum coding unit* or MCU. Each MCU contains at least one block of each image component, more if subsampling is used.

The Huffman coding stage can also be replaced with another algorithm for exploiting the statistics of the data called *arithmetic coding*. Arithmetic coding requires a separate decoder.

DPCM

Because of the nature of the DCT, each of the coefficients is the result of a differencing operation and is therefore normalized to center around zero. The exception is the first coefficient, referred to as the DC coefficient. This coefficient is the sum of the original values, rather than differences among them, and does not average to zero.

JPEG normalizes this value by subtracting each DC coefficient from the one before, then encoding the difference. The *Differential Pulse Code Modulation* or DPCM step adds the decoded DC coefficient of the previous block to the decoded difference value of the current one.

Quantization and Inverse Quantization

The quantization in JPEG uses tables with 64 possible quantization resolutions. Each position in the 8 x 8 block of DCT coefficients has a separately defined interval. The table is defined within the image file.

Research into the human visual system demonstrates a greater sensitivity to larger details and lower frequencies than smaller details and higher frequencies. As a consequence, there is an implicit assumption that low-frequency information in the image is a higher priority than high-frequency information. Though the quantization tables are not set by the standard, almost all tables have significantly smaller intervals in the first few, low-frequency coefficients. These intervals may be around 4 to 16 for the first few coefficients and be as high as 100 or more for later coefficients.

DCT and Inverse DCT

The DCT is defined for any size, but JPEG exclusively uses an 8 x 8 version. Of the 64 coefficients, 63 represent an estimate of the degree to which various horizontal and vertical frequencies are present in the block. The first coefficient alone is the zero-frequency, or DC, coefficient. It is the average of the values in the block.

Type and Color Conversion, Interleaving, and Sampling

The JPEG format itself also does not specify a color space. However, the JFIF uses a standard, subsampled color space.

Because the human visual system has less resolution for color than black and white, it makes sense to represent the color information at a lower resolution than the intensity. The YCbCr color space is one of many that represent the information in each pixel as intensity (Y) and color (Cb and Cr). This separation allows the intensity to be represented at full resolution while the color is reduced to half of the horizontal and/or vertical resolution.

There are several algorithms for reducing or increasing this resolution. Often, the sampling is combined with the color space conversion. The color space conversion is usually also responsible for converting between planar and interleaved data. The JPEG blocks all assume operation on a single color component. Before the data reaches the DCT, whether in YCbCr or another color space, the encoder must separate it into 8 x 8 blocks of one component each. Generally, the decoder must interleave this data again when reconstructing an interleaved RGB image.

Most RGB images are represented with 8 bits per color component, or 24 bits total. The image pixels are also unsigned, since they must always be positive. However, the DCT algorithms generally require that the data be 16 bits and signed as a matter of precision. Some DCT operations include the conversion, but in JPEG the data type conversion is more commonly combined with the color conversion.

As part of this conversion, a *level shift* must be performed. Each value has 128 subtracted from it when changing to signed and 128 added to it when changing back to unsigned. The resulting data range of the signed numbers centers on zero.

Figure 10.2 shows one possible order for executing these operations, but other orders are possible. For example, upsampling or downsampling can happen before the type conversion or after.

Progressive JPEG

Two methods are employed to allow the division of an encoded image into a series of scans of increasing detail. The encoder may choose to encode only a few of the coefficients in each scan and provide the starting and ending position of those coefficients. This method is called *spectral selection*. In later scans, additional sequences of coefficients are provided.

The encoder may also provide higher-order coefficient bits first, a technique called *successive approximation*. In each subsequent scan, one additional bit is provided.

Both of these methods for creating progressive images involve slightly modified calculations and treatment of the data and require different Huffman encoding functions.

Lossless JPEG

Lossless coding replaces the DCT with a prediction based only on the pixels above, to the left, and diagonally up and to the left. A predicted value is calculated using one of several hard-coded formulae. Pixels are encoded as the difference between the actual value and the predicted value.

Hierarchical JPEG

In the hierarchical mode, an image is encoded as a pyramid of images of varying resolutions. The first image is subsampled and encoded at the lowest resolution. Subsequent images are encoded as the difference between the previous resolution image, upsampled, and the current image.

The hierarchical mode requires removal of the DPCM stage from the second and subsequent resolutions, since the values to be encoded are already the result of a difference operation.

Hierarchical mode can be combined with progressive and lossless modes.

JPEG in Intel IPP

Intel IPP contains enough functions to optimize the majority of a JPEG encoder and decoder. Each of the blocks in Figure 10.2 is covered by at least one Intel IPP function. In most cases, there are several choices of functions that implement each block. Some functions implement exactly one block but others implement two or more. In many cases, there are performance benefits to integrating several steps of the codec into a single building block.

The implementation requires significant glue logic. Such logic is necessary to move data around, process control codes, decide on algorithms and tables, and so on. Furthermore, there are plenty of optional flavors of JPEG, and not all of them are covered completely by these functions.

Huffman Coding

Intel IPP provides Huffman encoding and decoding functions for decoding blocks of coefficients. No translation is performed for control codes, although the decoding functions extract control codes from the stream.

Two functions of Huffman encode blocks of coefficients into in a bit stream: `EncodeHuffman8x8_JPEG` and `EncodeHuffman8x8_Direct_JPEG`. The functions take two Huffman tables in specification structures as arguments, one each for AC and DC coefficients. The former also takes a state structure that maintains necessary buffers. The code tables are constructed from a standard JPEG format that can be preassembled or created by `EncodeHuffmanRawTableInit` based on frequency statistics. The versions of the function `GetHuffmanStatistics8x8` calculate these statistics for 8 x 8 blocks.

Progressive encoding requires four `EncodeHuffman8x8` functions, with the function modifiers `DCFirst`, `ACFirst`, `DCRefine`, and `ACRefine`. The `First` functions encode the high-order bits and/or the first sequence of coefficients for the first pass. The `Refine` functions encode additional bits, one at a time, and/or subsequent ranges of coefficients.

The functions that support decoding are analogs of the above. The functions `DecodeHuffman8x8` and `DecodeHuffman8x8_Direct` implement Huffman decoding for sequential JPEG images; four functions support progressive JPEG decoding.

Intel IPP does not support the optional arithmetic coding in JPEG.

Type and Color Conversion, Interleaving, and Sampling

To encode a 24-bit RGB image in JPEG as YCbCr 4:2:2, the encoder must perform four conversions before the transform stage. They are converting from RGB to YCbCr, de-interleaving the three channels, downsampling the color channels, and changing the data type from `Ipp8u` to `Ipp16s`. Figure 10.3 lists the Intel IPP functions involved in performing these four conversions. As indicated by the figure, there is some flexibility in the order of these operations.

There are about six ways to perform this set of conversions within Intel IPP. The methods differ in levels of integration. The options for encoding range from the single function `RGBToYCbCr422LS_JPEG_8u16s_C3P3R`, which executes all four operations in one call, to individual functions that perform each stage in separate calls. The advantage of the former is the performance and convenience of a single function. However, this monolithic operation may not be appropriate to many images—for example, those in a different color space—or to many algorithms, since there are numerous reasons to break this operation in pieces.

The set of functions in Intel IPP supports other color spaces. Only YCbCr is supported fully, with a single integrated function. But if you use `SampleDown` for sampling and `Sub128` for type conversion and level-shifting function, any one of the Intel IPP color space conversions can replace `RGBToYCbCr`. In many cases, you might need an additional interleaved-planar conversion, such as `Convert_8u_C3P3R`, and downsampling may or may not be required.

For each encoding function, there is an analogous decoding function that performs the inverse operation. Figure 10.4 lists the functions that decode a JPEG image that uses YCbCr 4:2:2 and indicates which operations they cover. The `SampleDown` functions are not exactly reversible.

Discrete Cosine Transform and Quantization

The DCT and quantization components have the same organization as the conversions. There are integrated versions and separated ones. However, there are fewer sensible ways to break down the three operations and, unlike the color space conversions, there are no variants within each operation, so there are fewer functions overall.

Figure 10.5 shows the four options for performing DCT and quantization for JPEG encoding. The Intel IPP contains a general size DCT, but for JPEG, all DCTs are 8 x 8. Likewise, the quantization functions, integrated or not, take 8 x 8 blocks.

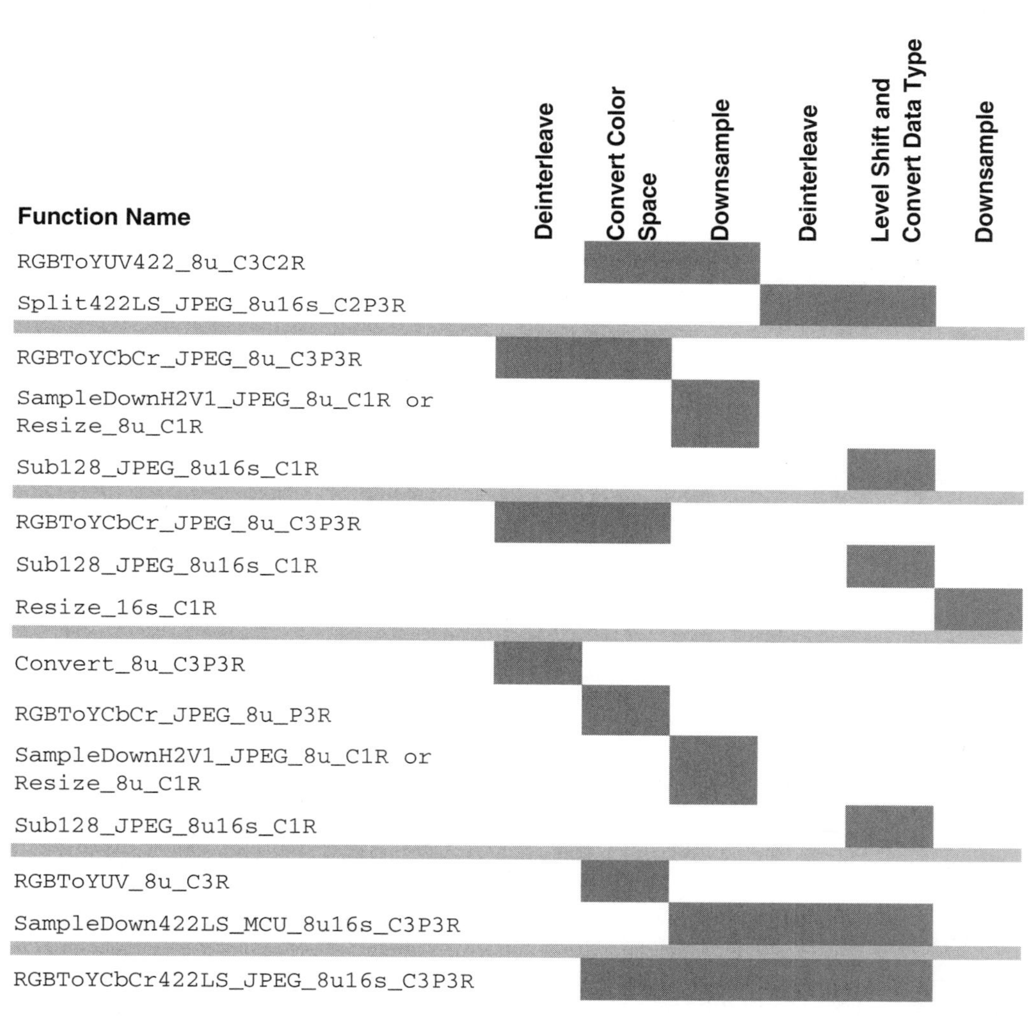

Figure 10.3 JPEG Encoding Functions for Color Space and Data Type Conversion and Sampling

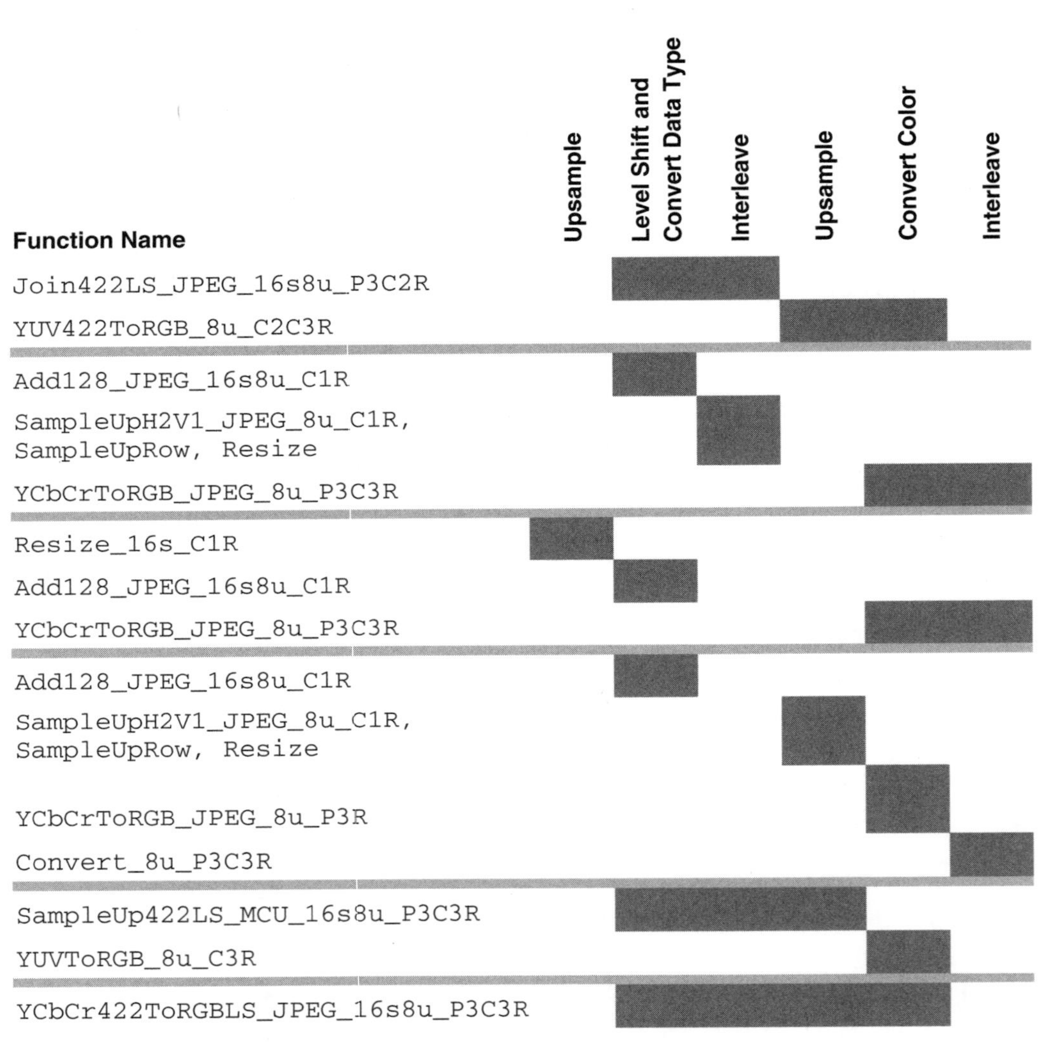

Figure 10.4 JPEG Decoding Functions for Color Space and Data Type Conversion and Sampling

The integrated function ippiDCTQuantFwd8x8LS_JPEG_8u16s_C1R performs the entire operation, including the type conversion that was listed in the previous section. The function ippiDCT8x8FwdLS_8u16s_C1R also performs the DCT and converts the type, and requires Quant8x8 or another function to perform the quantization. The function ippiDCT8x8Fwd_16s_C1 only performs the DCT, and unlike the previous two versions, does not support ROI. All 64 coefficients must be contiguous, both for the DCT and for the ippiQuantFwd8x8 function that works with it. This version is most compatible with the highly integrated conversions, such as ippiRGBToYCbCr422LS_JPEG_8u16s_C3P3R, from the previous section.

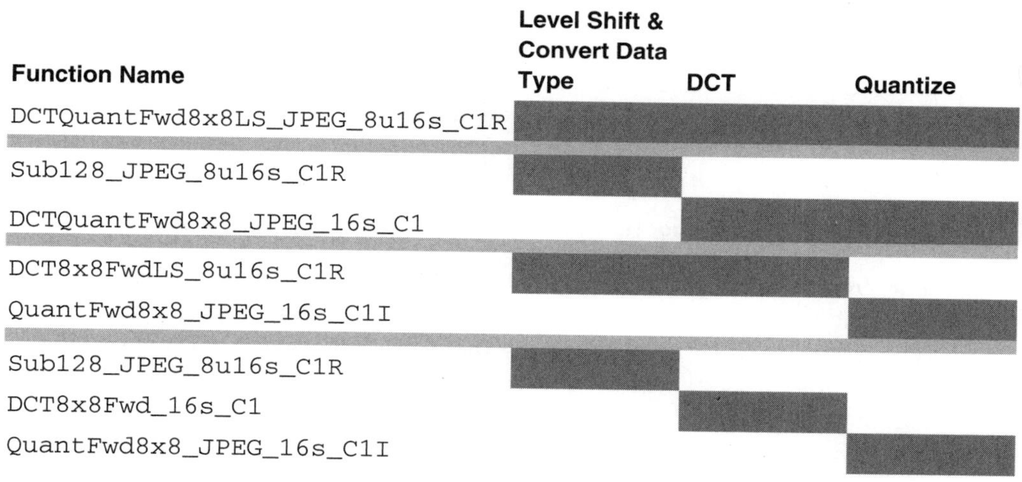

Function Name
Level Shift & Convert Data Type
DCT
Quantize
DCTQuantFwd8x8LS_JPEG_8u16s_C1R
Sub128_JPEG_8u16s_C1R
DCTQuantFwd8x8_JPEG_16s_C1
DCT8x8FwdLS_8u16s_C1R
QuantFwd8x8_JPEG_16s_C1I
Sub128_JPEG_8u16s_C1R
DCT8x8Fwd_16s_C1
QuantFwd8x8_JPEG_16s_C1I

Figure 10.5 JPEG Encoding Functions for DCT and Quantization

Figure 10.6 shows the analogous DCT and quantization functions for JPEG decoding.

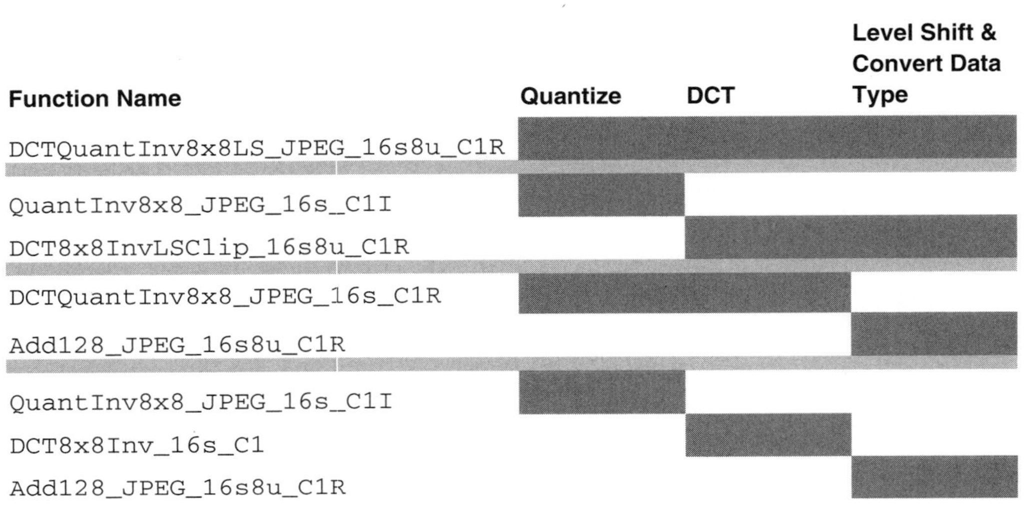

Function Name
Quantize
DCT
Level Shift & Convert Data Type
DCTQuantInv8x8LS_JPEG_16s8u_C1R
QuantInv8x8_JPEG_16s_C1I
DCT8x8InvLSClip_16s8u_C1R
DCTQuantInv8x8_JPEG_16s_C1R
Add128_JPEG_16s8u_C1R
QuantInv8x8_JPEG_16s_C1I
DCT8x8Inv_16s_C1
Add128_JPEG_16s8u_C1R

Figure 10.6 JPEG Decoding Functions for DCT and Quantization

Independent JPEG Group Library

The *Independent JPEG Group* (IJG) is a small association that wrote a reference implementation of the JPEG standard. This implementation, often called the IJG library or merely IJG, is widely used as a JPEG codec.

Because it is so widely used, this library has been modified to make use of Intel IPP JPEG functions and distributed as a sample. The IJG did not intend the original implementation to have high performance, so this modified version is considerably faster.

The advantage of modifying this existing library is that the numerous existing implementations based on IJG, even those that have diverged from the original source code, can mimic these modifications in the analogous modules. This modified IJG can also be used either as part of an existing JPEG implementation or as a starting point for a new one.

Interface and Usage

The IJG interface is simple but not very well documented. The key interface functions are listed in Table 10.1. Only a few function calls are necessary to create a functional encoder or decoder. Other function calls, such as to `jpeg_create_compress` and `jpeg_set_defaults`, are recommended to make initialization easier.

Table 10.1 IJG Encoding Functions

Function name	Description
Encoding	
`jpeg_stdio_dest`	Sets the output type and destination
`jpeg_start_compress`	Initializes the compression structure; writes data stream header
`jpeg_write_scanlines`	Compresses a given number of lines and writes them to output
`jpeg_finish_compress`	Finalizes and frees buffers
Decoding	
`jpeg_stdio_src`	Sets the input type and source
`jpeg_read_header`	Reads the entire header, including tables
`jpeg_start_decompress`	Initializes the compression structure
`jpeg_read_scanlines`	Reads and decompresses a given number of scan lines of data into memory
`jpeg_finish_decompress`	Finalizes and frees buffers

Two structures are of particular interest: `jpeg_compress_struct` and `jpeg_decompress_struct`. These structures are passed to almost every function listed in Table 10.1. They accumulate all information about the image, such as width and height, as well as flags for compression options. They also include the Huffman and quantization tables and state variables like the current scan line. Finally, they contain a dozen or more function pointers that dictate which functions are called to execute portions of the codec.

Some more interesting fields of these two structures are listed in Figure 10.7.

```
struct jpeg_decompress_struct
{
    struct jpeg_source_mgr * src;

    JDIMENSION image_width;        // image width in header
    JDIMENSION image_height;       // image height
    int num_components;            // # of color components
    J_COLOR_SPACE jpeg_color_space; // JPEG image color space
    J_COLOR_SPACE out_color_space; // decoded image color space

    // scaling ratio
    unsigned int scale_num, scale_denom;

    // algorithm variables determined by user
    J_DCT_METHOD dct_method;       // IDCT algorithm
    boolean do_fancy_upsampling;

    //  Computed by jpeg_start_decompress():
    JDIMENSION output_width;     // output image width
    JDIMENSION output_height;    // output image height
    …

    // State variables
    JDIMENSION output_scanline;
    …

    // Tables
    JQUANT_TBL * quant_tbl_ptrs[NUM_QUANT_TBLS];
    JHUFF_TBL * dc_huff_tbl_ptrs[NUM_HUFF_TBLS];
    JHUFF_TBL * ac_huff_tbl_ptrs[NUM_HUFF_TBLS];

    int data_precision;
    …

    // algorithm variables determined by bitstream
    boolean progressive_mode;
    boolean arith_code;
    …

    // structures containing indirect pointers
    struct jpeg_decomp_master * master;
    struct jpeg_d_main_controller * main;
    struct jpeg_d_coef_controller * coef;
    struct jpeg_d_post_controller * post;
    struct jpeg_input_controller * inputctl;
    struct jpeg_marker_reader * marker;
    struct jpeg_entropy_decoder * entropy;
    struct jpeg_inverse_dct * idct;
    struct jpeg_upsampler * upsample;
```

```
    struct jpeg_color_deconverter * cconvert;
    struct jpeg_color_quantizer * cquantize;
};

// example of indirect pointer structure:
struct jpeg_inverse_dct
{
    JMETHOD(void, start_pass, (j_decompress_ptr cinfo));
    inverse_DCT_method_ptr inverse_DCT[MAX_COMPONENTS];
};

// jpeg_compress_struct is very similar to
// jpeg_decompress_struct:
struct jpeg_compress_struct
{
    …
    JDIMENSION image_width;  // image width
    JDIMENSION image_height; // image height
    int input_components;   // # of color components in input

    J_COLOR_SPACE in_color_space; // input image color space

    // scaling ratio
    unsigned int scale_num, scale_denom;

    int data_precision;
    int num_components;
    J_COLOR_SPACE jpeg_color_space;
    …
};
```

Figure 10.7 Structures Controlling Image Encoding and Decoding by IJG

Most of these fields can be set by IJG routines to reasonable values. For example, the function `jpeg_create_compress` initializes a compression structure to zero, but with a gamma of 1.0. The function `jpeg_set_defaults` sets up Huffman and quantization tables, chooses a destination color space and data precision, and chooses otherwise popular coding options.

The fields that point to indirect pointer structures determine which algorithm is used for each step of the codec. Most calls to coding blocks, such as DCT, quantization, and color conversion, take place as indirect calls. Functions `jpeg_start_compress` and `jpeg_start_decompress` cause these functions to be initialized according to defaults. For compression, the function `jinit_compress_master` sets up a manager for each element in the `start_pass` field. The `prepare_for_pass` function then calls each manager to set up the module that will handle the actual execution of that module.

This internal structure of the code has advantages and disadvantages. On the plus side, it allows separation of individual blocks from coding flow, which permits addition of new features and functions without undue modification of higher-level functions. This is convenient when optimizing IJG. The most obvious downside of this method is poor readability, particularly with limited documentation.

A skeleton encoder and decoder are listed in Figure 10.8 to demonstrate these functions and structures.

```
myEncodeJPEG_8u_C3R(Ipp8u* pData, int step, IppiSize size)
{
    struct jpeg_compress_struct cinfo;
    jpeg_create_compress(&cinfo);

    // Set cinfo.in_color_space to match input image
    …

    // Sets up cinfo to a reasonable state
    jpeg_set_defaults(&cinfo);

    // Set fields in jpeg_compress_struct to match input image
    …

    // Open pFile and set it as output source
    …
    jpeg_stdio_dest(&cinfo, pFile);

    // Compress "height" lines of data in pData
    jpeg_start_compress(&cinfo, TRUE);
    jpeg_write_scanlines(&cinfo, pData, size.height);
    jpeg_finish_compress(&cinfo);

    jpeg_destroy_compress(&cinfo);

    // Close file
    …
}

myDecodeJPEG(Ipp8u** pData, IppiSize* pSize, … )
{
    struct jpeg_decompress_struct cinfo;
    …
```

```
    jpeg_create_decompress(&cinfo);

    // Open file & set it as input source
    ...
    jpeg_stdio_src(&cinfo, pFile);

    // Read header
    jpeg_read_header(&cinfo, TRUE);
    pSize->width = cinfo.image_width;
    pSize->height = cinfo.image_height;

    // Allocate buffer here
    *pData = ...

    // Decompress entire image
    jpeg_start_decompress(&cinfo);
    jpeg_read_scanlines(&cinfo, *pData, cinfo.image_height);
    jpeg_finish_decompress(&cinfo);

    jpeg_destroy_decompress(&cinfo);

    // Close file
    ...
}
```

Figure 10.8 Skeleton Code to Encode and Decode an Image with IJG

Two important examples of use of IJG are available for download from the Intel IPP Web site. One is an encoder, `cjpeg.c`, and the other a decoder, `djpeg.c`. Because the documentation on IJG is limited, as a practical matter these samples or utilities are required parts of the library. They are good guides to using the API.

Optimizing IJG

Optimization of IJG without changing the structure is a matter of creating wrappers for efficient versions of the functions. The code in Figure 10.9, which adds an efficient DCT implementation to IJG, is one good example. IJG performance is heavily dependent on DCT. Approximately 20 to 40 percent of the execution time is spent on the DCT, making it an obvious target for replacement.

The first step is to create a new version of the function. In this case, the behavior of the function `jpeg_idct_islow` is duplicated in the function `jpeg_idct_islow_intellib`. Code in `start_pass` sets the function pointer through which this function will be called, so this code is modified to instead use the new optimized function.

This function both performs an inverse DCT and dequantizes the coefficients, one of the few areas in which IJG is well designed for optimization. The main argument of the function is an array of 64 continuous 16-bit signed elements, `coef_block`. The output structure, `output_buf`, is an array of eight pointers to eight elements each. The variable `output_col` indicates an offset from that pointer to the eight coefficients. The expression `(output_buf[row] + output_col)[col]` retrieves one output value. The quantization table is passed in `compptr->dct_table` in JPEG-standard format.

The best function to perform this same operation is the efficient `ippiDCTQuantInv8x8LS_JPEG_16s8u_C1R`. The input is in the correct format already, both quantization table and input array, and the output is the right type. This function is called to place the result into another contiguous array, the local array `workspace`.

The subsequent copy is unfortunately necessitated by the data structure used for the function output. The output is arrayed somewhat strangely in eight rows of eight pixels. Presumably this allows the routine to place the out-of-bounds lines, those below the nominal height of the image, into dummy memory. The function `ippiDCTQuantInv8x8LS_JPEG_16s8u_C1R` is capable of returning each of the rows of eight pixels in noncontiguous memory, but the distance between them must be the same for all rows. Unfortunately, the dummy rows used in IJG are not placed immediately after the image rows. This is an example of how IJG is resistant to optimization. It would be better for the codec to use a larger image to handle the border instead of taking eight pointers to rows of pixels. If this mechanism weren't used to handle the border, the function would instead take a single pointer to the beginning of the block and a constant stride between each pair of rows. This is the sort inefficiency that motivates the JPEG sample described below.

With a little more effort, you can apply a similar method to the forward version of the transform. The only difference is that the existing function, `forward_DCT`, expects a quantization in natural order, but the relevant function takes a zig-zag order table. For efficiency, code in the DCT manager makes a copy of the quantization table in zig-zag order and places it in the compression structure.

```
// Indirect function pointer initialization
start_pass (j_decompress_ptr cinfo)
{
...
    if(cinfo->UseIPP) {
        method_ptr = jpeg_idct_islow_intellib;
    } else {
        method_ptr = jpeg_idct_islow;
    }
...
}

// original inverse DCT function
GLOBAL(void)
jpeg_idct_islow (j_decompress_ptr cinfo,
        jpeg_component_info * compptr,
        JCOEFPTR coef_block,
        JSAMPARRAY output_buf, JDIMENSION output_col)
{
...
}

// Optimized inverse DCT function
GLOBAL(void)
jpeg_idct_islow_intellib(
    j_decompress_ptr     cinfo,
    jpeg_component_info* compptr,
    JCOEFPTR             coef_block,
    JSAMPARRAY           output_buf,
    JDIMENSION           output_col)
{
    // Relevant types
    // JCOEFPTR = short* = Ipp16s*
    // JSAMPARRAY = JSAMPROW* = JSAMP** = short** = Ipp16s**
    // JDIMENSION = int
    // DCTSIZE is always 8

    int row;
    int *wsptr, *output;
    // DCTSIZE2 = DCTSIZE * DCTSIZE = 64
    Ipp8u workspace[DCTSIZE2];
```

```
    ippiDCTQuantInv8x8LS_JPEG_16s8u_C1R(coef_block,
        workspace, 8, (Ipp16u*)compptr->dct_table);

    wsptr = (int*)workspace;
    for(row = 0; row < DCTSIZE; row++)
    {
        output=(int*)(output_buf[row]+output_col);
        *output++=*wsptr++;
        *output=*wsptr++;
    }

    // A more efficient solution, but only works for some
    // images. Eliminates the need for a copy.
    // ippiDCTQuantInv8x8LS_JPEG_16s8u_C1R(inptr,
    //      output_buf[0]+output_col,
    //      output_buf[1]-output_buf[0],
    //      (Ipp16u*)compptr->dct_table);

    return;
    // ******************
}

// Adding a table entry for the forward DCT
jinit_forward_dct (j_compress_ptr cinfo)
{
...
    if(cinfo->UseIPP) {
        fdct->pub.forward_DCT = forward_DCT_intellib;
    } else {
        fdct->pub.forward_DCT = forward_DCT;
    }
...
}

start_pass_fdctmgr (j_compress_ptr cinfo)
{
...
```

```
    if(cinfo->UseIPP)
    {
        // reorder table to zig-zag
        for(i = 0; i < DCTSIZE2; i++)
        {
            rawqtbl[i] = (unsigned char)
                qtbl->quantval[izigzag_index[i]];
        }
        // build encoder quant table
        ippiQuantFwdTableInit_JPEG_8u16u(rawqtbl,dtbl);
    }
    else
    {
...
}
```

Figure 10.9 Speeding up IJG by Replacing the DCT

Other functional blocks also benefit from optimization along similar lines. The obvious blocks are color conversion and Huffman coding. Huffman coding is usually the second-most time-consuming block in a JPEG codec.

Table 10.2 lists the most interesting modifications to IJG. The functions that end with `_intellib` are replacements for existing IJG functions.

Table 10.2 Modifications Made to IJG to use Intel® Integrated Performance Primitives (Intel® IPP)

File name	Functions Modified	Comment
`jccolor.c`	`rgb_ycc_convert_intellib, rgb_gray_convert_intellib, cmyk_ycck_convert_intellib, jinit_color_converter`	Encoder color conversion functions modified to use Intel IPP.
`jdcolor.c`	`ycc_rgb_convert_intellib, ycck_cmyk_convert_intellib, jinit_color_deconverter`	Decoder color conversion functions modified to use Intel IPP.
`jcdctmgr.c`	`forward_DCT_intellib, jinit_forward_dct, start_pass_fdctmgr`	Forward DCT function modified to use Intel IPP DCT. An array with raw quantization coefficients added in function `start_pass_fdctmgr`.
`jidctint.c`	`jpeg_idct_islow_intellib`	Inverse DCT function modified to use `DCTInv`.
`jcsample.c`	`h2v1_downsample_intellib, h2v2_downsample_intellib, jinit_downsampler`	Downsampling functions modified to call Intel IPP downsampling functions.
`jdsample.c`	`h2v1_fancy_upsample_intellib, h2v2_fancy_upsample_intellib, jinit_upsampler`	Upsampling functions modified to call Intel IPP upsampling functions.
`jchuff.c`	`start_pass_huff, jpeg_make_c_derived_tbl_intellib, dump_buffer_intellib, flush_bits_intellib, encode_one_block_intellib, emit_restart_intellib, encode_mcu_huff_intellib, finish_pass_huff, htest_one_block_intellib, encode_mcu_gather_intellib, jpeg_gen_optimal_table_intellib, finish_pass_gather`	Several functions modified to use Intel IPP Huffman coding functions.
`jdhuff.c`	`start_pass_huff_decoder, jpeg_make_d_derived_tbl_intellib, process_restart, decode_mcu_intellib, jinit_huff_decoder`	Several functions modified to use Intel IPP Huffman decoding functions.

JPEG sample

The Intel IPP also has its own JPEG encoder and decoder, referred to as the JPEG sample. This sample encodes and decodes color and grayscale JPEG images. It supports decoding of thumbnails and reduced images, and encoding and decoding of progressive JPEG images. Like IJG, it supports color space conversions and sampling operations, which are technically pre-processing or post-processing operations.

The sample reads directly from files in the JFIF file format. Other file formats, such as TIFF or FlashPix†, require that the JPEG data be extracted into memory first.

This sample was originally based upon the discontinued Intel® JPEG library. Much of the code in that library that was optimized but aging ungracefully was replaced with calls to Intel IPP.

Interface and Usage

The JPEG sample has a very minimal interface, inherited from the JPEG library. Table 10.3 lists the four essential functions. The JPEG sample interface is described in detail in the manual that is included with the sample. This document also explains and demonstrates in more detail how to use the JPEG sample.

Table 10.3 The JPEG Sample Interface

Function name	Description
`ijlInit`	Initialize the `JPEG_CORE_PROPERTIES` structure. Must be called before every image read.
`ijlFree`	Release the `JPEG_CORE_PROPERTIES` structure and memory allocated by `ijlInit`.
`ijlRead`	Read an image, header, or image data from memory or file
`ijlWrite`	Write an image, header, or image data to memory or file

Figure 10.10 shows a simple example of how to read a JFIF file or JPEG image in memory with the JPEG sample. After initializing the `jcprops` structure with the `ijlInit` function, the code calls the `ijlRead` function twice. The first call reads the header of the image and places the relevant image parameters into the structure. Based on that information, the code can allocate memory for the bitmap that will be created and fill in the parameters for that

image. The second call to `ijlRead` then reads the bit stream, decodes it, and places the resulting image in the memory pointed to by `jcprops.DIBBytes`.

```
JPEG_CORE_PROPERTIES jcprops;
ijlInit(&jcprops);

// Set jcprops.JPGFile or jcprops.JPGBytes

ijlRead(&jcprops, IJL_JFILE_READPARAMS);

// Allocate image according to:
//  jcprops.JPGWidth
//  jcprops.JPGHeight
//  jcprops.JPGChannels

// Set up the following properties of the DIB
//   jcprops.DIBWidth
//   jcprops.DIBHeight
//   jcprops.DIBChannels
//   jcprops.DIBColor
//   jcprops.DIBPadBytes
//   jcprops.DIBBytes (the memory buffer)
//   jcprops.JPGColor

jerr = ijlRead(&jcprops, IJL_JFILE_READWHOLEIMAGE);
```

Figure 10.10 Decoding an Image with the JPEG Sample

Optimizing the JPEG Sample

The code for the JPEG sample predates the Intel IPP. As such, although the structure of the code is amenable to low-level optimization, it was not written with the Intel IPP API in mind. It is therefore an honest example of optimizing a well-designed JPEG codec. Because the Intel IPP functions were designed with this aim, they fit very naturally into the structure.

Figure 10.11 shows a portion of the unmodified inner loop of the encoder side of the JPEG sample. The input data has been converted to `Ipp16s` and has been broken down into the JPEG color space. The data is arranged in an MCU that comprises one or more 8 x 8 blocks. This section of code performs the DCT, the quantization, and the Huffman encoding on an entire MCU. The calls to the individual functions, `fDCT8x8`, fQnt8x8, and EncodeHuffman8x8, are not changed as part of the optimization. Inside these functions are calls to Intel IPP.

Options for DCT are few. The single function ippiDCT8x8Fwd_C1I performs exactly the DCT needed, an in-place 8 x 8 DCT. Because the quantization table argument of the function ippiQuantFwd8x8_JPEG_16s_C1I is in a JPEG standard format, the same is true for quantization.

For Huffman encoding, two additional steps are necessary. For one, the position within the bitstream is maintained in the STATE structure. The position information returned by the Intel IPP Huffman encoder must be returned to that state. The other is that the HUFFMAN_TABLE structure must include the AC and DC tables and the Huffman state structure in the Intel IPP format.

```
if(!jprops->raw_coefs || jprops->raw_coefs->data_type)
{
    /* Perform forward DCTs on a whole MCU */
    for(k = 0; k < tot_8x8_in_MCU; k++)
    {
        fDCT8x8(MCUptr + (k << 6));
    }
}

/* Quantize and encode the whole MCU */
for(k = 0; k < scan->ncomps; k++)
{
    for(l = 0; l < blocks_per_MCU[k]; l++)
    {

        if(!jprops->raw_coefs ||
            jprops->raw_coefs->data_type)
        {
            fQnt8x8(MCUptr,q_table[k]);
        }

        /* huffman encode */
        jerr = EncodeHuffman8x8(
            MCUptr,
            (Ipp16s*)&scan->dc_diff[k],
            dc_table[k],
            ac_table[k],
            state,
            0);
```

```
            if(IJL_OK != jerr)
            {
                goto Exit;
            }

            MCUptr += DCTSIZE2;

        } /* for blocks_per_MCU */
    }   /* for scan->ncomps */

...

OWNFUN(IJLERR) fDCT8x8(Ipp16s* pSrcDst)
{
    IppStatus status;

    status = ippiDCT8x8Fwd_16s_C1I(pSrcDst);
    if(ippStsNoErr != status)
    {
        return IJL_INTERNAL_ERROR;
    }

    return IJL_OK;
} /* fDCT8x8() */

OWNFUN(IJLERR) fQnt8x8(
    Ipp16s* pSrcDst,
    Ipp16u* pEncQuantTbl)
{
    IppStatus status;

    status =
        ippiQuantFwd8x8_JPEG_16s_C1I(pSrcDst,pEncQuantTbl);
    if(ippStsNoErr != status)
    {
        return IJL_BAD_QUANT_TABLE;
    }

    return IJL_OK;
} /* fQnt8x8() */

OWNFUN(IJLERR) EncodeHuffman8x8(
    Ipp16s* pSrc, Ipp16s* pLastDC,
    HUFFMAN_TABLE* pDcTable,
    HUFFMAN_TABLE* pAcTable,
    STATE* pState, int bIsLast)
{
    int pos = 0;
    IppStatus status;
    IJLERR jerr = IJL_OK;
```

```
    /* protect against buffer overrun */
    if(pState->entropy_bytes_left <= 128)
    {
        if(NULL == pState->file)
        {
            jerr = IJL_BUFFER_TOO_SMALL;
            goto Exit;
        }

        jerr = Flush_Buffer_To_File(pState);
        if(IJL_OK != jerr)
            goto Exit;
    }

    status = ippiEncodeHuffman8x8_JPEG_16s1u_C1(
        pSrc,
        pState->cur_entropy_ptr,
        pState->entropy_bytes_left,
        &pos,
        pLastDC,
        pDcTable->u.pEncHuffTbl,
        pAcTable->u.pEncHuffTbl,
        pState->u.pEncHuffState,
        bIsLast);

    if(ippStsNoErr != status)
    {
        jerr = IJL_INTERNAL_ERROR;
    }

    pState->cur_entropy_ptr += pos;
    pState->entropy_bytes_left -= pos;
    pState->entropy_bytes_processed += pos;

Exit:

    return jerr;
} /* EncodeHuffman8x8() */
```

Figure 10.11 DCT, Quantization, and Huffman Coding for JPEG Sample Encoder

JPEG 2000

Research on image compression has evolved in the decade since the JPEG codec, and the hardware constraints have loosened significantly. Therefore, after a long process of competitive submissions, the JPEG body settled on a definition for the intended replacement for the JPEG codec, JPEG 2000. This standard is to be the next generation of JPEG. Despite the name, though, JPEG 2000 is not currently enjoying the same wide acceptance or even awareness.

JPEG 2000 follows fundamentally the same coding paradigm: transform, quantize, and apply a variable-length code. However, almost every element of the codec is different in some way.

One difference is that the codec has been reorganized from four unequal and not-quite-orthogonal methods to two symmetric methods. In JPEG 2000, there are two paths: reversible, or integer, and nonreversible, or real. The reversible path is analogous to the lossless method, and the nonreversible path is analogous to the DCT-based methods. The variations on these methods, progressive and hierarchical, and other options are handled in the last coding stage, *tier-2 coding*.

Another difference is that the terminology has been completely changed. Specific names for codec blocks, such as DCT, have largely been replaced by generally descriptive names, such as *intercomponent transform*.

A third difference is that several of the blocks, while performing the same function as the analogous JPEG block, behave very differently. For example, the variable-length code is completely different and more closely resembles that of the bit-by-bit progressive JPEG method. Also, the DCT at the core of JPEG has been replaced by a wavelet transform, which has a broad impact on other components. The color conversion is very similar to that in JPEG, but is explicitly defined as a part of the standard rather than a post-processing or preprocessing step.

There are a few other differences, such as the extensive support for tiling, variable-sized code blocks, ROI, and shifting sampling grid. This section explains JPEG 2000 in some detail.

JPEG 2000 Codec Components

Figure 10.12 shows the components of a JPEG 2000 codec. Each component is described in turn below.

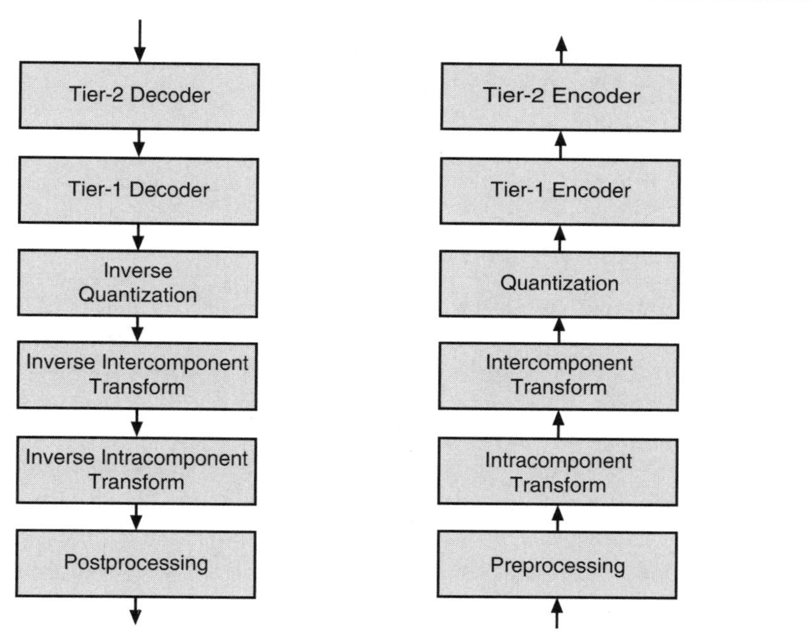

Figure 10.12 Components of a JPEG 2000 Implementation

Pre-processing and Post-processing

This stage is a simple normalization, akin to the level shift in JPEG. In the encoder, a bias is subtracted from the unsigned pixel data to center the data around zero. In the decoder, this same bias is added to restore the data to pixel range, typically zero to 255.

Intercomponent Transform

Images compressed by JPEG 2000 are made up of one or more components, which are generally color planes. As its name implies, the *intercomponent transform* or ICT is a transform that operates on the first three components of an image together. It is essentially a color-space transform that assumes that the first three components are the red, green, and blue channels of an image.

There are two types of ICT: the irreversible color transform, also called ICT, and the reversible color transform, or RCT. The former is a floating-point method and is identical to the RGB-to-YCrCb conversion from JPEG. The latter is an integer approximation of that conversion:

$$Y = \frac{1}{4} (R + 2G + B)$$

$$Cr = B - G$$

$$Cb = R - G$$

Intracomponent Transform

The transform block in JPEG 2000 is called the *intracomponent transform*. It is a wavelet transform, one of the two wavelet transforms supported by the standard. The reversible wavelet transform is called the 5/3 transform. It is integer-only and allows lossless coding. The nonreversible transform is called the 9/7 transform.

The wavelet transform, like the DCT, converts a signal into frequency information. In contrast to other frequency transforms, it maintains a spatial component, so that each coefficient indicates both an amount of frequency and a rough location for it. The advantage is that different frequencies can have a different amount of data allocated to them. Because locality is more important for higher frequency information, the higher the frequency, the more data is allocated to that frequency band, or *sub-band*.

Further, because the locality of frequency information is still represented in the position of the data, there is no need to divide the image into 8 x 8 blocks. The visual effect is to remove the discontinuity at the edge of these blocks.

The structure of this transform is such that at each level, the low-frequency block, or the raw image in the first iteration, is divided into smaller blocks of half the width and height. The blocks, or sub-bands, are high or low frequency in vertical or horizontal direction. This process is repeated for a certain number of levels. The number of levels of the transform is configurable, and is somewhat dictated by the size of the image. Figure 10.13 shows this sub-band structure.

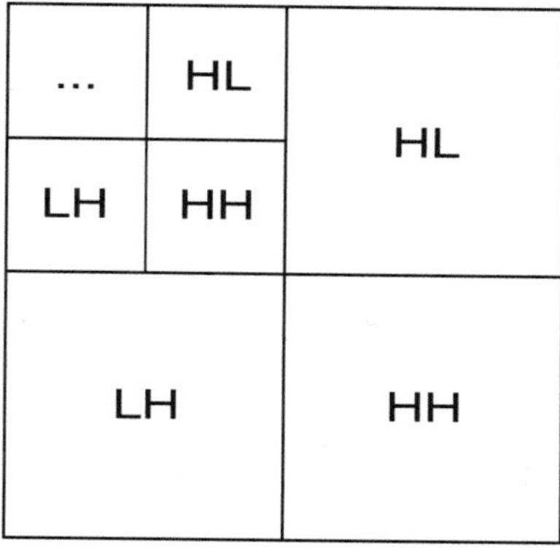

Figure 10.13 Sub-bands in JPEG 2000

Quantization

Quantization remains the lossy-compression step that removes the most data in advance of entropy coding. It is division by step size, rounded toward zero. For the reversible transform, this division is always by one. In JPEG 2000, the quantization factor is different for each sub-band.

Tier-1 Coding

The variable-length coding in JPEG 2000 is referred to as the *tier-1 coding*. The entropy coding is performed on bit planes, using a three-pass state machine. After that, arithmetic coding is applied to the output or part of it.

This component is generally the second-most time-consuming portion of the coding process.

Tier-2 Coding

The result of tier-1 coding is a series of packets representing one bit-plane, one sub-band, one color component, and one *precinct*, or block. The last stage of coding, called *tier-2 coding* in the literature, determines which packets to include and in what order. This stage controls the size/quality tradeoffs and data rate for transmitted images.

JPEG 2000 in Intel IPP

In terms of the number of functions, Intel IPP covers roughly half of the functions necessary to assemble a JPEG 2000 codec. In terms of performance, most of the performance-critical functions are contained in Intel IPP, so about 80 to 90 percent of the time spent in the codec should be spent in Intel IPP functions.

Preprocessing and Postprocessing

No function to perform this level shift currently exists. The shift is essentially the same as that in JPEG, but JPEG 2000 processing is generally done on either 32-bit signed integers or 32-bit floating-point numbers. Neither data type is currently supported.

Intercomponent Transform

The RCT is implemented explicitly in functions `ippiRCTFwd_JPEG2K` and `ippiRCTInv_JPEG2K`. The ICT is mathematically the same as `ippiRGBToYCbCr_JPEG` and `ippiRGBToYUV`, but the 32-bit data types are not currently supported by Intel IPP.

Intracomponent Transform

The Intel IPP has eight wavelet functions for JPEG 2000, such as `ippiWTFwdCol_D97_JPEG2K`. They support, orthogonally, the 5/3 and 9/7 wavelet transforms, forward and inverse transforms, and rows and columns. The integer 5/3 transform is supported for 16-bit and 32-bit signed integers. The 9/7 transform is supported for 32-bit floating point.

Quantization

The quantization step is not the same as in JPEG, since the block size is not set to 8 x 8 and the data type is generally different. However, quantization and its inverse are not particularly complex operations.

Tier-1 and Tier-2 Coding

The Intel IPP has a broad set of entropy coding functions of the form `ippiEncode*_JPEG2K` and `ippiDecode*_JPEG2K` to perform tier-1 encoding and decoding.

Tier-2 coding is mostly decision-making. The logic to implement it is not performance critical.

JPEG 2000 sample

Just as for JPEG, there is a sample that makes use of Intel IPP to implement JPEG 2000. The codec encodes a limited subset of JPEG 2000 images and decodes a slightly broader spectrum of images. The main goal is to show how to integrate Intel IPP functions in JPEG 2000 codec development.

The encoder sample takes a device-independent bitmap (DIB) as input. It uses only the integer or reversible encoding, though the supporting classes enable encoding of more image types. It employs the RCT and the 5/3 wavelet transform.

The decoding support is a little stronger than the encoding. For example, the Tier-1 encoder class, `PacketEncoder`, supports only 32-bit signed integer data, but the decoder class also supports 32-bit floating-point data as well.

Interface and Usage

Major elements of the JPEG 2000 sample interface are listed in Table 10.4.

For the tier-1 coding, the key functions include `EncodeTriplet` and `Encode` in `PacketEncoder` and `DecodeTriplet` and `Decode` in `PacketDecoder`. These functions place a single sub-band or three sub-bands into a bitstream, or extract one or three sub-bands from one.

The templated functions `fwd<>` and `inv<>` wrap the wavelet transforms. The forward transform breaks a single color component into a tree of sub-bands in an `SBTree` object. The number of levels in the `SBTree` determines how many levels of sub-band are calculated. The inverse transform reconstructs an image plane from a tree of sub-bands.

The functions `rctFwdC3P3` and `rctInvP3C3` perform the integer-only reversible color transform. The functions `ictFwdC3P3` and `ictInvP3C3` perform the floating-point irreversible color transform.

The code in Figure 10.14 shows the key portions of an abbreviated encoder using these classes and methods. This code encodes a bitmap in an `imageC3` object. The encoding is exclusively reversible integer coding, so there is no quantization, the intracomponent transform is the 5/3 wavelet, and the reversible color transform is used.

Table 10.4 Classes for the JPEG 2000 Sample

Class name	Description
Coding:	Command line options interpreter.
SBTree	Storage for sub-band tree, the output of the wavelets
WTFwd, WTInv	Templates for one-level wavelet transforms
PacketEncoder, PacketDecoder	Packets encoder and decoder
PHDecoder	Packet headers decoder.
Utilities:	
BoxInfo, Marker	Parsing and composing of jp2 file.
CmdOptions	Command line options interpreter.
DibFile	Access to bitmap files.
ImageC3, ImageP3	Storage for raster image data in 32-bit signed format.
MapFile	Access to file through mapping in memory.

```
void encode(const CmdOptions &options)
{
    ...

    // Preprocessing
    levShiftFwdC3I(imgC3.Data(), imgC3.LineStep(),
                   imgC3.Width(), imgC3.Height(), 7);

    // Optional Intracomponent Transform
    if(options.IsUseMCT())
        rctFwdC3P3(imgC3.Data(), imgC3.LineStep(),
            imgP3.Channels(), imgP3.LineStep(), width, height);
    else
        copyC3P3(imgC3.Data(), imgC3.LineStep(),
            imgP3.Channels(), imgP3.LineStep(), width, height);

    ...

    // Intracomponent Transform
    SBTree<Ipp32s> sbTreeC0(width, height, level);
    SBTree<Ipp32s> sbTreeC1(width, height, level);
    SBTree<Ipp32s> sbTreeC2(width, height, level);
```

```
    fwd<WT53>(imgP3.Channel(0), sbTreeC0, ippWTFilterFirstLow);
    fwd<WT53>(imgP3.Channel(1), sbTreeC1, ippWTFilterFirstLow);
    fwd<WT53>(imgP3.Channel(2), sbTreeC2, ippWTFilterFirstLow);

    // Tier-1 and Tier-2 coding
    ...
    // Encode lowest wavelet level
    PacketEncoder encoder(stream);
    encoder.Encode(sbTreeC0.LxLy());
    encoder.Encode(sbTreeC1.LxLy());
    encoder.Encode(sbTreeC2.LxLy());

    // Encode remaining levels
    for(k = level - 1; k >= 0; k--)
    {
        encoder.EncodeTriplet(sbTreeC0.HxLy(k),
            sbTreeC0.LxHy(k), sbTreeC0.HxHy(k));
        encoder.EncodeTriplet(sbTreeC1.HxLy(k),
            sbTreeC1.LxHy(k), sbTreeC1.HxHy(k));
        encoder.EncodeTriplet(sbTreeC2.HxLy(k),
            sbTreeC2.LxHy(k), sbTreeC2.HxHy(k));
    }
    ...
}
```

Figure 10.14 Encoding an Image with the JPEG 2000 Sample

Decoding any JPEG 2000 image is significantly more complicated than encoding using this one type. For one, the code blocks can be in any order and the number of possible tags is large. Further, the number of options is greater, since the JPEG 2000 image can be reversible or nonreversible, has flexibility on tiles and location in the coding grid, and may use quantization.

Optimizing the JPEG 2000 Sample

In the JPEG 2000 sample, the file `pp.h` contains wrappers for many functions. Figure 10.15 lists the code for two of these wrappers.

```
...
inline void rctFwdC3P3(const Ipp32s* src, int srcStep,
    Ipp32s** dst, int dstStep, int width, int height)
{
    IppiSize roiSize = {width, height};
    ippiRCTFwd_JPEG2K_32s_C3P3R(src, srcStep, dst, dstStep,
        roiSize);
}
...
class WT53
{
public:
    static void fwdRow(const Ipp32s* src, int srcStep,
        Ipp32s* low, int lowStep,
        Ipp32s* high, int highStep,
        IppiSize dstRoiSize,
        IppiWTFilterFirst phase)
    {
        ippiWTFwdRow_B53_JPEG2K_32s_C1R(src, srcStep,
            low, lowStep, high, highStep, dstRoiSize, phase);
    }

    static void fwdCol(const Ipp32s* src, int srcStep,
        Ipp32s* low, int lowStep,
        Ipp32s* high, int highStep,
        IppiSize dstRoiSize,
        IppiWTFilterFirst phase)
    {
        ippiWTFwdCol_B53_JPEG2K_32s_C1R(src, srcStep,
            low, lowStep, high, highStep, dstRoiSize, phase);
    }
...
};
```

Figure 10.15 Wrappers for Forward RCT and 5/3 Wavelet Functions in Intel® Integrated Performance Primitives (Intel® IPP)

The RCT functions are used directly by the encoder, but the wavelet transform is embedded within several layers of templated classes. These classes automatically handle multiple levels of sub-bands, wrap the column and row wavelet transforms into a single two-dimensional operation, and place the data into an `SBTree` object. Further, the templates allow expansion into additional data types.

MPEG-2

This section describes the video portion of the MPEG-2 standard. Chapter 7 describes MPEG-1 audio, known as MP3, and MPEG-2 audio, known as AAC.

MPEG-2 is intended for high-quality, high-bandwidth video. It is most prominent because it is used for DVD and HDTV video compression. Computationally, good encoding is expensive but can be done in real time by current processors. Decoding an MPEG-2 stream is relatively easy and can be done by almost any current processor or, obviously, by commercial DVD players.

MPEG-2 players must also be able to play MPEG-1. MPEG-1 is very similar, though the bit stream differs and the motion compensation has less resolution. It is used as the video compression on VCDs.

MPEG-2 is a complicated format with many options. It includes seven profiles dictating aspect ratios and feature sets, four levels specifying resolution, bit rate, and frame rate, and three frame types. The bit stream code is complex and requires several tables. However, at its core are computationally complex but conceptually clear compression and decompression elements. These elements are the focus of this section.

MPEG-2 Components

MPEG-2 components are very similar to those in JPEG. MPEG-2 is DCT based, and uses Huffman coding on the quantized DCT coefficients. However, the bit stream format is completely different, as are all the tables. Unlike JPEG, MPEG-2 also has a restricted, though very large, set of frame rates and sizes. But the biggest difference is the exploitation of redundancy between frames.

There are three types of frames in MPEG: I (intra) frames, P (predicted) frames, and B (bidirectional) frames. There are several consequences of frame type, but the defining characteristic is how prediction is done. Intra frames do not refer to other frames, making them suitable as key frames. They are, essentially, self-contained compressed images. By contrast, P frames are predicted by using the previous P or I frame, and B frames are predicted using the previous and next P or I frame. Individual blocks in these frames may be intra or non-intra, however.

MPEG is organized around a hierarchy of blocks, macroblocks, slices, and frames. Blocks are 8 pixels high by 8 pixels wide in a single channel.

Macroblocks are a collection of blocks 16 pixels high by 16 pixels wide and contain all three channels. Depending on subsampling, a macroblock contains 6, 8, or 12 blocks. For example, a YCbCr 4:2:0 macroblock has four Y blocks, one Cb and one Cr.

Following are the main blocks of an MPEG-2 codec, in encoding order. Figure 10.16 shows how these blocks relate to one another.

Motion Estimation and Compensation

The key to the effectiveness of video coding is using earlier and sometimes later frames to predict a value for each pixel. Image compression can only use a block elsewhere in the image as a base value for each pixel, but video compression can aspire to use an image of the same object. Instead of compressing pixels, which have high entropy, the video compression can compress the differences between similar pixels, which have much lower entropy.

Objects and even backgrounds in video are not reliably stationary, however. In order to make these references to other video frames truly effective, the codec needs to account for motion between the frames. This is accomplished with motion estimation and compensation. Along with the video data, each block also has motion vectors that indicate how much that frame has moved relative to a reference image. Before taking the difference between current and reference frame, the codec shifts the reference frame by that amount. Calculating the motion vectors is called *motion estimation* and accommodating this motion is called *motion compensation*.

This motion compensation is an essential and computationally expensive component in video compression. In fact, the biggest difference between MPEG-1 and MPEG-2 is the change from full-pel to half-pel accuracy. This modification makes a significant difference in quality at a given data rate, but also makes MPEG-2 encode very time-consuming.

DCT

Like JPEG, MPEG is DCT-based. The codec calculates a DCT on each 8 x 8 block of pixel or difference information of each image. The frequency information is easier to sort by visual importance and quantize, and it takes advantage of regions of each frame that are unchanging.

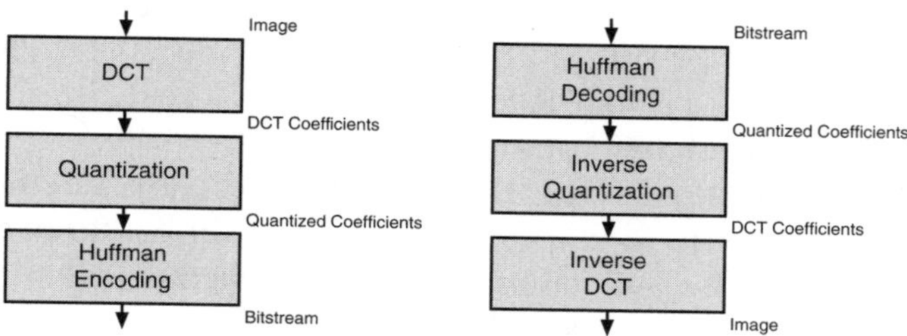

a) I Frame Encode and Decode

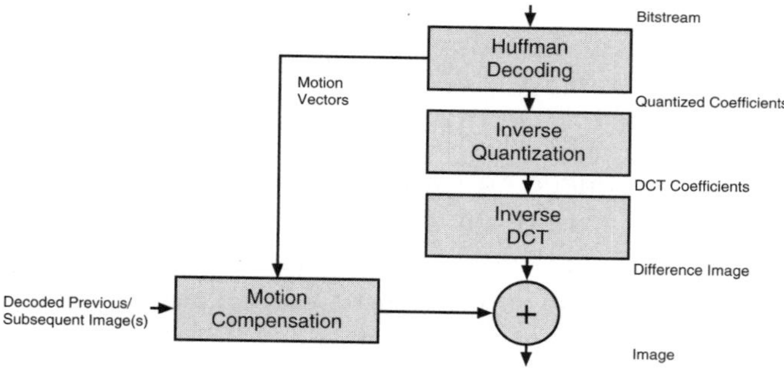

b) P/B Frame Decode

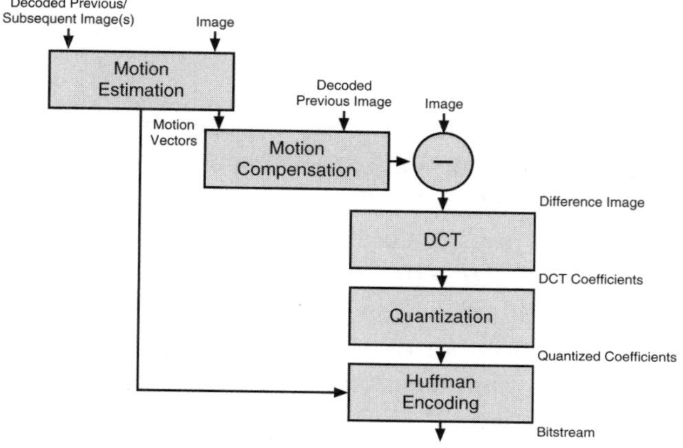

c) P/B Frame Encode

Figure 10.16 High-Level MPEG-2 Encoder and Decoder Blocks

Quantization

Quantization in MPEG is different for different block types. There are different matrices of coefficient-specific values for intra and non-intra macroblocks, as well as for color and intensity data. There is also a scale applied across all matrices. Both the scale and the quantization matrix can change each macroblock.

For intra blocks, the DC, or zero-frequency, coefficient is quantized by dropping the low 0 to 3 bits; that is, by shifting it right by zero to three bits. The AC coefficients are assigned into quantization steps according to the global scale and the matrix. The quantization is linear.

For non-intra blocks, the DC component contains less important information and is more likely to tend toward zero. Therefore, the DC and AC components are quantized in the same way, using the non-intra quantization matrix and scale.

Huffman Coding

In order for reduced entropy in the video data to become a reduced data rate in the bit stream, the data must be coded using fewer bits. In MPEG, as with JPEG, that means a Huffman variable-length encoding scheme. Each piece of data is encoded with a code the length of which is inversely related to its frequency. Because of the complexity of MPEG-2, there are dozens of tables of codes for coefficients, block types, and other information.

For intra blocks, the DC coefficient is not coded directly. Instead, the difference between it and a predictor is used. This predictor is either the DC value of the last block if present and intra, or a constant average value otherwise.

Two scan matrices are used to order the DCT coefficients. One does a zig-zag pattern that is close to diagonally symmetric for blocks that are not interlaced; the other does a modified zig-zag for interlaced blocks. These matrices put the coefficients in order of increasing frequency in an attempt to maximize lengths of runs of data.

The encoder codes run-level data for this matrix. Each run-level pair represents the number of consecutive occurrences of a certain level. The more common pairs have codes in a Huffman table. Less common codes, such as runs of more than 31, are encoded as an escape code followed by a 6-bit run and 12-bit level.

MPEG-2 in Intel IPP

Intel IPP provides a very efficient sample encoder and decoder for MPEG-2. Due to the number of variants, it is only a sample and not a compliant codec.

Each side of the codec includes hundreds of Intel IPP function calls. The bulk of the code in the sample is for bit stream parsing and data manipulation, but the bulk of the time is spent decoding the pixels. For this reason, almost all of the Intel IPP calls are concentrated in the pixel decoding blocks. In particular, the meatiest functions are the `Macroblock_*` functions:

```
Macroblock_420_I_field
Macroblock_420_P_field
Macroblock_420_B_field
Macroblock_420_I_frame
Macroblock_420_P_frame
Macroblock_420_B_frame
Macroblock_422
Macroblock_444
```

Macroblock Coding and Decoding

For decoding, two Intel IPP functions are of primary importance. Between them they implement a large portion of an MPEG-2 decoder, at least for intra blocks.

The first function is `ippiReconstructDCTBlock_MPEG2` for non-intra blocks and `ippiReconstructDCTBlockIntra_MPEG2` for intra blocks. These functions decode Huffman data, rearrange it, and dequantize it. The source is the Huffman-encoded bit stream pointing to the top of a block and the destination is an 8 x 8 block of consecutive DCT coefficients.

The Huffman decoding uses separate tables for AC and DC codes, formatted in the appropriate Intel IPP Spec structure. The scan matrix argument specifies the zig-zag pattern to be used. The functions also take two arguments for the quantization, a matrix and a scale factor. Each element is multiplied by the corresponding element in the quantization matrix, then by the global scale factor.

The function ReconstructDCTBlockIntra also takes two arguments for processing the DC coefficient: the reference value and the shift. The function adds the reference value, which is often taken from the last block, to the DC coefficient. The DC coefficient is shifted by the shift argument, which should be zero to three bits as indicated above.

The second main function is the inverse DCT. The two most useful DCT functions are ippiDCT8x8InvLSClip_16s8u_C1R for intra blocks and ippiDCT8x8Inv_16s_C1R for non-intra blocks. The versions without level-shift and clipping can also be used. This former function inverts the DCT on an 8 x 8 block then converts the data to Ipp8u with a level shift. The output values are pixels. The latter function inverts the DCT and leaves the result in Ipp16s; the output values are difference values. The decoder must then add these difference values to the motion-compensated reference block.

Figure 10.17 shows these functions decoding a 4:2:0 intra macroblock in the MPEG-2 decoder sample. The input is a bit stream and several pre-calculated tables. The DCT outputs the pixel data directly in an image plane. The four blocks of Y data are arrayed in a 2 x 2 square in that image, and the U and V blocks are placed in analogous locations in the U and V planes. This output can be displayed directly by the correct display, or the U and V planes can be upsampled to make a YCbCr 4:4:4 image, or the three planes can be converted by other Intel IPP functions to RGB for display.

```
ippiReconstructDCTBlockIntra_MPEG2_32s(
    &video->bitstream_current_data,
    &video->bitstream_bit_ptr,
    pContext->vlcTables.ippTableB5a,
    pContext->Table_RL,
    scan_1[pContext->PictureHeader.alternate_scan],
    q_scale[pContext->PictureHeader.q_scale_type]
        [pContext->quantizer_scale],
    video->curr_intra_quantizer_matrix,
    &pContext->slice.dct_dc_y_past,
    pContext->curr_intra_dc_multi,
    pContext->block.idct, &dummy);

ippiReconstructDCTBlockIntra_MPEG2_32s(
    …
    pContext->block.idct+64, &dummy);
…
// Repeat two more times for other Y blocks
ippiReconstructDCTBlockIntra_MPEG2_32s(
    …
```

```
    VIDEO_FRAME_BUFFER* frame =
        &video->frame_buffer.frame_p_c_n
            [video->frame_buffer.curr_index];

    // Inverse DCT and place in 16x16 block of image
    ippiDCT8x8InvLSClip_16s8u_C1R(
        pContext->block.idct,
        frame->Y_comp_data + pContext->offset_l,
        pitch_Y, 0, 0, 255);
    ippiDCT8x8InvLSClip_16s8u_C1R(
        pContext->block.idct,
        frame->Y_comp_data + pContext->offset_l + 8,
        pitch_Y, 0, 0, 255);
    ippiDCT8x8InvLSClip_16s8u_C1R(
        pContext->block.idct,
        frame->Y_comp_data + pContext->offset_l + 8*pitch_Y,
        pitch_Y, 0, 0, 255);
    ippiDCT8x8InvLSClip_16s8u_C1R(
        pContext->block.idct,
        frame->Y_comp_data +
            pContext->offset_l + 8*pitch_Y + 8,
        pitch_Y, 0, 0, 255);
…
    ippiReconstructDCTBlockIntra_MPEG2_32s(
        &video->bitstream_current_data,
        &video->bitstream_bit_ptr,
        pContext->vlcTables.ippTableB5b,
        pContext->Table_RL,
        scan_1[pContext->PictureHeader.alternate_scan],
        q_scale[pContext->PictureHeader.q_scale_type]
            [pContext->quantizer_scale],
        video->curr_chroma_intra_quantizer_matrix,
        &pContext->slice.dct_dc_cb_past,
        pContext->curr_intra_dc_multi,
        pContext->block.idct, &i1);

    ippiReconstructDCTBlockIntra_MPEG2_32s(
        …
        &pContext->slice.dct_dc_cr_past,
        pContext->curr_intra_dc_multi,
        pContext->block.idct + 64,&i2);

    ippiDCT8x8InvLSClip_16s8u_C1R (
        pContext->block.idct,
        frame->U_comp_data + pContext->offset_c,
        pitch_UV, 0,0,255);
```

```
ippiDCT8x8InvLSClip_16s8u_C1R (
    pContext->block.idct + 64,
    frame->V_comp_data + pContext->offset_c,
    pitch_UV, 0,0,255);
```

Figure 10.17 Decoding an MPEG-2 Intra Macroblock

The `dummy` parameter to the first `ippiReconstructDCTBlock` call is not used here but can be used for optimization. If the value returned is 1, then only the DC coefficient is nonzero and the inverse DCT can be skipped. If it is less than 10, then all the nonzero coefficients are in the first 4 x 4 block, and a 4 x 4 inverse DCT can be used.

The `ippiDCT8x8Inv_16s8u_C1R` functions could be called instead of the `ippiDCT8x8InvLSClip_16s8u_C1R` because data is clipped to the 0-255 range by default.

In the non-intra case, the pointer to the quantization matrix can be 0. In that case, the default matrices will be used.

The functions `ippiDCT8x8Inv_AANTransposed` can do an inverse DCT on pre-transposed data. To use these, pass a transposing scan matrix to `ippiReconstructBlock`, which essentially performs the transposition for free. These functions also take as an input the last parameter of the `ippiReconstructBlock` functions and perform no DCT or a 4 x 4 DCT, if appropriate.

These functions also support an alternative layout for YUV data, a hybrid layout in which there are two planes, Y and UV. The UV plane consists of U and V data interleaved. In this case, there is one 16 x 8 block of UV data per macroblock. The functions `ippiDCT8x8Inv_AANTransposed_16s_P2C2R` and `ippiDCT8x8Inv_AANTransposed_16s8u_P2C2R` support this alternative layout DCT. The `ippiMC16x8UV_8u_C1` and `ippiMC16x8BUV_8u_C1` functions support motion compensation.

On the encoding side, there are almost-analogous functions for each of the decode functions listed above. For intra blocks, the forward DCT function `ippiDCT8x8Fwd_8u16s_C1R` converts a block of `Ipp8u` pixels into `Ipp16s` DCT coefficients. Then the function `ippiQuantIntra_MPEG2` performs quantization, and the function `ippiPutIntraBlock` calculates the run-level pairs and Huffman encodes them. The parameters for these last two functions are very similar to those for their decoding counterparts.

For inter blocks, the function ippiDCT8x8Fwd_16s_C1R converts the difference information into DCT coefficients, the function ippiQuant_MPEG2 quantizes, and the function ippiPutNonIntraBlock calculates and encodes the run-level pairs.

Motion Estimation and Compensation

Motion estimation by the encoder is very computationally intensive, since it generally requires repeated evaluation of the effectiveness of candidate motion compensation vectors. However the possible motion vectors are chosen, using a fast evaluation function speeds up the algorithm. The Intel IPP functions ippiSAD16x16, ippiSqrDiff16x16, and ippiSqrDiff16x16 compare blocks from one frame against motion-compensated blocks in a reference frame. ippiSAD calculates the sum of absolute differences between the pixels, while ippiSqrDiff calculates the sum of squared differences. The Intel IPP sample uses the former.

Once the encoder has finished searching the space of possible motion vectors, it can use the many ippiGetDiff functions to find the difference between the current frame and the reference frame after motion compensation.

Both the encoder and decoder need a motion compensation algorithm. Intel IPP-based algorithms use ippiMC to combine the reference frame with the decoded difference information. Figure 10.18 shows such an algorithm for a macroblock from a 4:2:0 B-frame.

```
// Determine whether shift is half or full pel
//  in horizontal and vertical directions
// Motion vectors are in half-pels in bitstream
// The bit code generated is:
// FF = 0000b; FH = 0100b; HF = 1000b; HH = 1100b
flag1 = pContext->macroblock.prediction_type |
    ((pContext->macroblock.vector[0]  & 1) << 3) |
    ((pContext->macroblock.vector[1]  & 1) << 2);
flag2 = pContext->macroblock.prediction_type|
    ((pContext->macroblock.vector[0]  & 2) << 2) |
    ((pContext->macroblock.vector[1]  & 2) << 1);
flag3 = pContext->macroblock.prediction_type|
    ((pContext->macroblock.vector[2]  & 1) << 3) |
    ((pContext->macroblock.vector[3]  & 1) << 2);
flag4 = pContext->macroblock.prediction_type|
    ((pContext->macroblock.vector[2]  & 2) << 2) |
```

```
        ((pContext->macroblock.vector[3]  & 2) << 1);

    // Convert motion vectors from half-pels to full-pel
    // also convert for chroma subsampling
    // down, previous frame
    vector_luma[1] = pContext->macroblock.vector[1] >>1;
    vector_chroma[1] = pContext->macroblock.vector[1] >>2;

    // right, previous frame
    vector_luma[0] = pContext->macroblock.vector[0] >> 1;
    vector_chroma[0] = pContext->macroblock.vector[0] >> 2;

    // down, subsequent frame
    vector_luma[3] = pContext->macroblock.vector[3] >> 1;
    vector_chroma[3] = pContext->macroblock.vector[3] >> 2;

    // right, subsequent frame
    vector_luma[2] = pContext->macroblock.vector[2] >> 1;
    vector_chroma[2] = pContext->macroblock.vector[2] >> 2;


    offs1 =
        (pContext->macroblock.motion_vertical_field_select[0] +
            vector_luma[1] + pContext->row_l) * pitch_y +
            vector_luma[0] + pContext->col_l,

    offs2 =
        (pContext->macroblock.motion_vertical_field_select[1] +
            vector_luma[3] + pContext->row_l) * pitch_y +
            vector_luma[2] + pContext->col_l,

    i = ippiMC16x16B_8u_C1(
        ref_Y_data1 + offs1, ptc_y, flag1,
        ref_Y_data2 + offs2, ptc_y, flag3,
        pContext->block.idct, 32,
        frame->Y_comp_data + pContext->offset_l,
        ptc_y, 0);
    assert(i == ippStsOk);

    offs1 =
        (pContext->macroblock.motion_vertical_field_select[0] +
            vector_chroma[1] + pContext->row_c)* pitch_uv +
            vector_chroma[0] + pContext->col_c;

    offs2 =
        (pContext->macroblock.motion_vertical_field_select[1] +
            vector_chroma[3] + pContext->row_c)* pitch_uv +
            vector_chroma[2] + pContext->col_c;

    i = ippiMC8x8B_8u_C1(
```

```
        ref_U_data1 + offs1, ptc_uv, flag2,
        ref_U_data2 + offs2, ptc_uv, flag4,
        pContext->block.idct+256,16,
        frame->U_comp_data + pContext->offset_c,
        ptc_uv, 0);
    assert(i == ippStsOk);
    i = ippiMC8x8B_8u_C1(
        ref_V_data1 + offs1, ptc_uv,flag2,
        ref_V_data2 + offs2, ptc_uv,flag4,
        pContext->block.idct+320,16,
        frame->V_comp_data + pContext->offset_c,
        ptc_uv, 0);
    assert(i == ippStsOk);
```

Figure 10.18 MPEG-2 Bidirectional Motion Compensation

The first step is to convert the motion vectors from half-pel accuracy to full-pel accuracy, because the half-pel information is passed into the `ippiMC` functions as a flag. The code drops the least-significant bit of each motion vector and uses it to generate this flag. The starting point of each reference block is then offset vertically and horizontally by the amount of the motion vector.

Because this code handles bi-directional prediction, the code repeats all these steps for two separate motion vectors and two separate reference frames. This is the last decoding step, so the code places the result directly in the YCbCr output frame.

Color Conversion

The standard Intel IPP color conversion functions include conversions to and from YCbCr 4:2:2, 4:2:0, and 4:4:4. Because they are in the general color conversion set, these functions are called `RGBToYUV422` / `YUV422ToRGB`, `RGBToYUV420` / `YUV420ToRGB`, and `RGBToYUV` / `YUVToRGB`. These functions support interleaved and planar YCbCr data. Figure 10.19 shows a conversion of decoded MPEG-2 pixels into RGB for display.

```
src[0] = frame->Y_comp_data +
    pContext->Video[0].frame_buffer.video_memory_offset;
src[1] = frame->V_comp_data +
    pContext-Video[0].frame_buffer.video_memory_offset/4;
src[2] = frame->U_comp_data +
    pContext->Video[0].frame_buffer.video_memory_offset/4;
srcStep[0] = frame->Y_comp_pitch;
srcStep[1] = pitch_UV;
srcStep[2] = pitch_UV;

ippiYUV420ToRGB_8u_P3AC4R(src, srcStep, video_memory +
    pContext->Video[0].frame_buffer.video_memory_offset/4,
    roi.width<<2, roi);
```

Figure 10.19 Converting YCbCr 4:2:0 to RGB for Display

Other Topics

The three codecs presented here do not do justice to the extensive video codec support in Intel IPP. In addition to MPEG-2, Intel has samples using Intel IPP for MPEG-1, MPEG-4, DV, H.263, and H.264. These samples show how to use the special-purpose Intel IPP functions for those codecs as well as the more-general video coding and arithmetic functions.

Further Reading

The JPEG "pink book" (Pennebaker and Mitchell 1992) is the definitive text for JPEG. Adams (2002) wrote an excellent article summarizing JPEG 2000, explaining each block at a good level of detail. *Video Demystified* (Jack 2001) is a very comprehensive text for video compression in general and H.261, H.263, DV, and MPEG-1 and MPEG-2 in particular.

Chapter 11

Graphics and Physics

Intel® Integrated Performance Primitives (Intel® IPP) includes an extensive set of functions that performs vector and matrix arithmetic to support calculations for three-dimensional geometry of the sort required by computer graphics and physical modeling. These operations are particularly geared toward operation on small vectors and small square matrices, orders three through six. This chapter is an introduction to these functions and their applications.

The formulae and algorithms required by these domains tend to be involved and require multiple matrix and vector functions, as well as multiple branches and sign tests. Often, it is difficult enough just to achieve and demonstrate a correct result. Trying to additionally make them as efficient as possible, which requires the use of SIMD instructions, can be a formidable task. In addition to correctness and adopting new functions and their rules, it requires managing the data structures, arrays, and temporary buffers required to vectorize the code. For this reason, this chapter describes and then demonstrates the process of converting a formula or algorithm that is implemented directly in C code into code that efficiently uses Intel IPP. This demonstration includes several demonstrations of performance improvements using these techniques.

The algorithms are both representative and important in themselves. Hopefully, some will find the implementations of these algorithms to be valuable. The examples should be extensive enough to provide a small toolkit of algorithms as well as teach how to implement new algorithms with Intel IPP.

Background

This first section introduces some technical background and support software used in this chapter. The support software consists of the classes and interfaces that make up the framework within which algorithms for graphics and physics are implemented.

Geometry for Graphics and Physics

To the extent possible, the examples in this chapter are accompanied by all the necessary equations and explanation to understand them. Below is some background for three-dimensional geometry that will be helpful.

Geometric Object Parameters

Here are parameterizations for some three-dimensional geometric objects and the notations used in this chapter:

- A point is defined by three coordinates, (x, y, z).
- A directional vector is defined by three values, (dx, dy, dz).
- A line segment is defined by two points, P_0 and P_1.
- A triangle is defined by three points, P_0, P_1, and P_2.
- A ray is defined by point and a direction. A ray can be formulated as $R(t) = P_0+Dt$, where P_0 and D are the point and directional vectors.
- A plane is defined by three non-collinear points. A plane can be parameterized by four variables, A, B, C, and D, using the equation $Ax + By + Cz + D = 0$. The A, B, and C are components of a vector N (perpendicular to the plane) and D is the negative of the dot product of N and a point on the plane.
- A model is constructed of smaller objects. The objects in this chapter are composed entirely of triangles, but more complex polygons are also common.

Transforms

A point (x,y,z) can be treated as a three-dimensional vector and manipulated with matrix operations. The usual operation is multiplication by a 3 x 3 matrix. Several transforms can be defined this way. For example, a scaling transform would be the following:

$$\begin{bmatrix} x & y & z \end{bmatrix} \begin{bmatrix} S_x & & \\ & S_y & \\ & & S_z \end{bmatrix} = \begin{bmatrix} S_x x & S_y y & S_z z \end{bmatrix}$$

It is also possible to perform rotation around any axis with a matrix multiplication. Rotation about the z-axis by an angle θ is performed by

$$\begin{bmatrix} x & y & z \end{bmatrix} \begin{bmatrix} \cos(\theta) & -\sin(\theta) & \\ \sin(\theta) & \cos(\theta) & \\ & & 1 \end{bmatrix} = \begin{bmatrix} \cos(\theta)x + \sin(\theta)y & \cos(\theta)y - \sin(\theta)x & z \end{bmatrix}$$

Translation of an object can be performed two ways. It is possible to deviate from the multiplicative-transform framework and merely add a constant:

$$\begin{bmatrix} x & y & z \end{bmatrix} + \begin{bmatrix} T_x & T_y & T_z \end{bmatrix} = \begin{bmatrix} T_x + x & T_y + y & T_z + z \end{bmatrix}$$

Usually, the convenience and performance of a single transform matrix takes precedence. For this reason, coordinates are usually expressed as four-dimensional vectors, with the fourth dimension set to 1. Points expressed this way are called homogenous coordinates. The advantage is that translations can be expressed as a convenient matrix-vector multiplication:

$$\begin{bmatrix} x & y & z & 1 \end{bmatrix} \begin{bmatrix} 1 & & & \\ & 1 & & \\ & & 1 & \\ T_x & T_y & T_z & 1 \end{bmatrix} = \begin{bmatrix} T_x + x & T_y + y & T_z + z & 1 \end{bmatrix}$$

For directional vectors, the fourth coordinate is zero because translation is meaningless for a directional vector.

An object defined by an array of points can be transformed by a single matrix multiplication against that array, treated as a two-dimensional matrix.

Model and View

The coordinate system used for a model can be considered fixed. Several objects may each have a model space and would overlap if placed directly. The model-view transform converts points in the model space to the view space. The transform is usually expressed as a 4 x 4 matrix and is performed as a matrix multiplication.

Normals

A normal of a geometric object is a vector perpendicular to that object. The normal of a two-dimensional object describes the direction that the object is facing. One-dimensional objects have an infinite number of normals in three-space. While points have no sensible normal, normals are often set for vertices in a three-dimensional scene to reduce discontinuities in a surface.

The normal of a triangle can be calculated as $(P_1 - P_0) \times (P_2 - P_0)$. As noted previously, the normal of a plane is part of its common parameterization.

If an object is transformed with a matrix M, the corresponding transform for the normals of that object is $(M^{-1})^T$, the transpose of the inverse of M.

3DS structure and 3DS object

Examples in this chapter rely on various objects that are loaded from the 3DS file format. A 3DS file is composed of chunks of data. Each chunk represents one element of a scene, such as a view, light, material, background, or object. Objects are further decomposed into triangle meshes, lights, and cameras. The core of the object is the triangle mesh, which encompasses the vertices and triangles or polygons that define the object's shape.

The `Object3DS` class, defined in Figure 11.1, encapsulates this data. The member function `Load` reads a .3ds file into member arrays. The geometric data for the file is placed in arrays of `VertexData` and `TrianglesData` structures. The array of `VertexData` structures `m_vertexData` is a list of all the vertices in the object in no particular order. Data for each vertex includes a location in three-space (`x, y, z`), a normal (`nx, ny, nz`), a color (`r, g, b`), and a texture coordinate (`tu, tv`).

The connections between these vertices are captured in the array of `TrianglesData` structures `m_trianglesData`. Each structure in this array is three indices into the `m_vertexData` array, representing the three corners of a single triangle. For example, the first vertex of the first triangle is:

`m_vertexData[m_trianglesData[0].firstIndex].`

The indices should be in order in consideration of some applications but may not be.

This arrangement of data is geared toward conservation of memory and rapid display of the model, rather than host-based manipulation. The reader was written to load the objects into memory without regard to optimization of the subsequent operations. Therefore, using this data layout results in more realistic examples. The intent of the multiple data types and layouts supported by Intel IPP matrix operations is to work on such data in-place, with limited copying and reformatting.

This is also the class that includes the examples.

```
typedef struct {
    float               x;
    float               y;
    float               z;
    float               nx;
    float               ny;
    float               nz;
    float               r;
    float               g;
    float               b;
    float               tu;
    float               tv;
    long                flag;
} VertexData;

typedef struct {
    unsigned long       firstIndex;
    unsigned long       secondIndex;
    unsigned long       thirdIndex;
} TrianglesData;

typedef struct {
    float A, B, C, D;
} PlaneData;

…

class Object3DS
{
    private:
        static unsigned char ReadByte(FILE *file);
```

```
        static int ReadInt(FILE *file);
        static long ReadLong(FILE *file);
        static unsigned int ReadSectionID(FILE *file);
        static unsigned long ReadSizeLevel(FILE *file);
        static unsigned long ReadUnknownLevel(FILE *file);
        static unsigned long ReadLocalMatrix(FILE* pFile);
        int AddTexture(char* fileName);
        unsigned long ReadTextures(FILE* pFile);
        unsigned long ReadVertexMaterial(FILE* pFile,
            int shiftTriangles);
        unsigned long ReadTriangles(FILE* pFile);
        unsigned long ReadVertex(FILE* pFile);
        unsigned long ReadMeshLevel(FILE* pFile);
        unsigned long ReadObjectLevel(FILE* pFile);
        unsigned long ReadTextFileName(FILE* pFile);
        unsigned long ReadTextureMap(FILE* pFile);
        unsigned long ReadMaterialColor(FILE* pFile,
            ColorData *colorData);
        unsigned long ReadMaterialName(FILE* pFile);
        unsigned long ReadMaterial(FILE* pFile);
        unsigned long ReadDataLevel(FILE* pFile);
        int ReadVersion(FILE* pFile);

        LocalBuffer m_buffer_;

    public:
        Object3DS();
        ~Object3DS();
        int Load(FILE* pFile);
        void Normalize();
        …
        int     m_numVertex;
        int     m_shiftVertex;
        int     m_numTriangles;
        int     m_numMaterial;
        int     m_numTextureFiles;
        TextureData         m_globalTexture;
        char*               m_globalBitmap;
        unsigned long       m_sizeGlobalBitmap;
        VertexData*         m_vertexData;
        TrianglesData*      m_trianglesData;
        MaterialData*       m_materialData;
};
```

Figure 11.1 Declaration of the `Object3DS` Class

3DS OpenGL† Viewer

Another class, Render3DS, takes an Object3DS instance and renders it to a view. This class contains all the view information, including the size of the viewport, the orientation of the camera, the scene lighting information, and the model-view transformation. The class declaration and some function definitions are contained in Figure 11.2.

The most important member of this class is ModelViewMatrix. This matrix represents the transform between the model space and the view space. This matrix can be modified directly, but the member functions Rotate, Translate, and Scale are provided to transform the view more easily. The arguments taken by these functions are also mouse-friendly, and expect mouse location and movement values as input.

The Render3DS class uses OpenGL† to perform the display. OpenGL has the advantages of being easy to use, relatively fast, and available on multiple platforms, including Linux†. Other than its use of OpenGL, Render3DS is platform-neutral.

The ModelViewMatrix is laid out as an OpenGL transformation matrix. Every time the view is modified using OpenGL, the resulting view transformation matrix is recaptured, as in this code segment from the Translate method:

```
glMatrixMode(GL_MODELVIEW);
glLoadIdentity();
glTranslatef(out[0], out[1], 0.0f);
glMultMatrixf(ModelViewMatrix);
glGetFloatv(GL_MODELVIEW_MATRIX, ModelViewMatrix);
```

After a scene modification, the function Reshape sends the shape and state of the view to OpenGL. It sets up the viewport, sets the parameters and projection type, which is orthographic in this case, resets the projection matrix, and reloads the model-view matrix.

Finally, the function Display renders an Object3DS to the current OpenGL destination using the previous view information. If a mask is provided, it should have one entry per triangle; each triangle is filled only if its corresponding mask entry is nonzero.

```
class Render3DS
{
    public:

        typedef enum {PLANE, SIDE1, SIDE2, SIDE3} NormalType;

    private:

    typedef struct{
        int         GeomType;
        int         FillStyle;
        float       MatAmbient[4];
    } Style;

    float sizeXY, sizeZ;
    int x_prev,y_prev;
    static float pIdentity4f[16];

    Style style1, style2;

    float v_pointZ;
    float v_planeZ;
    int fill_;

    void Normalize(Object3DS& object);
    void InitLight (void);
    void InitStyle();
    void DrawObject(Object3DS& object, Style *pStyle,
                   char* pMask = 0);
…
    void DrawNormals(Object3DS& object, Style *pStyle,
        float r, float g, float b);

    void MakePlane();

    public:

    void SetFill(int fill = 1);
    float ModelViewMatrix[16];

    Render3DS(float* pViewMatrix4f = pIdentity4f);

    void GetBounds(const RECT *pWindowRect,
                   float *left, float* right,
                   float* top, float* bottom);
    float GetZMin() { return -sizeZ;}
    float GetZMax() { return sizeZ;}

    void Reset();
    void Set(float* pViewMatrix4f = pIdentity4f);
```

```
    void Reshape(RECT *pRect);
    void Rotate(int x, int y, int x_prev, int y_prev,
        RECT *pRect);
    void Translate(int x, int y, int x_prev, int y_prev,
        RECT *pRect);
    void Scale(int delta, RECT *pRect);
    void DisplayInit();
    void Display(Object3DS& object, char* pMask=0);
    void DisplayNormals(Object3DS& object,
        float r=1.0, float g=1.0, float b=1.0);
…
    void DisplayDone();

    void DrawTriangle(const float* pTriangle);
    void DrawLine(const float* pLine);

};

void Render3DS::Reshape(RECT *pRect)
{
    int w = pRect->right-pRect->left;
    int h = pRect->bottom-pRect->top;
    glViewport(pRect->left, pRect->top, pRect->right,
        pRect->bottom);
    glMatrixMode(GL_PROJECTION);
    glLoadIdentity();
    float left, right, top, bottom;
    GetBounds(pRect, &left, &right, &top, &bottom);
    glOrtho(left, right, bottom, top,
            -sizeZ, sizeZ);
    glMatrixMode(GL_MODELVIEW);
    glLoadMatrixf(ModelViewMatrix);
}

void Render3DS::Translate(int x, int y, int x_prev, int y_prev,
    RECT *pRect)
{
    int w = pRect->right-pRect->left;
    int h = pRect->bottom-pRect->top;
    float   norm;
    float   out[2];

    norm = (float)__min(h,w);
    out[0] = (2*x - 2*x_prev)/(norm);
    out[1] = (-2*y + 2*y_prev)/(norm);

    glMatrixMode(GL_MODELVIEW);
    glLoadIdentity();
```

```
    glTranslatef(out[0], out[1], 0.0f);
    glMultMatrixf(ModelViewMatrix);
    glGetFloatv(GL_MODELVIEW_MATRIX, ModelViewMatrix);
}

void Render3DS::Scale(int delta, RECT *pRect)
{
    int w = pRect->right-pRect->left;
    int h = pRect->bottom-pRect->top;
    float out = (float) 10.0f*(delta)/h;
    if (1+out> 0.0f) {
        sizeXY += sizeXY*out;
        sizeZ += sizeZ*out;
    }
    Reshape(pRect);
}

void Render3DS::Display(Object3DS& object, char* pMask)
{
    glPushMatrix ();
    DrawObject(object, &style1, pMask);
    glPopMatrix ();
}

void Render3DS::DrawObject(Object3DS& object,
    Style *pStyle, char* pMask)
{
    int i;
    glEnable(GL_NORMALIZE);
    glMaterialfv(GL_FRONT, GL_AMBIENT, pStyle->MatAmbient);

    TrianglesData* pTri;
    if (!pMask)
    {
        glPolygonMode (GL_FRONT_AND_BACK, pStyle->FillStyle);
        glBegin(GL_TRIANGLES);
        for (i=0; i< object.m_numTriangles; i ++)
        {
            pTri = &object.m_trianglesData[i];
            glNormal3fv(
                &(object.m_vertexData[pTri->firstIndex].nx));
            glVertex3fv(
                &(object.m_vertexData[pTri->firstIndex].x));

            glNormal3fv(
                &(object.m_vertexData[pTri->secondIndex].nx));
            glVertex3fv(
                &(object.m_vertexData[pTri->secondIndex].x));

            glNormal3fv(
```

```
                &(object.m_vertexData[pTri->thirdIndex].nx));
            glVertex3fv(
                &(object.m_vertexData[pTri->thirdIndex].x));
        }
        glEnd();
    }
    else
        for (i=0; i< object.m_numTriangles; i ++)
        {
            pTri = &object.m_trianglesData[i];
            if (pMask[i])
                glPolygonMode (GL_FRONT_AND_BACK, GL_FILL);
            else glPolygonMode (GL_FRONT_AND_BACK, GL_LINE);

            glBegin(GL_TRIANGLES);
            glNormal3fv(
                &(object.m_vertexData[pTri->firstIndex].nx));
            glVertex3fv(
                &(object.m_vertexData[pTri->firstIndex].x));

            glNormal3fv(
                &(object.m_vertexData[pTri->secondIndex].nx));
            glVertex3fv(
                &(object.m_vertexData[pTri->secondIndex].x));

            glNormal3fv(
                &(object.m_vertexData[pTri->thirdIndex].nx));
            glVertex3fv(
                &(object.m_vertexData[pTri->thirdIndex].x));
            glEnd();
        }

    glDisable(GL_NORMALIZE);
}
...
```

Figure 11.2 Declaration of `Render3DS` Class and Some Methods

Object Viewer Application

While the above code has been operating system-neutral, the user interface through which the objects are viewed and manipulated is specific to Microsoft Windows[†]. This simple application uses the `Object3DS` class to load and store the objects and the `Render3DS` class to render the object. The application allows the loading and viewing of objects, filled and wireframe, and displays the results of calculations made in this chapter. It also allows the rotation, translation, and scaling of the view and translation of the model.

Figure 11.3 shows a snapshot of this application running.

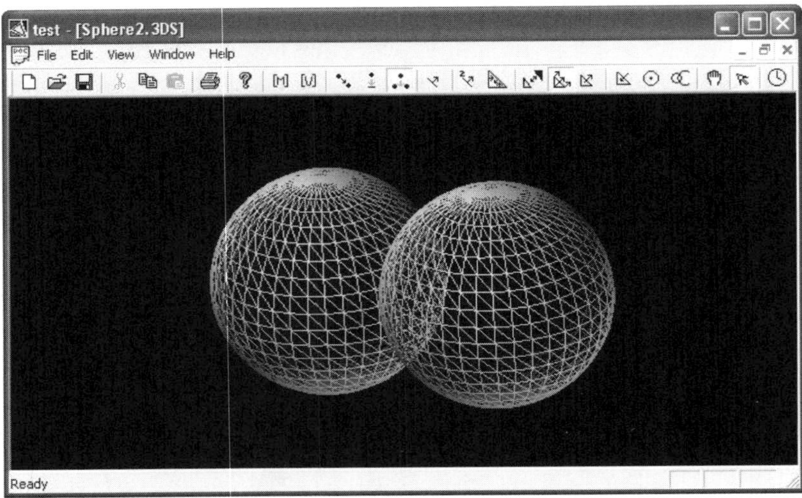

Figure 11.3 Object Viewer Application Showing the Object `sphere2.3ds`.

Programming Methodology

The examples in this chapter follow a methodology of loop removal that makes programming to Intel IPP matrix functions more manageable, particularly when converting from an existing implementation.

Matrix functions in the Intel IPP library have vector and vector-array versions, or matrix and matrix-array versions. For the same operation, using the array versions of each function is much more efficient than using the single-vector or single-matrix versions because of the overhead of the call and the internal setup for the operation.

For example, adding vectors of length three can be implemented two ways with Intel IPP matrix functions. Using the single-vector versions, such code might look like this:

```
for (int i=0; i<count; i++)
    ippmAdd_vv_32f_3x1(pSrc1[i],pSrc2[i],pDst[i]);
```

Using the vector-array versions, this loop is embedded in a single call:

```
ippmAdd_vava_32f_3x1(pSrc1, stride, pSrc2, stride,
    pDst, stride, count);
```

Figure 11.4 compares the performance of these two methods of calling Intel IPP for a matrix-vector multiplication with the performance of the same operation written in C. Lower numbers indicate a faster routine. According to this chart, even a run of eight vectors justifies using the vector-array version of this function.

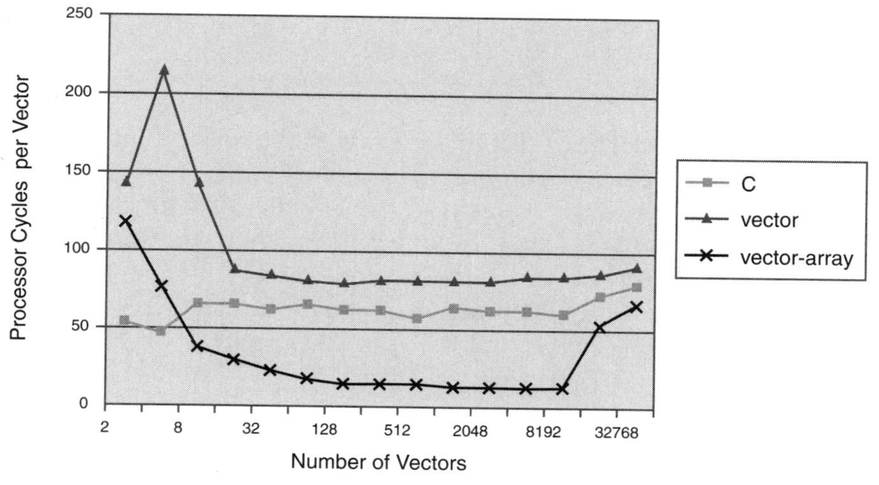

Figure 11.4 Graph of Performance for Three Implementations of Vector/Matrix Multiplication

Achieving this efficiency by making this conversion is daunting, and it is often difficult to make the resulting code mirror the original results. For this reason, the following methodology is useful for complex geometric algorithms of the sort usually required in graphics and physics:

1. Implement the formula using vector-vector, vector-matrix, and matrix-matrix functions. Use a big loop, and operate on single elements. The loop may be outside the function, and the function may already exist in some form.
2. Keep the same Intel IPP functions, but operate on elements of an array instead of single elements
3. Modify the Intel IPP functions and arguments to use the vector-array and matrix-array versions of the functions.

A further nuance that is essential in practice is the use of carefully sized temporary buffers. For a medium-sized array, say 5,000 vertices, efficient cache use dictates the use of buffers smaller than the entire array. A set of buffers only 256 vectors long fits comfortably in a typical first-level cache. Smaller buffers also take less memory, obviously. Figure 11.5 shows the performance of a typical function using a range of buffer sizes. The function used is:

```
ippmMul_mva_32f_4x4(pMatrix, 16,
    pVecSrc1, 16, pTmp1, 16, size);
ippmMul_mva_32f_4x4(pMatrix, 16,
    pVecSrc2, 16, pTmp2, 16, size);
ippmAdd_vava_32f_4x1(pTmp1, 16,
    pTmp2, 16, pVecDst, 16, size);
```

The vector plot uses the "v" versions of the above functions. The version with buffer operates on only 128 vectors at a time regardless of the total number of vectors. In this test, the effects of cache can be seen starting with arrays of size 1,024, and the performance deteriorates from there.

This methodology can be demonstrated with a small but typical vector math algorithm. This series of equations calculates the angle and axis of rotation between P_0 and P_1 around a center C:

$$V_0 = (P_0 - C) / |P_0 - C|$$

$$V_1 = (P_1 - C) / |P_1 - C|$$

$$A = V_0 \times V_1$$

$$\text{angle} = \arcsin(|A|)$$

This algorithm is most efficiently executed when performed on many points at once, assuming the points can be accessed as part of an array of structures, from an array of pointers to vectors, or as part of a structure of arrays.

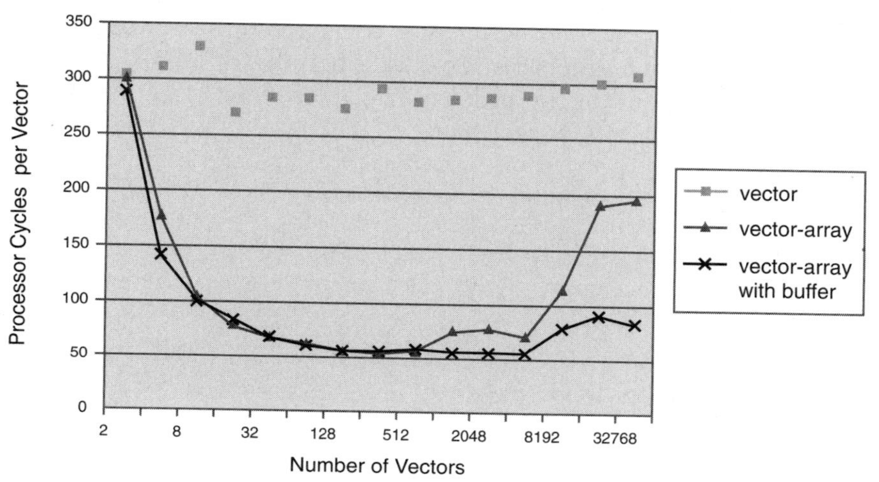

Figure 11.5 Graph of Performance of Code Sequence With and Without Buffer

Using the methodical approach above, you first write a completely scalar version of the code, using the vector-vector and vector-constant versions of the Intel IPP matrix functions. This code looks as follows:

```
function DoOnce(P0, P1, C)
  // V0 = (P0 - C) / |P0 - C|
  ippmSub_vv(P0, C, V0)
  ippmL2Norm_v(V0, tmp)
  ippmMul_vc(V0, 1.0/tmp, V0)

  // V1 = (P1 - C) / |P1 - C|
  ippmSub_vv(P1, C, V1)
  ippmL2Norm_v(V1, tmp)
  ippmMul_vc(V1, 1.0/tmp, V1)

  // A = V0 × V1
  ippmCrossProduct(V0, V1, A)

  // angle = arcsin(|A|)
  ippmL2Norm_v(A, tmp)
  ippsAsin(tmp, angle, 1)
```

This is pseudocode, and the arguments and function names have been simplified to illustrate the methodology, but the order of operations and function base names are accurate.

The next step is to convert the function to operation on multiple vectors instead of single vectors, without changing the structure of the function. Essentially, this is moving the loop from outside the function to inside the function. This requires a temporary buffer pTmp with one element per point in the input. That code, which assumes that the input is an array of points, is as follows:

```
function DoMany(pP0, pP1, C)
  for i=0 to N
      // V0 = (P0 - C) / |P0 - C|
      ippmSub_vv(pP0[i], C, pV0[i])
      ippmL2Norm_v(pV0[i], pTmp[i])
      ippmMul_vc(pV0[i], 1.0f/pTmp[i], pV0[i])

      // V1 = (P1 - C) / |P1 - C|
      ippmSub_vv(pP1[i], C, pV1[i])
      ippmL2Norm_v(pV1[i], pTmp[i])
      ippmMul_vc(pV1[i], 1.0f/pTmp[i], pV1[i])

      // A = V0 × V1
      ippmCrossProduct_v(pV0[i], pV1[i], pA[i])

      // angle = arcsin(|A|)
      ippmL2Norm_v(pA[i], pTmp[i])
      ippsAsin(pTmp[i], pAngle[i], 1)
```

As noted previously, it is important to reduce the amount of temporary storage used and keep the temporary storage and the input and output arrays in cache within each loop. For that reason, the next step is to add an additional inner loop and reduce the pTmp array to the size of that inner loop. The value of this loop is evident in the next code segment. The resulting function is as follows:

```
function DoMany2(pP0, pP1, C)
  for i=0 to N, step bufSize
      pV0curr = &pV0[i];
      pV1curr = &pV1[i];
      pP0curr = &pP0[i];
      pP1curr = &pP1[i];
      pACurr = &pA[i];
      pAngleCurr = &pAngle[i];

      for j=0 to bufSize
          // V0 = (P0 - C) / |P0 - C|
          ippmSub_vv(pP0Curr[j], C, pV0Curr[j], bufSize)
          ippmL2Norm_v(pV0Curr[j], pTmp[j], bufSize)
          ippmMul_vc(pV0Curr[j], 1.0/pTmp[j], pV0Curr[j])
```

```
        // V1 = (P1 - C) / |P1 - C|
        ippmSub_vv(pP1Curr[j], C, pV1Curr[j])
        ippmL2Norm_v(pV1Curr[j], pTmp[j])
        ippmMul_vc(pV1Curr[j], 1.0/pTmp[j], pV1Curr[j])

        // A = V0 × V1
        ippmCrossProduct_va(pV0Curr[j], pV1Curr[j],
            pACurr[j])

        // angle = arcsin(|A|)
        ippmL2Norm_v(pACurr[j], pTmp[j])
        ippsAsin(pTmp[j], pAngleCurr[j], 1)
```

The final step, to convert this code from the vector versions to the vector-array versions, becomes pretty easy. Mostly, it requires removing array subscripts and changing the descriptors in the function names.

Not shown in this pseudocode are the strides that most functions take that indicate the number of bytes between the beginnings of one vector and the next.

```
function DoManyFast()
  for i=0 to N, step bufSize
      pV0curr = &pV0[i];
      pV1curr = &pV1[i];
      pP0curr = &pP0[i];
      pP1curr = &pP1[i];
      pACurr = &pA[i];
      pAngleCurr = &pAngle[i];

      // V0 = (P0 - C) / |P0 - C|
      ippmSub_vav(pP0Curr, C, pV0Curr, bufSize)
      ippmL2Norm_va(pV0Curr, pTmp, bufSize)
      ippsDivCRev(1.0f, pTmp, bufSize)
      for j=0 to bufSize
          ippmMul_vc(pV0Curr[j], pTmp[j], pV0Curr[j])

      // V1 = (P1 - C) / |P1 - C|
      ippmSub_vav(pP1Curr, C, pV1Curr, bufSize)
      ippmL2Norm_va(pV1Curr, pTmp, bufSize)
      ippsDivCRev(1.0f, pTmp, bufSize)
      for j=0 to bufSize
          ippmMul_vc(pV1Curr[j], pTmp[j], pV1Curr[j])

      // A = V0 × V1
      ippmCrossProduct_va(pV0Curr, pV1Curr, pACurr,
          bufSize)
```

```
// angle = arcsin(|A|)
ippmL2Norm_va(pACurr, pTmp, bufSize)
ippsAsin(pTmp, pAngleCurr, bufSize)
```

Note that the unfortunate lack of an ippmMul_vav function reduces the efficiency of the divide portion of the code. Because the function doesn't exist, the calls to ippsDivCRev and ippmMul_vc may be best replaced with:

```
for j=0 to bufSize
    pV0Curr[j].x /= pTmp[j]
    pV0Curr[j].y /= pTmp[j]
    pV0Curr[j].z /= pTmp[j]
```

Geometry

This section walks through several examples of implementing geometric algorithms using Intel IPP.

These examples emphasize the geometry of the model rather than the view. While the math is essentially the same, it is reasonable to assume that almost all view-space calculations are done on a graphics card.

Transforming the Model

This example applies the view matrix onto the model. The routine uses the view matrix to transform the model itself then resets the view matrix to the identity matrix. Normally, when the view is generated, the graphics engine multiplies each of the vertices by the view matrix as part of the display process. In this example, each of the vertices of the model is multiplied by the view matrix before the model is rendered and the results are saved as the new model. At the same time, the normals are transformed by the inverse transpose of the view matrix.

As described above, the view matrix is saved in the Render3DS::ModelViewMatrix array. Every time a modification is made to the view, the modification is applied to this view matrix as well.

The variable m_vertexData points to an array of VertexData structures, which contain the x, y, and z coordinates of each vertex. This structure is defined in Figure 11.1. The first three elements are the x, y, and z coordinates, then there are several other elements including the vertex normal and color:

```
float x;
float y;
float z;
float nx;
...
```

To access these vertices in-place, the operation should start at the first x coordinate, &m_vertexData->x, or to use more appropriate syntax, &m_vertexData[0].x. The stride of this array is the distance from one x to the next, which is the size of the VertexData structure.

The view matrix is laid out to perform post-multiplication; that is, it expects dotprod(vector, viewMatrix). In order to pre-multiply vectors by the view matrix, that matrix must first be transposed. The Intel IPP function that performs this operation is ippmMul_mTva, which multiplies a transposed matrix against each of an array of vectors. Figure 11.6 shows this multiplication.

The operation is complicated slightly by the layout of the coordinate data. The in-place coordinate data isn't in homogenous coordinates because the value after z is more data instead of 1.0. That makes a two-step process to change the model necessary. With homogenous coordinates, the fourth row of the transform matrix, or fourth column, depending on matrix layout, is added to the resulting vector. To simulate this, after the 3 x 3 matrix multiplication, the last row of the matrix, starting at ModelViewMatrix[12], is added to each resulting vector. The function that performs this operation is ippmAdd_vav, which adds a single vector to each of an array of vectors.

For the resulting model to display correctly, the normals for each vertex must also undergo a transform. When the vertices of the model are transformed by a given matrix, the normals should be transformed by the inverse transpose of that matrix. Multiplying the normals in that way keeps them consistent with the new vertices.

The call to ippmInvert calculates this inverse matrix, and then the call to ippmMul_mva applies the transform to the nx, ny, and nz components of the normals. Because the transform of the vertices was transposed, this transform should not be, so the mva version of the function is used instead of the mTva. No addition is needed because normals are direction vectors whose fourth component in homogenous coordinates should be zero.

```
void CTestView::OnMutateModel()
{
    CTestDoc* pDoc = GetDocument();

    ippmMul_mTva_32f_3x3(
        m_render3DS_.ModelViewMatrix, sizeof(Ipp32f)*4,
        &pDoc->m_pData->m_vertexData->x, sizeof(VertexData),
        &pDoc->m_pData->m_vertexData->x, sizeof(VertexData),
        pDoc->m_pData->m_numVertex);
    ippmAdd_vav_32f_3x1(
        &pDoc->m_pData->m_vertexData->x, sizeof(VertexData),
        &m_render3DS_.ModelViewMatrix[12],
        &pDoc->m_pData->m_vertexData->x, sizeof(VertexData),
        pDoc->m_pData->m_numVertex);

    // Transform the normals
    Ipp32f pMatrixInv[16];
    ippmInvert_m_32f_4x4(m_render3DS_.ModelViewMatrix, 16,
        pMatrixInv, 16);

    ippmMul_mva_32f_3x3(
        pMatrixInv, sizeof(Ipp32f)*4,
        &pDoc->m_pData->m_vertexData->nx, sizeof(VertexData),
        &pDoc->m_pData->m_vertexData->nx, sizeof(VertexData),
        pDoc->m_pData->m_numVertex);

    // Reset the view matrix
    m_render3DS_.Reset();
    pDoc->Reinit();

    Invalidate(false);
}
...
```

Figure 11.6 Code for Transforming Vertices and Normals of a Model

Projection

Another interesting projection is the projection of all of the points of a model onto a plane. This operation flattens the model in the viewing plane, so the silhouette should remain unchanged until the model is rotated again. Like the previous example, this operation has the advantage that it doesn't matter how the vertices are laid out or what triangles each vertex is part of.

The first step is to calculate the matrix to be used for transformation. The easiest way conceptually to flatten the model is to transform it into the view space, then flatten the Z coordinate, then transform back into the model space. Mathematically, that can be expressed as:

$$M_{mv} * M_{flat} * M_{mv}^{-1} * V$$

M_{mv} is the view matrix, or `Render3DS::ModelViewMatrix`. The M_{flat} matrix is equal to an identity matrix with a zeroed-out Z component:

$$\begin{bmatrix} 1.0 & 0.0 & 0.0 & 0.0 \\ 0.0 & 1.0 & 0.0 & 0.0 \\ 0.0 & 0.0 & 0.0 & 0.0 \\ 0.0 & 0.0 & 0.0 & 1.0 \end{bmatrix}$$

The stride used for the matrix, 16, is the size of each row, or 4 elements times 4 bytes per element. It would be clearer but more verbose to use `4 * sizeof(Ipp32f)`.

The new normal is calculated by transforming a unit normal in the Z direction out of view space into model space. This is done by multiplying it by the view matrix, as in:

$$N = M_{mv} * \begin{bmatrix} 0.0 \\ 0.0 \\ 1.0 \end{bmatrix}$$

The normal is then set using `ippiSet`. The advantage of the imaging version of the set function is that it takes an array of three values for the three-channel set. In essence, this function performs the nonexistent operation `ippmSet_vva`.

The width of the image is set to 1 so that at each iteration the function will skip ahead by the stride. The stride is sizeof(VertexData) as it has been before. This operation, shown in Figure 11.7, could also be done in C.

```
void CTestView::OnProjectPlane()
{
    CTestDoc* pDoc = GetDocument();
    ASSERT_VALID(pDoc);

    m_projectPlane_ = !m_projectPlane_;

    if (!m_projectPlane_)
    {
        pDoc->Reload();
        Invalidate(false);
        return;
    }

    Ipp32f pMatrix[16], pMatrixTmp[16], pMatrixInv[16];
    Ipp32f pZNormal[4] = { 0.0f, 0.0f, 1.0f, 0.0f },
        pNormal[4];
    Ipp32f pZFlat[16] = {
        1.0f, 0.0f, 0.0f, 0.0f,
        0.0f, 1.0f, 0.0f, 0.0f,
        0.0f, 0.0f, 0.0f, 0.0f,
        0.0f, 0.0f, 0.0f, 1.0f};

    // Calculate the normal to the plane
    ippsCopy_32f(m_render3DS_.ModelViewMatrix, pMatrix, 16);
    ippmMul_mv_32f_4x4(pMatrix, 16, pZNormal, pNormal);

    // Calculate the transform matrix
    ippmInvert_m_32f_4x4(pMatrix, 16, pMatrixInv, 16);
    ippmMul_mm_32f_4x4(pMatrix, 16, pZFlat, 16,
        pMatrixTmp, 16);
    ippmMul_mm_32f_4x4(pMatrixTmp, 16, pMatrixInv, 16,
        pMatrix, 16);

    // Transform the vertices
    ippmMul_mva_32f_3x3(
        pMatrix, sizeof(Ipp32f)*4,
        &pDoc->m_pData->m_vertexData->x, sizeof(VertexData),
        &pDoc->m_pData->m_vertexData->x, sizeof(VertexData),
        pDoc->m_pData->m_numVertex);
```

```
    // Set all of the normals to the plane normal
    IppiSize sizeAsImage = { 1, pDoc->m_pData->m_numVertex };
    int stride = sizeof(VertexData);
    ippiSet_32f_C3R(pNormal,
        &pDoc->m_pData->m_vertexData[0].nx, stride,
        sizeAsImage);

    }
    Invalidate();
}
```

Figure 11.7 Projecting an Object onto a Plane

The result of this operation performed on a sphere is shown in Figure 11.8. The unmodified sphere is shown for reference, and the whole scene is rotated to show the flattened sphere more clearly.

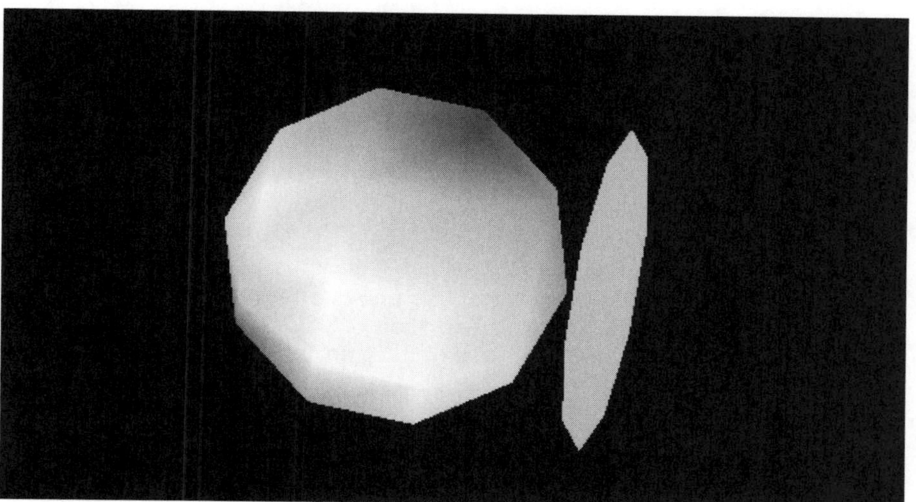

Figure 11.8 Object `sphere1.3ds`, Unmodified and Projected onto the Viewing Plane

Drawing in the View

A technique similar to the above can be used to insert an object that is fixed in the view rather than fixed in space. Figure 11.9 shows how to use the current mouse position to draw a triangle in model space that appears under the cursor.

The x- and y-coordinates are normalized to the range (-0.5, 0.5), then multiplied by the size of the window in model-space. The z-coordinate is set just inside the back clipping plane. A triangle is defined by shifting the x- and y-coordinates. The inverse of the view matrix is calculated with `ippmInvert_m`. Then each vertex of this triangle is multiplied by the view matrix, and the resulting triangle is rendered. Note that the 4 x 4 version of `ippmMul` is used, since the triangle vertices use homogenous coordinates.

```
GetClientRect(rect);
m_render3DS_.GetBounds(rect, &left, &right, &top, &bottom);
x = ((float)m_currMousePos_.x-(float)rect.Width()/2.0) /
    (float)rect.Width()*(right-left);
y = ((float)m_currMousePos_.y-(float)rect.Height()/2.0) /
    (float)rect.Height()*(bottom-top);
z = m_render3DS_.GetZMax()-0.01;
float pTriangle[12] = {
    x, y, z, 1.0,
    x+0.5, y-0.2, z, 1.0,
    x+0.2, y-0.5, z, 1.0 };
ippmInvert_m_32f_4x4(
    m_render3DS_.ModelViewMatrix, 4*4,
    pMatrixInv, 4*4);
ippmMul_mTva_32f_4x4(pMatrixInv, 4*4,
    pTriangle, 4*4, pTriangle, 4*4, 3);
m_render3DS_.DrawTriangle(pTriangle);
```

Figure 11.9 Drawing a Triangle Under the Cursor

Ray Tracing

Ray tracing is an alternate rendering method that inherently provides certain visual effects, such as shadows and refraction. It simulates the process of light reflection and transmission directly, by bouncing light rays on objects. The term generally refers to the process of tracing backward along a ray of light, bouncing off of objects, until it reaches a light source.

It is also possible to trace forward from a light source, illuminating objects; this process is sometimes referred to as *radiosity*.

A basic ray-tracing algorithm is:

1. For each pixel, trace a ray into the scene.
2. For each ray, calculate the first object it intersects.
3. For each ray-object intersection, do the following:
   - Send out rays in zero or more directions, up to a certain depth of recursion.
   - Trace a ray directly to each light.
   - Return the total amount and color of light reflected back along the ray.

Objects have reflectance parameters or functions that determine, for a given angle of incidence and angle of reflection, what percentage of light is reflected or in some cases refracted. Generally, each color component is reflected a different percentage.

This section walks through the first fundamental operation in the ray-tracing algorithm above: calculating which triangle, if any, a given ray hits. One algorithm for making this calculation is:

1. Precalculate the plane equation for each triangle.
2. Precalculate the plane equation for each side of each triangle.
3. For each ray, do these tasks:
   - For each triangle, calculate the location of the intersection of the ray with the plane of the triangle. Then, determine whether the intersection point lies inside the triangle.
   - Determine which triangle, if any, was struck first.

For the purposes of this calculation and the display of the results, the last step, finding the front-most triangle, is skipped, and all triangles hit will be highlighted.

Calculating the Plane Equation

The algorithm for calculating the intersection of rays with triangles requires that the formula for the triangle's plane be explicitly calculated. A plane can be defined with the formula

$$Ax + By + Cz + D = 0$$

The three values A, B, and C form a vector normal to the plane. The final parameter is the distance from the origin.

Calculating this plane from the three points of a triangle is done by taking the cross product of two sides, or

$$N = (P_1 - P_0) \times (P_2 - P_0)$$

Once the normal is calculated, the remaining parameter is the negative dot product of that normal with a point on the plane. That is,

$$D = -N \bullet P_0$$

The code in Figure 11.10 is a straightforward implementation of this calculation using the `Object3DS` structure. In this simple implementation, the tricky part is extracting the coordinates of each triangle vertex from the array of vertices. Each triangle is represented as three indices into the vertex array. In the previous examples, each vertex was transformed without regard to which triangle it was attached to. In this example, the three points of each triangle must be operated upon together. Because they are stored as an array of indices rather than an array of vectors, a vector of arrays, or an array of pointers, their level of indirection isn't supported directly by the Intel IPP matrix functions.

```
for (i=0; i<m_numTriangles; i++)
{
    pNormal = &(m_planeData[i].A);
    pD = &(m_planeData[i].D);
    // pTmp1 = P1 - P0
    pTmp1[0] =
        m_vertexData[m_trianglesData[i].secondIndex].x -
        m_vertexData[m_trianglesData[i].firstIndex].x;
    pTmp1[1] =
        m_vertexData[m_trianglesData[i].secondIndex].y -
        m_vertexData[m_trianglesData[i].firstIndex].y;
    pTmp1[2] =
        m_vertexData[m_trianglesData[i].secondIndex].z-
        m_vertexData[m_trianglesData[i].firstIndex].z;
    // pTmp2 = P2 - P0
    pTmp2[0] =
        m_vertexData[m_trianglesData[i].thirdIndex].x -
        m_vertexData[m_trianglesData[i].firstIndex].x;
    pTmp2[1] =
        m_vertexData[m_trianglesData[i].thirdIndex].y -
        m_vertexData[m_trianglesData[i].firstIndex].y;
    pTmp2[2] =
```

```
            m_vertexData[m_trianglesData[i].thirdIndex].z-
            m_vertexData[m_trianglesData[i].firstIndex].z;

        // pNormal = pTmp1 x pTmp2
        ippmCrossProduct_vv_32f_3x1(pTmp1, pTmp2, pNormal);

        // pD = -pNormal * P0
        ippmDotProduct_vv_32f_3x1(pNormal,
            &(m_vertexData[m_trianglesData[i].firstIndex].x),
            pD);
        *pD=-*pD;
    }
```

Figure 11.10 Straightforward Implementation of Plane Parameters Calculation

The next step is to create an embedded loop representing the operation on one buffer-size of data. This code lays the foundation for use of vector-array operations, and also produces a performance improvement of about 25 percent. This code operates on arrays of vectors, but operates on them one at a time. The code is listed in Figure 11.11.

```
int i,j;
m_planeData = new PlaneData[m_numTriangles];
const int bufSize = 256;
Ipp32f *pNormal, pTmp1[3*bufSize], pTmp2[3*bufSize], *pD;
int loopSize = bufSize;

for (i=0; i<m_numTriangles; i+=bufSize)
{
    if (i>m_numTriangles-bufSize)
        loopSize = m_numTriangles - i;

    for (j=0; j<loopSize; j++)
    {
        int p1 = m_trianglesData[i+j].firstIndex;
        int p2 = m_trianglesData[i+j].secondIndex;
        int p3 = m_trianglesData[i+j].thirdIndex;

        pTmp1[j*3] =
            m_vertexData[p2].x - m_vertexData[p1].x;
        pTmp1[j*3+1] =
            m_vertexData[p2].y - m_vertexData[p1].y;
        pTmp1[j*3+2] =
            m_vertexData[p2].z - m_vertexData[p1].z;

        pTmp2[j*3] =
```

```
            m_vertexData[p3].x - m_vertexData[p1].x;
        pTmp2[j*3+1] =
            m_vertexData[p3].y - m_vertexData[p1].y;
        pTmp2[j*3+2] =
            m_vertexData[p3].z - m_vertexData[p1].z;
    }
    for (j=0; j<loopSize; j++)
    {
        int p1 = m_trianglesData[i+j].firstIndex;
        pNormal = &(m_planeData[i+j].A);
        pD = &(m_planeData[i+j].D);
        ippmCrossProduct_vv_32f_3x1(
            pTmp1+j*3, pTmp2+j*3, pNormal);
        ippmDotProduct_vv_32f_3x1(pNormal,
            &(m_vertexData[p1].x),
            pD);
        *pD=-*pD;
    }
```

Figure 11.11 Intermediate Implementation of Plane Parameters Calculation

From this point, it is simple to convert the cross product from the one-vector version to the vector-array version. A code listing of this modification is shown in Figure 11.12. Unfortunately, the dot product still uses the one-vector version. It requires one point from the triangle, and that point can still only be accessed indirectly using the index from the `m_trianglesData` array.

```
    IppStatus st = ippmCrossProduct_vava_32f_3x1(
        pTmp1, 3*sizeof(Ipp32f),
        pTmp2, 3*sizeof(Ipp32f),
        (float*)&m_planeData[i], sizeof(PlaneData),
        loopSize);
    for (j=0; j<loopSize; j++)
    {
        int p1 = m_trianglesData[i+j].firstIndex;
        pNormal = &(m_planeData[i+j].A);
        pD = &(m_planeData[i+j].D);
        ippmDotProduct_vv_32f_3x1(pNormal,
            &(m_vertexData[p1].x),
            pD);
        *pD=-*pD;
    }
```

Figure 11.12 Replacing `ippmCrossProduct_vv` with `ippmCrossProduct_vava`

The final step is to extract the data into a temporary array before performing any of the operations. This code is listed in Figure 11.13. This initial copy makes the data contiguous and allows the use of vector-array versions of `ippmSub` and `ippmDotProd`.

Since all of the vertex data is contiguous and all the strides are the same, there is another performance advantage to be gained. The function `ippsSub_32f` has much less overhead in the inner loop than `ippmSub_vava`, since the latter has to increment each pointer by the stride on each loop, while the former can expect contiguous data.

The assignment of the negative of the dot product is executed in three steps: the dot product, the negation, and the assignment. The dot product is done by the function `ippmDotProduct_vava`, which fills the array `pD` with the fourth plane parameter for each triangle. Then the entire array `pD` is negated by the function `ippsMulC_32f_I`, an in-place multiplication by a constant. Finally, the function `ippiCopy_32f_C1C4R` copies the array `pD` into the array of plane data, skipping three elements—the other three plane parameters—after each write. That function is intended to write a single channel into four-channel data, which is exactly what is required here.

Once these modifications are made, the cost of the explicit copy is almost entirely absorbed by the advantage of a faster subtraction. This method is similar in performance to the earlier code after the modification in Figure 11.12. However, the `pVert1`, `pVert2`, and `pVert3` arrays are important to the subsequent code, to be developed in the next section. Additionally, extracting this data into an unpacked array is a simple and clean way to implement the code.

```
for (i=0; i<m_numTriangles; i+=bufSize)
{
    if (i>m_numTriangles-bufSize)
        loopSize = m_numTriangles - i;
    for (j=0; j<loopSize; j++)
    {
        int p1 = m_trianglesData[i+j].firstIndex;
        int p2 = m_trianglesData[i+j].secondIndex;
        int p3 = m_trianglesData[i+j].thirdIndex;
        pVert1[j*4]  = m_vertexData[p1].x;
        pVert1[j*4+1]  = m_vertexData[p1].y;
        pVert1[j*4+2]  = m_vertexData[p1].z;
        pVert2[j*4]  = m_vertexData[p2].x;
        pVert2[j*4+1]  = m_vertexData[p2].y;
        pVert2[j*4+2]  = m_vertexData[p2].z;
```

```
            pVert3[j*4] = m_vertexData[p3].x;
            pVert3[j*4+1] = m_vertexData[p3].y;
            pVert3[j*4+2] = m_vertexData[p3].z;
        }

//      IppStatus st = ippmSub_vava_32f_3x1(
//          pVert2, 4*sizeof(Ipp32f),
//          pVert1, 4*sizeof(Ipp32f),
//          pTmp1, 4*sizeof(Ipp32f), loopSize);
        ippsSub_32f(pVert2, pVert1, pTmp1, loopSize);

//      st = ippmSub_vava_32f_3x1(
//          pVert3, 4*sizeof(Ipp32f),
//          pVert1, 4*sizeof(Ipp32f),
//          pTmp2, 4*sizeof(Ipp32f), loopSize);
        ippsSub_32f(pVert3, pVert1, pTmp1, loopSize);

        st = ippmCrossProduct_vava_32f_3x1(
            pTmp1, 4*sizeof(Ipp32f),
            pTmp2, 4*sizeof(Ipp32f),
            (float*)&m_planeData[i], 4*sizeof(Ipp32f),
            loopSize);
        st = ippmDotProduct_vava_32f_3x1(
            (float*)&m_planeData[i], 4*sizeof(Ipp32f),
            pVert1, 4*sizeof(Ipp32f),
            pD, loopSize);
        ippsMulC_32f_I(-1.0, pD, loopSize);
        ippiCopy_32f_C1C4R(pD, loopSize*sizeof(Ipp32f),
            (float*)&m_planeData[i].D,
            loopSize*4*sizeof(Ipp32f),
            size);
```

Figure 11.13 Final Implementation of Plane Parameters Calculation

Since the time spent on the initial copy is about 20 percent of the total execution time, in some cases it would be worthwhile to make a more persistent copy of the data. In this case, since the calculation of plane equations happens only when the model is changed, it would be necessary to recopy the model data every time. Alternatively, a table of pointers to vertices can be calculated from the table of indices; while expensive, this need be done only once. Once created, this table could be used to extract the vertex data using the function `ippmCopy_va_32f_LS`. Such a pointer table can be calculated and used as shown in Figure 11.14.

Unfortunately, this modification does not produce higher-performing code. Rather, due to the performance of the ippmCopy_va_32f_LS function, the performance degrades relative to the code in Figure 11.13.

```
// One-time pointer table initialization
for (i=0; i<m_numTriangles; i++)
{
    pPtrs1[i] =
        &m_vertexData[m_trianglesData[i].firstIndex].x;
    pPtrs2[i] =
        &m_vertexData[m_trianglesData[i].secondIndex].x;
    pPtrs3[i] =
        &m_vertexData[m_trianglesData[i].thirdIndex].x;
    }
}
...
for (i=0; i<m_numTriangles; i+=bufSize)
{
    if (i>m_numTriangles-bufSize)
        loopSize = m_numTriangles - i;

    ippmCopy_va_32f_LS(
        (const float**)pPtrs1, 0, sizeof(Ipp32f),
        pVert1, 4*sizeof(Ipp32f), sizeof(Ipp32f),
        3, loopSize);
    ippmCopy_va_32f_LS(
        (const float**)pPtrs2, 0, sizeof(Ipp32f),
        pVert2, 4*sizeof(Ipp32f), sizeof(Ipp32f),
        3, loopSize);
    ippmCopy_va_32f_LS(
        (const float**)pPtrs3, 0, sizeof(Ipp32f),
        pVert3, 4*sizeof(Ipp32f), sizeof(Ipp32f),
        3, loopSize);
    ...
}
```

Figure 11.14 Creating and Using a Pointer Table

Table 11.1 lists this result and relative performance for the other four versions of code in this section, taken on one example model.

Table 11.1 Rotation Functions in Intel® Integrated Performance Primitives (Intel® IPP)

Code Version	Relative Performance
Figure 11.10	1.00
Figure 11.11	0.76
Figure 11.12	0.64
Figure 11.13	0.67
Figure 11.14	0.9

Figure 11.15 shows the normals calculated for each triangle in an object. The normals are each drawn starting from the center of the triangle and proceeding in the direction of the normal vector.

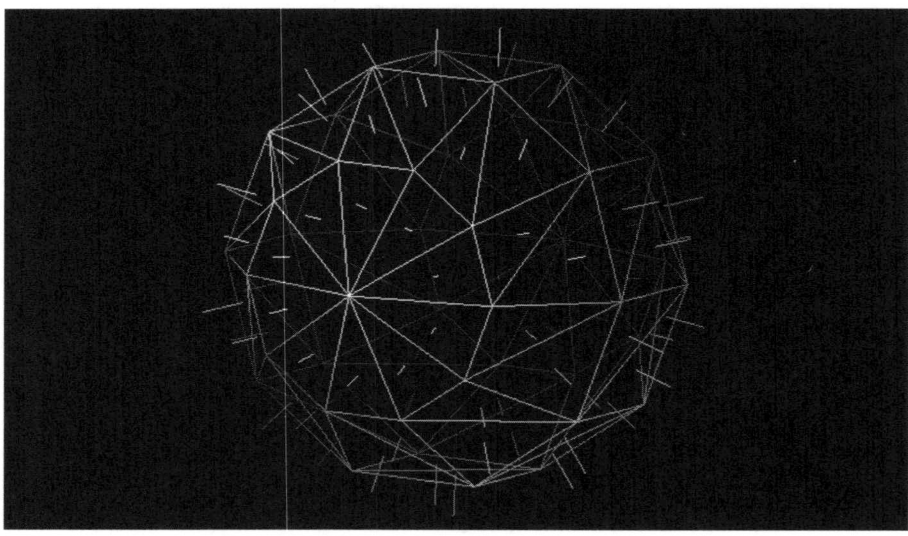

Figure 11.15 Triangle Normals for Object `sphere1.3ds`

Pre-calculating the Planes for Each Side of the Triangle

The next step in intersecting a ray and a triangle is to pre-calculate the plane equations for each side of each triangle. That is, it is necessary to find the three planes normal to the triangle that contains the three sides.

These planes will later be used to determine whether a point lies inside or outside the triangle.

The three planes are calculated in a manner similar to the planes of the triangles in the previous section. Instead of the two vectors $(P_1 - P_0)$ and $(P_2 - P_0)$, this calculation will use the vectors $(P_a - P_b)$, where $a \neq b$, and the triangle normal N. The equations are:

$$N_0 = (P_1 - P_2) \times N$$

$$D_0 = -N_0 \bullet P_0$$

$$N_1 = (P_2 - P_0) \times N$$

$$D_1 = -N_1 \bullet P_1$$

$$N_2 = (P_0 - P_1) \times N$$

$$D_2 = -N_2 \bullet P_2$$

The order of the subtractions of points doesn't matter, since there is no guarantee that the points are in the right order anyway. Therefore, after the plane equations are determined, the sign must be set appropriately. This is done by taking the dot product of the plane vector and a point that is known to be on the inside of the plane; in this case, the point is the third vertex of the triangle. If the result of that dot product is negative, the plane parameters are negated.

The code in Figure 11.16 follows immediately after the code from the previous section. The `pTmp1` array already contains the results of `P2-P1` and the `pTmp2` array contains `P3-P1`. The arrays `pVert1`, `pVert2`, and `pVert3` are arrays of vectors, and each `pVertN[j*4]` is the start of the `N`th vertex of triangle `j`.[1]

The steps taken in this code are the same as in Figure 11.10 through Figure 11.13, with the exception of the sign correction. Refer to the details associated with those figures for further explanation.

---

[1] Since the vertex arrays only contain a subset of the total vertices in the object, from a broader perspective they contain the vertices of triangle `i+j`, where `i` is another loop variable.

```
//--------------------------------
        // pTmp1 = P2 - P1

        // Plane 3 normal = pTmp1 x triangle normal
        st = ippmCrossProduct_vava_32f_3x1(
            pTmp1, 4*sizeof(Ipp32f),
            (float*)&m_planeData[i], 4*sizeof(Ipp32f),
            (float*)&m_side3Plane[i], 4*sizeof(Ipp32f),
            loopSize);

        // Plane 3 D = -Plane 3 normal * P1
        st = ippmDotProduct_vava_32f_3x1(
            (float*)pVert1, 4*sizeof(Ipp32f),
            (float*)&m_side3Plane[i], 4*sizeof(Ipp32f),
            pD, loopSize);
        ippsMulC_32f_I(-1.0f, pD, loopSize);
        st = ippiCopy_32f_C1C4R(pD, loopSize*sizeof(Ipp32f),
            (float*)&m_side3Plane[i].D,
            loopSize*4*sizeof(Ipp32f),
            size);

        // if ((Plane 3 normal * P3) < 0)
        //      Plane 3 normal = - Plane 3 normal
        st = ippmDotProduct_vava_32f_4x1(
            (float*)pVert3, 4*sizeof(Ipp32f),
            (float*)&m_side3Plane[i], 4*sizeof(Ipp32f),
            pD, loopSize);
        for (j=0; j<loopSize; j++)
        {
            if (pD[j]<0.0f)
            {
                m_side3Plane[i+j].A = -m_side3Plane[i+j].A;
                m_side3Plane[i+j].B = -m_side3Plane[i+j].B;
                m_side3Plane[i+j].C = -m_side3Plane[i+j].C;
                m_side3Plane[i+j].D = -m_side3Plane[i+j].D;
            }
        }

//--------------------

        // pTmp2 = P3 - P1

        // Plane 2 normal = pTmp2 x triangle normal
        st = ippmCrossProduct_vava_32f_3x1(
            pTmp2, 4*sizeof(Ipp32f),
            (float*)&m_planeData[i], 4*sizeof(Ipp32f),
            (float*)&m_side2Plane[i], 4*sizeof(Ipp32f),
            loopSize);
```

```
        // Plane 2 D = -Plane 2 normal * P3
        st = ippmDotProduct_vava_32f_3x1(
             (float*)pVert3, 4*sizeof(Ipp32f),
             (float*)&m_side2Plane[i], 4*sizeof(Ipp32f),
             pD, loopSize);
        ippsMulC_32f_I(-1.0f, pD, loopSize);
        st = ippiCopy_32f_C1C4R(pD, loopSize*sizeof(Ipp32f),
             (float*)&m_side2Plane[i].D,
             loopSize*4*sizeof(Ipp32f), size);

        // if ((Plane 2 normal * P2) < 0)
        //       Plane 2 normal = - Plane 2 normal
        st = ippmDotProduct_vava_32f_4x1(
             (float*)pVert2, 4*sizeof(Ipp32f),
             (float*)&m_side2Plane[i], 4*sizeof(Ipp32f),
             pD, loopSize);
        for (j=0; j<loopSize; j++)
        {
             if (pD[j]<0.0f)
             {
                  m_side2Plane[i+j].A = -m_side2Plane[i+j].A;
                  m_side2Plane[i+j].B = -m_side2Plane[i+j].B;
                  m_side2Plane[i+j].C = -m_side2Plane[i+j].C;
                  m_side2Plane[i+j].D = -m_side2Plane[i+j].D;
             }
        }

//-----------------------------

        // pTmp1 = P3 - P1
        st = ippmSub_vava_32f_3x1(
             pVert3, 4*sizeof(Ipp32f),
             pVert2, 4*sizeof(Ipp32f),
             pTmp1, 4*sizeof(Ipp32f), loopSize);

        // Plane 1 normal = pTmp1 x triangle normal
        st = ippmCrossProduct_vava_32f_3x1(
             pTmp1, 4*sizeof(Ipp32f),
             (float*)&m_planeData[i], 4*sizeof(Ipp32f),
             (Ipp32f*)&m_side1Plane[i], 4*sizeof(Ipp32f),
             loopSize);

        // Plane 1 D = -Plane 1 normal * P2
        st = ippmDotProduct_vava_32f_3x1(
             (float*)pVert2, 4*sizeof(Ipp32f),
             (float*)&m_side1Plane[i], 4*sizeof(Ipp32f),
             pD, loopSize);
        ippsMulC_32f_I(-1.0f, pD, loopSize);
        st = ippiCopy_32f_C1C4R(pD, loopSize*sizeof(Ipp32f),
```

```
        (float*)&m_side1Plane[i].D,
        loopSize*4*sizeof(Ipp32f), size);

    // if ((Plane 1 normal * P1) < 0)
    //      Plane 1 normal = - Plane 1 normal
    st = ippmDotProduct_vava_32f_4x1(
        (float*)pVert1, 4*sizeof(Ipp32f),
        (float*)&m_side1Plane[i], 4*sizeof(Ipp32f),
        pD, loopSize);
    for (j=0; j<loopSize; j++)
    {
        if (pD[j]<0.0f)
        {
            m_side1Plane[i+j].A = -m_side1Plane[i+j].A;
            m_side1Plane[i+j].B = -m_side1Plane[i+j].B;
            m_side1Plane[i+j].C = -m_side1Plane[i+j].C;
            m_side1Plane[i+j].D = -m_side1Plane[i+j].D;
        }
    }
```

Figure 11.16 Code to Calculate the Planes for Each Side of a Triangle

The results of this code are displayed in Figure 11.17. The normal for each side of each triangle is drawn starting at the center of that side. Each normal should be inside the triangle for which it is a normal, coplanar with that triangle, and perpendicular to the side it touches.

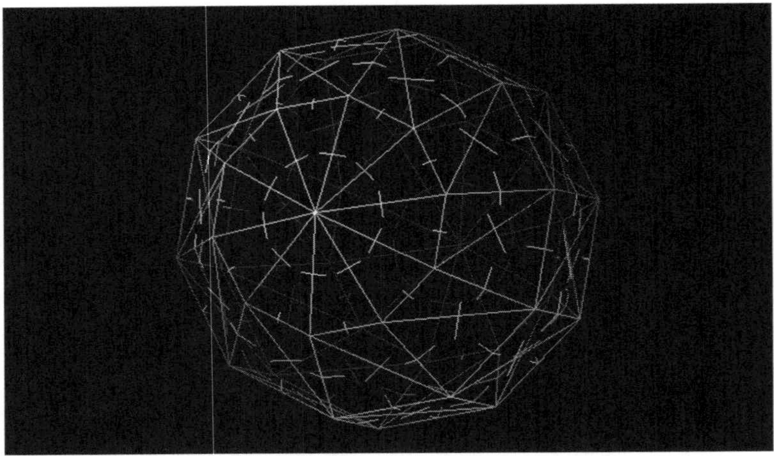

Figure 11.17 Normals for Each Side of Each Triangle

Intersecting a Ray and a Plane

Each ray passing from the imaging plane into the scene has to be compared against some or all of the triangles. The function in this example compares a ray against all of the triangles in an object.

The first half of the ray-triangle intersection algorithm is the ray-plane intersection. Once you have the point of intersection of a ray and the plane on which a triangle lies, you can then determine whether that point lies inside a triangle on that plane.

A ray is defined by two parameters, a point on the ray and a direction. Keep in mind that, in homogenous coordinates, the point's fourth coordinate is 1, while the direction's fourth coordinate is 0.

As a function of t, the ray $R(t) = P_0 + Dt$, where P_0 and D are the point and directional vectors.

Using this parameterization, the formula for calculating value t at which the ray intersects the triangle plane T is

$$t = -\frac{T \bullet P_0}{T \bullet D}.$$

The location of the intersection in 3-space is then found by plugging this value for t back into the ray equation. When the ray is parallel to the plane, the directional vector D and the plane normal N are normal to each other, and therefore their dot product, the denominator T•D, is zero. In this case, there is no intersection.

The code in Figure 11.18 calculates the dot product of the `pStart` vector and the vector-array of triangle planes, then calculates the dot product of `pDir` and the planes, then divides the two. The next step is to calculate the ray-plane intersection points by plugging t back into the ray equation $R(t) = P_0 + t*D$. Since the `ippmMul_vav` function doesn't exist, this operation is done by hand. Note that it is here that the value of t is negated.

```
for (i=0; i<m_numTriangles; i+=bufSize)
{
    if (i>m_numTriangles-bufSize)
        loopSize = m_numTriangles - i;
    ippmDotProduct_vav_32f_4x1(
        (const float*)&m_planeData[i],
        4*sizeof(Ipp32f), pStart,
        pTmp1, loopSize);
    ippmDotProduct_vav_32f_4x1(
```

```
        (const float*)&m_planeData[i],
        4*sizeof(Ipp32f), pDir,
        pTmp2, loopSize);
    ippsDiv_32f(pTmp2, pTmp1, pT, loopSize);

    for (j=0; j<loopSize; j++)
    {
        pPoint[j*4]   = pStart[0]-pT[j]*pDir[0];
        pPoint[j*4+1] = pStart[1]-pT[j]*pDir[1];
        pPoint[j*4+2] = pStart[2]-pT[j]*pDir[2];
        pPoint[j*4+3] = 1.0;
    }
```

Figure 11.18 Code to Calculate the Intersection of a Ray and a Plane

Determining Whether a Point is Inside a Triangle

Once the intersection point is determined, that point can be compared against each of the three sides to determine whether it is in the interior direction from that side. Recall that the formula for a plane is

$$Ax + By + Cz + D = 0.$$

If the dot product between a vector S_n = [A, B, C, D] and a vector P = [x, y, z, 1] is zero, the point is on that plane. If it is greater than zero, it is on one side of the plane, and if it is less than zero, it is on the other side. Since the pre-calculation code forced the interior side to be the greater-than-zero side, a point is on the inside of the triangle if

$$S_0 \bullet P > 0 \text{ and } S_1 \bullet P > 0 \text{ and } S_2 \bullet P > 0$$

The code in Figure 11.19 implements this test. The first test is to determine whether the ray intersected the plane at all. If an element `pTmp2` is zero, that means that the denominator of the calculation of `pT` for that element was zero, and there was no intersection. This fact is determined by comparing each element of pTmp2 against the constant 0.0 using `ippiCompareC`. The result is saved in the mask array `pMask`. Since `ippiCompareC` supports an equality test but not an inequality test, the result is logically negated.

The three plane operations proceed in the same way. Each takes the dot product of the plane equation for one triangle side against the point of intersection with the triangle. This is done with the vector-array version of the code, `ippmDotProduct_vava`. Then the compare function is used to test whether the results were greater than zero. The results of that compare function are stored in the temporary array pMaskTmp so they can be ANDed with the mask pMask. At the end, the mask is non-zero for all triangles with which the ray intersected.

```
st = ippiCompareC_32f_C1R(
    pTmp2, loopSize*sizeof(Ipp32f), 0.0,
    &pMask[i], loopSize*sizeof(Ipp32f),
    imSize, ippCmpEq);
ippsNot_8u_I(&pMask[i], loopSize);

st = ippmDotProduct_vava_32f_4x1(
    (float*)&m_side1Plane[i], 4*sizeof(Ipp32f),
    pPoint, 4*sizeof(Ipp32f),
    pT, loopSize);
st = ippiCompareC_32f_C1R(
    pT, loopSize*sizeof(Ipp32f), 0.0,
    pMaskTmp, loopSize*sizeof(Ipp32f),
    imSize, ippCmpGreater);
ippsAnd_8u_I(pMaskTmp, &pMask[i], loopSize);

st = ippmDotProduct_vava_32f_4x1(
    (float*)&m_side2Plane[i], 4*sizeof(Ipp32f),
    pPoint, 4*sizeof(Ipp32f),
    pT, loopSize);
st = ippiCompareC_32f_C1R(
    pT, loopSize*sizeof(Ipp32f), 0.0,
    pMaskTmp, loopSize*sizeof(Ipp32f),
    imSize, ippCmpGreater);
ippsAnd_8u_I(pMaskTmp, &pMask[i], loopSize);

st = ippmDotProduct_vava_32f_4x1(
    (float*)&m_side3Plane[i], 4*sizeof(Ipp32f),
    pPoint, 4*sizeof(Ipp32f),
    pT, loopSize);
st = ippiCompareC_32f_C1R(
    pT, loopSize*sizeof(Ipp32f), 0.0,
    pMaskTmp, loopSize*sizeof(Ipp8u),
    imSize, ippCmpGreater);
ippsAnd_8u_I(pMaskTmp, &pMask[i], loopSize);
```

Figure 11.19 Code to Determine Whether a Point Lies Inside a Triangle

Figure 11.20 shows the results of the ray-triangle intersection algorithm run on a model. A ray was traced from the point under the cursor. Triangles for which the resulting mask entry was zero were drawn in wireframe, while triangles for which the mask entry was nonzero were filled. The front triangle is brighter because its normal faces forward.

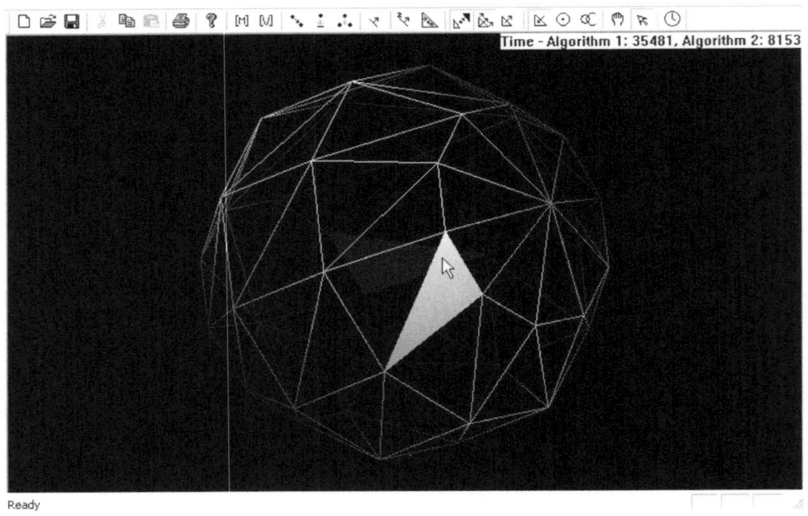

Figure 11.20 Triangles That Intersect a Ray Traced from the Cursor

Normally, ray tracing uses some method of culling the triangles tested for intersection, such as intersection with a bounding sphere. Because of the efficiency of vector-based implementation of the ray trace, it is likely to be more efficient to reduce the search space by testing bounding spheres or rectangles of entire blocks, rather than individual triangles. Few modifications would be required to make this method skip blocks for which the ray failed to intersect the bounding object, particularly if the block size were equal to or a multiple of the buffer size.

Physics

This section shows the same programming methodology and matrix functionality applied to two problems in the area of physics. The first is the calculation of the center of mass of a three-dimensional object. The second is collision detection between two objects constructed of triangles.

Calculating Center of Mass

In order to calculate the rotational effect of an impact on an object, it is necessary to know the center of gravity or center of mass of the object. The calculation of center of mass can be vectorized. Furthermore, it is an involved formula with variables that are somewhat hard to keep straight. It is complicated enough to justify a first programming pass to make a version that operates on single vectors before proceeding to calls on vector arrays.

Arguably, the performance of this algorithm is not as important for a rigid body, since the center of mass will remain in the same place relative to the model. For a deformable body, on the other hand, the performance is certainly salient.

This algorithm calculates the center of mass of a hollow object. The steps are as follows:

1. For each triangle, do the following:
   - Calculate the mass of the triangle
   - Add the mass to the total body mass
   - Calculate the center of mass of the triangle
   - Multiply the mass with each coordinate of the center
2. Sum the results for each triangle.
3. Divide the sum by the total mass of the body.

Figure 11.21 shows the first cut of the implementation of this algorithm.

The first step is to calculate the mass of the triangle. Assuming uniform density and unit thickness, the mass of a triangle is equal to its area. The area of a triangle can be calculated from the lengths of two of its sides with this equation:

$$M = |(P_1 - P_0) \times (P_2 - P_0)| / 2$$

Since the magnitude is taken after the cross product, the order of pixels is irrelevant. The function `ippmL2Norm` is used to calculate the magnitude of the cross product results.

This equation is implemented using scalar subtraction because the points can only be referenced indirectly using the indices in the `TrianglesData` structure.

The next step is to calculate the center of mass of the triangle. The center of mass is the average of the three vertices, or

$$C = (P_0 + P_1 + P_2)/3$$

The differences between P_0 and the other two vertices have already been calculated, so the code takes advantage of this fact. The center can be calculated in this way instead:

$$C = (P_0 + (P_1 - P_0) + P_0 + (P_2 - P_0) + P_0)/3 = P_0 + (S_{10} + S_{20})/3$$

The number of operations is the same in the two equations, but S_{10} and S_{20} already exist in a contiguous array, so the vector-array versions of functions can be applied later.

```
void Object3DS::CalcCenterOfMass(float* pPoint,
    float* pMass, int algorithm)
{
    int i;
    IppStatus st;

    Ipp32f pCenterBody[4]={0.0f, 0.0f, 0.0f, 1.0f};
    Ipp32f massBody = 0.0f;

    for (i = 0; i<m_numTriangles; i++)
    {
        //P0, P1 and P2 are vertices of the current triangle
        Ipp32f *pP0 = (Ipp32f*)&m_vertexData[
                      m_trianglesData[i].firstIndex];
        Ipp32f *pP1 = (Ipp32f*)&m_vertexData[
                      m_trianglesData[i].secondIndex];
        Ipp32f *pP2 = (Ipp32f*)&m_vertexData[
                      m_trianglesData[i].thirdIndex];
        //S10, S20 are vectors that start at P0 and
        // end at P1 and P2 respectively

        Ipp32f S10[3], S20[3], tmp[3], CenterTriangle[3],
            MassTriangle=0;

        //compute S10 and S20 coordinates:
        // S10 = P1 - P0, S20 = P2 - P0
```

```
        S10[0] = pP1[0] - pP0[0];
        S10[1] = pP1[1] - pP0[1];
        S10[2] = pP1[2] - pP0[2];
        S20[0] = pP2[0] - pP0[0];
        S20[1] = pP2[1] - pP0[1];
        S20[2] = pP2[2] - pP0[2];

        //find the mass of the triangle:
        // if density  = 1 than mass = area = |S10 x S20|/2
        st = ippmCrossProduct_vv_32f_3x1(S10, S20, tmp);
        st = ippmL2Norm_v_32f_3x1(tmp, &MassTriangle);
        MassTriangle /= 2.0f;

        //find the center of triangle's mass:
        // CenterTriangle = P0 + (S10 + S20)/3
        st = ippmAdd_vv_32f_3x1(S10, S20,
                CenterTriangle);
        st = ippmMul_vc_32f_3x1(CenterTriangle,
                1.0f/3.0f, CenterTriangle);

        CenterTriangle[0] += pP0[0];
        CenterTriangle[1] += pP0[1];
        CenterTriangle[2] += pP0[2];

        pCenterBody[0] += CenterTriangle[0] * MassTriangle;
        pCenterBody[1] += CenterTriangle[1] * MassTriangle;
        pCenterBody[2] += CenterTriangle[2] * MassTriangle;

        massBody += MassTriangle;
    }

    pPoint[0] = pCenterBody[0] / massBody;
    pPoint[1] = pCenterBody[0] / massBody;
    pPoint[2] = pCenterBody[0] / massBody;

    *pMass = massBody;
}
```

Figure 11.21 Initial Code to Calculate the Center of Mass

Introducing the Intel IPP vector-array functions into this code segment provides the biggest performance gain. The `CrossProduct`, `L2Norm`, `Add`, and `Multiply` calls can be directly replaced by the vector-array versions of those functions. The scalar division by 2.0 to find the mass of the triangle can be replace by a call to `ippsDivC`. Finally, the accumulation of the body mass is replaced by ippsSum. Figure 11.22 shows these modifications.

Note that even though the masses and centers of mass of the triangles are in arrays, their product can be taken only with scalar multiplication because of the lack of an ippmMul_vav function.

```
for (i = 0; i<m_numTriangles; i++)
{
    //P0, P1 and P2 are vertices of the current triangle
    Ipp32f *pP0 = (Ipp32f*)&m_vertexData[
                  m_trianglesData[i].firstIndex];
    Ipp32f *pP1 = (Ipp32f*)&m_vertexData[
                  m_trianglesData[i].secondIndex];
    Ipp32f *pP2 = (Ipp32f*)&m_vertexData[
                  m_trianglesData[i].thirdIndex];

    //compute S10 and S20 coordinates:
    // S10 = P1 - P0, S20 = P2 - P0
    pS10[i*4] = pP1[0] - pP0[0];
    pS10[i*4+1] = pP1[1] - pP0[1];
    pS10[i*4+2] = pP1[2] - pP0[2];
    pS20[i*4] = pP2[0] - pP0[0];
    pS20[i*4+1] = pP2[1] - pP0[1];
    pS20[i*4+2] = pP2[2] - pP0[2];
}

int count = m_numTriangles;
int stride = sizeof(Ipp32f)*4;

//find the mass of the triangle
// density  = 1 so mass = area = |S10 x S20|/2
st = ippmCrossProduct_vava_32f_3x1(
    pS10, stride, pS20, stride,
    pTmp, stride, count);
st = ippmL2Norm_va_32f_3x1(
    pTmp, stride, pMassTriangle, count);
ippsDivC_32f_I(2.0f, pMassTriangle, count);

//find the center of triangle's mass:
// CenterTriangle = P0 + (S10 + S20)/3
st = ippmAdd_vava_32f_3x1(
    pS10, stride, pS20, stride,
    pCenterTriangle, stride, count);
st = ippmMul_vac_32f_3x1(
    pCenterTriangle, stride, 1.0f/3.0f,
    pCenterTriangle, stride, count);

for (i = 0; i<m_numTriangles; i++)
{
```

```
        Ipp32f *pP0 = (Ipp32f*)&m_vertexData[
                     m_trianglesData[i].firstIndex];
        pCenterTriangle[i*4] += pP0[0];
        pCenterTriangle[i*4+1] += pP0[1];
        pCenterTriangle[i*4+2] += pP0[2];
    }

    //add the result to the center of mass:
    //pCenterBody += MassTriangle * CenterTriangles
    for (i = 0; i < m_numTriangles; i++)
    {
        pCenterBody[0] +=
            pCenterTriangle[i*4] * pMassTriangle[i];
        pCenterBody[1] +=
            pCenterTriangle[i*4+1] * pMassTriangle[i];
        pCenterBody[2] +=
            pCenterTriangle[i*4+2] * pMassTriangle[i];

        }
        //add triangle's mass to the body's mass
        ippsSum_32f(pMassTriangle, count, &massTmp,
                   ippAlgHintNone);
        massBody += massTmp;
    }
```

Figure 11.22 Center of Mass Code Using Vector-Array functions

It is important to the performance of the routine that the temporary buffers `pS10`, `pS20`, `pCenterTriangle`, `pMassTriangle`, and `pTmp` all fit in cache. For models of a few thousand triangles or more, the buffers must be smaller than the entire model, and an additional loop is added to accommodate the smaller buffers. Even for smaller models, using an additional inner loop might be beneficial because of the lower memory requirements.

Figure 11.23 shows this modification to the center of mass code.

```
    for (i = 0; i<m_numTriangles; i+=bufSize)
    {
        if (i+bufSize > m_numTriangles)
            loopSize = m_numTriangles-i;
        for (j=0; j<loopSize; j++)
        {
            //P0, P1 and P2 are vertices of the current
            // triangle
            Ipp32f *pP0 = (Ipp32f*)&m_vertexData[
                m_trianglesData[i+j].firstIndex];
```

```
        Ipp32f *pP1 = (Ipp32f*)&m_vertexData[
            m_trianglesData[i+j].secondIndex];
        Ipp32f *pP2 = (Ipp32f*)&m_vertexData[
            m_trianglesData[i+j].thirdIndex];

        //compute S10 and S20 coordinates:
        // S10 = P1 - P0, S20 = P2 - P0
        pS10[j*4] = pP1[0] - pP0[0];
        pS10[j*4+1] = pP1[1] - pP0[1];
        pS10[j*4+2] = pP1[2] - pP0[2];
        pS20[j*4] = pP2[0] - pP0[0];
        pS20[j*4+1] = pP2[1] - pP0[1];
        pS20[j*4+2] = pP2[2] - pP0[2];
    }

    int count = loopSize;
    int stride = sizeof(Ipp32f)*4;

    //find the mass of the triangle
    // density  = 1 so mass = area = |S10 x S20|/2
    st = ippmCrossProduct_vava_32f_3x1(
        pS10, stride, pS20, stride,
        pTmp, stride, count);
    st = ippmL2Norm_va_32f_3x1(
        pTmp, stride, pMassTriangle, count);
    ippsDivC_32f_I(2.0f, pMassTriangle, count);

    //find the center of triangle's mass:
    // CenterTriangle = P0 + (S10 + S20)/3
    st = ippmAdd_vava_32f_3x1(
        pS10, stride, pS20, stride,
        pCenterTriangle, stride, count);
    st = ippmMul_vac_32f_3x1(
        pCenterTriangle, stride, 1.0f/3.0f,
        pCenterTriangle, stride, count);

    for (j=0; j<loopSize; j++)
    {
        Ipp32f *pP0 = (Ipp32f*)&m_vertexData[
              m_trianglesData[i+j].firstIndex];
        pCenterTriangle[j*4] += pP0[0];
        pCenterTriangle[j*4+1] += pP0[1];
        pCenterTriangle[j*4+2] += pP0[2];
    }

    //add the result to the center of mass:
    //pCenterBody += MassTriangle * CenterTriangles
    for (j=0; j<loopSize; j++)
    {
        pCenterBody[0] +=
```

```
            pCenterTriangle[j*4] * pMassTriangle[j];
        pCenterBody[1] +=
            pCenterTriangle[j*4+1] * pMassTriangle[j];
        pCenterBody[2] +=
            pCenterTriangle[j*4+2] * pMassTriangle[j];
    }

    //add triangle's mass to the body's mass
    ippsSum_32f(pMassTriangle, count, &massTmp,
            ippAlgHintNone);
    massBody += massTmp;
}
```

Figure 11.23 Center of Mass Code Modified to Use Smaller Temporary Buffers

A further modification is possible. In the loop that calculates the differences between triangle vertices, it is possible to load a temporary array with the values of P0. This array can then be used to remove the loop containing these lines:

```
pCenterTriangle[j*4] += pP0[0];
pCenterTriangle[j*4+1] += pP0[1];
pCenterTriangle[j*4+2] += pP0[2];
```

The loop is replaced with the single function call:

```
st = ippmAdd_vava_32f_3x1(
    pP0, stride, pCenterTriangle, stride,
    pCenterTriangle, stride, count);
```

The performance is about the same, since that point array is used only once.

Figure 11.24 shows the results of this algorithm on a sample model. A filled triangle has been drawn in the scene to indicate the center of mass.

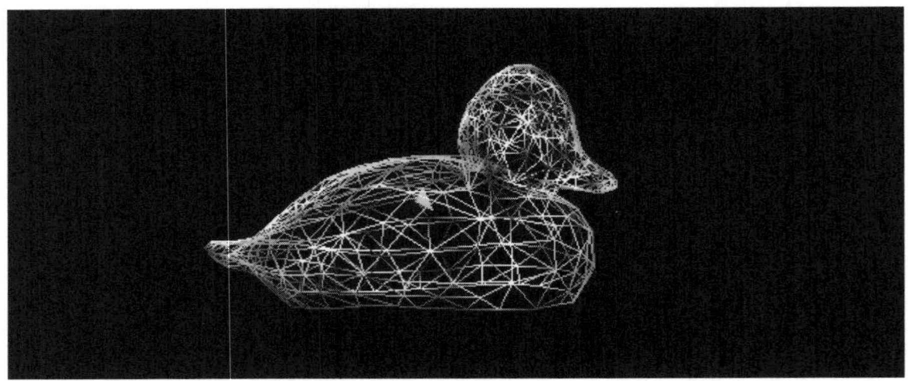

Figure 11.24 Calculated Center of Mass of Object `duck.3ds`[2]

Line Segment-Triangle Intersection

With minor modifications, the ray-triangle intersection code from the ray-tracing section above can be adapted to line segment-triangle intersection. Unlike rays, line segments are realizable physically, and collision detection depends on such intersection of physical objects.

The difference between the ray and line-segment versions of the algorithm is that the line segment is of finite length, so the algorithm must check that the intersection point lies between the endpoints of the line segment.

To implement this in the easiest possible way, the argument `pStart` to `IntersectRay` is interpreted as one endpoint of the line segment, and the direction vector `pEnd` is assumed to be equal to the distance between `pStart` and the other endpoint. If that is true, then

$$R(t) = P_0+Dt$$

$$R(0) = P_0$$

$$R(1) = P_0 + D = P_1$$

[2] This model was provided by 3DCafe.com.

To determine whether intersection point lies between the endpoints, the routine should check whether the calculated `t` lies between 0 and 1. The code in Figure 11.25 does this check with `ippiCompareC_32f_C1R`. The values in pT need to be negated to be valid, so the code checks that the values `pT[i]` lie between 0 and -1.

```
void Object3DS::IntersectLineSeg(float* p1,
    float* p2, unsigned char* pMask)
{
    float pStart[4],pDir[4];
    pStart[0] = p1[0];
    pStart[1] = p1[1];
    pStart[2] = p1[2];
    pStart[3] = 1.0;
    pDir[0] = p2[0]-p1[0];
    pDir[1] = p2[1]-p1[1];
    pDir[2] = p2[2]-p1[2];
    pDir[3] = 0.0;

    IntersectRay(pStart, pDir, pMask, 1, 1);
}

void Object3DS::IntersectRay(float* pStart, float* pDir,
    unsigned char* pMask, int algorithm, int lineSeg)
{
    ...
            // Modification for line-segment intersection
            if (lineSeg)
            {
                st = ippiCompareC_32f_C1R(
                    pT, loopSize*sizeof(Ipp32f), 0.0f,
                    pMaskTmp, loopSize*sizeof(Ipp8u),
                    imSize, ippCmpLessEq);
                ippsAnd_8u_I(pMaskTmp, &pMask[i], loopSize);

                st = ippiCompareC_32f_C1R(
                    pT, loopSize*sizeof(Ipp32f), -1.0f,
                    pMaskTmp, loopSize*sizeof(Ipp8u),
                    imSize, ippCmpGreaterEq);

                ippsAnd_8u_I(pMaskTmp, &pMask[i], loopSize);
            }
    ...
}
```

Figure 11.25 Code to Calculate the Intersection of a Line Segment and an Object

Triangle-Triangle Intersection

A triangle intersects another triangle if any one of the sides of one triangle intersects the body of the other triangle. Using the `IntersectLineSeg` function, calculating the intersection of two arrays of triangles is simple, because the function can check a triangle side in one object against every triangle in another object.

This is implemented by iterating through every triangle in one object. For each side in the triangle, the routine calls `IntersectLineSeg` on the other object. If any entry of the generated mask is nonzero, the mask for that triangle is also set. Then the mask is accumulated for the second object.

```
void Object3DS::IntersectObject(Object3DS& obj,
    unsigned char* pMask, unsigned char* pMaskOther)
{
    int i=0;
    int p1, p2, p3;
    int len = m_numTriangles,
        otherLen = obj.m_numTriangles;

    Ipp8u* pMaskTmp = ippsMalloc_8u(IPP_MAX(len, otherLen));
    Ipp8u max;
    for (i=0; i<len; i++)
    {
        IppiSize size = {otherLen, 1};
        p1 = m_trianglesData[i].firstIndex;
        p2 = m_trianglesData[i].secondIndex;
        p3 = m_trianglesData[i].thirdIndex;

        obj.IntersectLineSeg(
            (float*)&m_vertexData[p1],
            (float*)&m_vertexData[p2], pMaskTmp);
        ippiMax_8u_C1R(pMaskTmp, otherLen, size, &max);
        pMask[i] |= max;
        ippsOr_8u_I(pMaskTmp, pMaskOther, otherLen);

        obj.IntersectLineSeg(
            (float*)&m_vertexData[p2],
            (float*)&m_vertexData[p3], pMaskTmp);
        ippiMax_8u_C1R(pMaskTmp, otherLen, size, &max);
        pMask[i] |= max;
        ippsOr_8u_I(pMaskTmp, pMaskOther, otherLen);

        obj.IntersectLineSeg(
            (float*)&m_vertexData[p3],
            (float*)&m_vertexData[p1], pMaskTmp);
        ippiMax_8u_C1R(pMaskTmp, otherLen, size, &max);
        pMask[i] |= max;
```

```
        ippsOr_8u_I(pMaskTmp, pMaskOther, otherLen);
    }

    for (i=0; i<otherLen; i++)
    {
        IppiSize size = {len, 1};
        p1 = obj.m_trianglesData[i].firstIndex;
        p2 = obj.m_trianglesData[i].secondIndex;
        p3 = obj.m_trianglesData[i].thirdIndex;

        IntersectLineSeg(
            (float*)&obj.m_vertexData[p1],
            (float*)&obj.m_vertexData[p2], pMaskTmp);
        ippiMax_8u_C1R(pMaskTmp, len, size, &max);
        pMaskOther[i] |= max;
        ippsOr_8u_I(pMaskTmp, pMask, len);

        IntersectLineSeg(
            (float*)&obj.m_vertexData[p2],
            (float*)&obj.m_vertexData[p3], pMaskTmp);
        ippiMax_8u_C1R(pMaskTmp, len, size, &max);
        pMaskOther[i] |= max;
        ippsOr_8u_I(pMaskTmp, pMask, len);

        IntersectLineSeg(
            (float*)&obj.m_vertexData[p3],
            (float*)&obj.m_vertexData[p1], pMaskTmp);
        ippiMax_8u_C1R(pMaskTmp, len, size, &max);
        pMaskOther[i] |= max;
        ippsOr_8u_I(pMaskTmp, pMask, len);
    }
    ippsFree(pMaskTmp);
}
```

Figure 11.26 Code to Calculate Intersecting Triangles for Two Compound Objects

One optimization to this code is possible. Every triangle-triangle intersection results in two side-triangle intersections. Therefore, it is possible to skip one of the six side-triangle intersection checks, improving the performance of the routine by about one-sixth.

Figure 11.27 shows the results of this algorithm applied to two pairs of objects. All triangles that intersect with a triangle in the other object are filled; the remaining triangles are outlined.

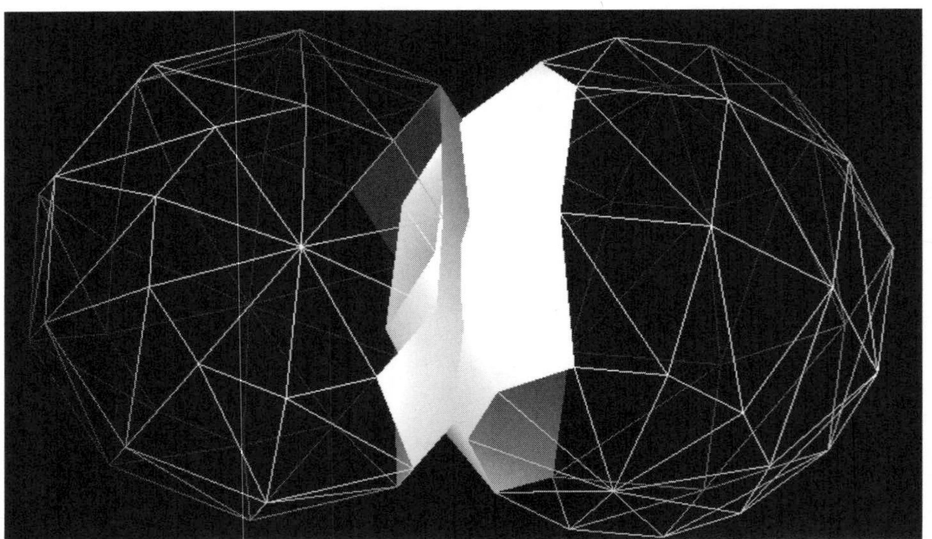

a) sphere1.3ds

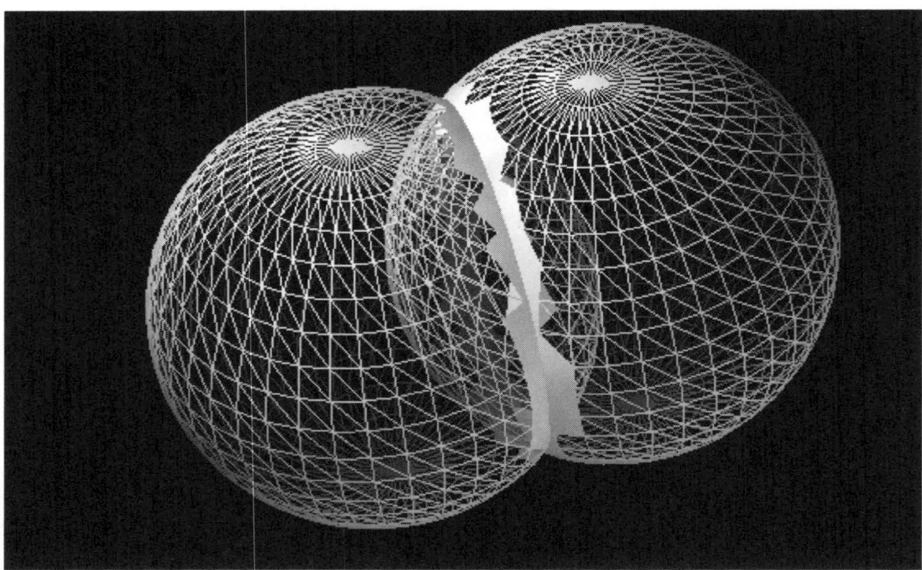

b) sphere2.3ds

Figure 11.27 Triangle-by-Triangle Intersection of Two Objects

Further Reading

Computer Graphics (Foley et al. 1990) is the broadest and most useful reference for computer graphics overall. *Mathematics for 3D Game Programming and Computer Graphics* (Lengyel 2002) is an extremely valuable guide to the mathematics of geometry, ray tracing, illumination, and physics. *Procedural Elements for Computer Graphics* (Rogers 1985) contains good technical descriptions of algorithms for graphics. Many of the algorithms are commonly implemented in graphics cards now. *An Introduction to Ray Tracing* (Glassner 1989) describes some core algorithms and some interesting algorithms for ray tracing.

OpenGL Programming Guide (Woo et al. 1997) is the official guide for programming OpenGL[†], and pretty much the only reference you need.

Chapter 12

Special-Purpose Domains

This chapter is a brief introduction to several previously unaddressed functional areas in the Intel® Integrated Performance Primitives (Intel® IPP). It covers three areas: strings, cryptography, and computer vision. For each of the areas, it provides a short explanation of the technology area, the breadth and intent of functional support provided in that area, and short examples of use of those functions. The goal is to provide an introduction to each area with enough examples to give you a running start.

Strings

Intel IPP 4.0 and later provide a set of general operations that are intended for use on character strings. These functions are, by and large, significantly faster than the standard library equivalents and can be used to make high-performance replacements for them.

All of these functions operate on 8-bit characters, type `Ipp8u`. Many of them also operate on 16-bit characters (types `Ipp16u` and `Ipp16s`) useful for Unicode characters. In all but a few cases, such as the capitalization functions, it does not matter whether the data is a text string or not. Therefore, some string functions might have more general applicability.

Table 12.1 String Functions for Intel® Integrated Performance Primitives (Intel® IPP) , `string.h`, STL Strings, and `CString/CStringT`

Intel IPP Functions	`string.h` Functions	string, basic_string Methods (C++ STL)	CString / CStringT Members (Windows†/ MFC†)
`Copy`	`strcpy, strcat, strncat`	`append, assign, copy, replace, substr`	`Right`
`Find`	`strstr`	`find`	`Find,` *`Replace`*
`FindC`	`strlen, strchr`	`find`	`Find`
`FindRevC`	`strrchr`	`rfind`	`ReverseFind`
`FindCAny`	`strpbrk,` *`strtok`*`, strcspn`	`find_first_of`	`FindOneOf,` *`Remove, SpanExcluding, Tokenize`*
`FindRevCAny`		`find_last_of`	
`Insert`		`insert`	`Insert,` *`Replace`*
`Remove`			`Delete,` *`Replace`*
`Compare`	`strcmp, strncmp`	`compare`	`Compare`
`CompareIgnoreCase CompareIgnoreCaseLatin`			`CompareNoCase`
`Equal`			
`TrimC, TrimCAny`			`Trim`
`TrimStartCAny`			`TrimLeft`
`TrimEndCAny`			`TrimRight`
`ReplaceC`			
`Uppercase, UppercaseLatin`	`toupper (char)`		`MakeUpper`
`Lowercase, LowercaseLatin`	`tolower (char)`		`MakeLower`
`Hash`			
`Concat, ConcatC`			
`SplitC`			

Note: Italicized functions are only partly implemented by the Intel IPP string function. All Intel IPP functions listed have the prefix `ipps`.

The operations supported are basic operations common across several string implementations, both function-based and object-based. Table 12.1 lists the correspondence between the Intel IPP string functions and three widely used string implementations: the C functions in `string.h`, the C++ standard template library class `string`, and the MFC[†] class `CString`. While there is not a one-to-one correspondence between the Intel IPP functions and other library functions, the Intel IPP functions provide most of the operations needed to implement a replacement for any of these.

C Strings

C string functions are those in `string.h`, such as `strlen` and `strcmp`.

Intel IPP uses the more recent interpretation of string, with a separate pointer and length, rather than the traditional null-terminated C string. In order to implement null-terminated strings, most functions first determine the length of the string, then use the length for the subsequent call or calls.

Figure 12.1 lists implementations of several of the C string functions. The function `my_strlen` uses the `ippsFindC` function to find the first occurrence of a zero in the string. The index of that zero is the length of the null-terminated string. Since the string is known to be null-terminated, the length of the string is passed as an extremely large number.

Rather than incurring the extra overhead of a call to the function `my_strlen`, subsequent functions use the `STRLEN` macro, which assigns the length of the first argument to the second argument. Functions that take a maximum length—one such example is `my_strncat`—must instead use the `ippsFindC` function with the maximum length as the string length. If the index of the first zero is greater than or equal to the maximum length, `ippsFindC` will return -1 and exactly that maximum number of characters should be copied or searched.

In C++, it would be more convenient to create an inline version instead of a macro. The macro can't return the length since the Intel IPP function returns its result in an argument rather than the return value. An inline function could return the length properly, on the stack.

```
#define STRMAX ((1<<30) - 1)

int my_strlen(char* cs)
{
    int index;

    ippsFindC_8u((Ipp8u*)cs, STRMAX, 0, &index);

    return index;
}

#define STRLEN(s,i) ippsFindC_8u((s), STRMAX,0,&(i))

char* my_strcpy(char* s, char* ct)
{
    int len;
    STRLEN((Ipp8u*)ct,len);

    ippsCopy_8u((Ipp8u*)ct,(Ipp8u*)s,len+1);

    return s;
}

char* my_strncat(char* s, char* ct, int n)
{
    int slen, ctlen;
    STRLEN((Ipp8u*)s, slen);

    ippsFindC_8u((Ipp8u*)ct, n, 0, &ctlen);
    if (ctlen == -1) ctlen = n;

    ippsCopy_8u((Ipp8u*)ct, (Ipp8u*)s+slen, ctlen);
    *(s+slen+ctlen) = 0;

    return s;
}

int my_strcmp(char* cs, char* ct)
{
    int cslen, ctlen;
    STRLEN((Ipp8u*)cs, cslen);
    STRLEN((Ipp8u*)ct, ctlen);

    int res;
    ippsCompare_8u((Ipp8u*)cs, (Ipp8u*)ct,
        IPP_MIN(cslen, ctlen), &res);
    if ((res == 0) && (cslen != ctlen))
        res = cslen-ctlen;

    // res is specified to be >0, ==0, or <0
```

```
    return res;
}

char* my_strchr(char* cs, char c)
{
    int index, len;

    STRLEN((Ipp8u*)cs, len);
    ippsFindC_8u((Ipp8u*)cs, len, c, &index);

    if (index == -1) return 0;
    else return &cs[index];
}

char* my_strpbrk(char* cs, char* ct)
{
    int index, cslen, ctlen;

    STRLEN((Ipp8u*)cs, cslen);
    STRLEN((Ipp8u*)ct, ctlen);
    ippsFindCAny_8u((Ipp8u*)cs, cslen,
        (Ipp8u*)ct, ctlen, &index);

    if (index == -1) return 0;
    else return &cs[index];
}
...
```

Figure 12.1 Implementations of Some `string.h` Functions Using Intel® Integrated Performance Primitives (Intel® IPP)

C++ Standard Template Library Strings

The Standard Template Library (STL) of C++ includes a templated general string class, `basic_string`. This string class provides iterators, containers, and broad search and modification functions for arbitrary lists of data. The class `string` is an alias for optimization for character strings. It is defined as `basic_string<char>`.

Most Intel IPP string functionality is most appropriate to this `string` class. This section shows an implementation of several member functions, in a simplified nontemplate STL-like string implementation. Figure 12.2 lists the code for several of these functions.

Almost every operation in the STL library is overloaded. Each operation can take a `basic_string`, an iterator, or an array with one or more parameters. This implementation has no template to compare to `basic_string` and no iterators. Therefore, the version that takes the array with the most flexible position and length parameters is used as the example. Each of the overloaded functions could be implemented by calling this version.

This code lists only `string` functions that map directly to Intel IPP string functions. As a result, each function contains only argument checking and a single call to Intel IPP. In a few cases, there is a position parameter. This parameter must be added to the relevant string pointer and subtracted from the length passed to Intel IPP. It must also be checked against the length to avoid passing an invalid pointer.

```
my_size_type mystring::find(const char* s, int pos,
    my_size_type n) const
{
    if (pos >= length_) return -1;
    my_size_type index;

    ippsFind_8u((Ipp8u*)pString_+pos, length_-pos,
        (Ipp8u*)s, n, &index);
    return index;
}

my_size_type mystring::find_first_of(const char* s,
    int pos, my_size_type n) const
{
    if (pos >= length_) return -1;
    my_size_type index;

    ippsFindCAny_8u((Ipp8u*)pString_+pos, length_-pos,
        (Ipp8u*)s, n, &index);
    return index;
}

int mystring::compare(my_size_type p0, my_size_type n0,
    const char *s, my_size_type pos) const
{
    if (p0 >= length_) return -1;
    int res;

    ippsCompare_8u((Ipp8u*)pString_+p0, (Ipp8u*)s+pos,
        IPP_MIN(n0, length_-p0), &res);

    // res is specified to be >0, ==0, or <0
    return res;
```

```
}

mystring& mystring::insert(my_size_type p0,
    const char *s, my_size_type n)
{
    if (p0 >= length_) return *this;

    ippsInsert_8u_I((Ipp8u*)s, n,
        (Ipp8u*)pString_, &length_, p0);

    return *this;
}
```

Figure 12.2 Partial Implementation of STL-Like String Class

MFC Strings

The Microsoft Foundation Classes† (MFC) also include a widely-used string class. This class, `CString`, is very similar to the STL string class. Its recent replacement, the templated `CStringT` class, appears even more so, since it is a templated class that supports multiple fundamental types rather than just character strings.

The primary difference between the methods in `CString` and those in `string` is that the functions in the latter tend to take fewer arguments, even to the point of taking null-terminated strings without lengths. But the underlying functionality is very similar, so the example code in Figure 12.3 shows only a single, more difficult method, `Replace`. This function replaces any occurrences of one null-terminated input string with the second null-terminated string.

There are three cases that this function must handle for string replacement: the replacement string is either larger, smaller, or the same length as the string to be replaced. The simplest case is that in which the strings are the same length. In this case, the code repeatedly calls `ippsFind` to find the next occurrence of the input string and `ippsCopy` to copy the new string on top of it.

If the replacement string is smaller, an additional step is required to remove the extra portion of the old string. The function `ippsRemove` is used to remove the difference. For example, if the old string is eight characters and the new one five, ippsRemove deletes three characters and shifts the remaining string left to compensate.

Finally, if the replacement string is larger, the operation requires two passes. The first pass determines the ultimate length of the new string then allocates a new string of that length and copies the data into it. The second pass acts much like the previous case, by first copying a same-size portion of the replacement string, then inserting the remaining characters with ippsInsert.

This method demonstrates ippsInsert, but it would be more efficient to perform the second pass entirely with copies. Alternating copies into the newly allocated data from the original data and from the replacement string, though slightly more complicated, would require fewer copies.

```
int myCString::Replace(const char* oldStr,
    const char* newStr)
{
    int oldLen, newLen;
    STRLEN((Ipp8u*)oldStr,oldLen);
    STRLEN((Ipp8u*)newStr,newLen);

    int index=0, relInd;
    ippsFind_8u((Ipp8u*)pString_+index, length_-index,
        (Ipp8u*)oldStr, oldLen, &relInd);
    index+= relInd;
    if (oldLen == newLen)
        while (relInd != -1)
        {
            ippsCopy_8u((Ipp8u*)newStr,
                (Ipp8u*)pString_+index, newLen);
            index += newLen;
            ippsFind_8u((Ipp8u*)pString_+index,
                length_-index,
                (Ipp8u*)oldStr, oldLen, &relInd);
            index+= relInd;
        }
    else if (newLen < oldLen)
        while (relInd != -1)
        {
            ippsCopy_8u((Ipp8u*)newStr,
                (Ipp8u*)pString_+index, newLen);
            ippsRemove_8u_I((Ipp8u*)pString_, &length_,
                index+newLen,oldLen-newLen);
            pString_[length_] = 0;

            index += newLen;
            if (index >= length_) break;
```

```
            ippsFind_8u((Ipp8u*)pString_+index,
                length_-index,
                (Ipp8u*)oldStr, oldLen, &relInd);
            index+= relInd;
        }
    else
    {
        int count=0;
        while (relInd != -1)
        {
            count++;
            ippsFind_8u((Ipp8u*)pString_+index,
                length_-index,
                (Ipp8u*)oldStr, oldLen, &relInd);
            index+= oldLen + relInd;
        }
        if (count != 0)
            Expand_(length_ + count*(newLen-oldLen));
        index = 0;
        ippsFind_8u((Ipp8u*)pString_+index,
            length_-index,
            (Ipp8u*)oldStr, oldLen, &relInd);
        index+= relInd;
        while (relInd != -1)
        {
            ippsCopy_8u((Ipp8u*)newStr,
                (Ipp8u*)pString_+index, oldLen);
            ippsInsert_8u_I((Ipp8u*)newStr+oldLen,
                newLen-oldLen,
                (Ipp8u*)pString_, &length_, index+oldLen);
            index += newLen;
            if (index >= length_) break;
            ippsFind_8u((Ipp8u*)pString_+index,
                length_-index,
                (Ipp8u*)oldStr, oldLen, &relInd);
            index+= relInd;
        }
    }

    return index;
    return 0;
}
```

Figure 12.3 Implementation of `myCString::Replace` Function

Cryptography

Cryptography is the processing of data to conceal any of the information it contains. Algorithms for encoding data are usually complicated and almost always time-consuming. Intel IPP cryptography is a set of fast implementations of standard algorithms in this area.

Cryptography is different from other sections of Intel IPP. Designing custom cryptographic algorithms is generally a mistake. Using proprietary cryptography methods in the hope of keeping them private, known as "security by obscurity", has been shown to fail again and again. For this reason, even in Intel IPP it makes sense to emphasize complete implementations of established algorithms over primitive components. While the cryptographic domain includes some primitive components, the domain has about a dozen popular algorithms implemented completely. The functions can be divided into four groups: symmetric encryption algorithms, public key encryption algorithms, hashing functions, and primitives.

For U.S. export control reasons, the cryptographic functions in Intel IPP 4.0 are in a separate package that includes only the `ippCP` static and dynamic libraries, header files, and manuals. Along with those development tools, there are a number of helpful examples, approximately one for each algorithm. Therefore, this section and the examples herein will be kept relatively short, and handle some areas not covered by that code.

Big Numbers

The primitive layer of the cryptographic domain has the following groups of functions:

- Big number modulo arithmetic, including efficient powers
- Secure random number generation
- Prime-number generation

The security of cryptography schemes are generally based on the expense of attempting randomly to decrypt balanced with the practicality of the time to correctly encrypt and decrypt. For this reason, large integers are the core of many cryptographic schemes. Big numbers in this case are generally more than 64 bits long and less than 4,096.

The big number functions in Intel IPP operate on the `IppsBigNum` structure. This structure is important for most cryptographic algorithms, because it is used to store almost all keys and blocks of data passed to Intel IPP cryptographic functions.

Unfortunately, using the `IppsBigNum` structure directly is a little clumsy. For this reason, Figure 12.4 lists one way to wrap this structure in a more-convenient C++ class that interacts cleanly with Intel IPP functions.

```
class BigNum
{
    private:
        IppsBigNum* pNum_;
        int length_;

    public:
        BigNum(int length);
        ~BigNum();

        void Set(int sign, const unsigned int* pData);
        void Get(int* sign, unsigned int* pData) const;
        void Zero();
        void Randomize(int len=-1);

        IppsBigNum* GetBN() const { return pNum_; }
        int GetLength() const { return length_; }

        void Print() const;
};

BigNum::BigNum(int length)
{
    int bufSize;
    length_ = length;

    ippsBigNumBufferSize(length_, &bufSize);

    pNum_ = (IppsBigNum*)ippsMalloc_8u(bufSize);

    ippsBigNumInit(length_, pNum_);
}

BigNum::~BigNum()
{
    if (pNum_) ippsFree(pNum_);
}

void BigNum::Set(int sign, const unsigned int* pData)
```

```
{
    ippsSet_BN((IppsBigNumSGN)(sign>0), length_,
        pData, pNum_);
}

void BigNum::Get(int* sign, unsigned int* pData) const
{
    int dummy;
    IppsBigNumSGN sgn;
    ippsGet_BN(&sgn, &dummy, pData, pNum_);
    if ((int)sgn) *sign = 1;
    else *sign = -1;
}

void BigNum::Zero()
{
    Ipp32u* pZero = ippsMalloc_32u(length_);
    ippsZero_16s((Ipp16s*)pZero, length_*2);
    ippsSet_BN((IppsBigNumSGN)0, length_, pZero, pNum_);
}

void BigNum::Randomize(int len)
{
    // Seed RNG with low 32 bits of CPU clock.
    int i;
    Ipp32u seed  = ippCoreGetCpuClocks() % (((Ipp64s)1<<32)-1);
    srand(seed);

    Ipp32u* pRand = ippsMalloc_32u(length_);
    for (i = 0; i < length_; i++)
        pRand[i] = (Ipp32u)rand() + (((Ipp32u)rand())<<16);

    // Pad with zeros if passed a length
    if (len != -1)
        ippsSet_32s(0, (Ipp32s*)pRand+len, length_ - len);

    // Fill *this with generated random number
    Set(1, pRand);

    ippsFree(pRand);
}

void BigNum::Print() const
{
    Ipp32u* pData = ippsMalloc_32u(length_);
    int dummy;
    Get(&dummy, pData);
```

```
    for (int i=0; i<length_; i++)
        printf("%x ",pData[i]);
    printf("\n");

    ippsFree(pData);
}
```

Figure 12.4 Partial Implementation of a BigNum Class

The BigNum class conveniently is shown with the basic functions. The constructor initializes the internal IppsBigNum instance; if there were a function BigNumInitAlloc, it would hardly be necessary. Passing an array of unsigned integers to the Set function sets the data. The Get function returns the same data in a similar array. The key GetBN function can be used to extract the internal IppsBigNum to pass it into Intel IPP.

The function Randomize is indispensable. Most cryptographic functions need to be seeded with some unpredictable data. Creation of secure random numbers and large primes, particularly keys, consumes a lot of entropy. This function allows automatic creation of any quantity of random data to fill the BigNum instance.

Public-Key Cryptography

Public-key cryptography allows an entity that wishes to receive secure transmissions to create a system for encrypting data that can only be read by that entity. Such an entity creates a pair of keys based on large primes. The public key is published or provided to any other entity that wishes to send a secure transmission. The private key and primes are kept secret and are used to decode any transmissions encoded with the public key.

The result is an easy and secure transmission method that anyone with the public key can use. Further, if some authority certifies the identity of the owner of the public key, then this method doubles as part of an identity certification scheme, since only the person certified can read the encrypted messages.

Intel IPP supports two types of public-key cryptography schemes, RSA and DSA. Figure 12.5 shows a key-generation class for RSA. This class creates all keys necessary to encrypt and decrypt RSA in and puts them in the structure IppsRSA.

```
class RSAKeyGen
{
   private:
       int keyLen_, primeLen_;
       IppsRSA* pRSAEncKey_;
       IppsRSA* pRSADecKey_;

   public:
       RSAKeyGen(int keyLen, int primeLen);
       ~RSAKeyGen();

       void GenerateKeys();
       IppsRSA* GetPublicKey() const
       { return pRSAEncKey_; }
       IppsRSA* GetPrivateKey() const
       { return pRSADecKey_; }
};

int gen_t(int kp)
{
    int t;

    t = 27;
    if(kp>150) t = 18;
    if(kp>200) t = 15;
    if(kp>250) t = 12;
    if(kp>300) t = 9;
    if(kp>350) t = 8;
    if(kp>400) t = 7;
    if(kp>450) t = 6;
    return t;
}
void RSAKeyGen::GenerateKeys()
{
    int sign, i;
    Ipp32u pSeed[10];
    BigNum content(keyLen_/2), seed(10),
        publicKey((keyLen_+31)/32);

    // Initialize publicKey to reasonable value
    publicKey.Zero();
    publicKey.Randomize(keyLen_/32);
```

```
    // Generate some random data for content and seed
    content.Randomize();
    seed.Randomize();
    seed.Get(&sign, pSeed);

    IppStatus st = ippsRSAKeyGen(publicKey.GetBN(),
        content.GetBN(), pSeed, gen_t(primeLen_),
        keyLen_, primeLen_, pRSADecKey_);

    // Create the public (encode) key from the private
    // (decode) key
    int length;
    Ipp32u *pData = ippsMalloc_32u((keyLen_+31)/32);
    ippsRSAKeyGet(pData, &length, IppsRSAKeyN,
        pRSADecKey_);
    ippsRSAKeySet(pData, length, IppsRSAKeyN,
        pRSAEncKey_);
    ippsRSAKeyGet(pData, &length, IppsRSAKeyE,
        pRSADecKey_);
    ippsRSAKeySet(pData, length, IppsRSAKeyE,
        pRSAEncKey_);
}

RSAKeyGen::~RSAKeyGen()
{
    if (pRSAEncKey_) ippsFree(pRSAEncKey_);
    if (pRSADecKey_) ippsFree(pRSADecKey_);
}

IppStatus myRSAInitAlloc(IppsExpMethod method,
    int k, int kp, IppsRSAType flag, IppsRSA **pKey)
{
    int bufSize[4];

    ippsRSABufferSizes(method, k, kp,
        flag, &bufSize[0], &bufSize[1], &bufSize[2],
        &bufSize[3]);
    Ipp32u* pBuf =
        ippsMalloc_32u(bufSize[0]+bufSize[1]+bufSize[2]+
        bufSize[3]);

    *pKey = (IppsRSA*)pBuf;
    return ippsRSAInit(method, k, kp, flag,
        pBuf+bufSize[3], pBuf+bufSize[3]+bufSize[0],
        pBuf+bufSize[3]+bufSize[0]+bufSize[1], *pKey);
}
```

```
RSAKeyGen::RSAKeyGen(int keyLen, int primeLen):
    keyLen_(keyLen), primeLen_(primeLen)
{
    myRSAInitAlloc(IppsSlidingWindows,
        keyLen_, primeLen_, IppsRSAPrivate, &pRSADecKey_);
    myRSAInitAlloc(IppsSlidingWindows,
        keyLen_, primeLen_, IppsRSAPublic, &pRSAEncKey_);
}

char pTextSource[1024] =
    "Gallia est omnis divisa in partes tres, quarum "
    "unam incolunt Belgae, aliam Aquitani, tertiam "
    "qui ipsorum lingua Celtae, nostra Galli appellantur. "
    "Hi omnis lingua, institutis, legibus inter se differunt. "
    "Gallos ab Aquitanis Garumna flumen, a Belgis Matrona "
    "et Sequana dividit. ";

void main()
{
    IppStatus st;
    static int keyLen = 256;
    RSAKeyGen keyGen(keyLen, keyLen/2);
    keyGen.GenerateKeys();

    BigNum plaintext(keyLen/32), cyphertext(keyLen/32),
        decodedtext(keyLen/32);

    char pTextDest[1024];
    int sign, i;
    for (i=0; i<strlen(pTextSource)+1; i+=keyLen/8)
    {
        plaintext.Set(1,(Ipp32u*)&pTextSource[i]);
        st = ippsRSAEncrypt(plaintext.GetBN(),
            cyphertext.GetBN(), keyGen.GetPublicKey());

        st = ippsRSADecrypt(cyphertext.GetBN(),
            decodedtext.GetBN(), keyGen.GetPrivateKey());
        decodedtext.Get(&sign, (Ipp32u*)&pTextDest[i]);
    }

    // This code prepares the composite integer
    // and public key for distribution
    // These are needed for encryption
    Ipp32u pN[keyLen/32];
    Ipp32u pKey[keyLen/32];

    ippsRSAKeyGet(pN, &nLen, IppsRSAKeyN,
        keyGen.GetPublicKey());
    ippsRSAKeyGet(pKey, &pubKeyLen, IppsRSAKeyE,
```

```
        keyGen.GetPublicKey());
    for (i=0; i<nLen; i++)
        printf("%x ",pN[i]);
    printf("\n");
    for (i=0; i<pubKeyLen; i++)
        printf("%x ",pKey[i]);
    printf("\n");
}
```

Figure 12.5 `RSAKeyGen` Class Declaration, Definition, and Usage

The `IppsRSA` key structure can act as either a public, encrypting key or a private, decrypting key. To be a private key, a structure must have all the internals set: large integer, both primes, public key, and private key. A public key structure needs only the large integer and public key.

Generating and assembling the `IppsRSA` key structure is difficult, since it requires the allocation of four separate buffers. Until such time as an `ippsRSAInitAlloc` function is available, the `myRSAInitAlloc` function creates a fully allocated RSA structure.

The function `ippsRSAKeyGen` needs considerable entropy to operate in the seed and content string. In addition, the key needs to contain a starting "probable prime" value. This function uses the `BigNum` method `Randomize` to generate all of these values.

The `t` argument to `ippsRSAKeyGen` determines how rigorously the key generator should check whether the suspected primes are truly primes. The longer the key is, the higher this argument must be for a certain probability of primality. The function `gen_t` provides a reasonable value for `t`.

The code in the `main` function demonstrates the use of the functions `ippsRSAEncrypt` and `ippsRSADecrypt`. Both have extremely simple interfaces. Their arguments are the key structure and two `IppsBigNum` structures, input and output. These big numbers must be the length of the key. Any data to be encrypted needs to be packed into a big number first.

This use of the same `RSAKeyGen` object to create both the public and private keys is convenient but unrealistic. In the common use case for RSA, the key's creator must publish the public key and large integer for someone else to encrypt a message. The last portion of the code shows how to print the large integer N and the public key. Once published, they can be read and reentered into a public key in an `IppsRSA` structure.

Other Cryptographic Support in Intel® Integrated Performance Primitives (Intel® IPP)

Intel IPP supports many other algorithms in addition to the above. The following is an almost complete listing of the algorithms supported in Intel IPP 4.0.

Symmetric cryptography:

- Data Encryption Standard (DES) and Triple Data Encryption Standard (TDES)
- Rijndael, Blowfish, and Twofish block ciphers

Hash and data authentication algorithm (DAA) functions:

- MD5, HMAC-MD5
- SHA1, SHA256/384/512, HMAC-SHA1, HMAC-SHA256/384/512
- DAADES, DAATDES
- DAARijdael, DAABlowfish, DAATwofish

Public key cryptography:

- Infrastructure functions such as pseudorandom number generation (PNRG) and prime number generation
- Digital Signature Algorithm (DSA)

Computer Vision

In addition to the general image processing functions discussed in Chapters 8 and 9, Intel IPP includes a domain comprised of computer-vision oriented functions. These functions are in the areas of:

- Statistics: norm, mean, median, standard deviation, histograms
- Analysis functions and filters: erode and dilate, blur, Laplace, Sobel, distance transform, pyramid
- Feature detection: edge, corner, template matching
- Motion detection and understanding: motion templates

Many of these functions are closely associated with the Open Source Computer Vision Library (OSCVL), currently available online (Intel 2003b). The histories of this library and the Intel IPP computer vision domain are intertwined, and the OSCVL uses Intel IPP as its optimization layer.

This section demonstrates edge detection, pyramids, and template matching. The examples make extensive use of the `Image8u` class from Chapter 8 and the `LocalBuffer` class used in Chapter 10.

Edge Detection

Perhaps the most important low-level vision task is detection of edges in the image. Edges are visual discontinuities of brightness, color, or both. They are usually detected by an automated operation on a small region of pixels. Interpreted correctly, they convey higher-level scene information, particularly the boundaries of objects in the scene.

The Canny edge detector is one of the more complex edge detection systems, but it is a prominent and successful detector. The Canny detector actually requires three steps: differentiation of the image, suppression of values that are non-maximal along a line, and thresholding those values with hysteresis along a line. In Intel IPP, the first step, calculating the slopes of the image, is done before calling the `ippiCanny` function to perform the next two steps.

The output of the first step is two images, the x-slope and the y-slope, and they are both expected to be `Ipp16s`. For this reason the interface of the differentiating Sobel filters takes an `Ipp8u` image as input and produces an `Ipp16s` image as output. Two Sobel functions, `Sobel3x3_Dx` and `Sobel3x3_Dy`, must be called to generate both horizontal and vertical slopes.

Figure 12.6 lists a `Canny` class that follows the aforementioned steps to detect edges for an input image.

```
class Canny : public Filter
{
    private:
        Ipp32f lowThresh_, highThresh_;
        LocalBuffer buf_;

    protected:
        virtual int Go_(const Ipp8u* pSrc, int srcStep,
```

```
            Ipp8u* pDst, int dstStep,
            IppiSize dstROISize, int nChannels);

    public:
        void SetThresholds(Ipp32f low, Ipp32f high)
        { lowThresh_ = low; highThresh_ = high; }

        virtual IppiSize GetKernelSize() const;
        virtual IppiPoint GetAnchor() const;
};

int Canny::Go_(const Ipp8u* pSrc, int srcStep,
    Ipp8u* pDst, int dstStep,
    IppiSize dstROISize, int nChannels)
{
    if (nChannels != 1) return -1;

    // Allocate temporary images and buffers
    int bufSize;
    ippiCannyGetSize(dstROISize, &bufSize);
    int tmpSize = dstStep * dstROISize.height *
        sizeof(Ipp16s);
    buf_.SetMinAlloc(tmpSize*2 + bufSize);
    Ipp16s *pTmpX = (Ipp16s*)buf_.Alloc_8u(tmpSize);
    Ipp16s *pTmpY = (Ipp16s*)buf_.Alloc_8u(tmpSize);
    Ipp8u* pBuffer = buf_.Alloc_8u(bufSize);

    // Calculate derivative "images"
    IppStatus st;
    st = ippiSobel3x3_Dx_8u16s_C1R(pSrc, srcStep,
        pTmpX, dstStep*sizeof(Ipp16s), dstROISize);
    st = ippiSobel3x3_Dy_8u16s_C1R(pSrc, srcStep,
        pTmpY, dstStep*sizeof(Ipp16s), IPCV_ORIGIN_BL,
        dstROISize);

    // Calculate Edges
    st = ippiCanny_16s8u_C1R(pTmpX, dstStep*2,
        pTmpY, dstStep*2, pDst, dstStep, dstROISize,
        lowThresh_, highThresh_, pBuffer);

    buf_.ReleaseAll();
    return 0;
}

// Using Canny:

    Image8u image2;
    image2.CopySettings(&image);

    Canny canny;
```

```
canny.SetBorderMode(Filter::REPEAT);

canny.SetThresholds(0.0, 64.0);
canny.Go(&image, &image2);
image2.View("Edges - low threshold",0);
canny.SetThresholds(0.0, 256.0);
canny.Go(&image, &image2);
image2.View("Edges - medium threshold",0);
canny.SetThresholds(0.0, 512.0);
canny.Go(&image, &image2);
image2.View("Edges - high threshold",1);
```

Figure 12.6 Declaration, Definition, and Usage of `Canny` Edge Detection Class

The easiest way to implement the `Canny` class is to inherit the pointer math functions and border support from the `Filter` class developed in Chapter 9. The `Filter` class is appropriate since the input of the `Sobel` functions and the output of the `Canny` function are both `Ipp8u` images, and the `Sobel` filter requires a border just as other filters do. The filter takes care of all border operations and data conversions. The Canny class needs only four functions: `GetKernelSize`, which returns {3,3}; `GetAnchor`, which returns {1,1}; `SetThresholds`, which sets the Canny thresholds; and `Go_`, which performs the filtering.

The `Go_` function requires three temporary buffers. The `Canny` function requires a temporary buffer of a size returned by `CannyGetSize`. The outputs of the `Sobel` calls are placed in two temporary images to be passed to `Canny`. The output of `Canny` is returned in the destination array.

The figure also shows how to use this class to find edges in the image `image2`. Determining appropriate thresholds is nontrivial and difficult to do automatically. Figure 12.7 shows the results of this code, with three attempted thresholds. For this image, the middle threshold seems to outline the girl and the flowers without highlighting the texture of her shirt.

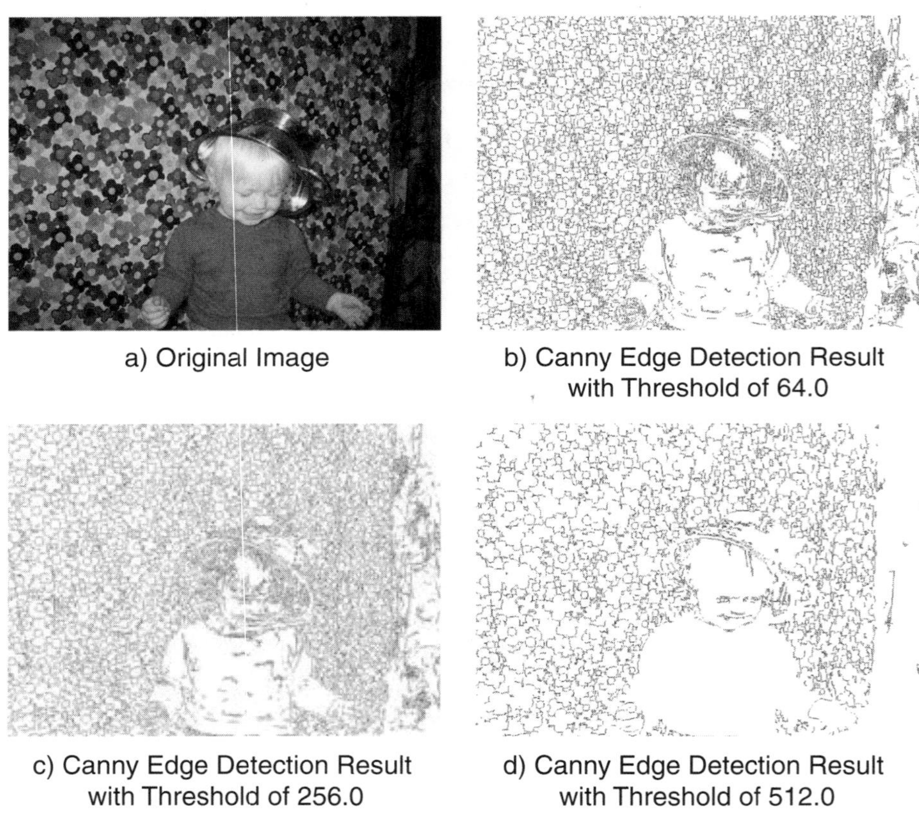

a) Original Image

b) Canny Edge Detection Result with Threshold of 64.0

c) Canny Edge Detection Result with Threshold of 256.0

d) Canny Edge Detection Result with Threshold of 512.0

Figure 12.7 Canny Edge Detection Results

Multi-resolution Analysis

When trying to find an object in a scene, size is as important a characteristic as shape or color. Even if you know exactly what shape or color an object is, you need to know how many pixels wide and tall it is. One easy way of performing an analysis without knowing this size is to perform the search on multiple resolutions of an image. Such a set of resolutions of an image is often called an image pyramid.

The lower-resolution images of a pyramid are significantly smaller than the original image. Typically, each level of the pyramid is reduced by a factor of two in each direction from the previous level. In this case, the total size of the whole pyramid is twice the size of the original image.

Therefore, the search time for an entire pyramid is roughly twice the search time for the original image. Ironically, it takes less time to search for larger versions of the object than smaller versions.

In Intel IPP, the core pyramid functions are `ippiPyrDown` and `ippiPyrUp`. The former blurs an image and down-samples it by two in each dimension. The latter up-samples the image and blurs it. Repeated application of the `PyrDown` function generates a pyramid, as in Figure 12.8. The pyramid that these functions create is called a *Gaussian pyramid* because the filter used to blur the image is a Gaussian blur.

```
class PyrGauss
{
    private:
        LocalBuffer buf;

    public:
        PyrGauss();
        ~PyrGauss();

        int PyrUp(Image8u* pSrc, Image8u* pDst);
        int PyrDown(Image8u* pSrc, Image8u* pDst);

        IppiSize GetDestSizeUp(Image8u* pSrc);
        IppiSize GetDestSizeDown(Image8u* pSrc);
};

class Pyramid8u
{
    public:
        enum { MaxLevels = 32 };

        Pyramid8u();
        ~Pyramid8u();
        Image8u* GetLevel(int level);
        void SetTopLevel(Image8u* pImage);

    private:
        static PyrGauss pyr_;

        Image8u* pImages[MaxLevels];
        void FreeAll_();

};

int PyrGauss::PyrDown(Image8u* pSrc, Image8u* pDst)
```

```
{
    IppiSize dstSize = GetDestSizeDown(pSrc);

    if (dstSize.width > pDst->GetSize().width) return -1;
    if (dstSize.height > pDst->GetSize().height) return -1;

    // Allocate temporary buffer
    int bufSize;
    IppStatus st;
    st = ippiPyrDownGetBufSize_Gauss5x5(
        pSrc->GetSize().width,
        ipp8u, pSrc->GetChannelCount(), &bufSize);
    if (st != 0) return -1;
    buf.SetMinAlloc(bufSize);
    Ipp8u* pBuffer = buf.Alloc_8u(bufSize);

    IppiSize srcSize = pSrc->GetSize();
    // Round source size to even
    srcSize.width &= ~1;
    srcSize.height &= ~1;

    switch (pDst->GetChannelCount())
    {
        case 1:
            st = ippiPyrDown_Gauss5x5_8u_C1R(
                pSrc->GetData(), pSrc->GetStride(),
                pDst->GetData(), pDst->GetStride(),
                srcSize, pBuffer);
            break;
        case 3:
            st = ippiPyrDown_Gauss5x5_8u_C3R(
                pSrc->GetData(), pSrc->GetStride(),
                pDst->GetData(), pDst->GetStride(),
                srcSize, pBuffer);
            break;
        default:
            buf.ReleaseAll();
            return -1;
    }

    buf.ReleaseAll();
    if (st != 0) return -1;
    else return 0;
}

Image8u* Pyramid8u::GetLevel(int level)
{
    int i;
    if (level == 0) return pImages[0];
    if (level > MaxLevels) level = MaxLevels-1;
```

```
    for (i=1; i<=level; i++)
    {
        if (!pImages[i])
        {
            pImages[i] = new Image8u(
                pyr_.GetDestSizeDown(pImages[i-1]),
                pImages[i-1]->GetChannelCount());
            if ((pImages[i]->GetSize().width == 0) ||
                (pImages[i]->GetSize().height == 0))
                return 0;
            pyr_.PyrDown(pImages[i-1], pImages[i]);
        }
    }

    return pImages[level];
}
```

Figure 12.8 Declaration and Some of the Definition of Pyramid Classes

This example shows two classes, `PyrGauss` and `Pyramid8u`. The `PyrGauss` class calculates the next level up or down of a pyramid. The main task this class performs in wrapping the `PyrDown` and `PyrUp` functions is memory management. The Intel IPP pyramid functions require a temporary buffer. This class uses a persisting local buffer to avoid reallocating memory.

The `Pyramid8u` class merely manages an entire Gaussian pyramid for an image. Most of the logic is contained in the `GetLevel` function. This function generates a pyramid on demand, creating each lower level if necessary. The original image is externally maintained, and must persist for the lifetime of the `Pyramid8u` instance.

Figure 12.9 shows a five-level pyramid copied into a single image. It is possible to pack the entire pyramid into an image of the same height and twice the width of the original by laying out the levels in a spiral pattern.

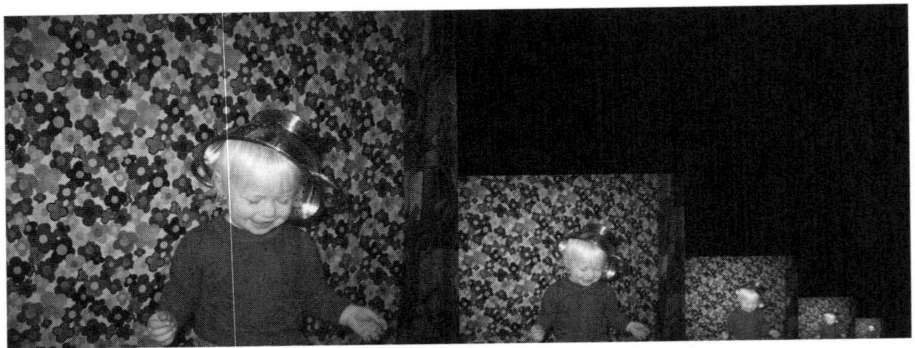

Figure 12.9 A Composite Image of a Five-Level Gaussian Image Pyramid

Pyramids are also used for lossless packing of an image, sometimes for analysis. In this case, each level of the pyramid is retained as the difference between an image and the reconstructed image from the next level down. The difference can be very small. The lowest layer of the pyramid is retained exactly. Such a structure is called a *Laplacian pyramid*.

Template Matching

In computer vision, a template is a canonical representation of an object used for finding the object in a scene. There are many ways to match the template, such as taking the pixel-by-pixel normalized sum of the squared difference between template and image.

Generally, the methods compare the template pixel by pixel to each region of the image. The output for each location in the image is how well the pixels in the region centered on that location matched the template. Correlation, which multiplies the template against the image region pixel by pixel, is one way. The sum of the products across a region indicates how well the template matches at that location.

The Intel IPP `ippiMatchTemplate` functions cover a host of methods of comparing a template to an image including correlation, squared difference, normalized correlation, and normalized squared difference. Figure 12.10 lists a `MatchTemplate` class that wraps the template searching methods with a simple interface.

```
class MatchTemplate
{
    private:
        LocalBuffer buf_;


    public:
        enum { SqDiff, SqDiffNormed, Corr, CorrNormed,
            Coeff, CoeffNormed };

        IppiSize GetDestSize(IppiSize srcSize,
            IppiSize templateSize) const
        {
            IppiSize dstSize = {
                srcSize.width+templateSize.width-1,
                srcSize.height+templateSize.height-1 };
            return dstSize;
        }

        int Go(const Image8u* pSrc,
            const Image8u* pTemplate,
            Ipp32f* pResult, int resultStep,
            int method);
};

int MatchTemplate::Go(const Image8u* pSrc,
    const Image8u* pTemplate,
    Ipp32f* pResult, int resultStep, int method)
{
    if (pSrc->GetChannelCount() != 1) return -1;
    if (pTemplate->GetChannelCount() != 1) return -1;

    int bufSize;
    switch (method)
    {
        case SqDiff:
            ippiMatchTemplateGetBufSize_SqDiff(
                pSrc->GetSize(), pTemplate->GetSize(),
                ipp8u, &bufSize);
            buf_.SetMinAlloc(bufSize);
            ippiMatchTemplate_SqDiff_8u32f_C1R(
                pSrc->GetConstData(), pSrc->GetStride(),
                pSrc->GetSize(),
                pTemplate->GetConstData(),
                pTemplate->GetStride(),
                pTemplate->GetSize(),
```

```
                pResult, resultStep,
                buf_.Alloc_8u(bufSize));
            break;
        case SqDiffNormed:

        ...

        default:
            buf_.ReleaseAll();
            return -1;
    }

    return 0;
}
```

Figure 12.10 `MatchTemplate` Class

The `MatchTemplate` class is very similar to other filters but is not a child of the `Filter` class because the output is type `Ipp32f`. It is possible to present it as a `Filter` by requiring a threshold step, or in some other way normalizing the result to `Ipp8u`. Alternatively, the class `Filter` could reasonably be expanded to provide `Ipp32f` output.

Figure 12.11 shows one way to use the `MatchTemplate` class to match a template to an image pyramid.

```
    int h=image.GetSize().height;
    int w=image.GetSize().width;

    Image8u edgeIm, tmpIm, borderIm;

    edgeIm.CopySettings(&image);

    Canny c;
    c.SetThresholds(0.0, 256.0);
    c.Go(&image, &edgeIm);

    IppiPoint kernel = {templateIm.GetSize().width/2,
        templateIm.GetSize().height/2};
    MatchTemplate mt;

    Pyramid8u pyr;
    pyr.SetTopLevel(&image);

    int resultStep;
    IppiSize resultSize;
    Ipp32f* pResult32f =
        ippiMalloc_32f_C1( w,h, &resultStep);
```

```
Image8u resultIm, resultIm2;
resultIm.CopySettings(&image);
resultIm2.CopySettings(&image);

BorderMaker b(templateIm.GetSize(), kernel);

int i,j,k;

for (i=0; i<5; i++)
{
    resultSize = pyr.GetLevel(i)->GetSize();
    edgeIm.InitAlloc(resultSize, 1);
    c.Go(pyr.GetLevel(i), &edgeIm);
    b.MakeBorderImage(&edgeIm, &borderIm,
        Filter::REFLECT);

    borderIm.View("Border image",0);

    mt.Go(&borderIm, &templateIm, pResult32f,
          resultStep, mt.CoeffNormed);

    ippiThreshold_LTValGTVal_32f_C1R(
        pResult32f, resultStep,
        pResult32f, resultStep,
        resultSize, 0.35f, 0.0f, 0.35f, 1.0f);
    ippiMulC_32f_C1IR(255.0f, pResult32f,
        resultStep, resultSize);
    resultIm.CopyFrom_R(pResult32f, resultSize.width,
        resultSize.height, resultStep, 0,0);
```

```
    resultIm2.Zero();
    for (j=kernel.y; j<resultSize.height-kernel.y; j++)
        for (k=kernel.x; k<resultSize.width-kernel.x; k++)
            if (*resultIm.GetData(k,j))
            {
                resultIm2.CopyFrom_R(&borderIm,
                    k, j,
                    templateIm.GetSize().width,
                    templateIm.GetSize().height,
                    k-kernel.x, j-kernel.y);
            }

    resultIm2.View("Result", 1, resultSize);
}
```

Figure 12.11 Using the `MatchTemplate` Class to Find an Object at Multiple Resolutions

This code compares a single template against each level of an image pyramid. First it initializes a Canny edge detector, a pyramid generator, a template matcher, and a border maker. Then, for five levels of an image pyramid, it finds edges and matches the edges against the template.

The `BorderMaker` class is a child of the `Filter` class that just provides the border functionality. The function `Go_` does nothing, but given a size and anchor for a kernel, it permits the use of the `MakeBorderImage` function. The `BorderMaker` class takes the place of deriving the `MatchTemplate` class from `Filter`.

Since the template is an outline shape, edge detection is done on each pyramid level, and then the edge probabilities are thresholded with the `Threshold_GTValLTVal` function. This detection is done with the `Canny` class, listed earlier. If, instead of calculating edges of each level of the pyramid, the pyramid were calculated on the edge image, the lower levels of the pyramid would contain blurry outlines. The template would not match those blurry outlines very well.

The tricky part is not choosing a template or matching method, it's choosing a threshold for whether an object matches or not. In this case, the threshold has been chosen by hand, though it was made easier by the use of a normalized template matching method. In practice, choosing a threshold for an arbitrary template is very difficult.

The threshold is usually important for detection, and in this case is essential for displaying the result. For display purposes, the result images are not the raw results of the template matching. They are the result of copying a template-sized block from the source image everywhere that the template result was above the threshold. This is done by the conditional call to the `resultIm2.CopyFrom_R` method.

The result of this code is shown in Figure 12.12.

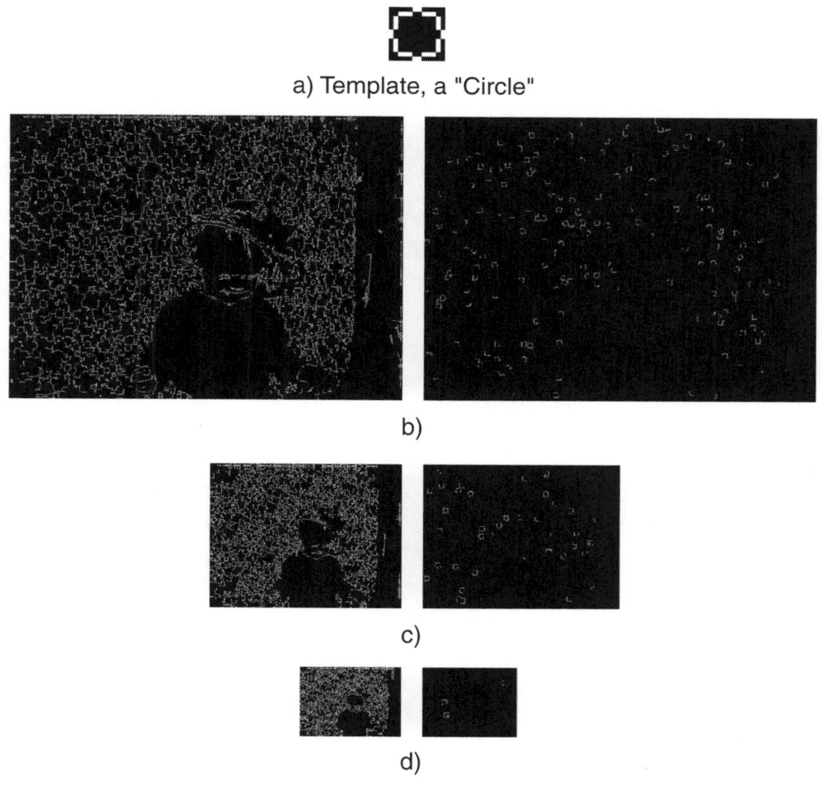

Figure 12.12 Template Matching Results

With the template in Figure 12.12 a), the procedure described finds circles of various sizes in an image. It should be apparent that plenty of circles were found, mostly the centers of flowers in the wallpaper. Many circles were not complete but were close enough because of a good size match and three good sides.

Note that the "before" pictures are slightly larger than the "after" pictures due to the border. The border is necessary to allow the output of the template matching to be the same size as the original level of the pyramid.

The circles are all approximately the same size, the size of the template. Since each pixel in the smaller images in the pyramid represents a larger image area, the template is actually finding larger circles in the lower, or smaller, pyramid images than in the larger images.

Further Reading

Cryptography: Theory and Practice (Stinson 1995) explains many of the algorithms supported in Intel IPP and breaks them down into pseudocode. It starts with plenty of background on the theory and mathematics behind them.

Many of the image processing texts listed at the end of Chapter 9 are also good computer vision and image analysis texts. *Pattern Classification and Scene Analysis* (Duda and Hart 1973), though a few decades old, is an excellent collection of pattern and image analysis methods.

References

Adams, M.D. 2002. The JPEG-2000 still image compression standard. http://www.ece.uvic.ca/~mdadams/papers/jpeg2000.pdf

Bracewell, R. N. 1986. *The Fourier Transform and Its Applications.* 2nd ed. New York: McGraw Hill.

Brandenburg, K. 1999. MP3 and AAC explained. *AES 17th International Conference on High Quality Audio Coding.*

Duda, R. O., and P. E. Hart. 1973. *Pattern Classification and Scene Analysis.* New York: John Wiley & Sons.

Foley, J., A. van Dam, S. Feiner, and J. Hughes. 1990. *Computer Graphics: Principles and Practice.* 2nd ed. Reading, MA: Addison Wesley.

Glassner, A. S., ed. 1989. *An Introduction to Ray Tracing.* London: Academic Press.

Ingle, V. K., and J. G. Proakis. 2000. *Digital Signal Processing Using Matlab*[†]. Pacific Grove, CA: Brooks/Cole.

Intel Corporation. 2003. *Signal processing.* Vol. 1 of *Intel® Integrated Performance Primitives for Intel® Architecture Reference Manual.* Santa Clara, CA: Intel Corporation. Portable Document Format.

Intel Corporation. 2003. *Image and video processing.* Vol. 2 of *Intel® Integrated Performance Primitives for Intel® Architecture Reference Manual.* Santa Clara, CA: Intel Corporation. Portable Document Format.

Intel Corporation. 2003. *Small matrices.* Vol. 3 of *Intel® Integrated Performance Primitives for Intel® Architecture Reference Manual.* Santa Clara, CA: Intel Corporation. Portable Document Format.

Intel Corporation. 2003. *Cryptography.* Vol. 4 of *Intel® Integrated Performance Primitives for Intel® Architecture Reference Manual.* Santa Clara, CA: Intel Corporation. Portable Document Format.

Jack, Keith. 2001 *Video Demystified.* 3rd ed. Eagle Rock, VA: LLH Technology Publishing.

Jain, A. K. 1989. *Fundamentals of Digital Image Processing*. Englewood Cliffs, NJ: Prentice Hall.

Klette, R., and P. Zamperoni. 1994. *Handbook of Image Processing Operators*. West Sussex, UK: John Wiley & Sons.

Lengyel, E. 2002. *Mathematics for 3D Game Programming and Computer Graphics*. Hingham, MA: Charles River Media.

Myler, H. R., and A. R. Weeks. 1993. *The Pocket Handbook of Image Processing Algorithms in C*. Englewood Cliffs, NJ: Prentice Hall.

Oppenheim, A. V., and R. W. Schafer. 1989. *Discrete-Time Signal Processing*. Englewood Cliffs, NJ: Prentice Hall.

Oppenheim, A. V., and A. S. Willsky. 1983. *Signals and Systems*. Englewood Cliffs, NJ: Prentice Hall.

Pan, D. 1995. A tutorial on MPEG/audio compression. *IEEE Multimedia*. Summer:60-74.

Pennebaker, W. B., and J. L. Mitchell. 1992. *JPEG Still Image Data Compression Standard*. New York: Chapman and Hall.

Roads, C. 1995. *The Computer Music Tutorial*. Cambridge, MA: The MIT Press.

Rogers, D. F. 1985. *Procedural Elements for Computer Graphics.* 2nd ed. New York: McGraw-Hill.

Rogers, D. F. 1990. *Mathematical Elements for Computer Graphics.* 2nd ed. New York: McGraw-Hill.

Stinson, D. R. 1995. *Cryptography: Theory and Practice*. Boca Raton, FL: CRC Press.

Strum, R. D., and D. E. Kirk. 1989. *First Principles of Discrete Systems and Digital Signal Processing*. Reading, MA: Addison Wesley.

Woo, M., J. Neider, T. Davis, and D. Shreiner. 1999. *OpenGL Programming Guide*. 3rd ed. Reading, MA: Addison Wesley.

Zolzer, U. 2002. *DAFX*. West Sussex, UK: John Wiley & Sons.

Index

D

E

F

G

J

T

"As the pace of technology introduction increases it's difficult to keep up. Intel Press has established an impressive portfolio. The breadth of topics is a reflection of both Intel's diversity as well as our commitment to serve a broad technical community.

I hope you will take advantage of these products to further your technical education."

Patrick Gelsinger
Senior Vice President and Chief Technology Officer
Intel Corporation

Turn the page to learn about titles from Intel Press for system developers

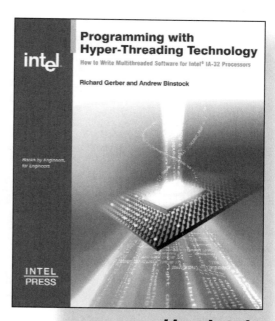

The Software Optimization Cookbook

High-performance Recipes for the Intel® Architecture

By Richard Gerber

ISBN 0-9712887-1-2

Through simple explanations and C/C++ code samples, an Intel trainer explains the techniques and tools you can use to improve the performance of applications for Intel® 32-bit processors. This book also includes tested recipes for those long nights of coding and testing.

Use performance tools and tested concepts to analyze and improve applications

Change-Based Test Management

Improving the Software Validation Process

By Jon Sistowicz and Ray Arell

ISBN 0-9717861-2-7

Two leading proponents of Change-Based Test Management (CBTM) at Intel Corporation provide software engineers and test specialists with a detailed explanation of how applying this new methodology significantly improves quality while reducing development time. This introduction to CBTM includes case studies and author insights help readers visualize CBTM in action.

"An essential book for any developer involved with software testing. Extremely practical."

Virginia Aldrich, Senior Software Engineer, Express Imaging Systems

Programming Itanium®-based Systems

Developing High Performance Applications for Intel's New Architecture

By Walter Triebel, Rick Booth, and Joseph Bissell

ISBN 0-9702846-2-4

To help developers harness the power of Intel's new line of very long instruction word (VLIW) processors, three experts provide insight into code development and optimization techniques, to include porting applications from other environments.

A programming guide for software application developers targeting the Itanium® processor family

About Intel Press

Intel Press is the authoritative source of timely, highly relevant, and innovative books to help software and hardware developers speed up their development process. We collaborate only with leading industry experts to deliver reliable, first-to-market information about the latest technologies, processes, and strategies.

Our products are planned with the help of many people in the developer community and we encourage you to consider becoming a customer advisor. If you would like to help us and gain additional advance insight to the latest technologies, we encourage you to consider the Intel Press Customer Advisor Program. You can **register** here:

www.intel.com/intelpress/register.htm

For information about bulk orders or corporate sales, please send email to **bulkbooksales@intel.com**.

Other Developer Resources from Intel

At these Web sites you can also find valuable technical information and resources for developers:

developer.intel.com	general information for developers
www.intel.com/IDS	content, tools, training, and the Early Access Program for software developers
www.intel.com/software/products	programming tools to help you develop high-performance applications
shale.intel.com/softwarecollege	the Intel Software College provides training tools and technologies from the people who know processors
www.intel.com/idf	world-wide technical conference, the Intel Developer Forum

INTEL PRESS